INJUSTICE
GODS AMONG US

VOLUME 1

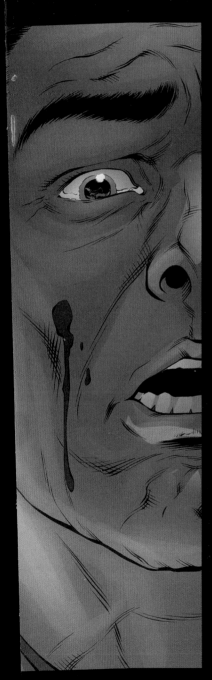

THIS STORY TAKES PLACE BEFORE
THE START OF THE GAME

Tom Taylor
Writer

Jheremy Raapack
Mike S. Miller
Bruno Redondo
Axel Gimenez
David Yardin
Tom Derenick
Marc Deering
Diana Egea
Artists

Andrew Elder
Alejandro Sanchez
David Yardin
David López and Santi Casas
of Ikari Studio
Colorists

Wes Abbott
Letterer

SUPERMAN Created by
JERRY SIEGEL and JOE SHUSTER.
By Special Arrangement
with the Jerry Siegel Family.

BASED ON THE VIDEOGAME
INJUSTICE: GODS AMONG US

Jim Chadwick Editor – Original Series
Sarah Gaydos Sarah Litt Assistant Editors – Original Series
Rachel Pinnelas Editor
Robbin Brosterman Design Director – Books
Louis Prandi Publication Design

Hank Kanalz Senior VP – Vertigo & Integrated Publishing

Diane Nelson President
Dan DiDio and Jim Lee Co-Publishers
Geoff Johns Chief Creative Officer
Amit Desai Senior VP – Marketing & Franchise Management
Amy Genkins Senior VP – Business & Legal Affairs
Nairi Gardiner Senior VP – Finance
Jeff Boison VP – Publishing Planning
Mark Chiarello VP – Art Direction & Design
John Cunningham VP – Marketing
Terri Cunningham VP – Editorial Administration
Larry Ganem VP – Talent Relations & Services
Alison Gill Senior VP – Manufacturing & Operations
Jay Kogan VP – Business & Legal Affairs, Publishing
Jack Mahan VP – Business Affairs, Talent
Nick Napolitano VP – Manufacturing Administration
Sue Pohja VP – Book Sales
Fred Ruiz VP – Manufacturing Operations
Courtney Simmons Senior VP – Publicity
Bob Wayne Senior VP – Sales

DC Comics, 1700 Broadway, New York, NY 10019
A Warner Bros. Entertainment Company.
Printed by Solisco Printers, Scott, QC, Canada. 1/12/15.
Third Printing. ISBN: 978-1-4012-4843-7

Library of Congress Cataloging-in-Publication Data

Taylor, Tom, 1978- author.
  Injustice : Gods among us, Volume 1 / Tom Taylor, Jheremy
Raapack, Mike S. Miller.
    pages cm
"Originally published in single magazine form as INJUSTICE Digital
Chapters 1-18."
  ISBN 978-1-4012-4843-7
1. Graphic novels. I. Raapack, Jheremy, illustrator. II. Miller, Mike S,
illustrator. III. Title. IV. Title: Gods among us, Volume 1.
  PN6727.T293I55 2013
  741.5'973—dc23
                                        2013021242

PART ONE

Jheremy Raapack Axel Gimenez Mike S. Miller Pencillers

Jheremy Raapack Marc Deering Mike S. Miller Inkers

Cover Art by Jheremy Raapack & Tony Aviña

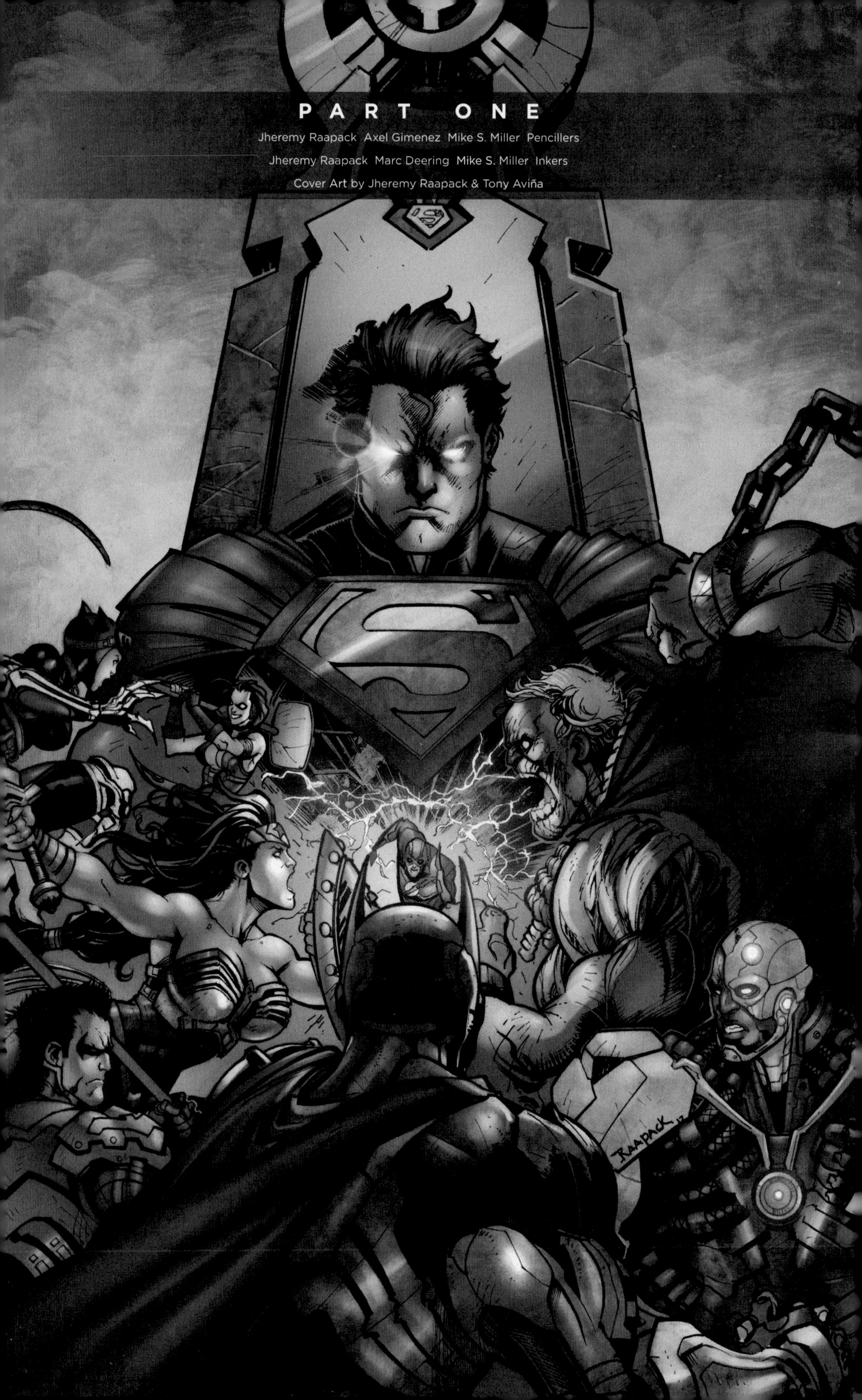
RAAPACK

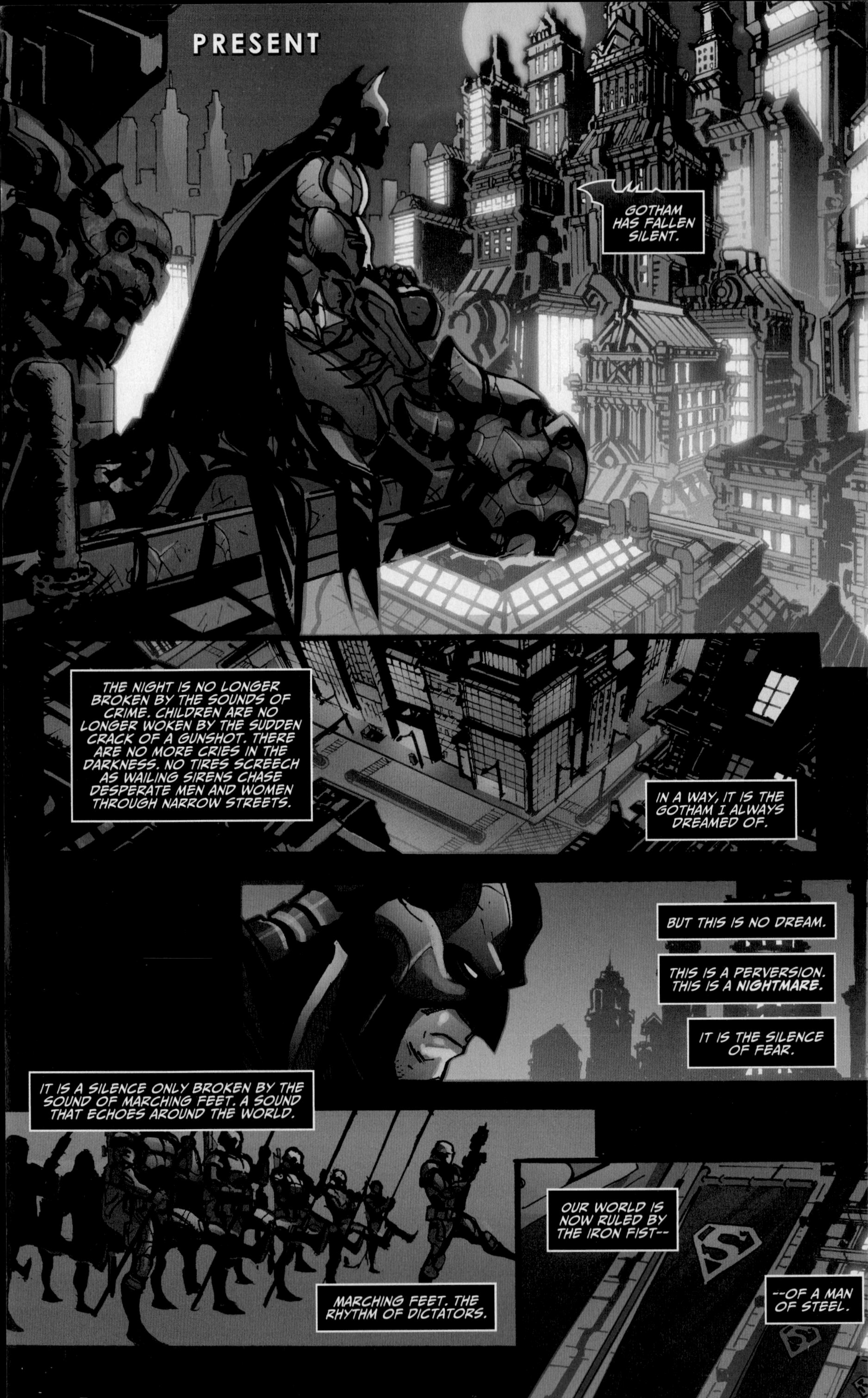
PRESENT
GOTHAM HAS FALLEN SILENT.
THE NIGHT IS NO LONGER BROKEN BY THE SOUNDS OF CRIME. CHILDREN ARE NO LONGER WOKEN BY THE SUDDEN CRACK OF A GUNSHOT. THERE ARE NO MORE CRIES IN THE DARKNESS. NO TIRES SCREECH AS WAILING SIRENS CHASE DESPERATE MEN AND WOMEN THROUGH NARROW STREETS.
IN A WAY, IT IS THE GOTHAM I ALWAYS DREAMED OF.
BUT THIS IS NO DREAM.
THIS IS A PERVERSION. THIS IS A **NIGHTMARE.**
IT IS THE SILENCE OF FEAR.
IT IS A SILENCE ONLY BROKEN BY THE SOUND OF MARCHING FEET. A SOUND THAT ECHOES AROUND THE WORLD.
MARCHING FEET. THE RHYTHM OF DICTATORS.
OUR WORLD IS NOW RULED BY THE IRON FIST--
--OF A MAN OF STEEL.

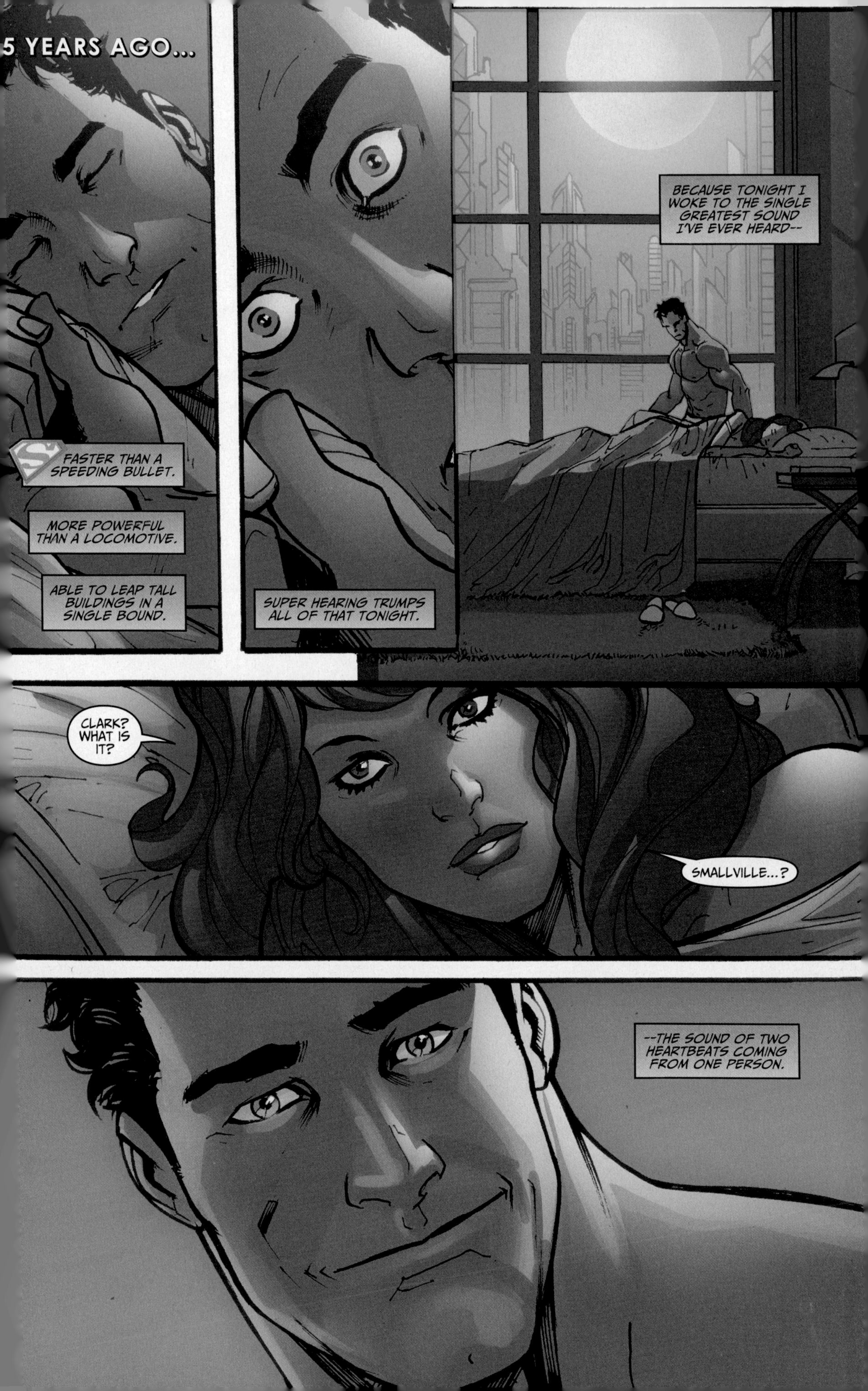
5 YEARS AGO...
FASTER THAN A SPEEDING BULLET.
MORE POWERFUL THAN A LOCOMOTIVE.
ABLE TO LEAP TALL BUILDINGS IN A SINGLE BOUND.
SUPER HEARING TRUMPS ALL OF THAT TONIGHT.
BECAUSE TONIGHT I WOKE TO THE SINGLE GREATEST SOUND I'VE EVER HEARD--
CLARK? WHAT IS IT?
SMALLVILLE...?
--THE SOUND OF TWO HEARTBEATS COMING FROM ONE PERSON.

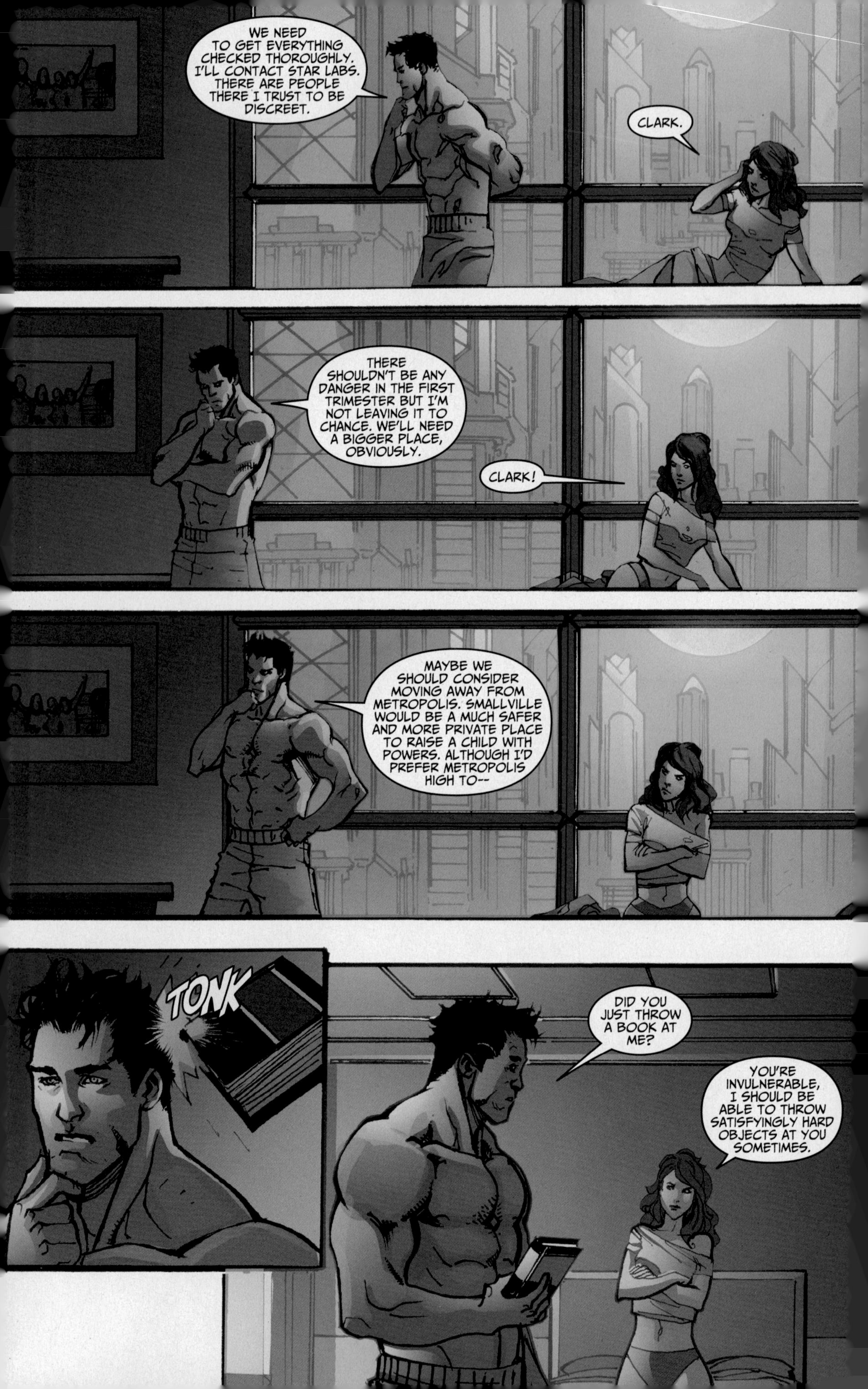
WE NEED TO GET EVERYTHING CHECKED THOROUGHLY. I'LL CONTACT STAR LABS. THERE ARE PEOPLE THERE I TRUST TO BE DISCREET.
CLARK.
THERE SHOULDN'T BE ANY DANGER IN THE FIRST TRIMESTER BUT I'M NOT LEAVING IT TO CHANCE. WE'LL NEED A BIGGER PLACE, OBVIOUSLY.
CLARK!
MAYBE WE SHOULD CONSIDER MOVING AWAY FROM METROPOLIS. SMALLVILLE WOULD BE A MUCH SAFER AND MORE PRIVATE PLACE TO RAISE A CHILD WITH POWERS. ALTHOUGH I'D PREFER METROPOLIS HIGH TO--
TONK
DID YOU JUST THROW A BOOK AT ME?
YOU'RE INVULNERABLE, I SHOULD BE ABLE TO THROW SATISFYINGLY HARD OBJECTS AT YOU SOMETIMES.

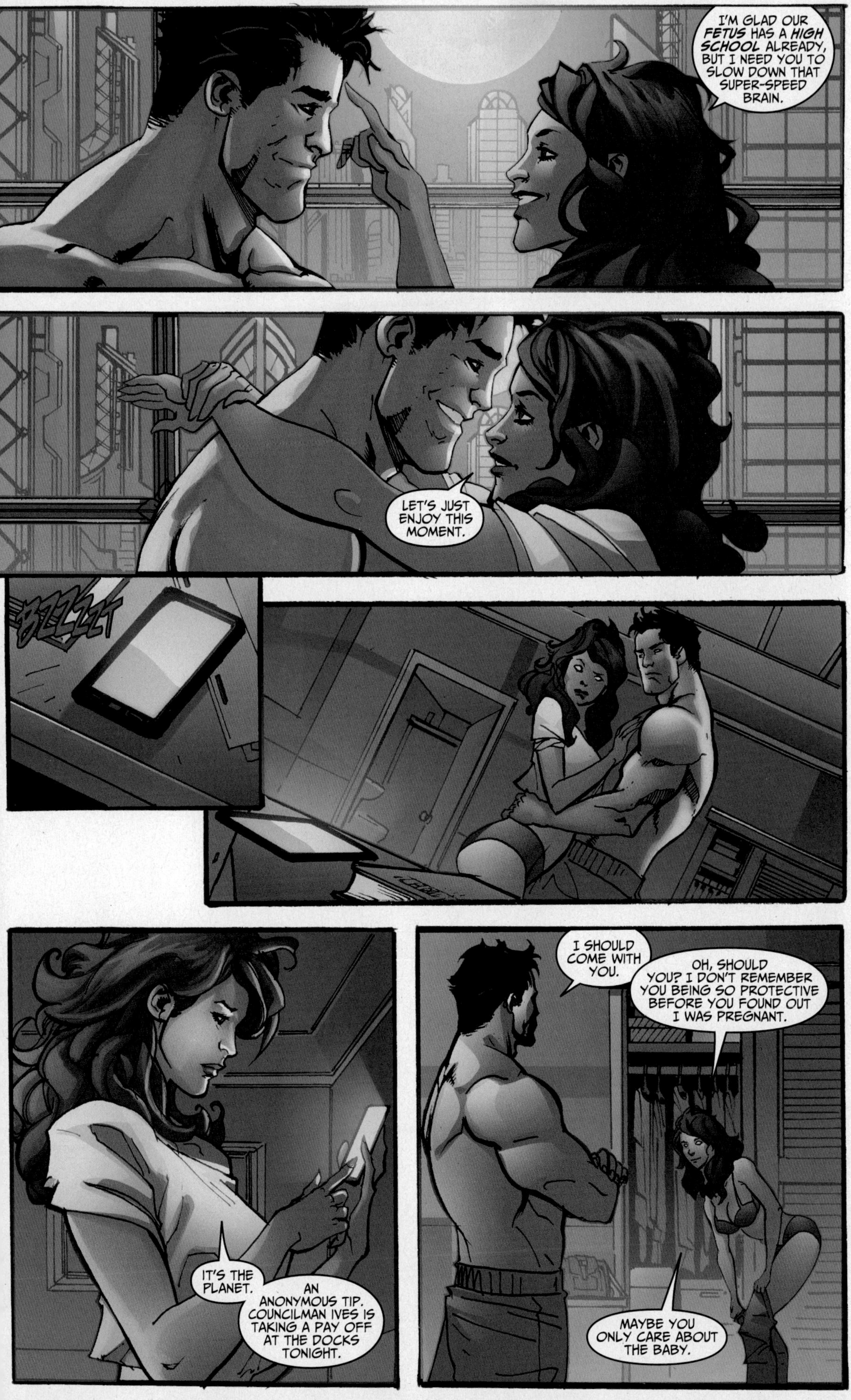
I'M GLAD OUR FETUS HAS A HIGH SCHOOL ALREADY, BUT I NEED YOU TO SLOW DOWN THAT SUPER-SPEED BRAIN.
LET'S JUST ENJOY THIS MOMENT.
BZZZZT
IT'S THE PLANET.
AN ANONYMOUS TIP. COUNCILMAN IVES IS TAKING A PAY OFF AT THE DOCKS TONIGHT.
I SHOULD COME WITH YOU.
OH, SHOULD YOU? I DON'T REMEMBER YOU BEING SO PROTECTIVE BEFORE YOU FOUND OUT I WAS PREGNANT.
MAYBE YOU ONLY CARE ABOUT THE BABY.

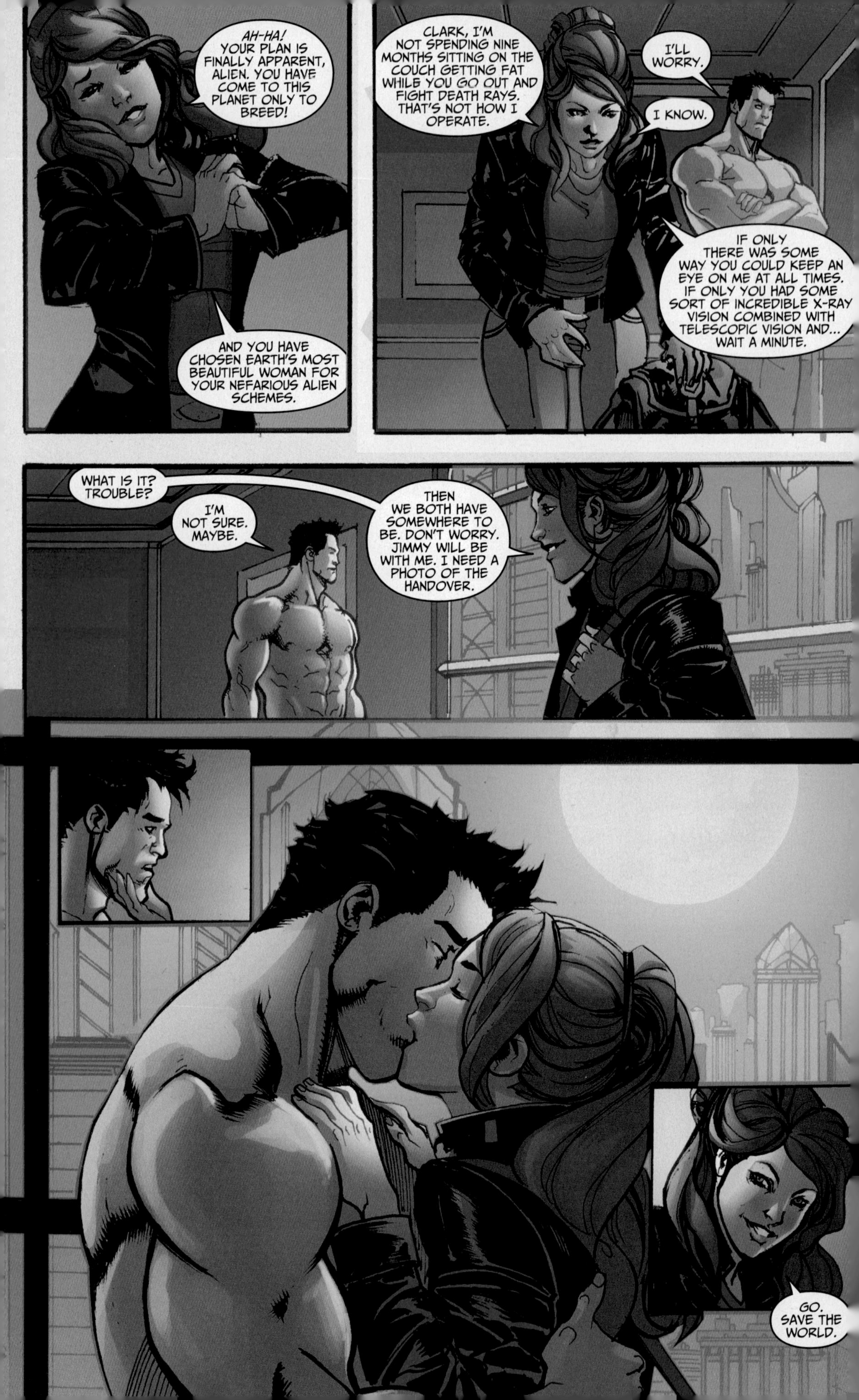
AH-HA! YOUR PLAN IS FINALLY APPARENT, ALIEN. YOU HAVE COME TO THIS PLANET ONLY TO BREED!
AND YOU HAVE CHOSEN EARTH'S MOST BEAUTIFUL WOMAN FOR YOUR NEFARIOUS ALIEN SCHEMES.
CLARK, I'M NOT SPENDING NINE MONTHS SITTING ON THE COUCH GETTING FAT WHILE YOU GO OUT AND FIGHT DEATH RAYS. THAT'S NOT HOW I OPERATE.
I'LL WORRY.
I KNOW.
IF ONLY THERE WAS SOME WAY YOU COULD KEEP AN EYE ON ME AT ALL TIMES. IF ONLY YOU HAD SOME SORT OF INCREDIBLE X-RAY VISION COMBINED WITH TELESCOPIC VISION AND... WAIT A MINUTE.
WHAT IS IT? TROUBLE?
I'M NOT SURE. MAYBE.
THEN WE BOTH HAVE SOMEWHERE TO BE. DON'T WORRY. JIMMY WILL BE WITH ME. I NEED A PHOTO OF THE HANDOVER.
GO. SAVE THE WORLD.

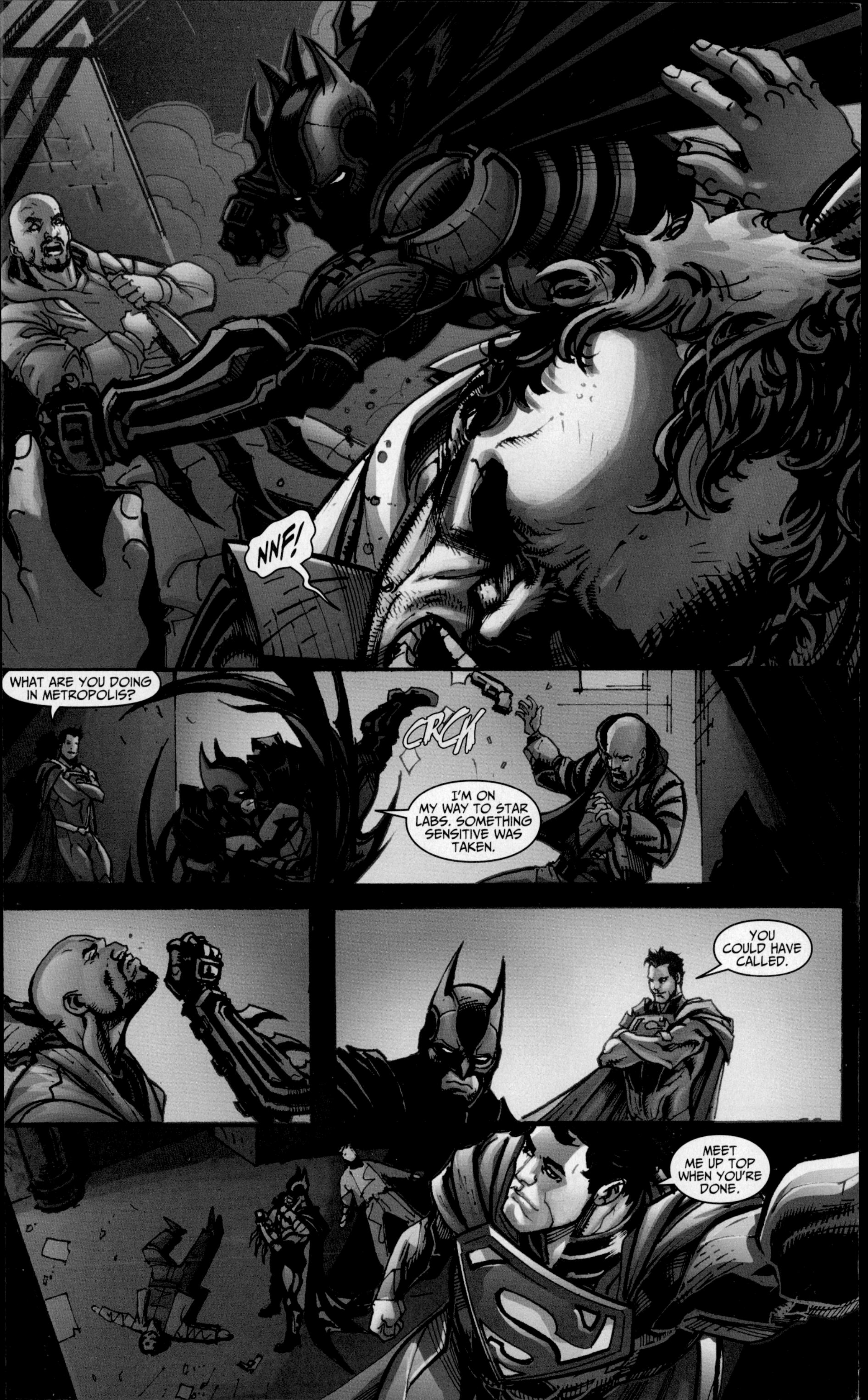
NNF!
WHAT ARE YOU DOING IN METROPOLIS?
CRCK
I'M ON MY WAY TO STAR LABS. SOMETHING SENSITIVE WAS TAKEN.
YOU COULD HAVE CALLED.
MEET ME UP TOP WHEN YOU'RE DONE.

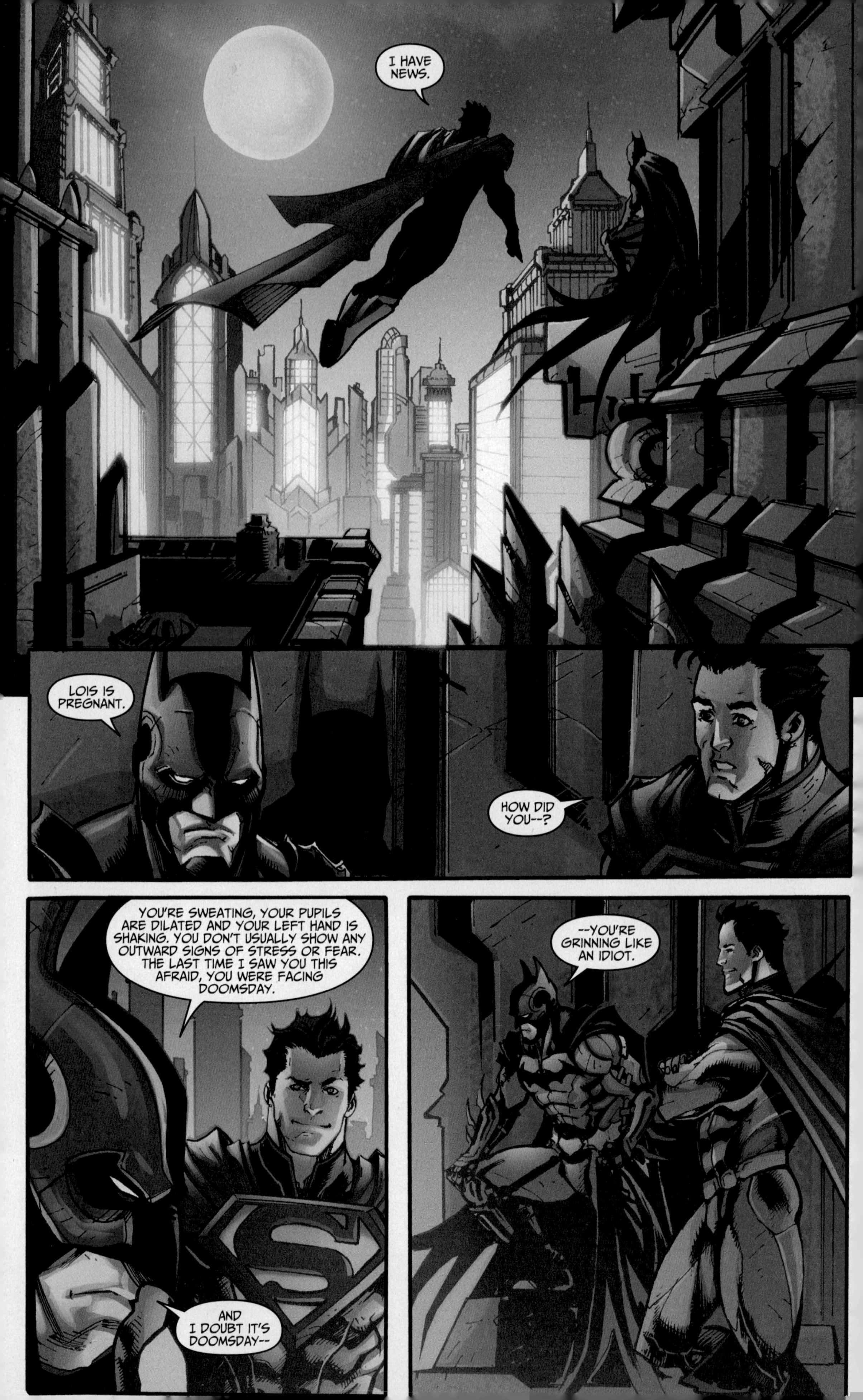
I HAVE NEWS.
LOIS IS PREGNANT.
HOW DID YOU--?
YOU'RE SWEATING, YOUR PUPILS ARE DILATED AND YOUR LEFT HAND IS SHAKING. YOU DON'T USUALLY SHOW ANY OUTWARD SIGNS OF STRESS OR FEAR. THE LAST TIME I SAW YOU THIS AFRAID, YOU WERE FACING DOOMSDAY.
AND I DOUBT IT'S DOOMSDAY--
--YOU'RE GRINNING LIKE AN IDIOT.

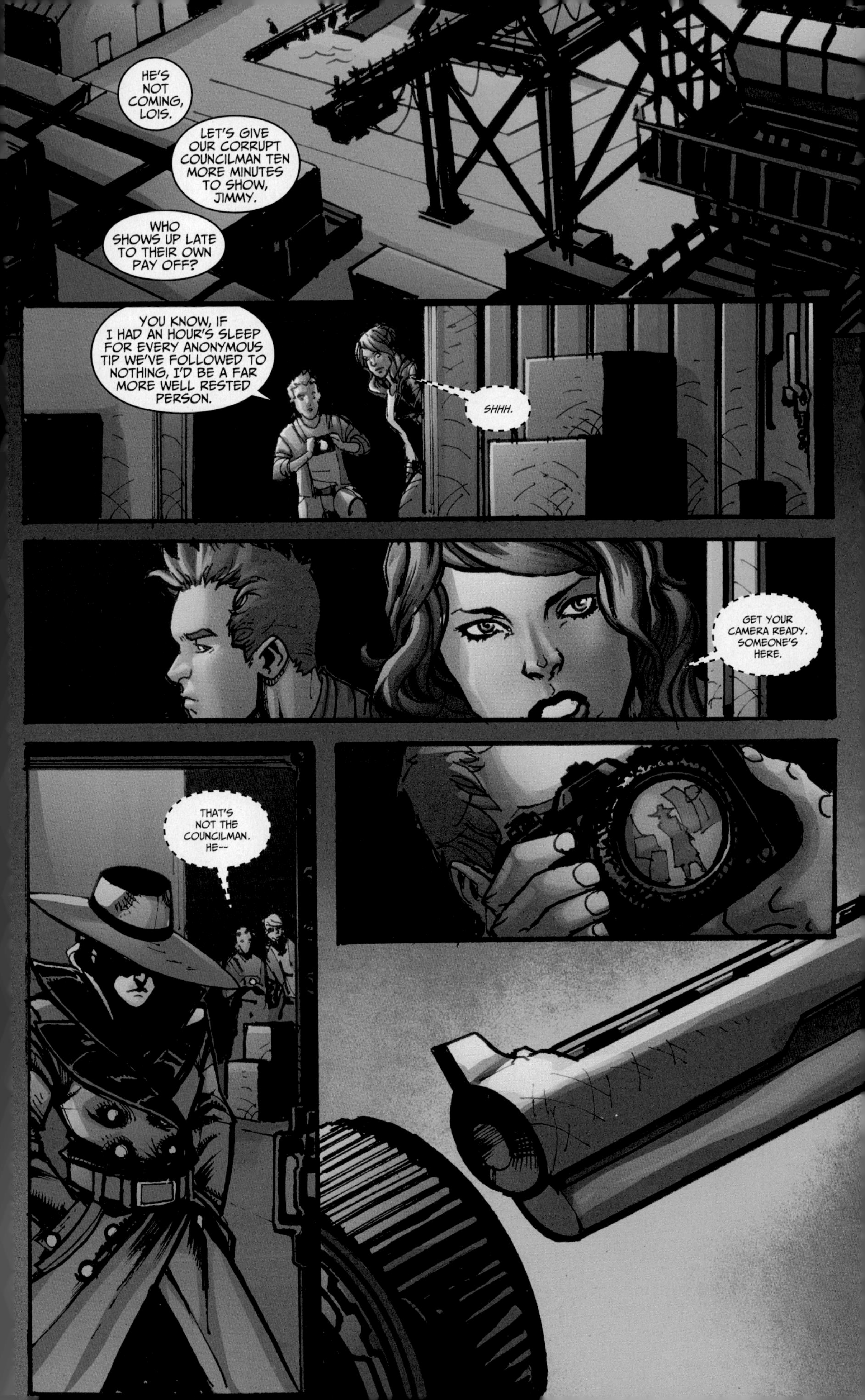
HE'S NOT COMING, LOIS.
LET'S GIVE OUR CORRUPT COUNCILMAN TEN MORE MINUTES TO SHOW, JIMMY.
WHO SHOWS UP LATE TO THEIR OWN PAY OFF?
YOU KNOW, IF I HAD AN HOUR'S SLEEP FOR EVERY ANONYMOUS TIP WE'VE FOLLOWED TO NOTHING, I'D BE A FAR MORE WELL RESTED PERSON.
SHHH.
GET YOUR CAMERA READY. SOMEONE'S HERE.
THAT'S NOT THE COUNCILMAN. HE--

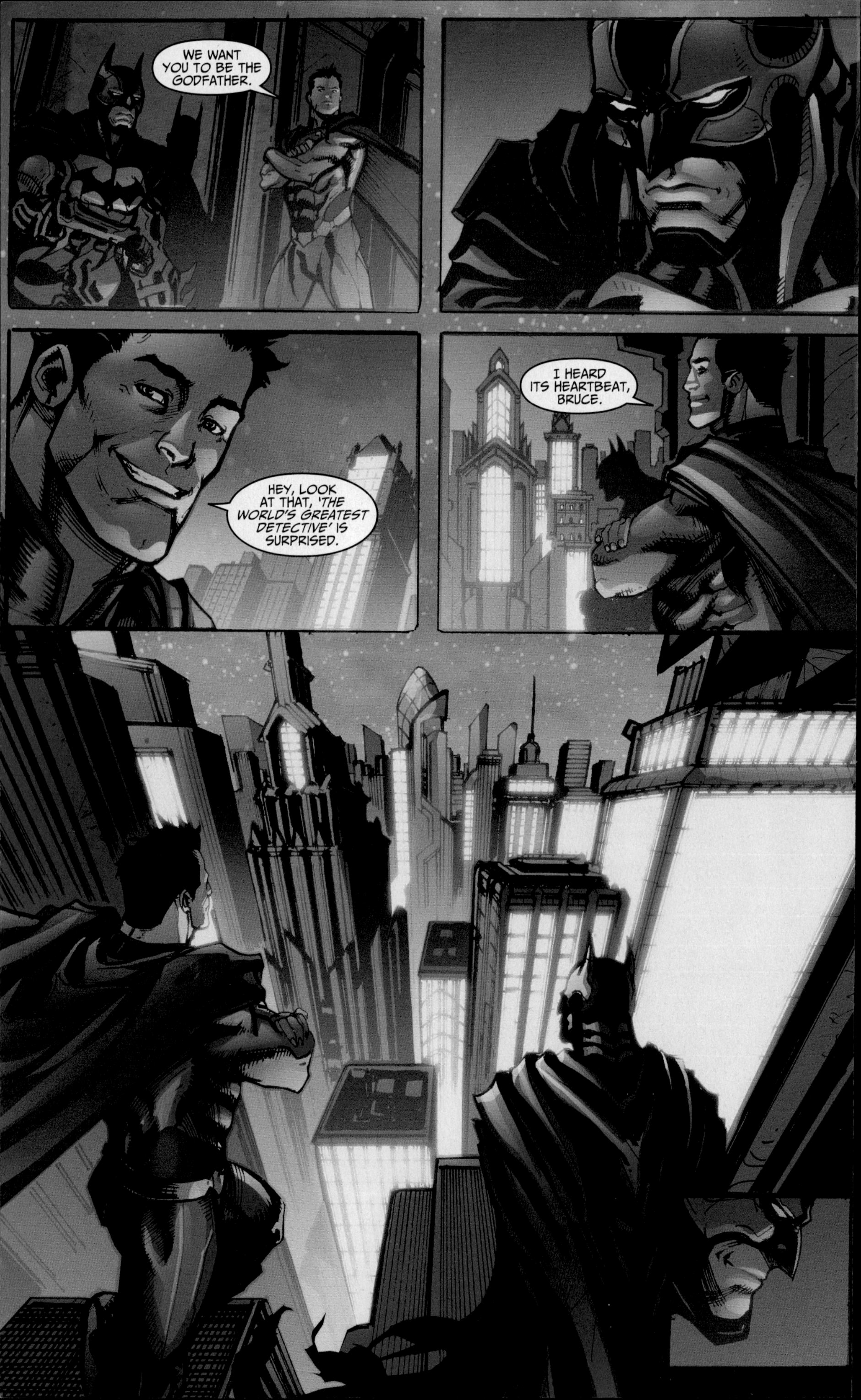
WE WANT YOU TO BE THE GODFATHER.
HEY, LOOK AT THAT, 'THE WORLD'S GREATEST DETECTIVE' IS SURPRISED.
I HEARD ITS HEARTBEAT, BRUCE.

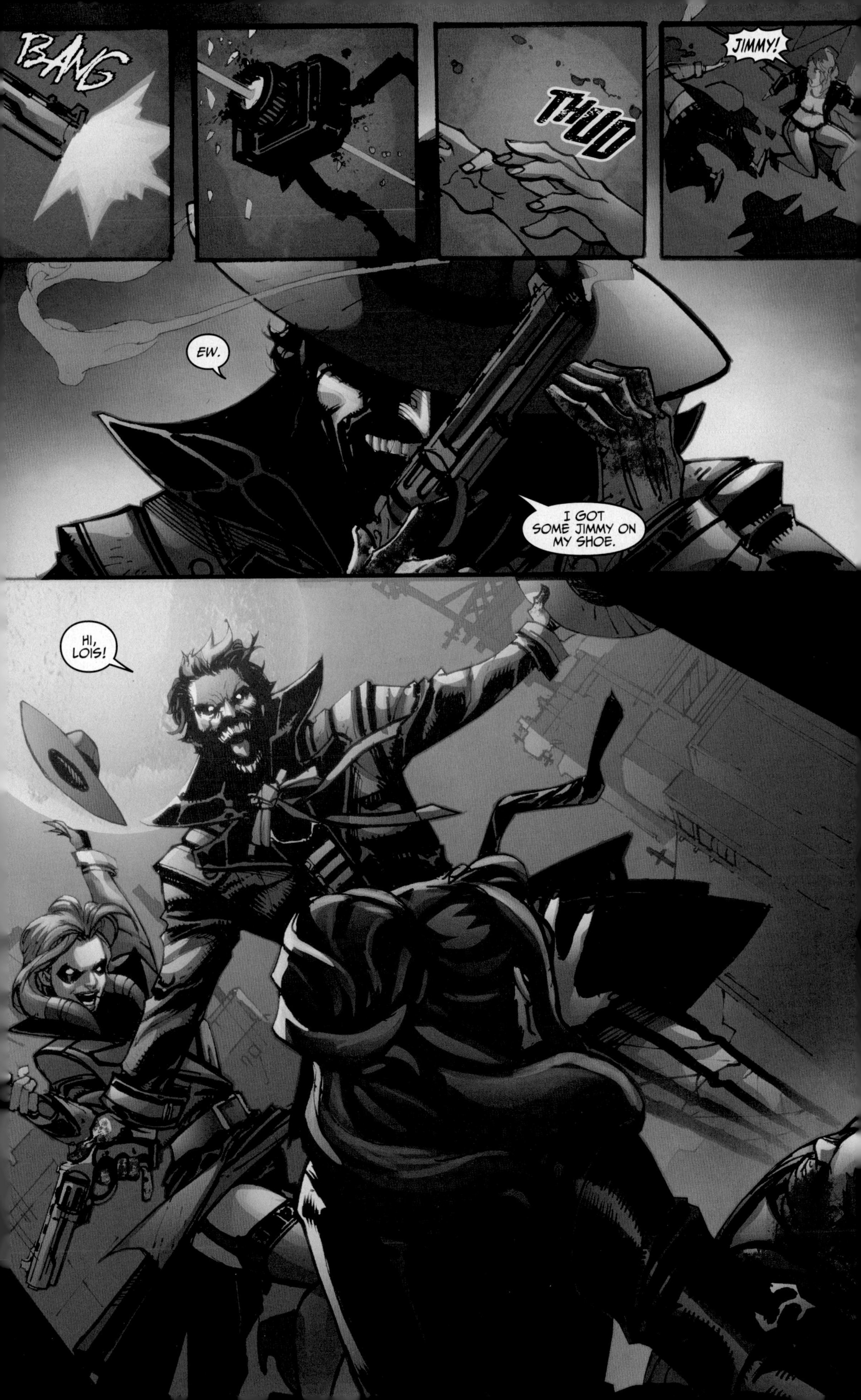
BANG
THUD
JIMMY!
EW.
I GOT SOME JIMMY ON MY SHOE.
HI, LOIS!

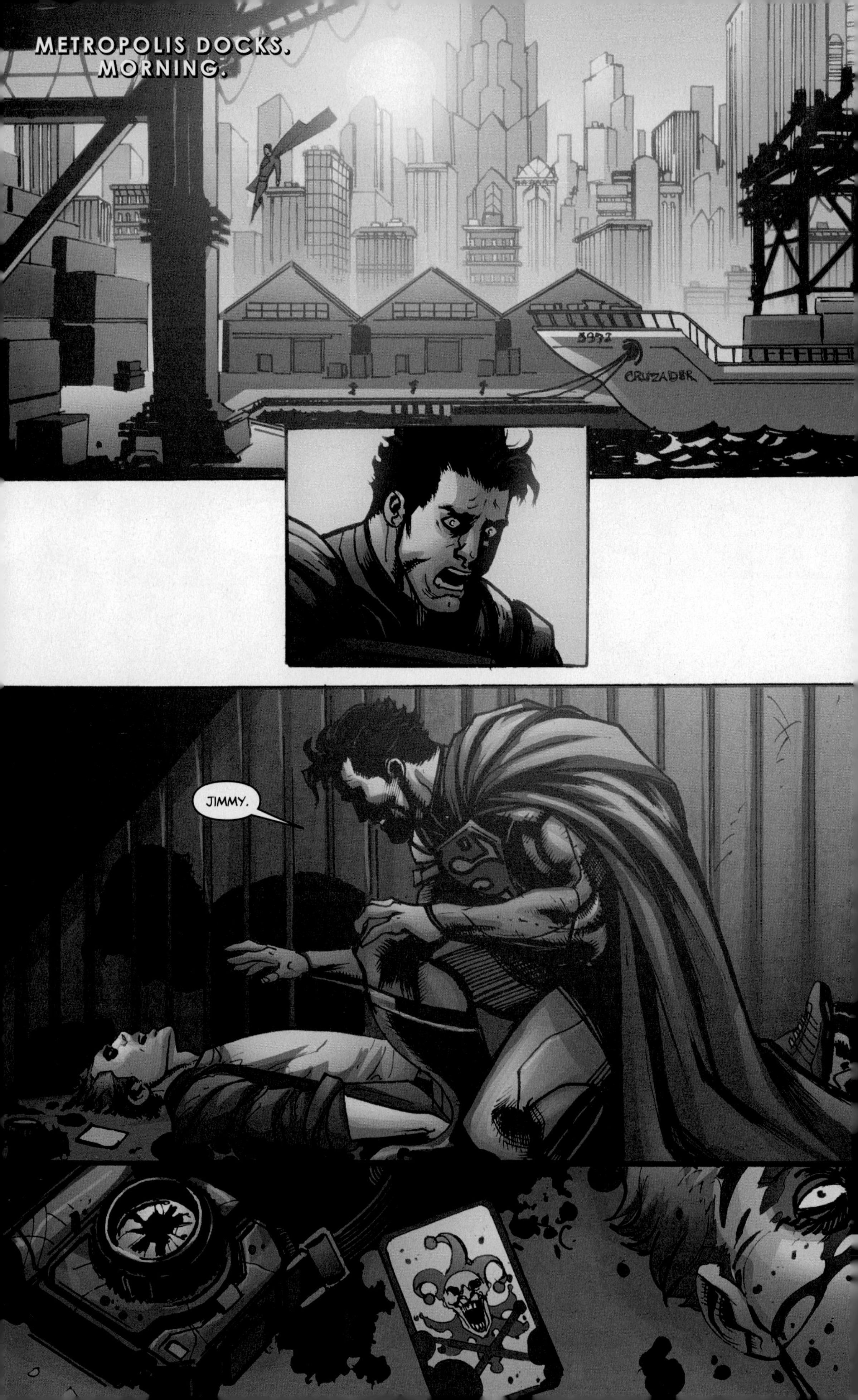
METROPOLIS DOCKS.
MORNING.
CRUZADER
JIMMY.

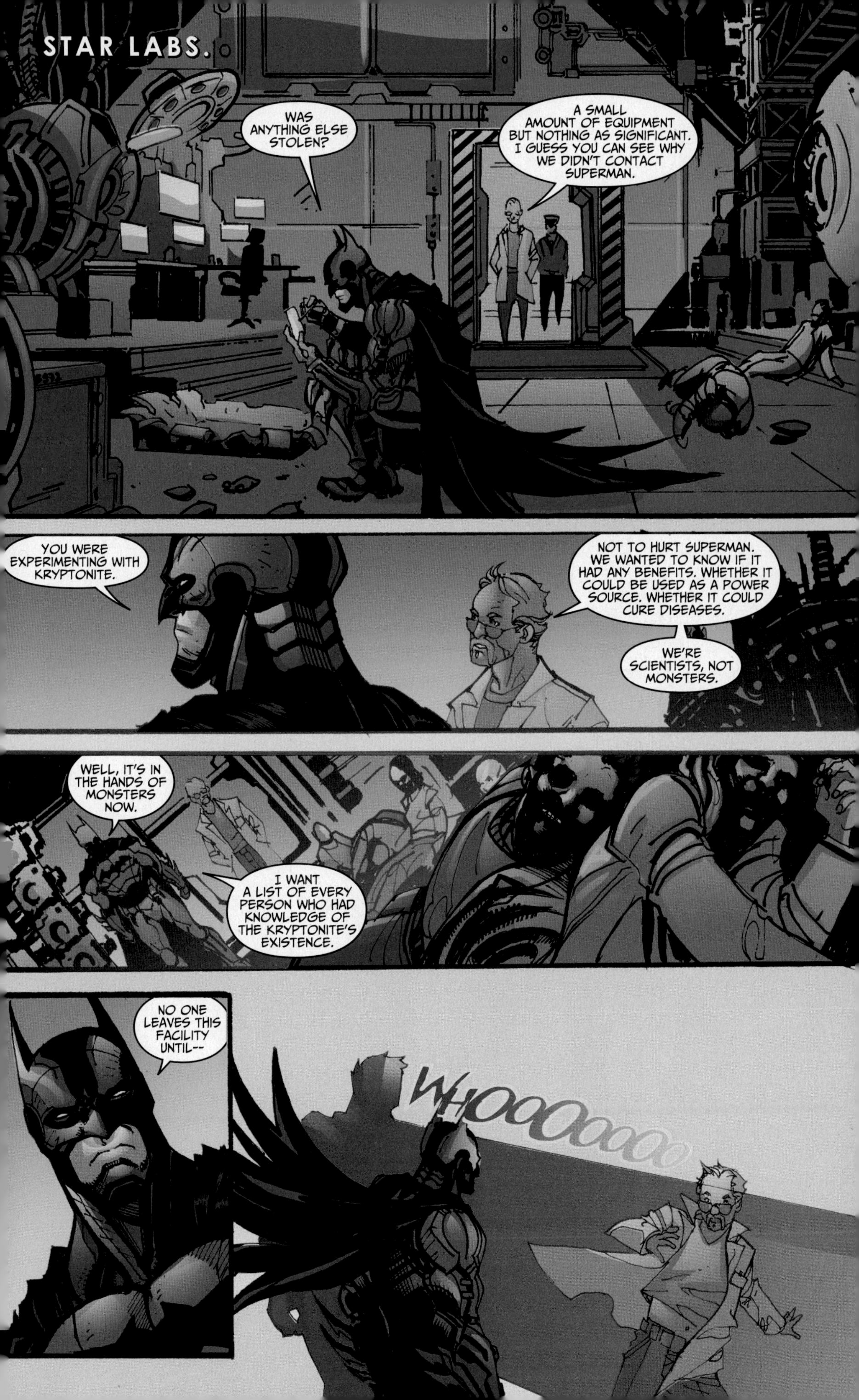
STAR LABS.
WAS ANYTHING ELSE STOLEN?
A SMALL AMOUNT OF EQUIPMENT BUT NOTHING AS SIGNIFICANT. I GUESS YOU CAN SEE WHY WE DIDN'T CONTACT SUPERMAN.
YOU WERE EXPERIMENTING WITH KRYPTONITE.
NOT TO HURT SUPERMAN. WE WANTED TO KNOW IF IT HAD ANY BENEFITS. WHETHER IT COULD BE USED AS A POWER SOURCE. WHETHER IT COULD CURE DISEASES.
WE'RE SCIENTISTS, NOT MONSTERS.
WELL, IT'S IN THE HANDS OF MONSTERS NOW.
I WANT A LIST OF EVERY PERSON WHO HAD KNOWLEDGE OF THE KRYPTONITE'S EXISTENCE.
NO ONE LEAVES THIS FACILITY UNTIL--
WHOOOOOOOO

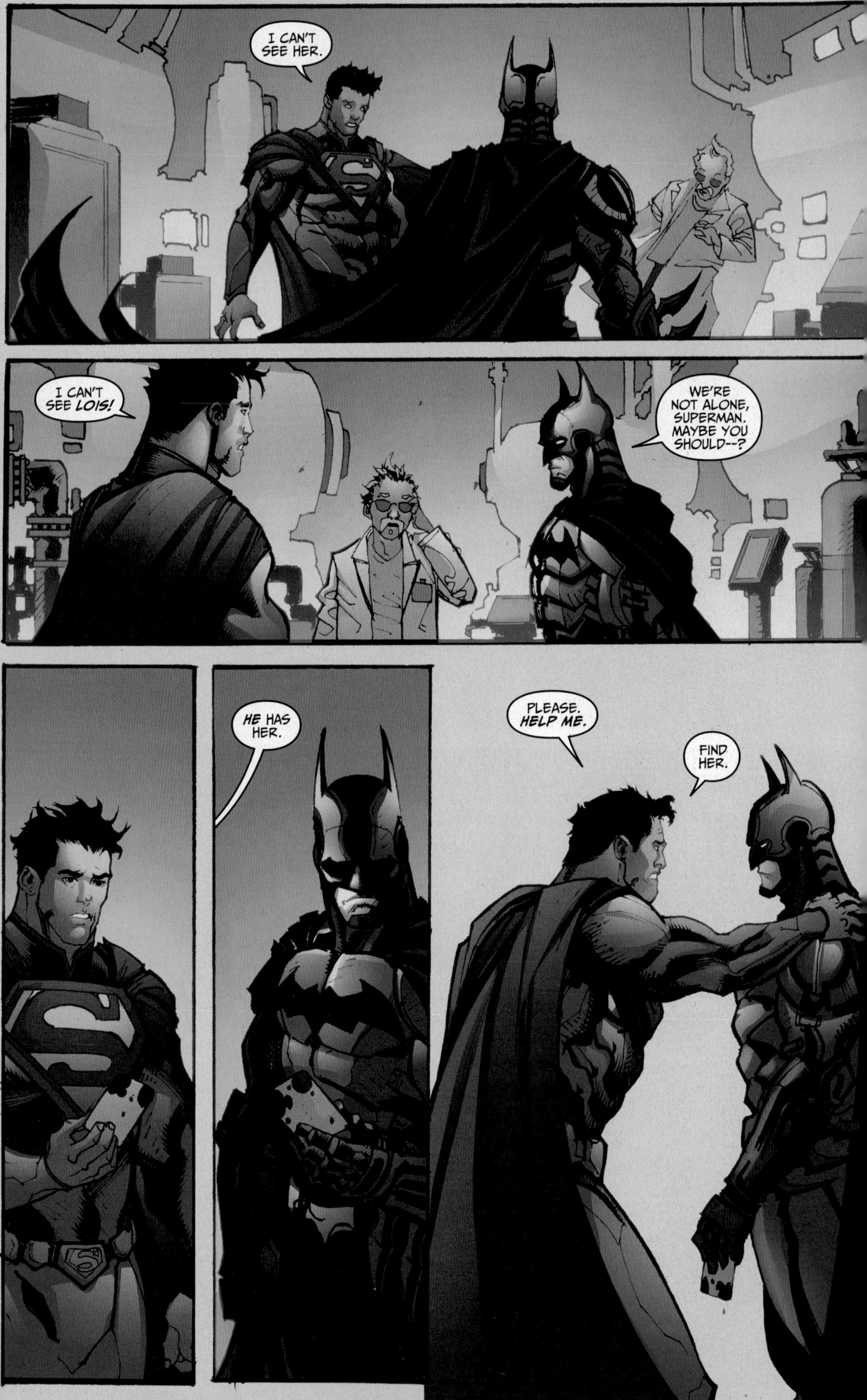
I CAN'T SEE HER.
I CAN'T SEE *LOIS!*
WE'RE NOT ALONE, SUPERMAN. MAYBE YOU SHOULD--?
HE HAS HER.
PLEASE. *HELP ME.*
FIND HER.

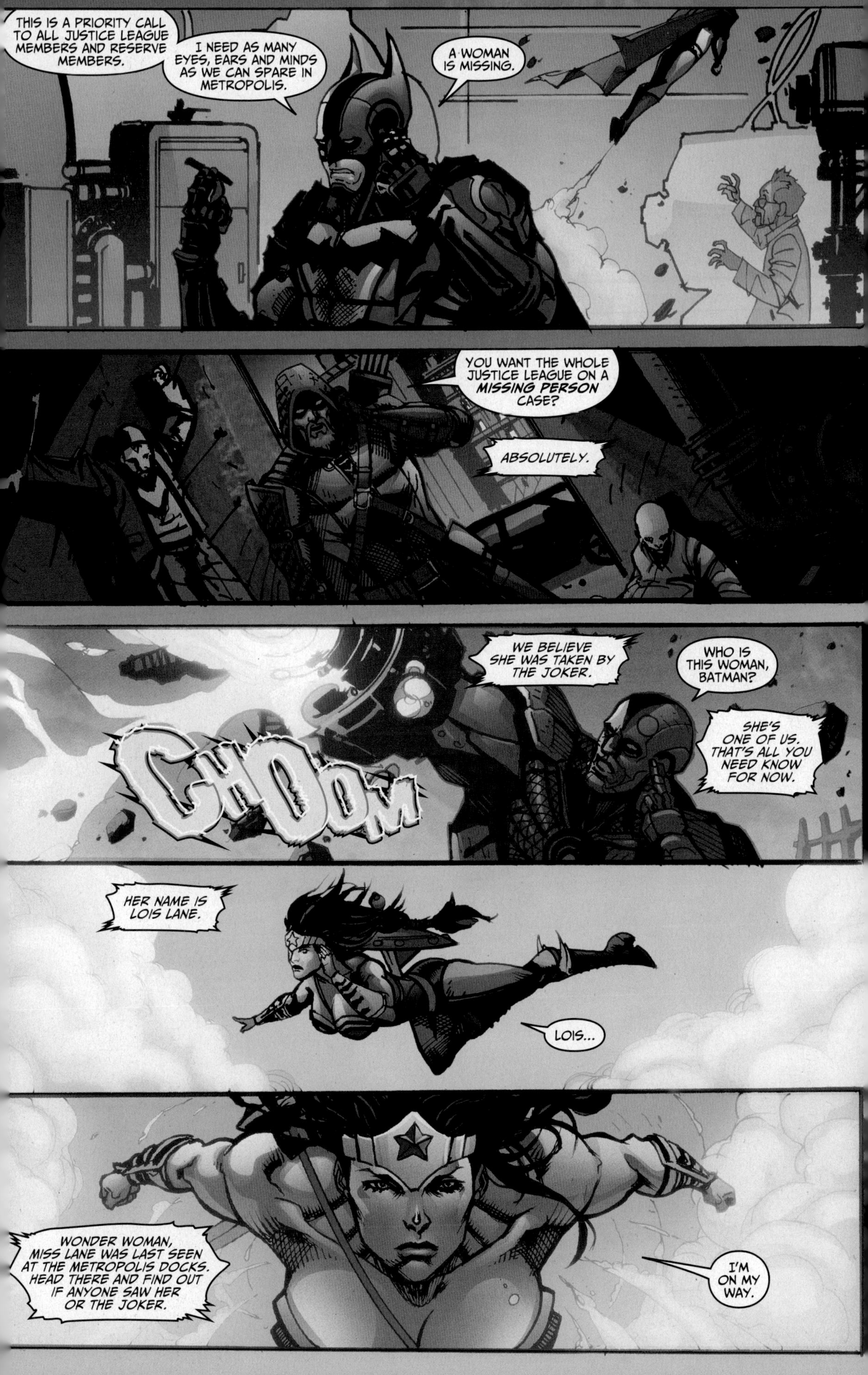

THIS IS A PRIORITY CALL TO ALL JUSTICE LEAGUE MEMBERS AND RESERVE MEMBERS.
I NEED AS MANY EYES, EARS AND MINDS AS WE CAN SPARE IN METROPOLIS.
A WOMAN IS MISSING.
YOU WANT THE WHOLE JUSTICE LEAGUE ON A *MISSING PERSON* CASE?
ABSOLUTELY.
WE BELIEVE SHE WAS TAKEN BY THE JOKER.
WHO IS THIS WOMAN, BATMAN?
SHE'S ONE OF US. THAT'S ALL YOU NEED KNOW FOR NOW.
CHOOOM
HER NAME IS LOIS LANE.
LOIS...
WONDER WOMAN, MISS LANE WAS LAST SEEN AT THE METROPOLIS DOCKS. HEAD THERE AND FIND OUT IF ANYONE SAW HER OR THE JOKER.
I'M ON MY WAY.

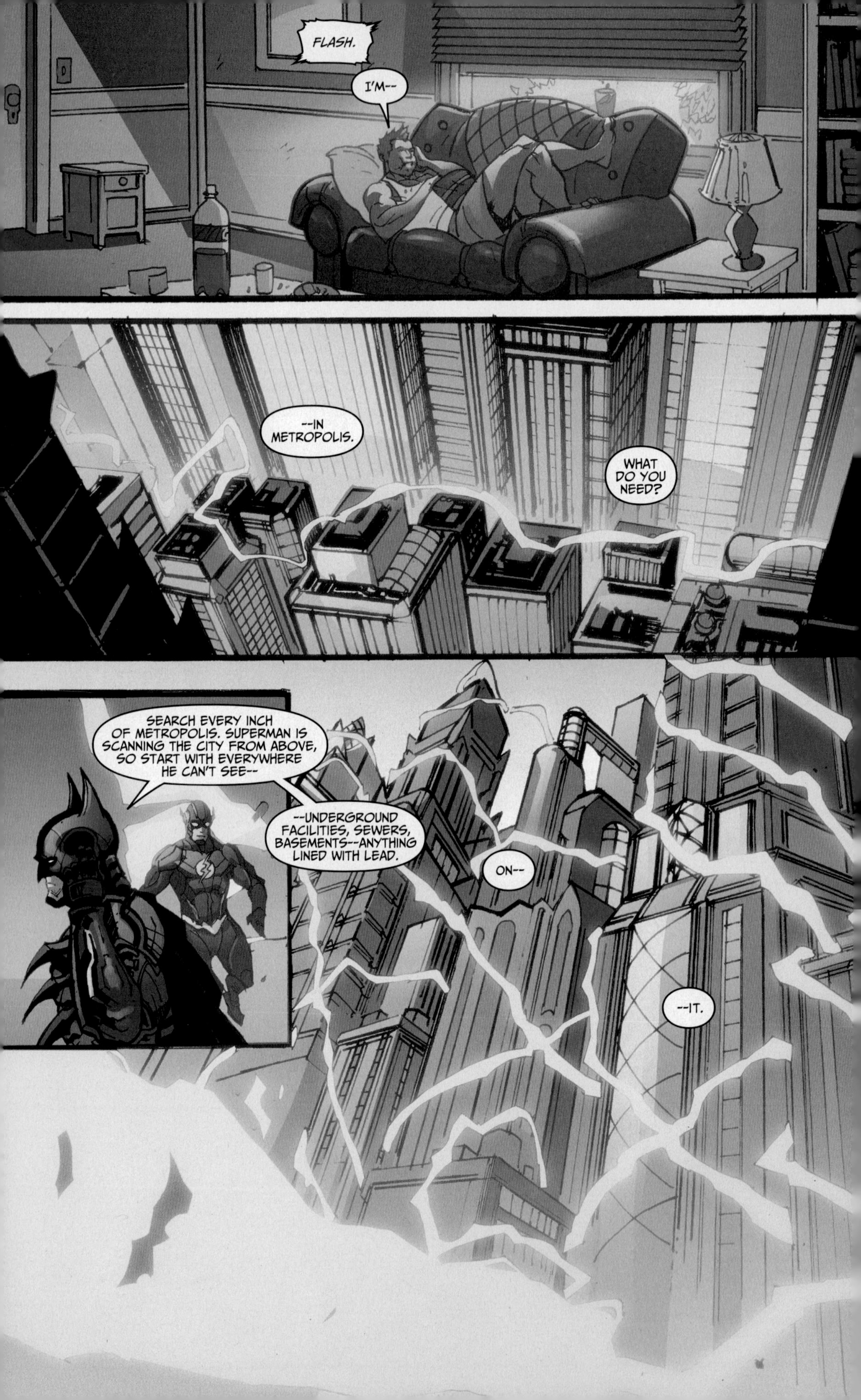
FLASH.
I'M--
--IN METROPOLIS.
WHAT DO YOU NEED?
SEARCH EVERY INCH OF METROPOLIS. SUPERMAN IS SCANNING THE CITY FROM ABOVE, SO START WITH EVERYWHERE HE CAN'T SEE--
--UNDERGROUND FACILITIES, SEWERS, BASEMENTS--ANYTHING LINED WITH LEAD.
ON--
--IT.

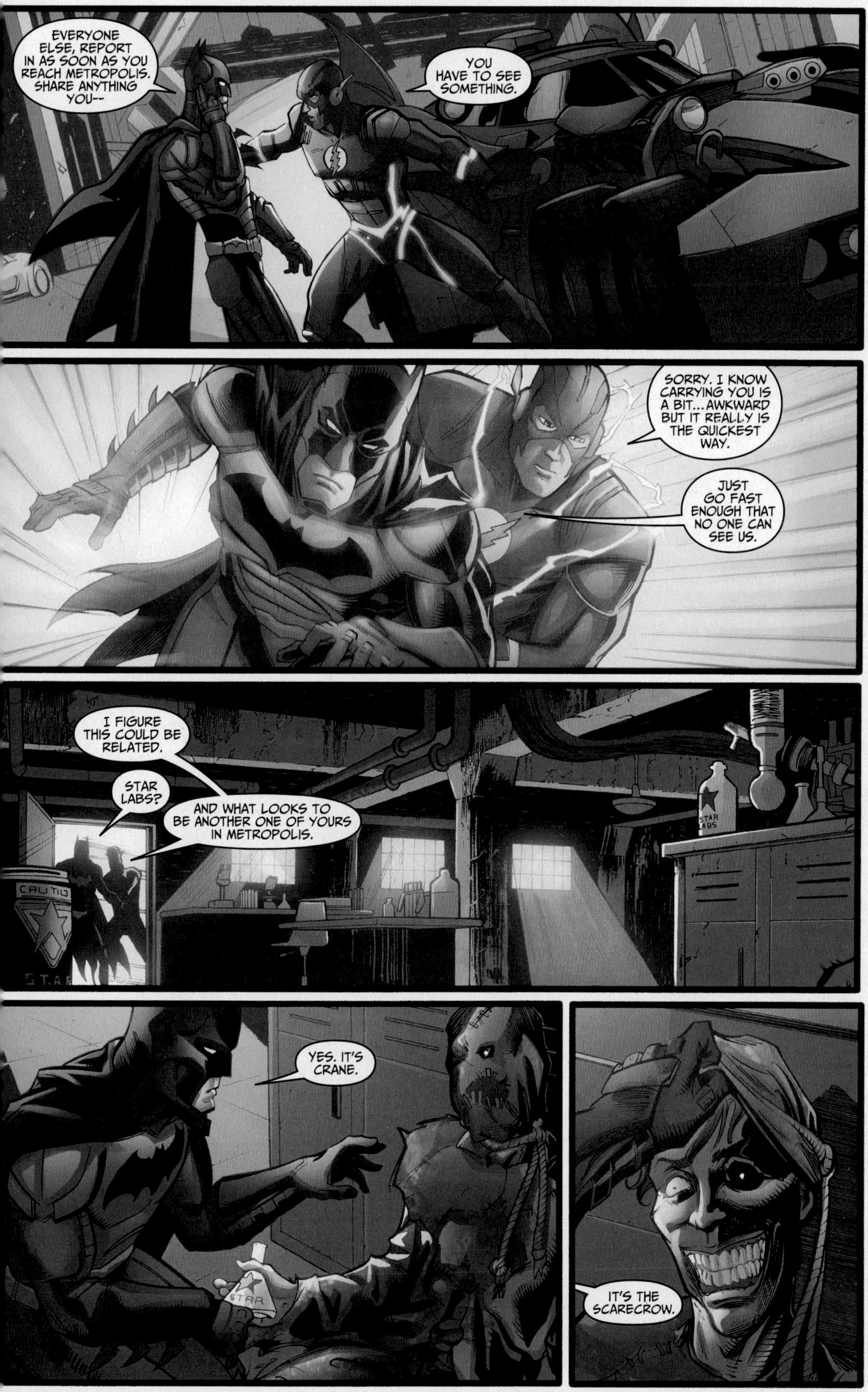
EVERYONE ELSE, REPORT IN AS SOON AS YOU REACH METROPOLIS. SHARE ANYTHING YOU--
YOU HAVE TO SEE SOMETHING.
SORRY. I KNOW CARRYING YOU IS A BIT... AWKWARD BUT IT REALLY IS THE QUICKEST WAY.
JUST GO FAST ENOUGH THAT NO ONE CAN SEE US.
I FIGURE THIS COULD BE RELATED.
STAR LABS?
AND WHAT LOOKS TO BE ANOTHER ONE OF YOURS IN METROPOLIS.
YES. IT'S CRANE.
IT'S THE SCARECROW.

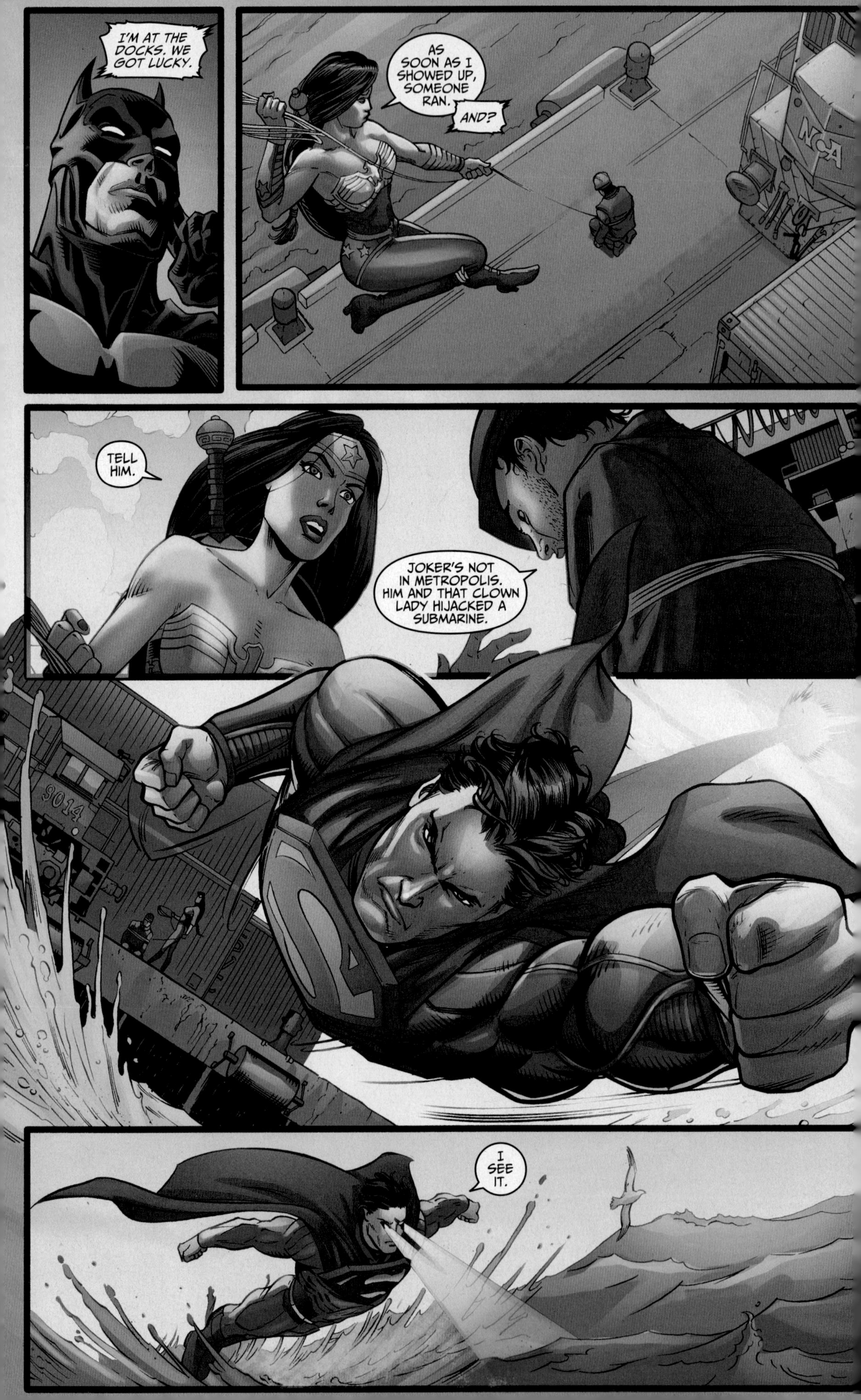
I'M AT THE DOCKS. WE GOT LUCKY.
AS SOON AS I SHOWED UP, SOMEONE RAN.
AND?
TELL HIM.
JOKER'S NOT IN METROPOLIS. HIM AND THAT CLOWN LADY HIJACKED A SUBMARINE.
I SEE IT.

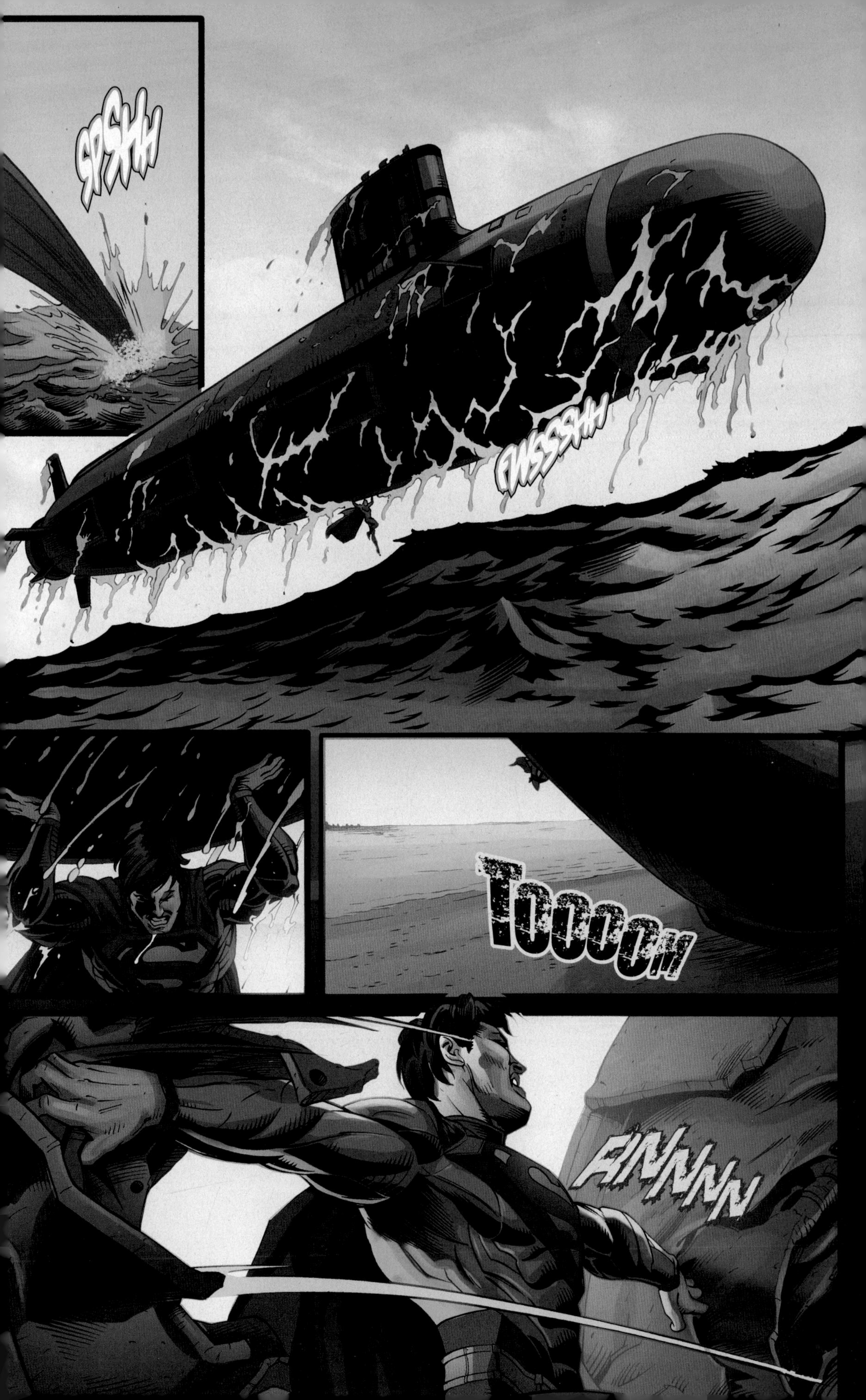
SPSHH
FWSSSHH
TOOOOOM
RNNNN

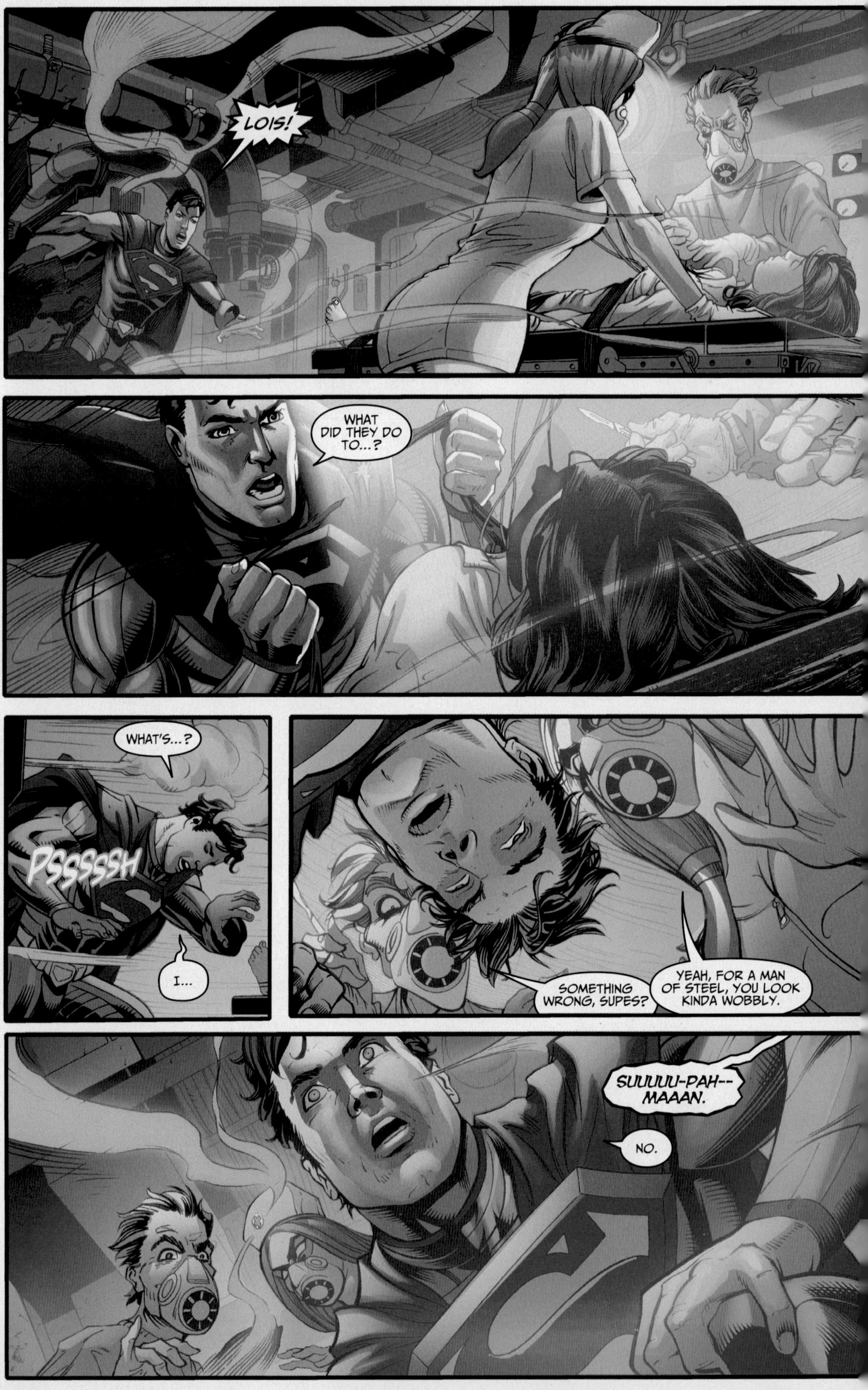
LOIS!
WHAT DID THEY DO TO...?
WHAT'S...?
PSSSSSH
I...
SOMETHING WRONG, SUPES?
YEAH, FOR A MAN OF STEEL, YOU LOOK KINDA WOBBLY.
SUUUUU-PAH-- MAAAN.
NO.

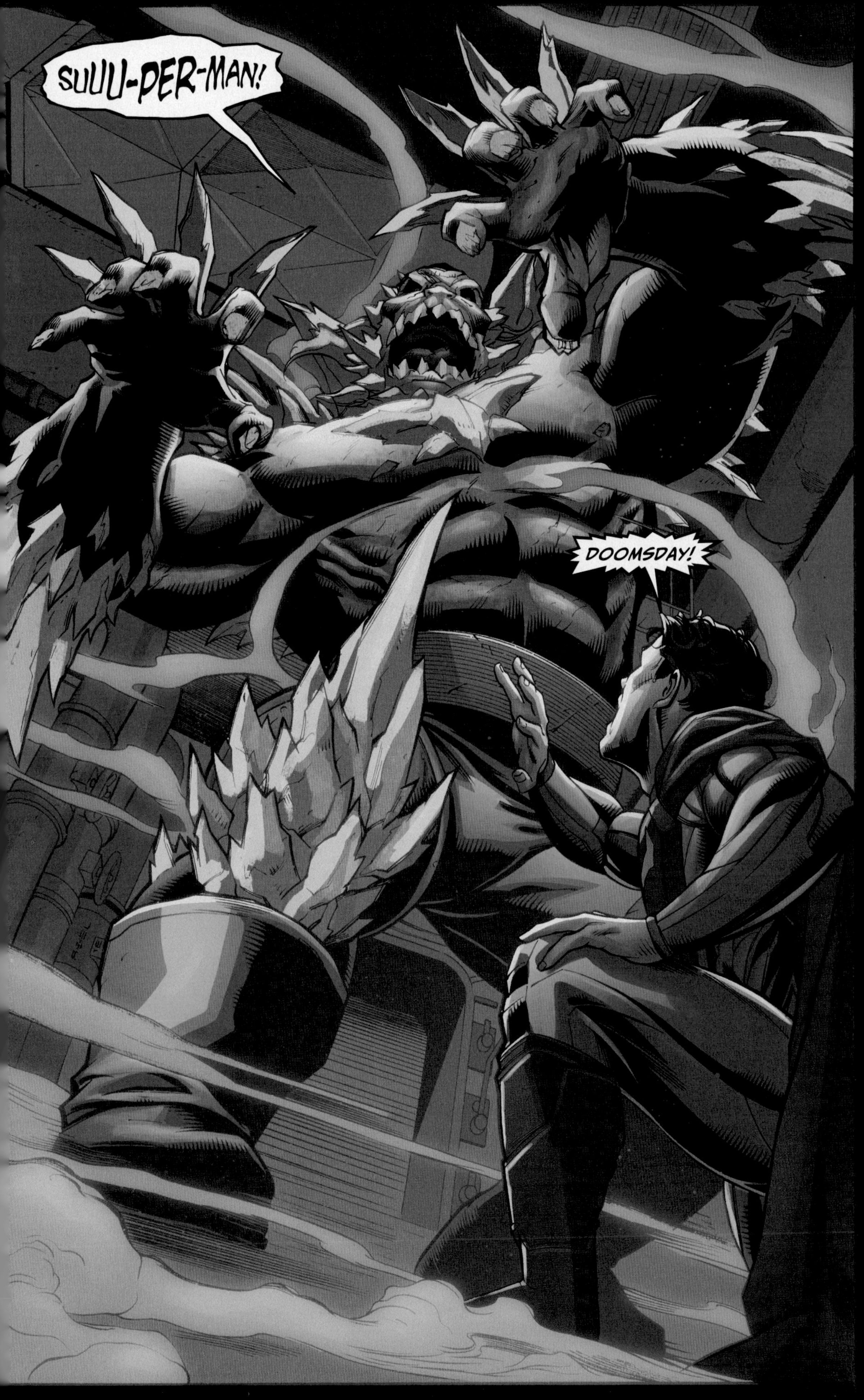
SUUU-PER-MAN!
DOOMSDAY!

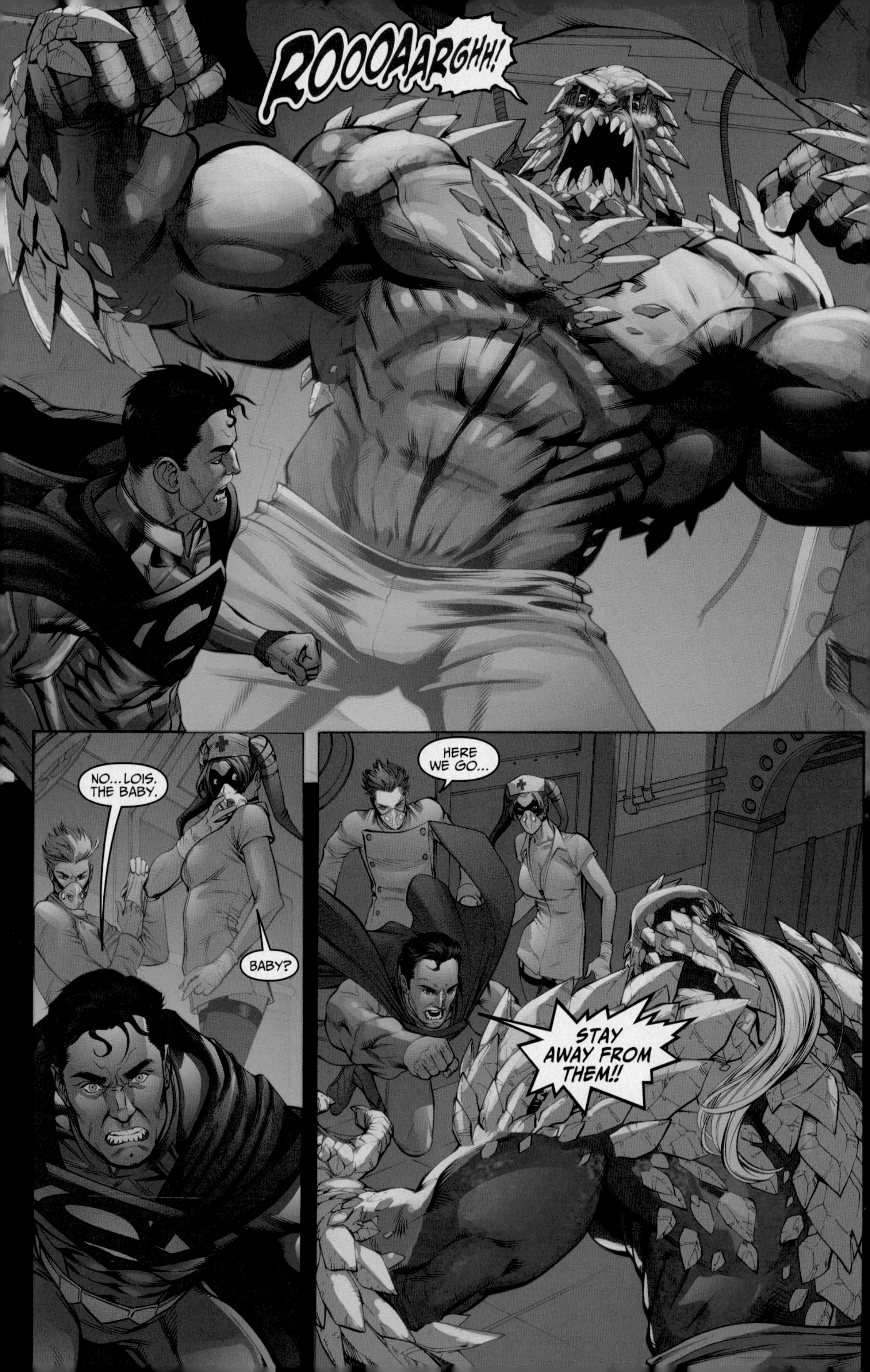
ROOOAARGHH!
NO...LOIS. THE BABY.
BABY?
HERE WE GO...
STAY AWAY FROM THEM!!

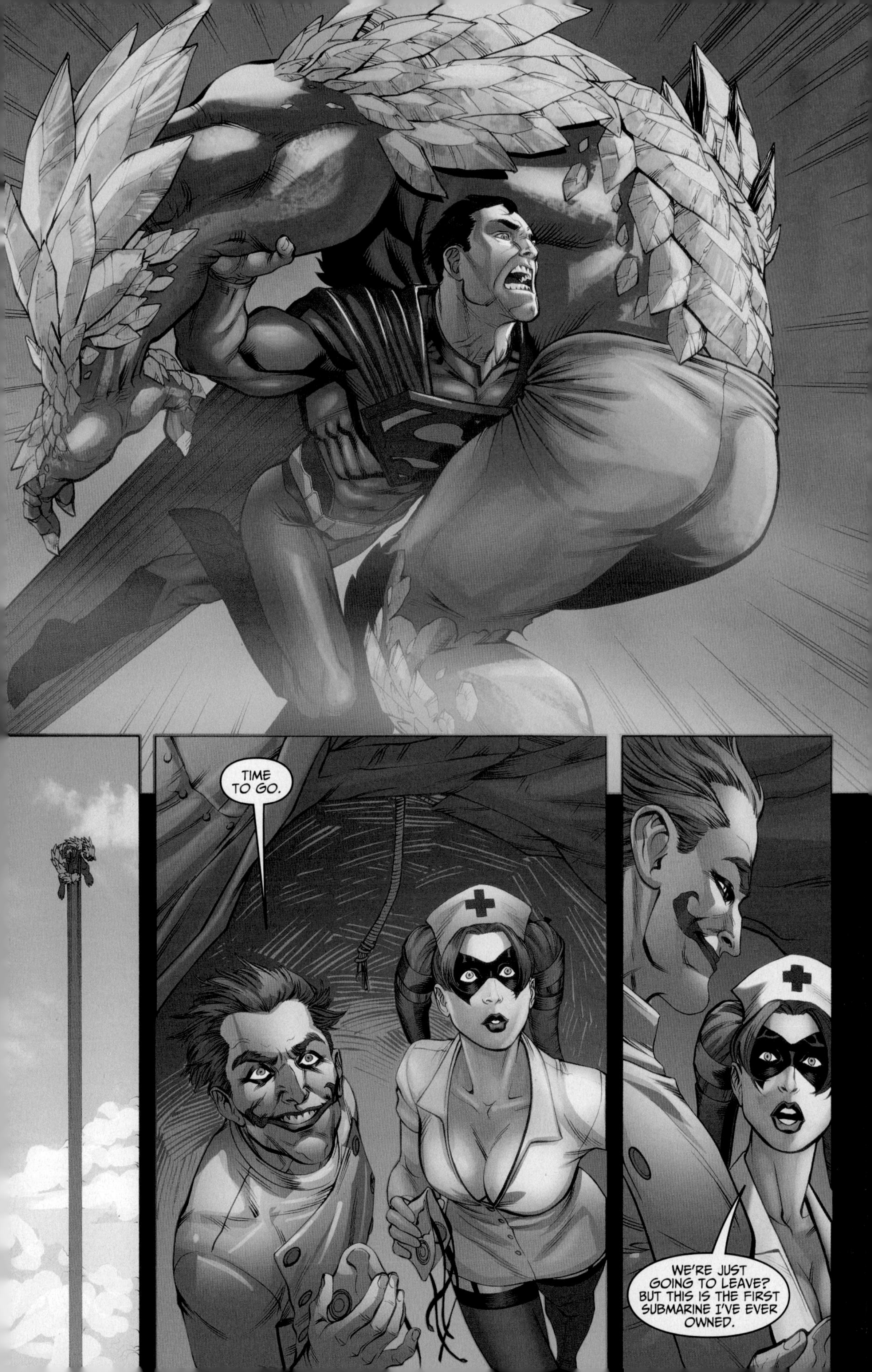
TIME TO GO.
WE'RE JUST GOING TO LEAVE? BUT THIS IS THE FIRST SUBMARINE I'VE EVER OWNED.

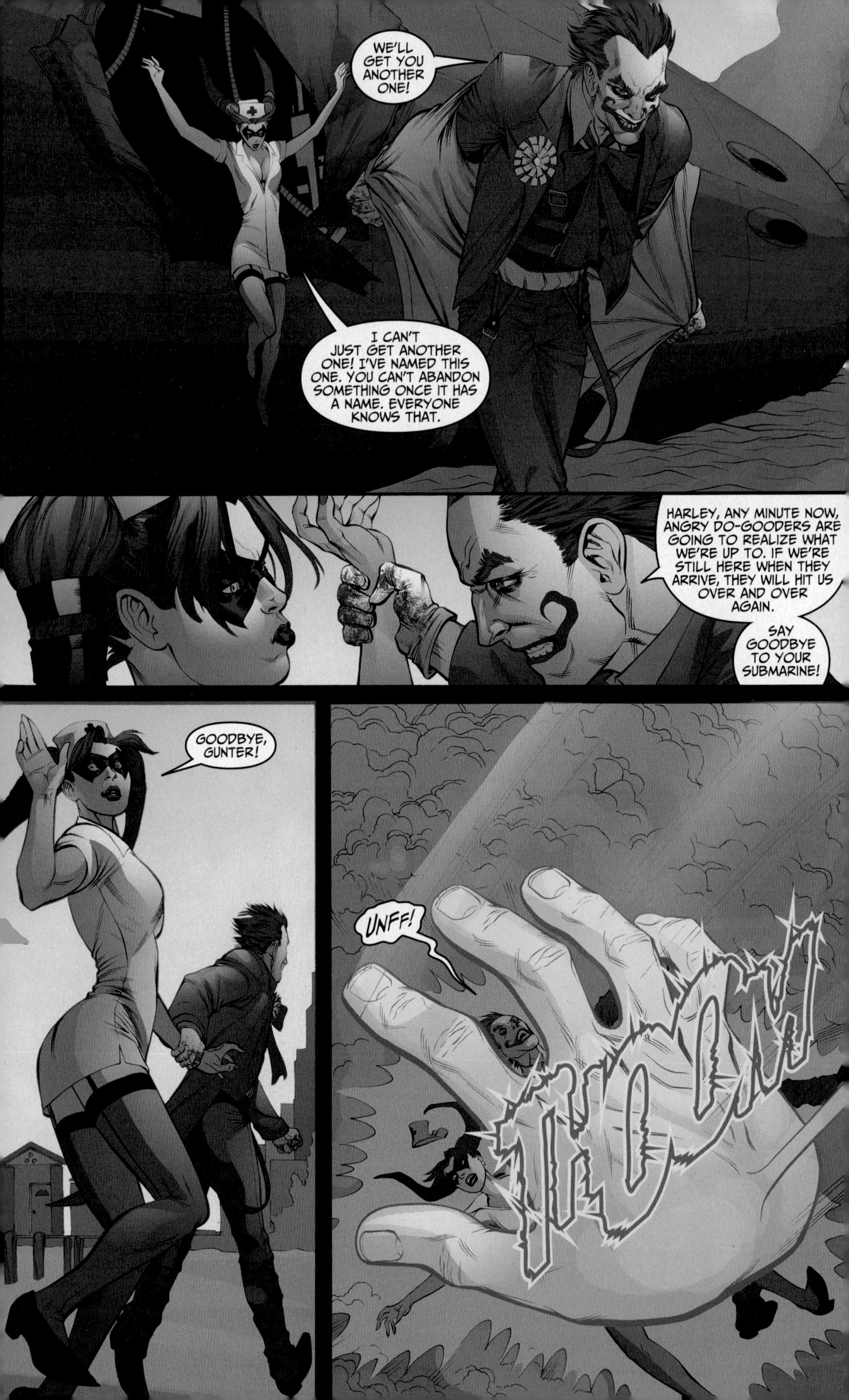
WE'LL GET YOU ANOTHER ONE!
I CAN'T JUST GET ANOTHER ONE! I'VE NAMED THIS ONE. YOU CAN'T ABANDON SOMETHING ONCE IT HAS A NAME. EVERYONE KNOWS THAT.
HARLEY, ANY MINUTE NOW, ANGRY DO-GOODERS ARE GOING TO REALIZE WHAT WE'RE UP TO. IF WE'RE STILL HERE WHEN THEY ARRIVE, THEY WILL HIT US OVER AND OVER AGAIN.
SAY GOODBYE TO YOUR SUBMARINE!
GOODBYE, GUNTER!
UNFF!

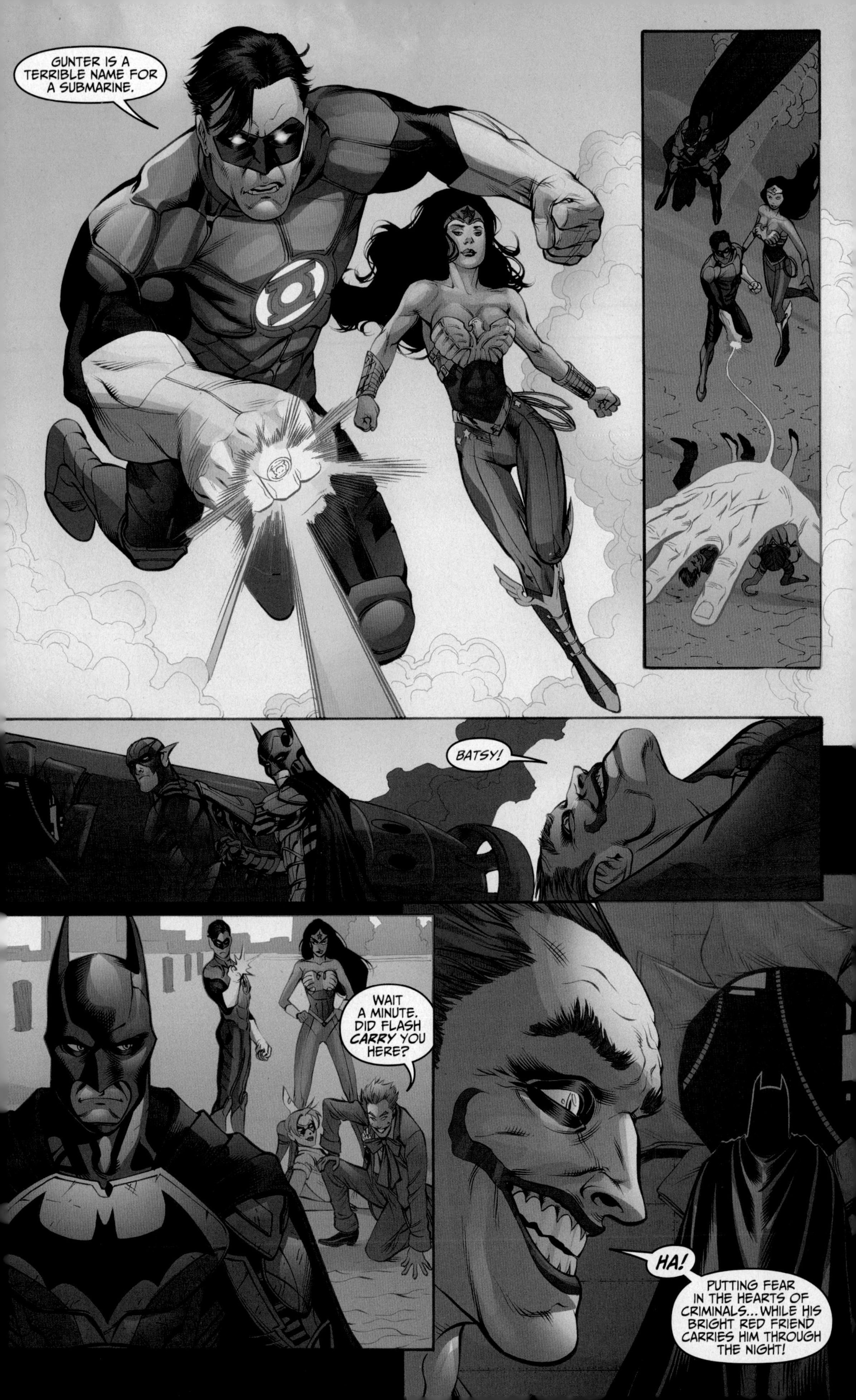
GUNTER IS A TERRIBLE NAME FOR A SUBMARINE.
BATSY!
WAIT A MINUTE. DID FLASH CARRY YOU HERE?
HA!
PUTTING FEAR IN THE HEARTS OF CRIMINALS... WHILE HIS BRIGHT RED FRIEND CARRIES HIM THROUGH THE NIGHT!

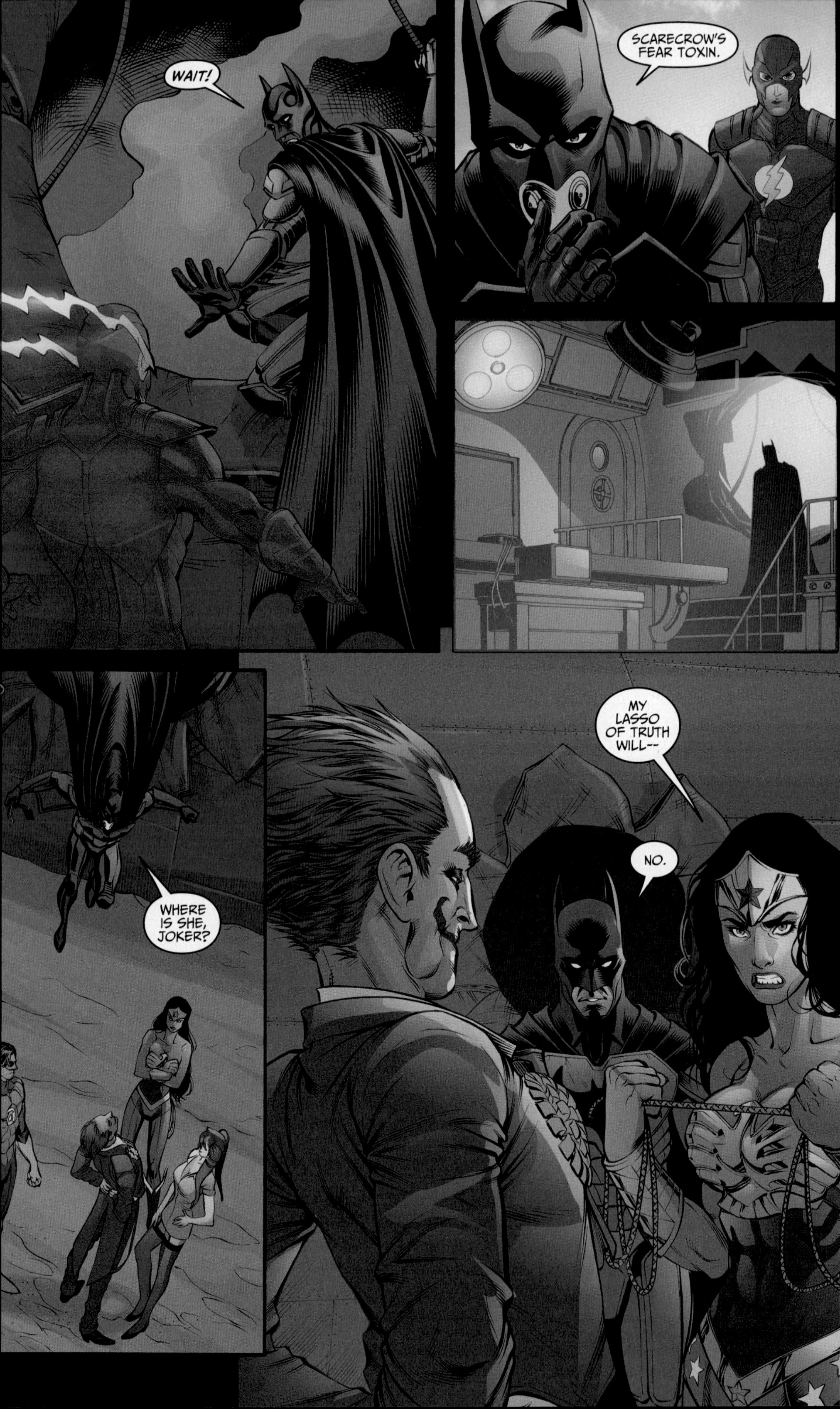
WAIT!
SCARECROW'S FEAR TOXIN.
WHERE IS SHE, JOKER?
MY LASSO OF TRUTH WILL--
NO.

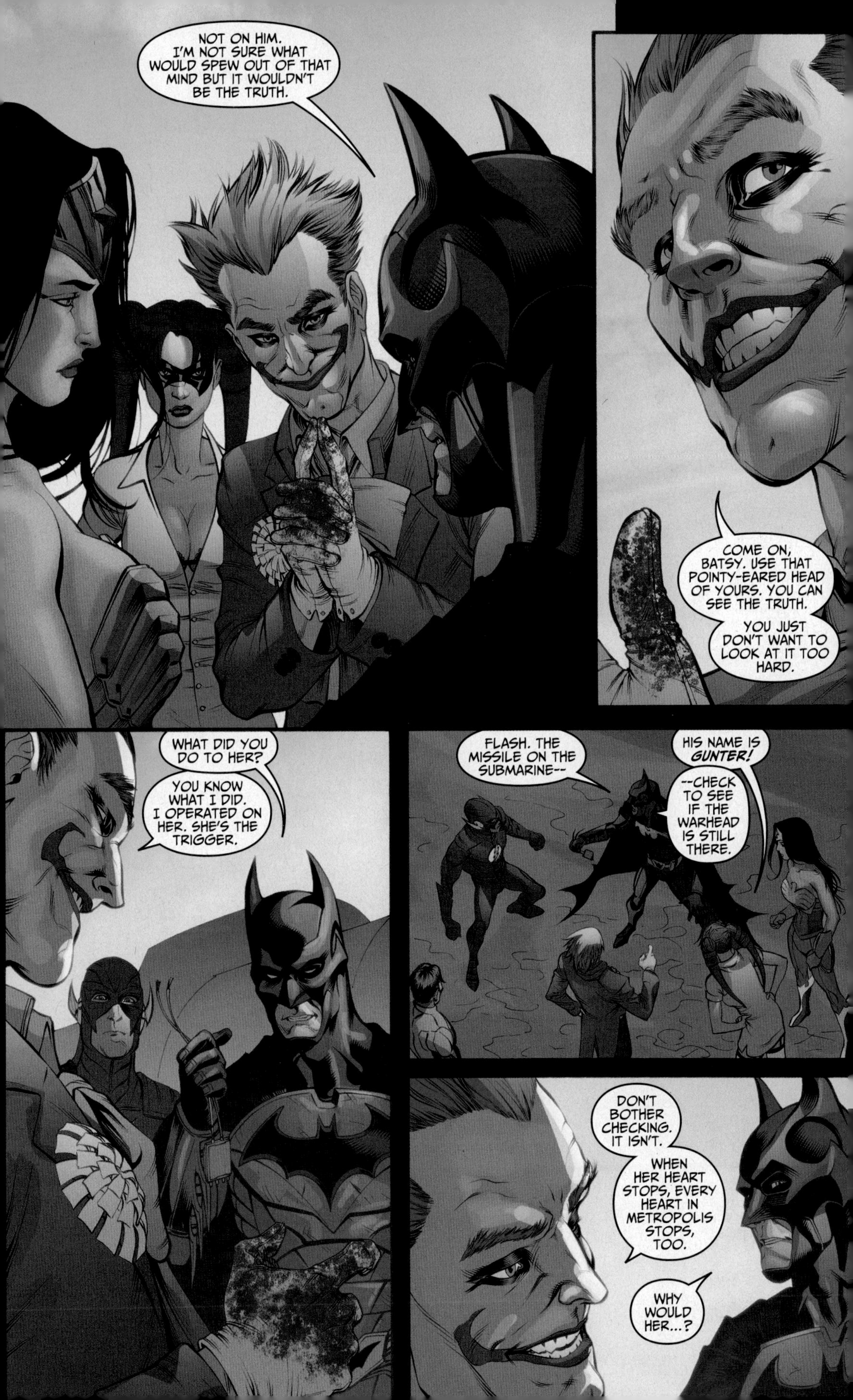
NOT ON HIM. I'M NOT SURE WHAT WOULD SPEW OUT OF THAT MIND BUT IT WOULDN'T BE THE TRUTH.
COME ON, BATSY. USE THAT POINTY-EARED HEAD OF YOURS. YOU CAN SEE THE TRUTH.
YOU JUST DON'T WANT TO LOOK AT IT TOO HARD.
WHAT DID YOU DO TO HER?
YOU KNOW WHAT I DID. I OPERATED ON HER. SHE'S THE TRIGGER.
FLASH. THE MISSILE ON THE SUBMARINE--
HIS NAME IS *GUNTER!*
--CHECK TO SEE IF THE WARHEAD IS STILL THERE.
DON'T BOTHER CHECKING. IT ISN'T.
WHEN HER HEART STOPS, EVERY HEART IN METROPOLIS STOPS, TOO.
WHY WOULD HER...?

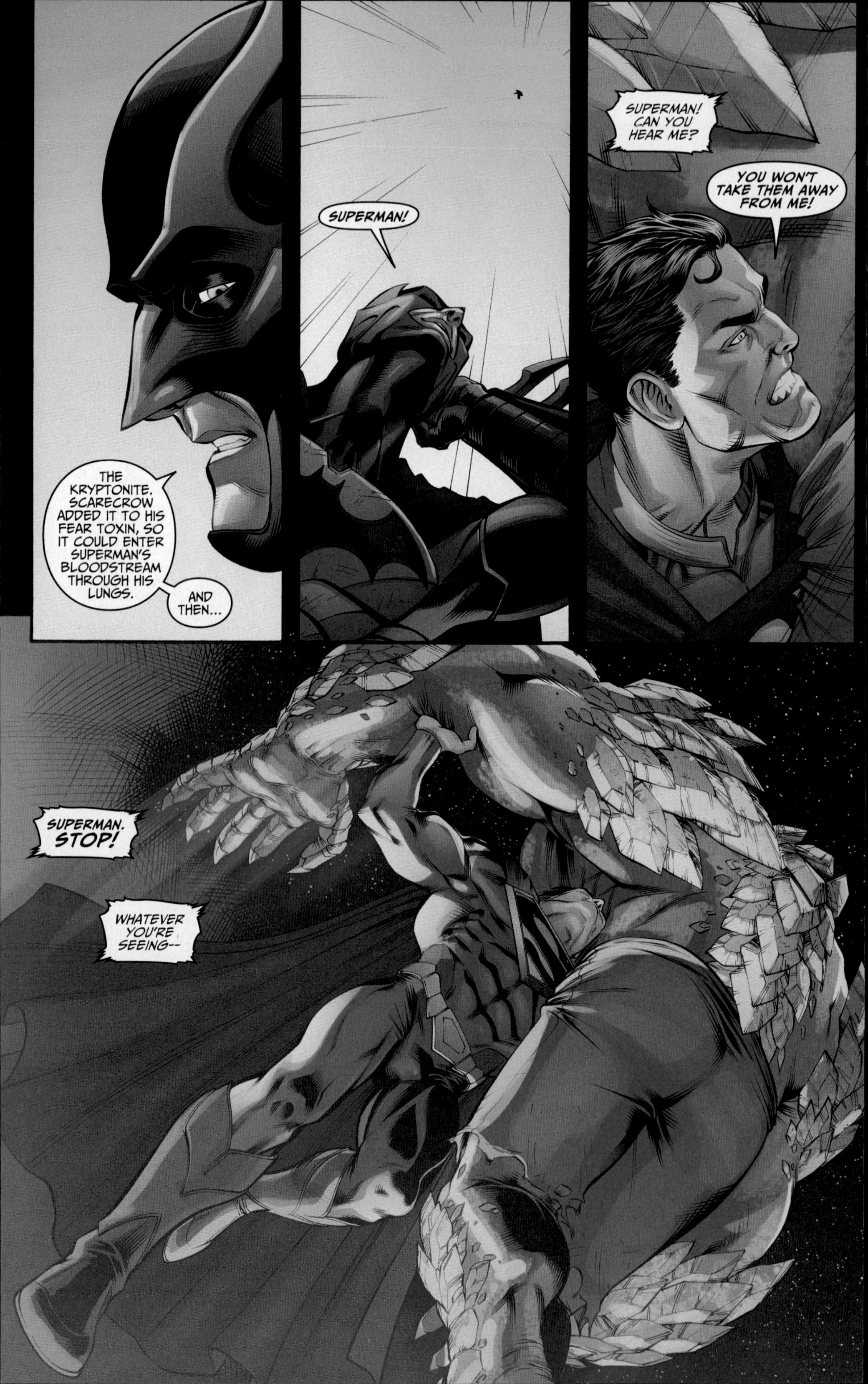
THE KRYPTONITE. SCARECROW ADDED IT TO HIS FEAR TOXIN, SO IT COULD ENTER SUPERMAN'S BLOODSTREAM THROUGH HIS LUNGS.
AND THEN...
SUPERMAN!
SUPERMAN! CAN YOU HEAR ME?
YOU WON'T TAKE THEM AWAY FROM ME!
SUPERMAN. STOP!
WHATEVER YOU'RE SEEING--

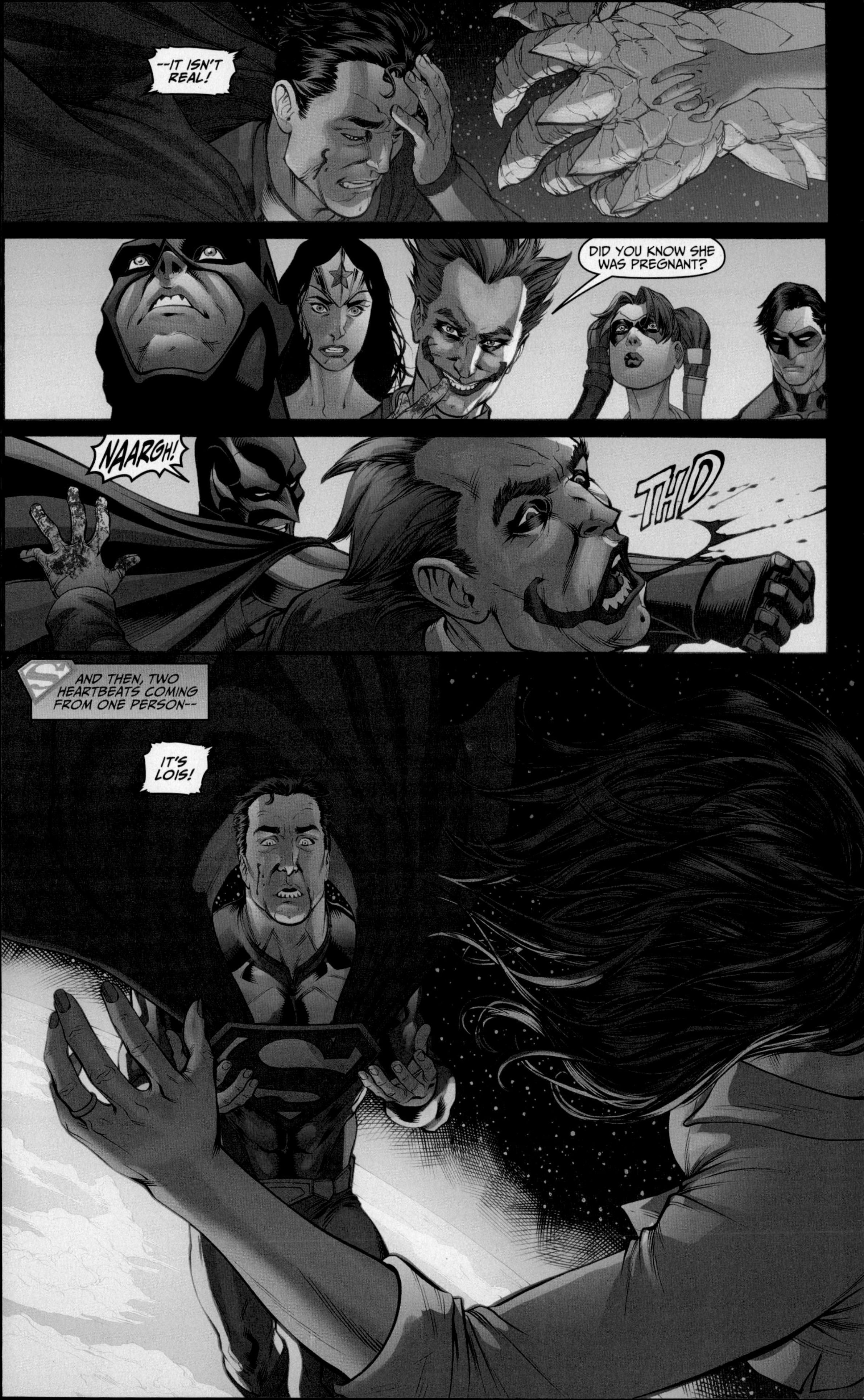
--IT ISN'T REAL!
DID YOU KNOW SHE WAS PREGNANT?
NAARGH!
THD
AND THEN, TWO HEARTBEATS COMING FROM ONE PERSON--
IT'S LOIS!

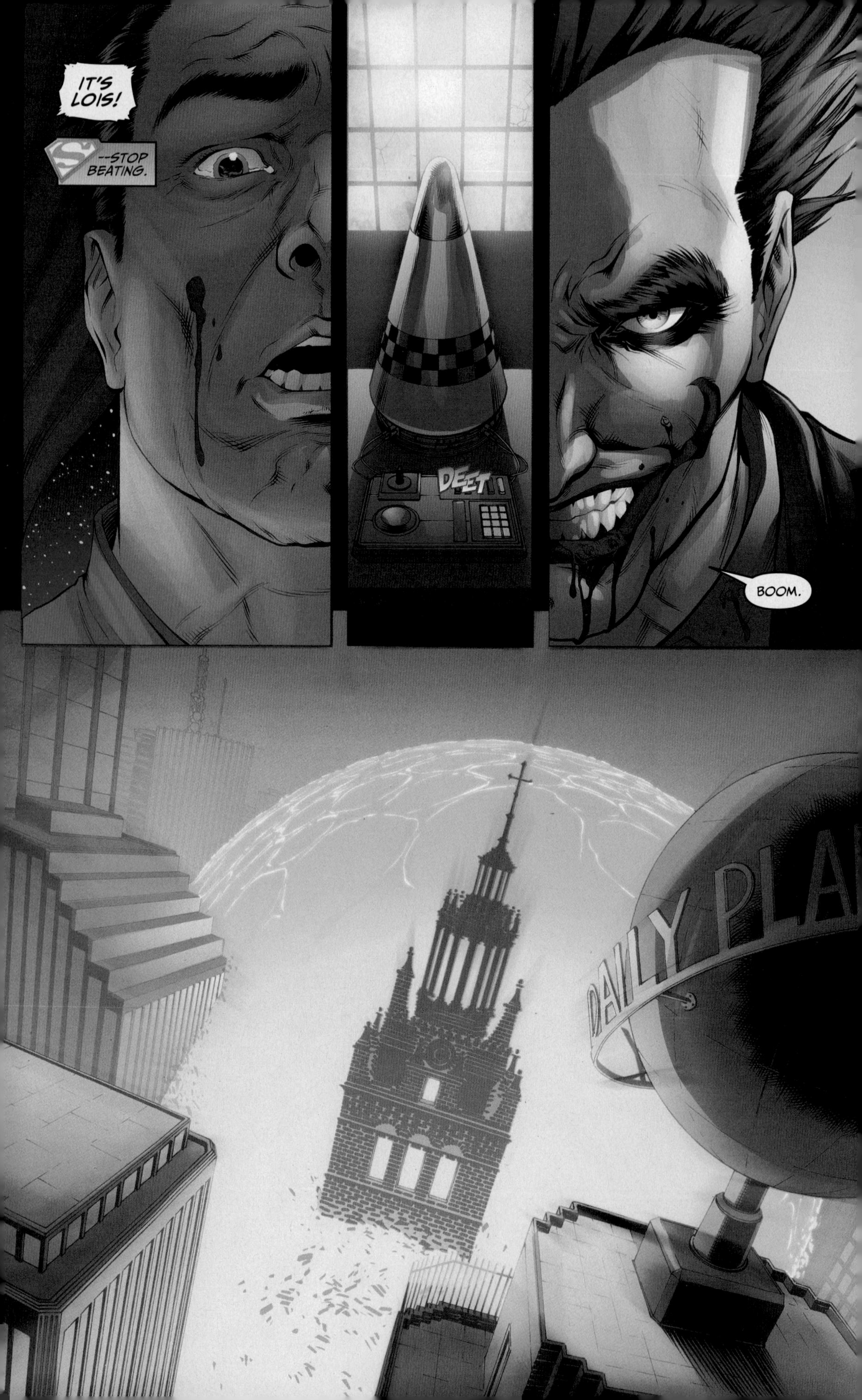
IT'S LOIS!
--STOP BEATING.
DEET
BOOM.
DAILY PLA

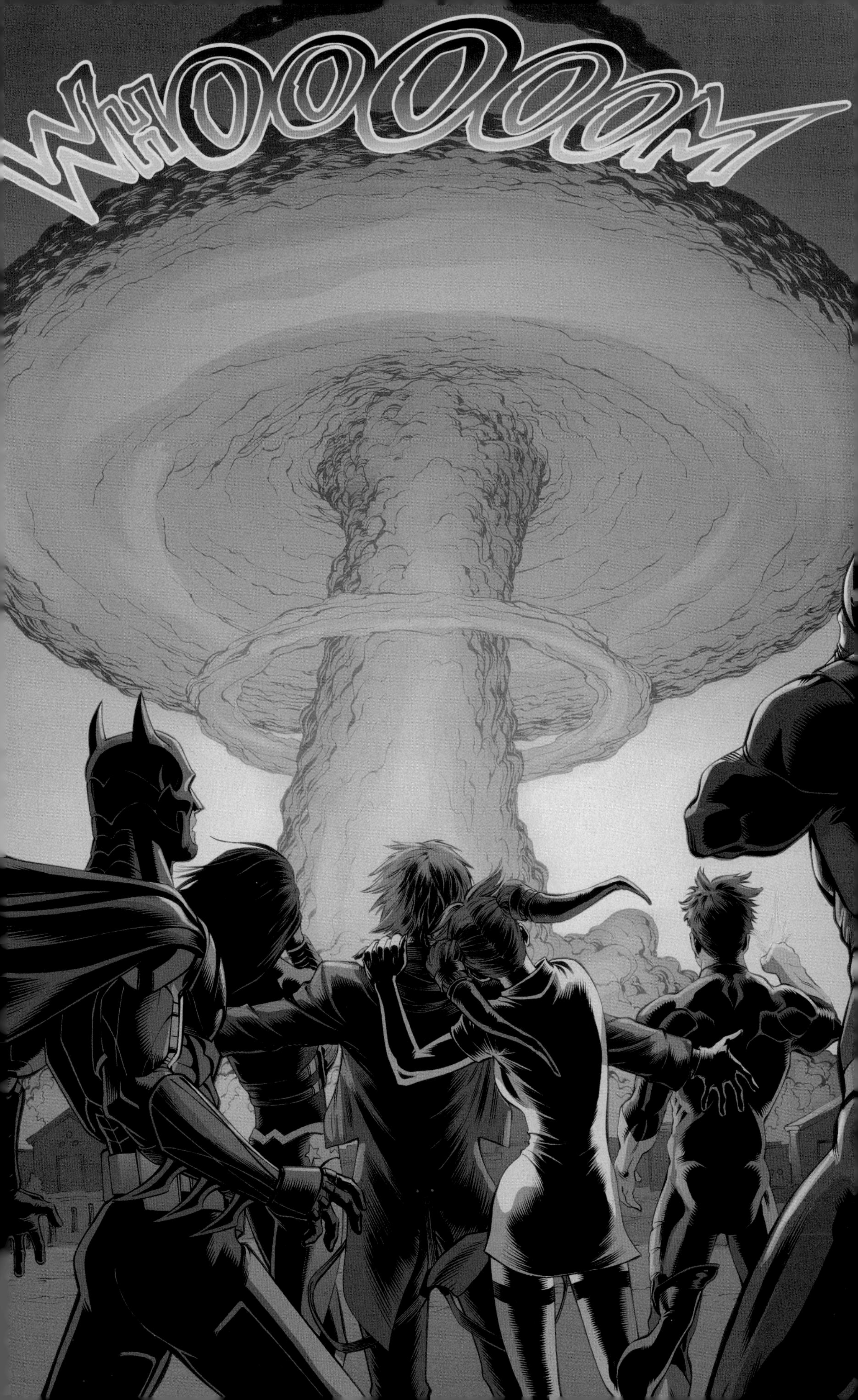
WHOOOOOM

PART TWO

Mike S. Miller Bruno Redondo Artists

Cover Art by Jheremy Raapack & Andrew Elder

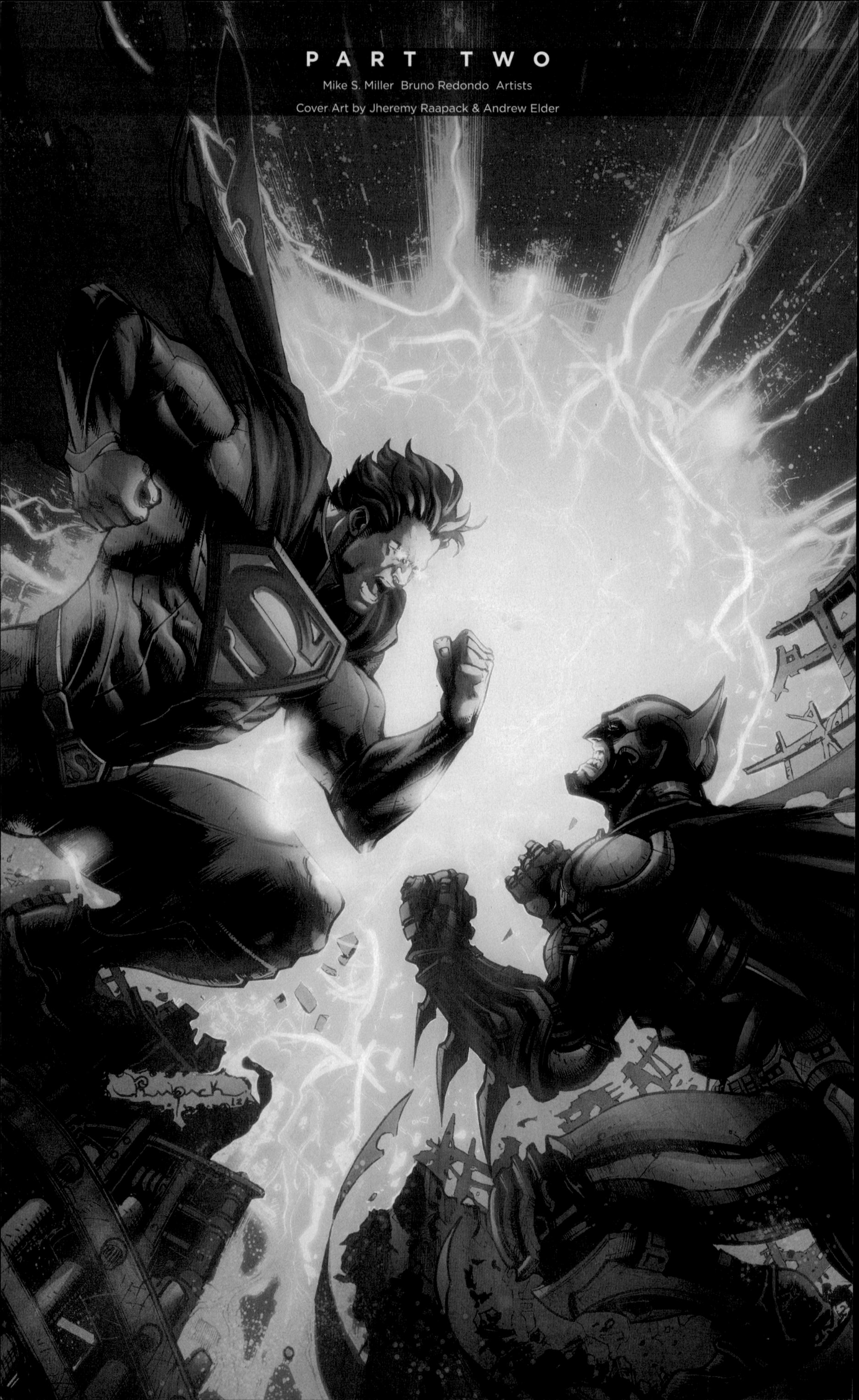

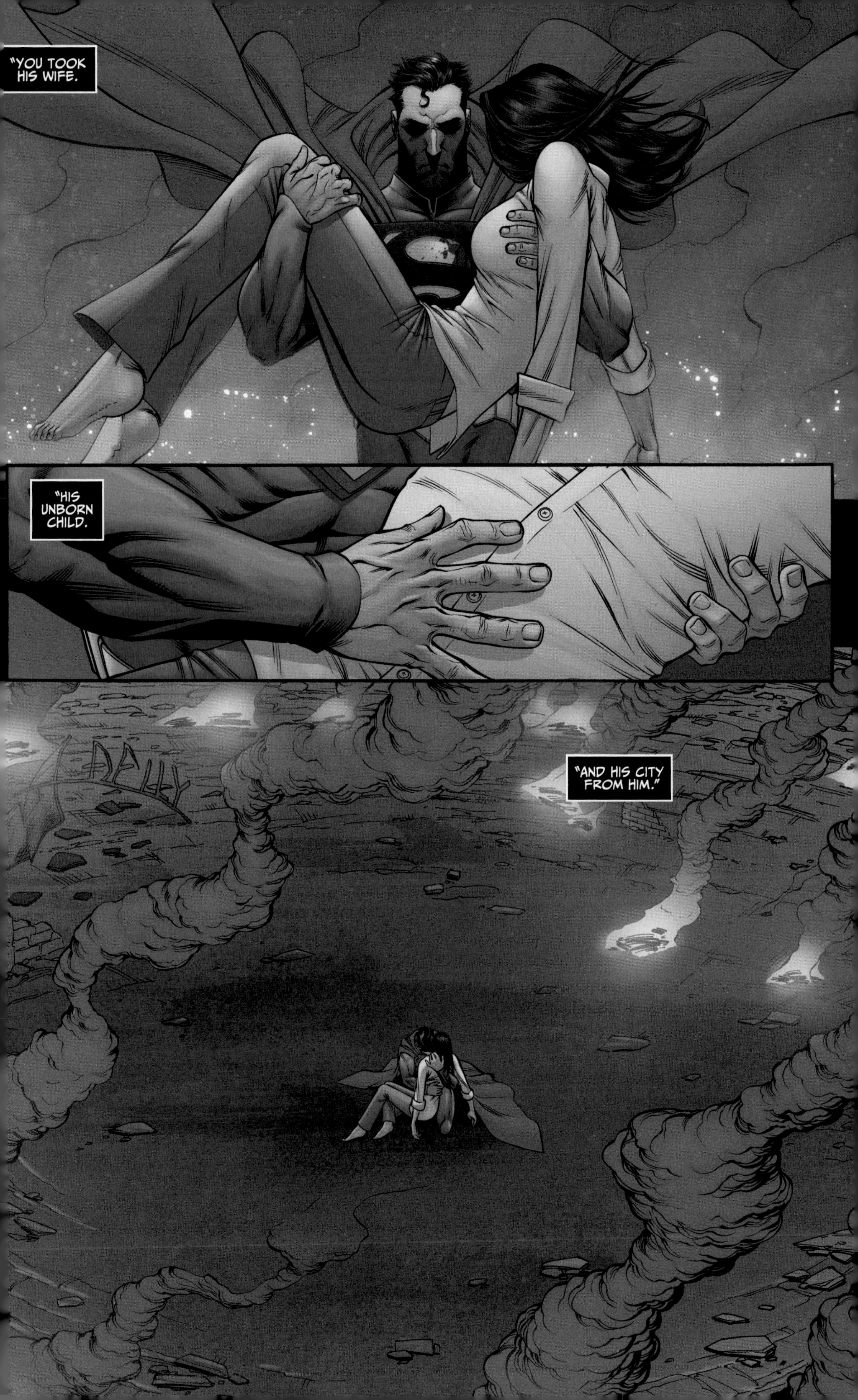
"YOU TOOK HIS WIFE.
"HIS UNBORN CHILD.
"AND HIS CITY FROM HIM."

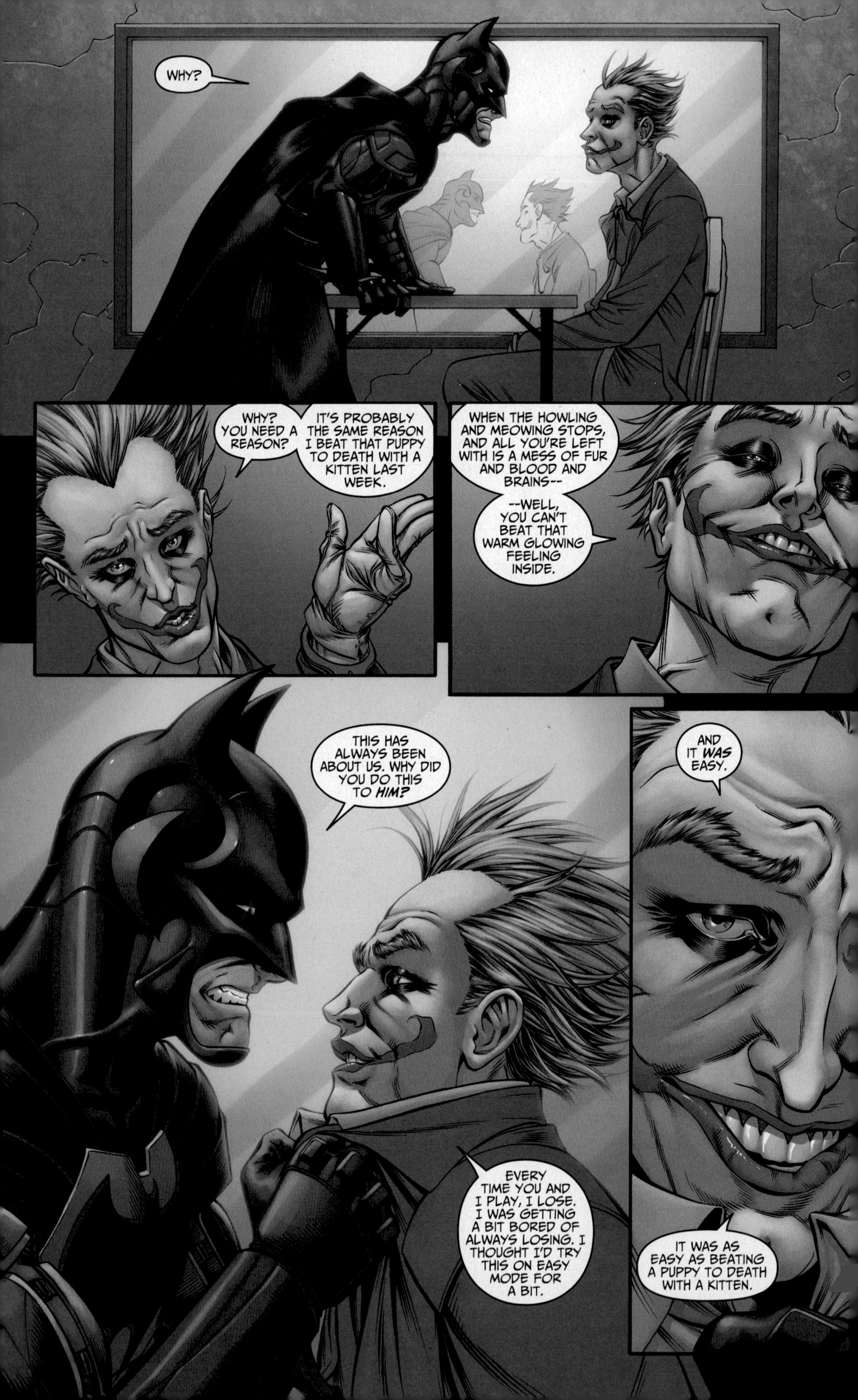
WHY?
WHY? YOU NEED A REASON?
IT'S PROBABLY THE SAME REASON I BEAT THAT PUPPY TO DEATH WITH A KITTEN LAST WEEK.
WHEN THE HOWLING AND MEOWING STOPS, AND ALL YOU'RE LEFT WITH IS A MESS OF FUR AND BLOOD AND BRAINS--
--WELL, YOU CAN'T BEAT THAT WARM GLOWING FEELING INSIDE.
THIS HAS ALWAYS BEEN ABOUT US. WHY DID YOU DO THIS TO *HIM?*
EVERY TIME YOU AND I PLAY, I LOSE. I WAS GETTING A BIT BORED OF ALWAYS LOSING. I THOUGHT I'D TRY THIS ON EASY MODE FOR A BIT.
AND IT *WAS* EASY.
IT WAS AS EASY AS BEATING A PUPPY TO DEATH WITH A KITTEN.

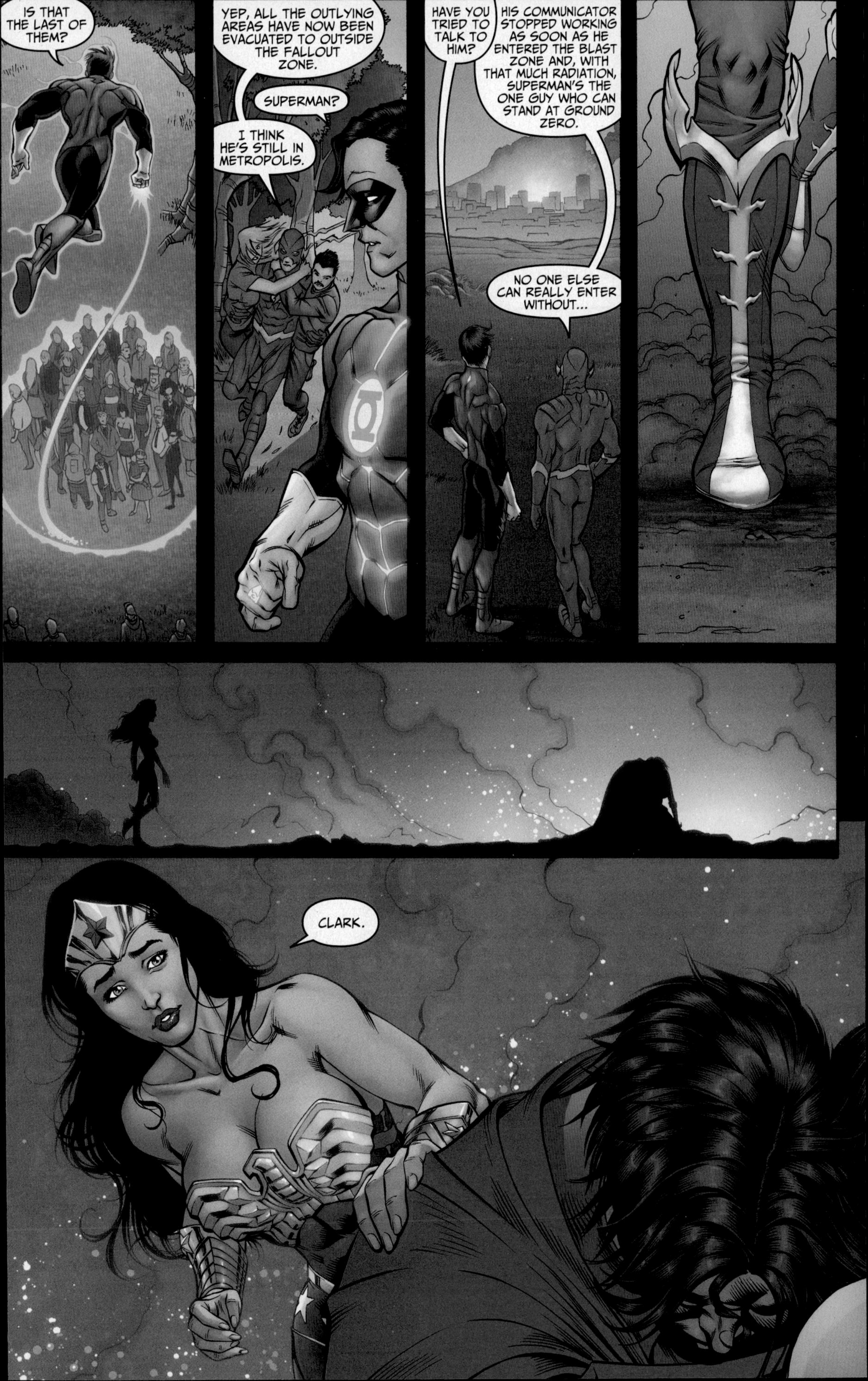
IS THAT THE LAST OF THEM?
YEP, ALL THE OUTLYING AREAS HAVE NOW BEEN EVACUATED TO OUTSIDE THE FALLOUT ZONE.
SUPERMAN?
I THINK HE'S STILL IN METROPOLIS.
HAVE YOU TRIED TO TALK TO HIM?
HIS COMMUNICATOR STOPPED WORKING AS SOON AS HE ENTERED THE BLAST ZONE AND, WITH THAT MUCH RADIATION, SUPERMAN'S THE ONE GUY WHO CAN STAND AT GROUND ZERO.
NO ONE ELSE CAN REALLY ENTER WITHOUT...
CLARK.

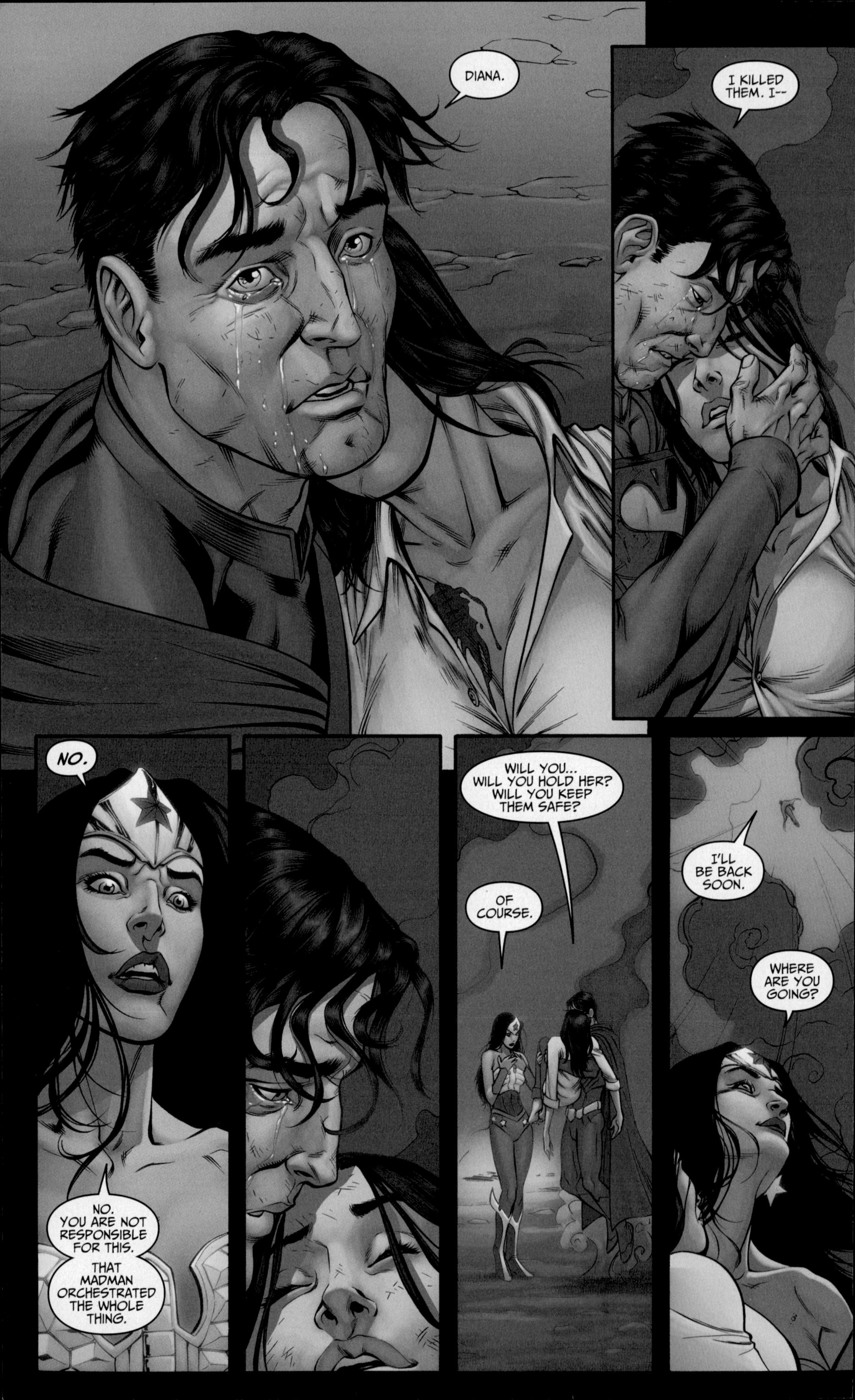
DIANA.
I KILLED THEM. I--
NO.
NO. YOU ARE NOT RESPONSIBLE FOR THIS.
THAT MADMAN ORCHESTRATED THE WHOLE THING.
WILL YOU... WILL YOU HOLD HER? WILL YOU KEEP THEM SAFE?
OF COURSE.
I'LL BE BACK SOON.
WHERE ARE YOU GOING?

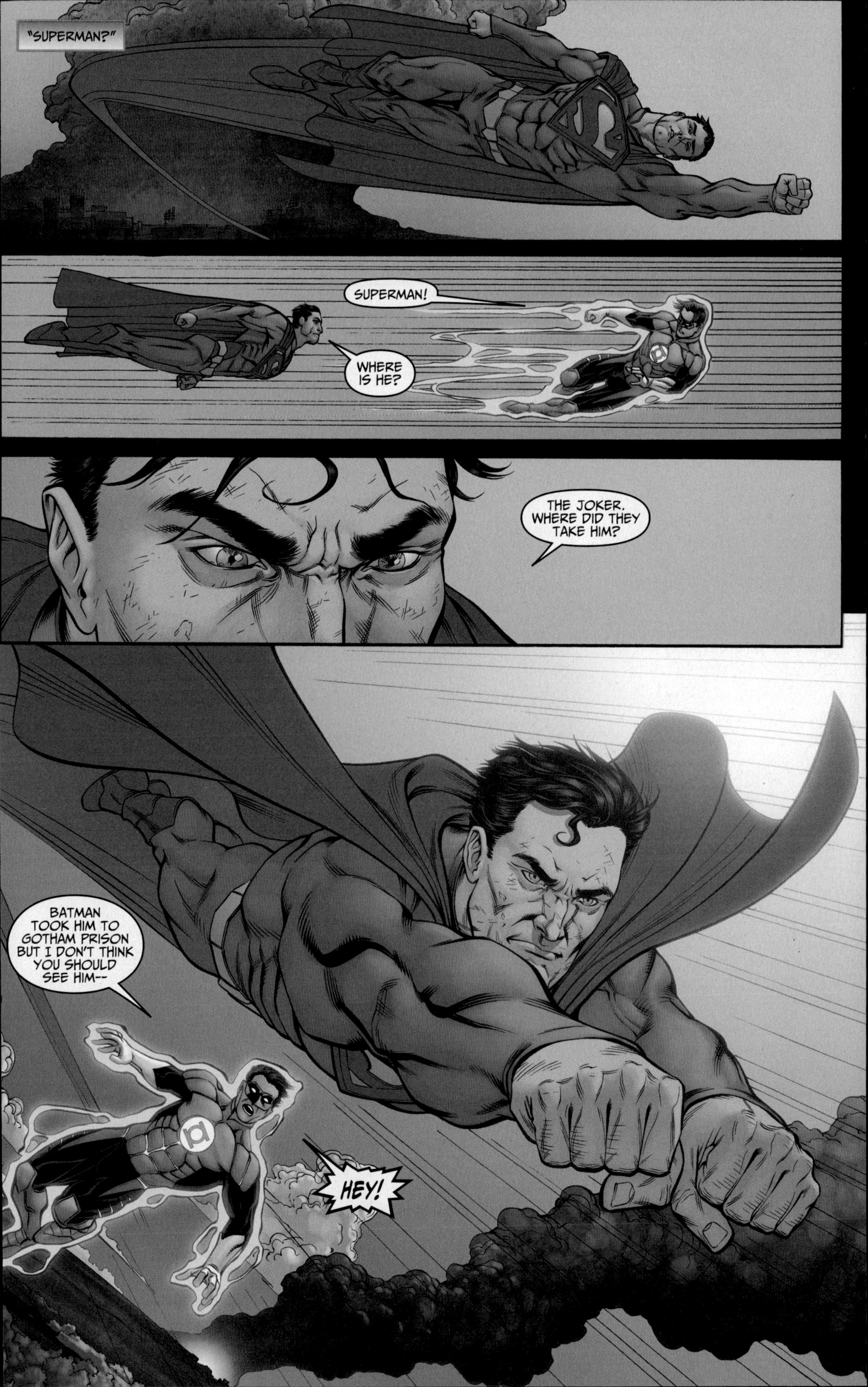
"SUPERMAN?"
SUPERMAN!
WHERE IS HE?
THE JOKER. WHERE DID THEY TAKE HIM?
BATMAN TOOK HIM TO GOTHAM PRISON BUT I DON'T THINK YOU SHOULD SEE HIM--
HEY!

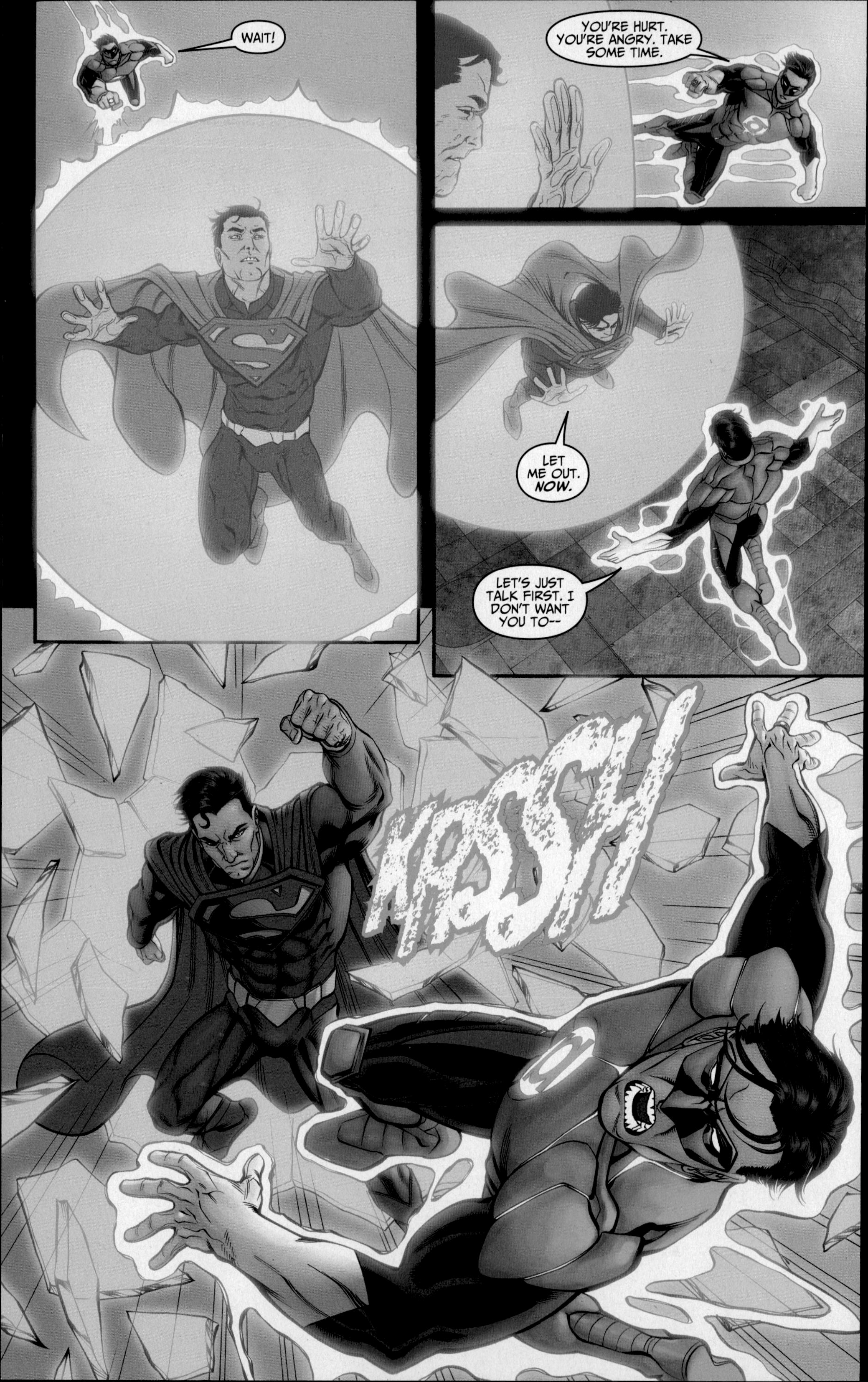
WAIT!
YOU'RE HURT. YOU'RE ANGRY. TAKE SOME TIME.
LET ME OUT. NOW.
LET'S JUST TALK FIRST. I DON'T WANT YOU TO--
KRRSSH

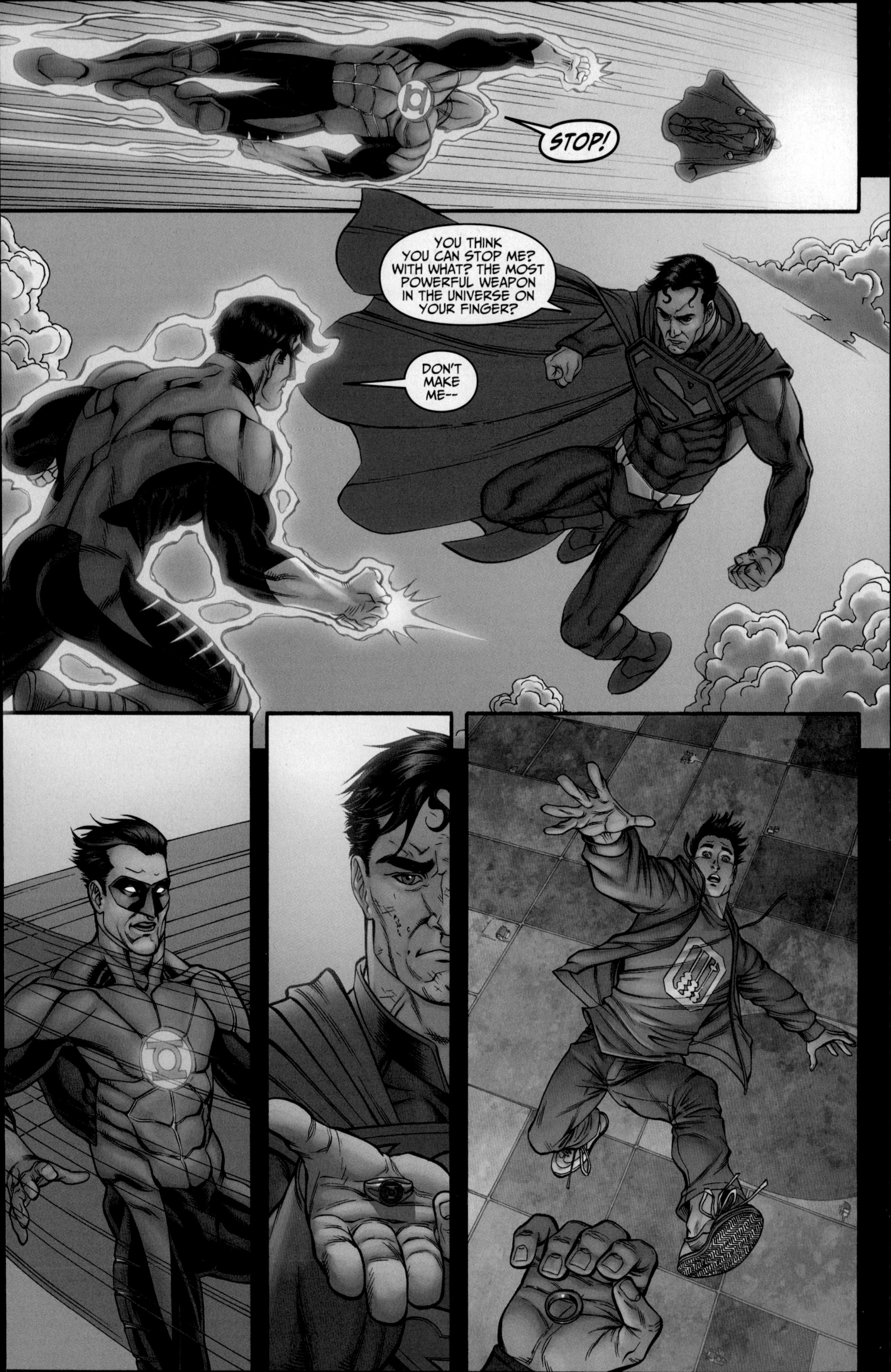
STOP!
YOU THINK YOU CAN STOP ME? WITH WHAT? THE MOST POWERFUL WEAPON IN THE UNIVERSE ON YOUR FINGER?
DON'T MAKE ME--

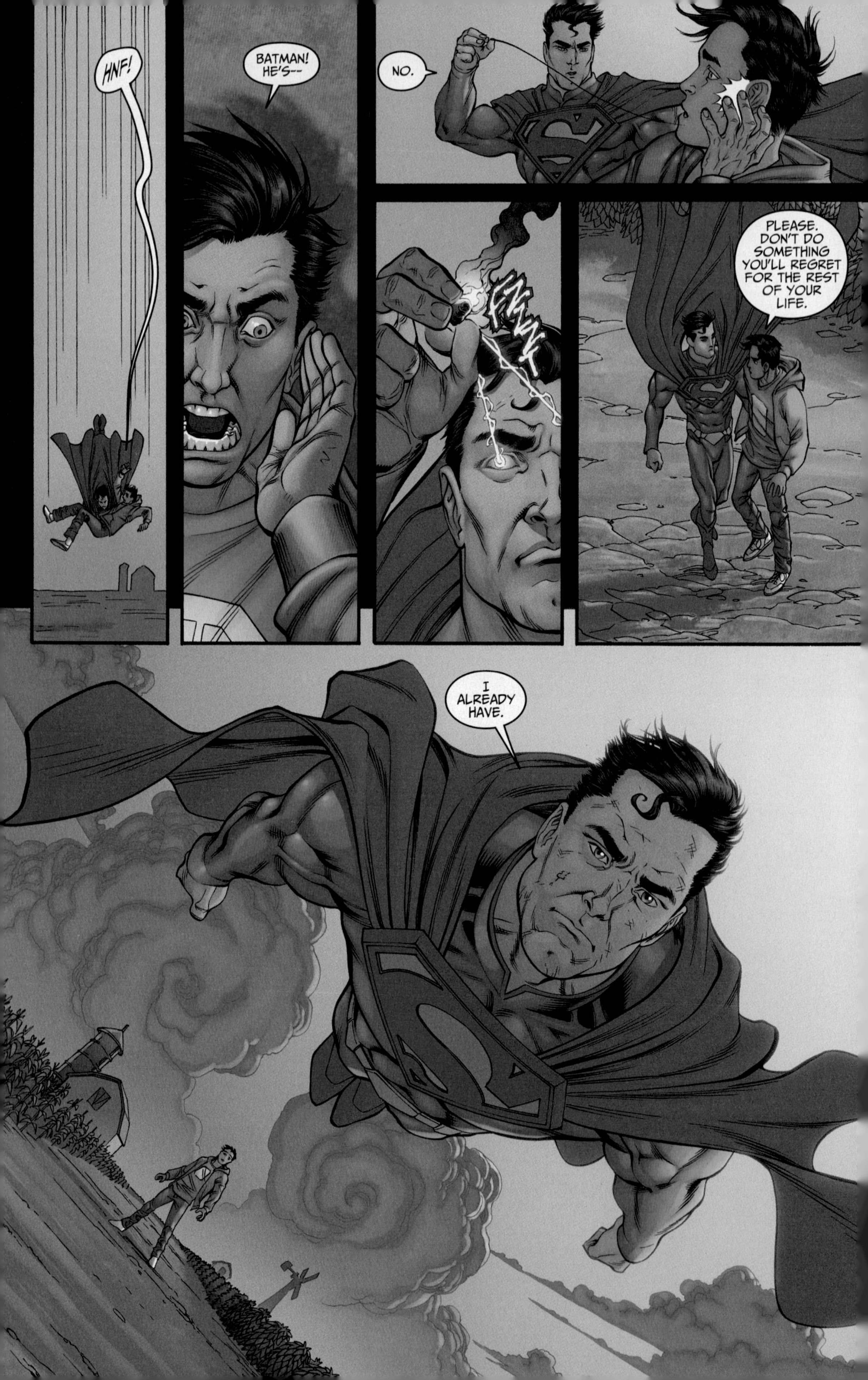
HNF!
BATMAN! HE'S--
NO.
FZZZT
PLEASE. DON'T DO SOMETHING YOU'LL REGRET FOR THE REST OF YOUR LIFE.
I ALREADY HAVE.

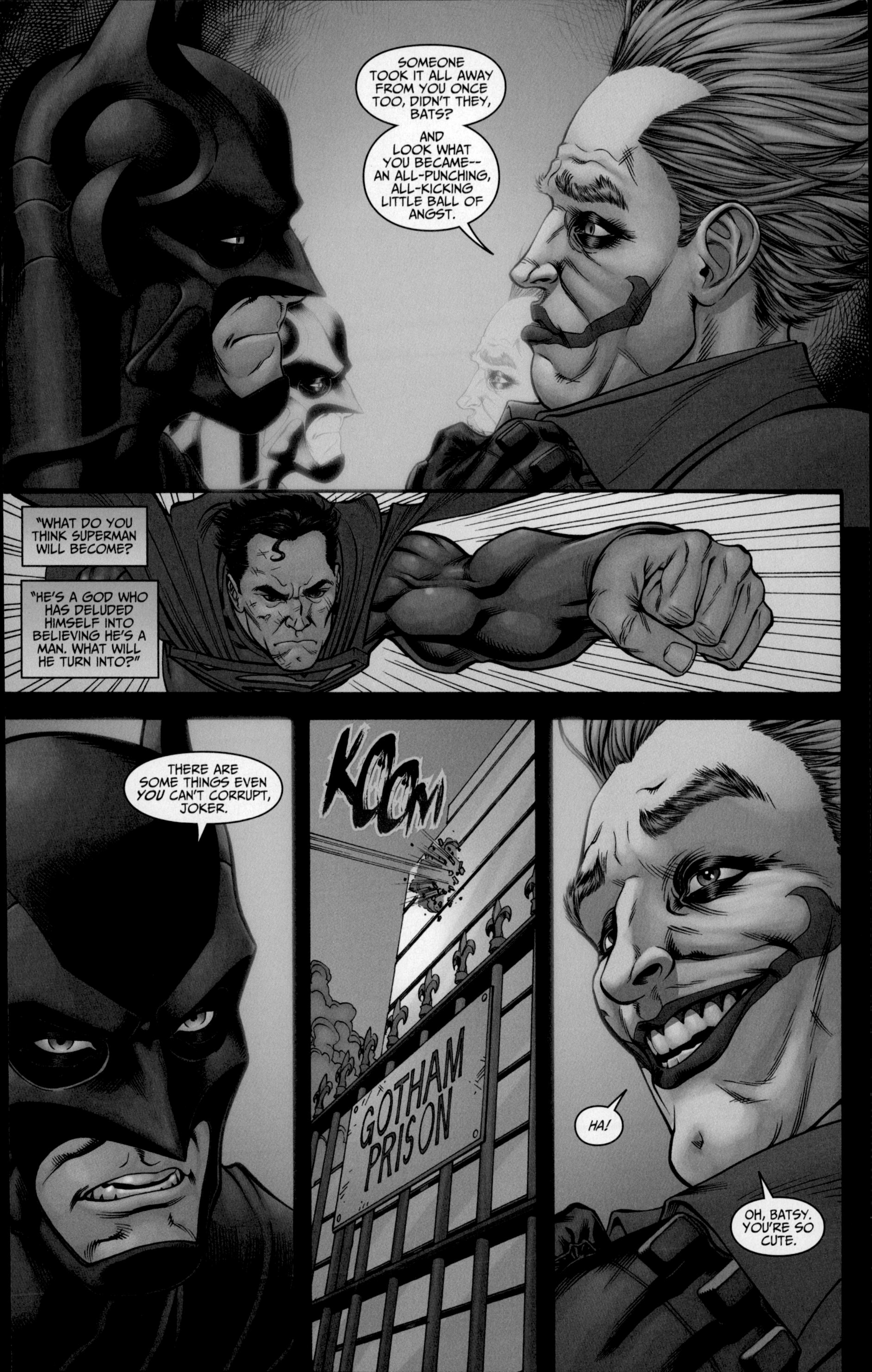
SOMEONE TOOK IT ALL AWAY FROM YOU ONCE TOO, DIDN'T THEY, BATS?
AND LOOK WHAT YOU BECAME-- AN ALL-PUNCHING, ALL-KICKING LITTLE BALL OF ANGST.
"WHAT DO YOU THINK SUPERMAN WILL BECOME?
"HE'S A GOD WHO HAS DELUDED HIMSELF INTO BELIEVING HE'S A MAN. WHAT WILL HE TURN INTO?"
THERE ARE SOME THINGS EVEN YOU CAN'T CORRUPT, JOKER.
KOOM
GOTHAM PRISON
HA!
OH, BATSY. YOU'RE SO CUTE.

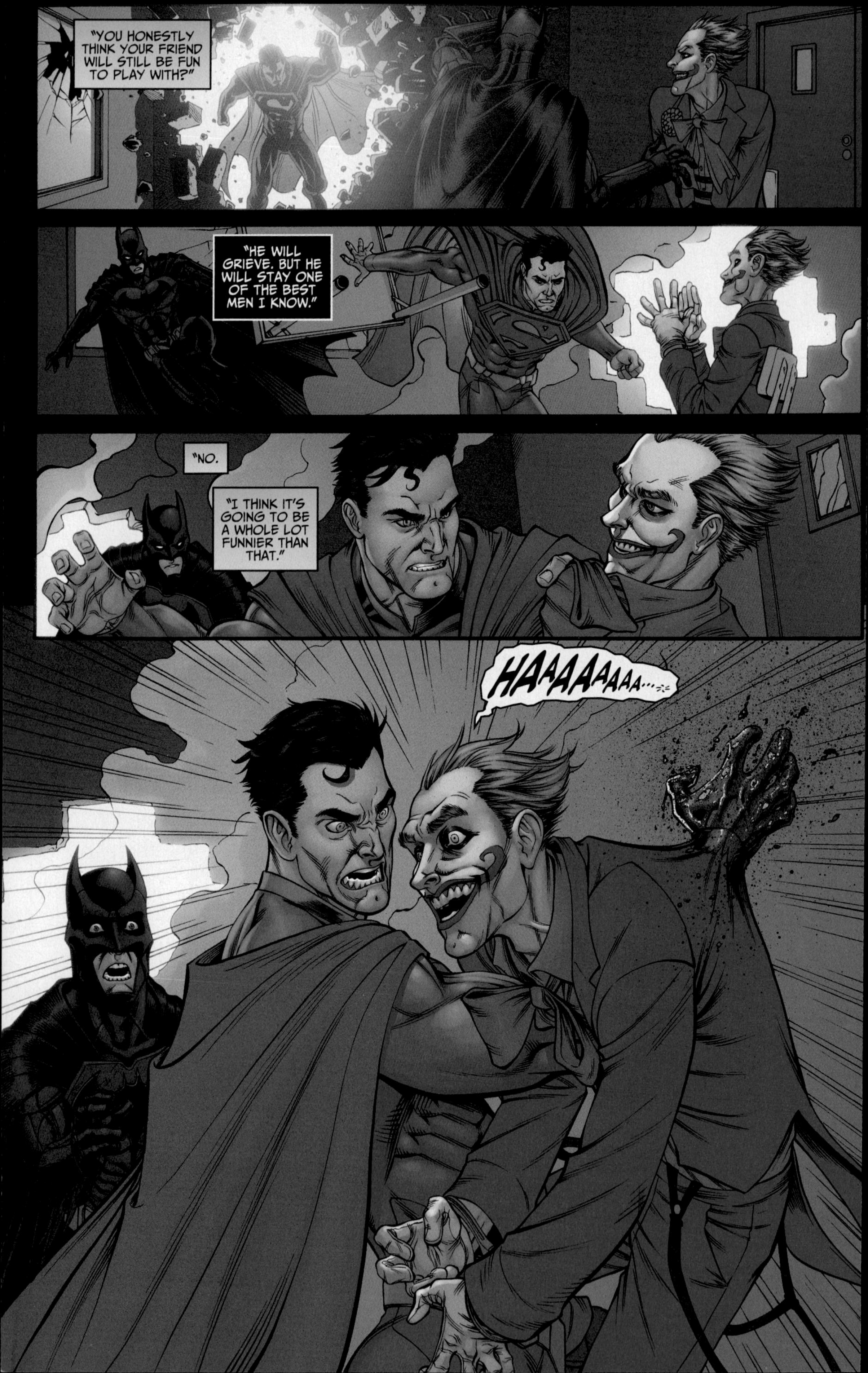
"YOU HONESTLY THINK YOUR FRIEND WILL STILL BE FUN TO PLAY WITH?"
"HE WILL GRIEVE. BUT HE WILL STAY ONE OF THE BEST MEN I KNOW."
"NO.
"I THINK IT'S GOING TO BE A WHOLE LOT FUNNIER THAN THAT."
HAAAAAAAA...

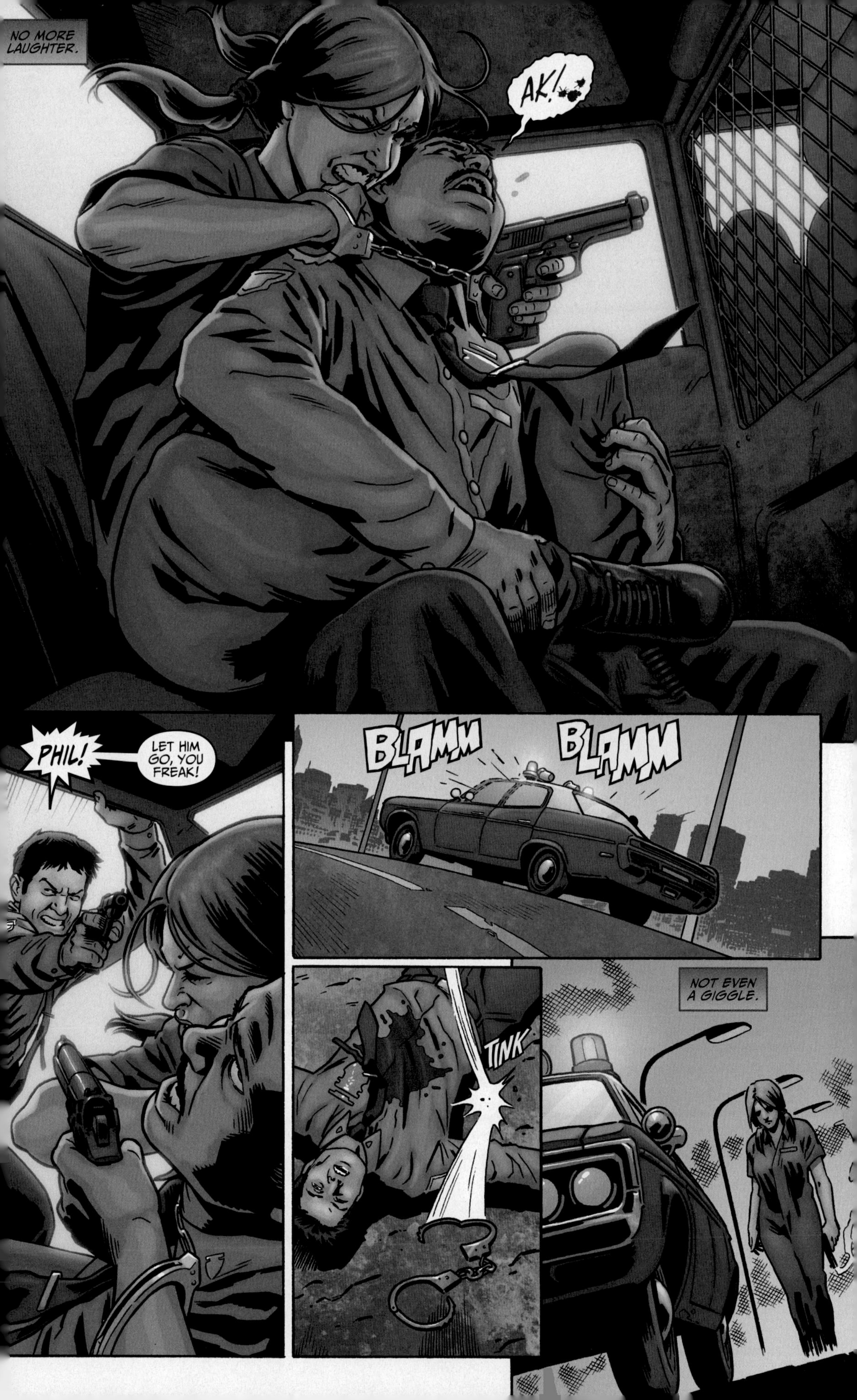
NO MORE LAUGHTER.
AK!
PHIL!
LET HIM GO, YOU FREAK!
BLAMM
BLAMM
TINK
NOT EVEN A GIGGLE.

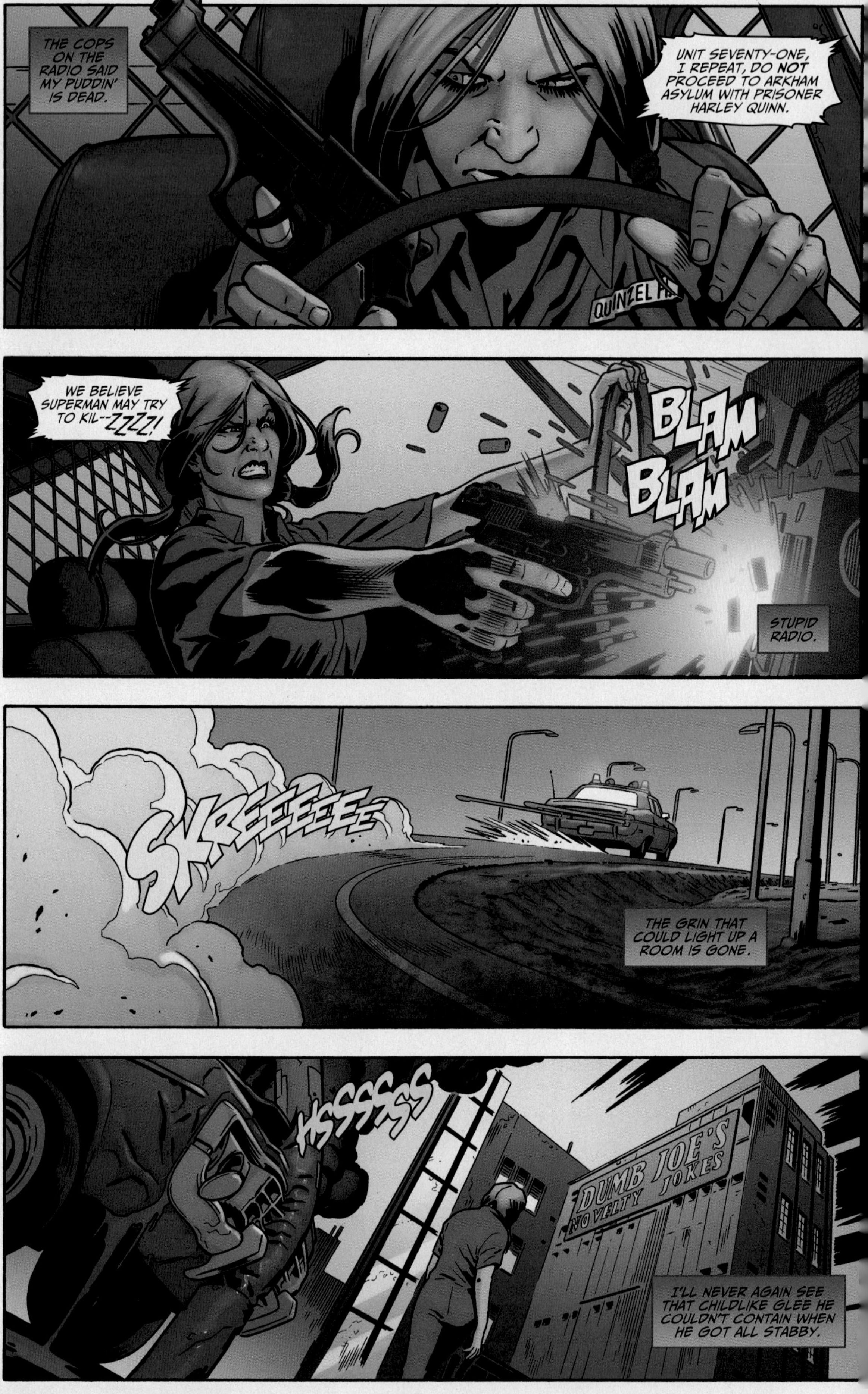
THE COPS ON THE RADIO SAID MY PUDDIN' IS DEAD.
UNIT SEVENTY-ONE, I REPEAT, DO NOT PROCEED TO ARKHAM ASYLUM WITH PRISONER HARLEY QUINN.
QUINZEL
WE BELIEVE SUPERMAN MAY TRY TO KIL--ZZZZ!
BLAM
BLAM
STUPID RADIO.
SKREEEEEEE
THE GRIN THAT COULD LIGHT UP A ROOM IS GONE.
HSSSSSS
DUMB JOE'S
NOVELTY JOKES
I'LL NEVER AGAIN SEE THAT CHILDLIKE GLEE HE COULDN'T CONTAIN WHEN HE GOT ALL STABBY.

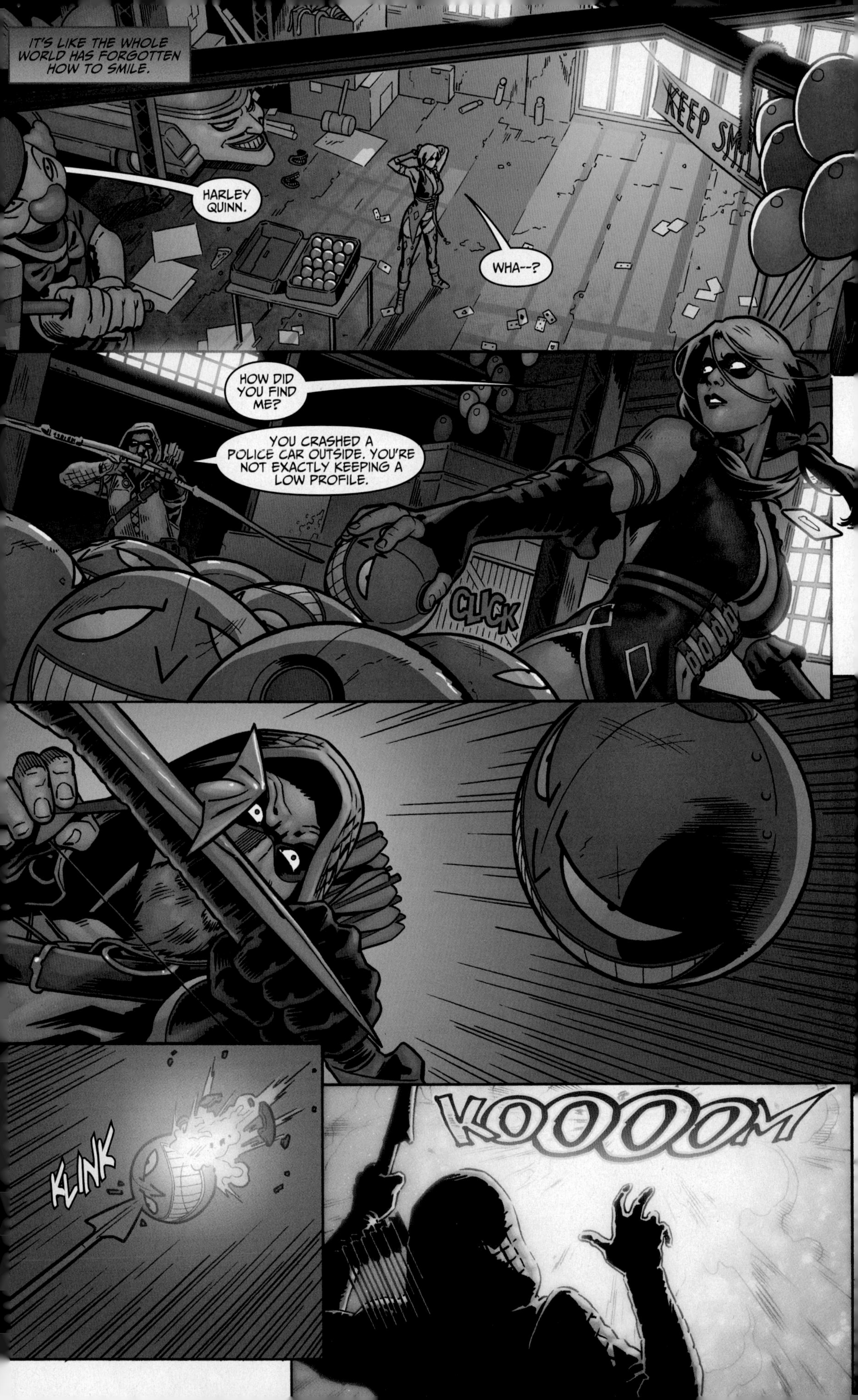
IT'S LIKE THE WHOLE WORLD HAS FORGOTTEN HOW TO SMILE.
KEEP SMI
HARLEY QUINN.
WHA--?
HOW DID YOU FIND ME?
YOU CRASHED A POLICE CAR OUTSIDE. YOU'RE NOT EXACTLY KEEPING A LOW PROFILE.
CLICK
KLINK
KOOOOM

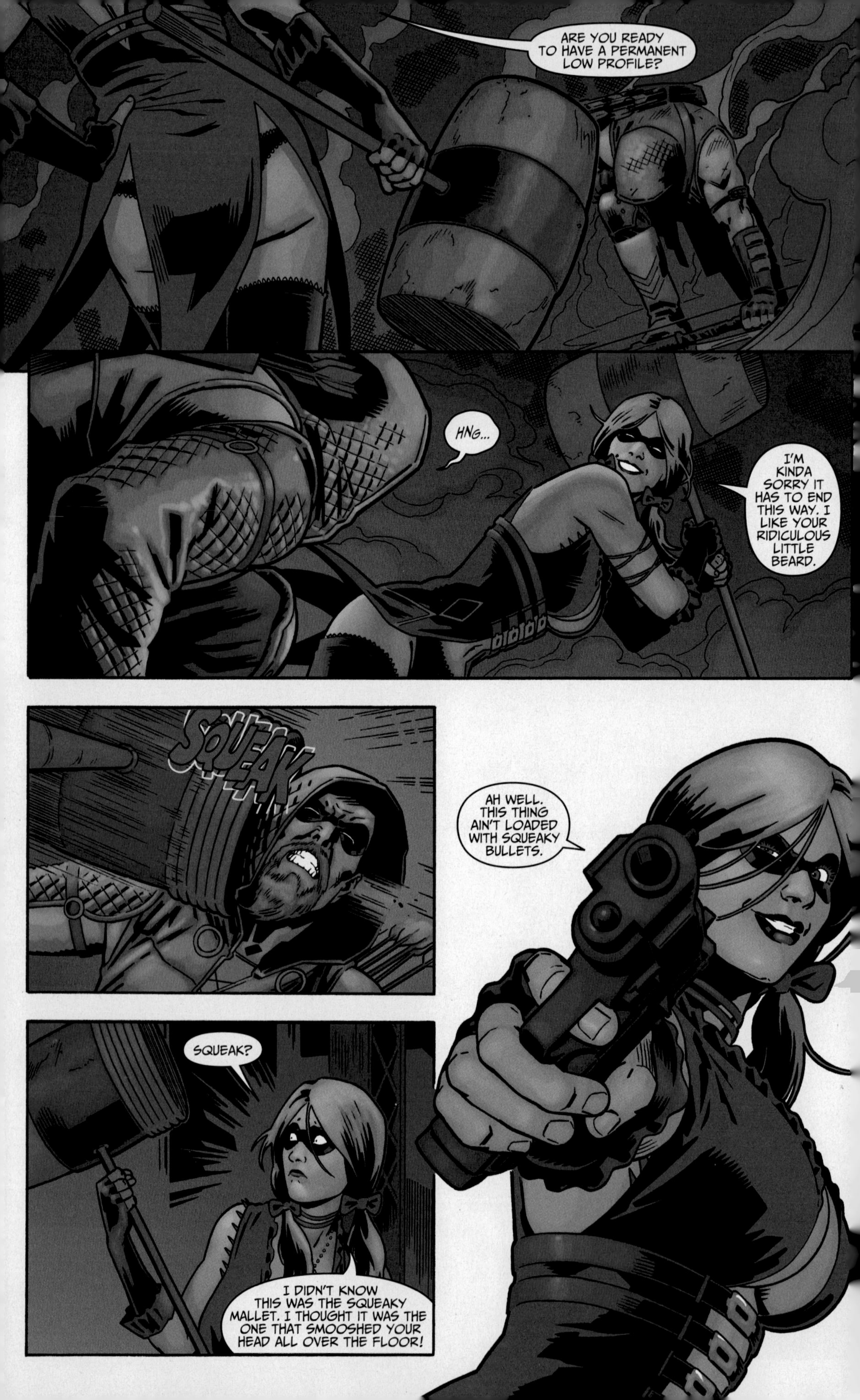
ARE YOU READY TO HAVE A PERMANENT LOW PROFILE?
HNG...
I'M KINDA SORRY IT HAS TO END THIS WAY. I LIKE YOUR RIDICULOUS LITTLE BEARD.
SQUEAK
SQUEAK?
I DIDN'T KNOW THIS WAS THE SQUEAKY MALLET. I THOUGHT IT WAS THE ONE THAT SMOOSHED YOUR HEAD ALL OVER THE FLOOR!
AH WELL. THIS THING AIN'T LOADED WITH SQUEAKY BULLETS.

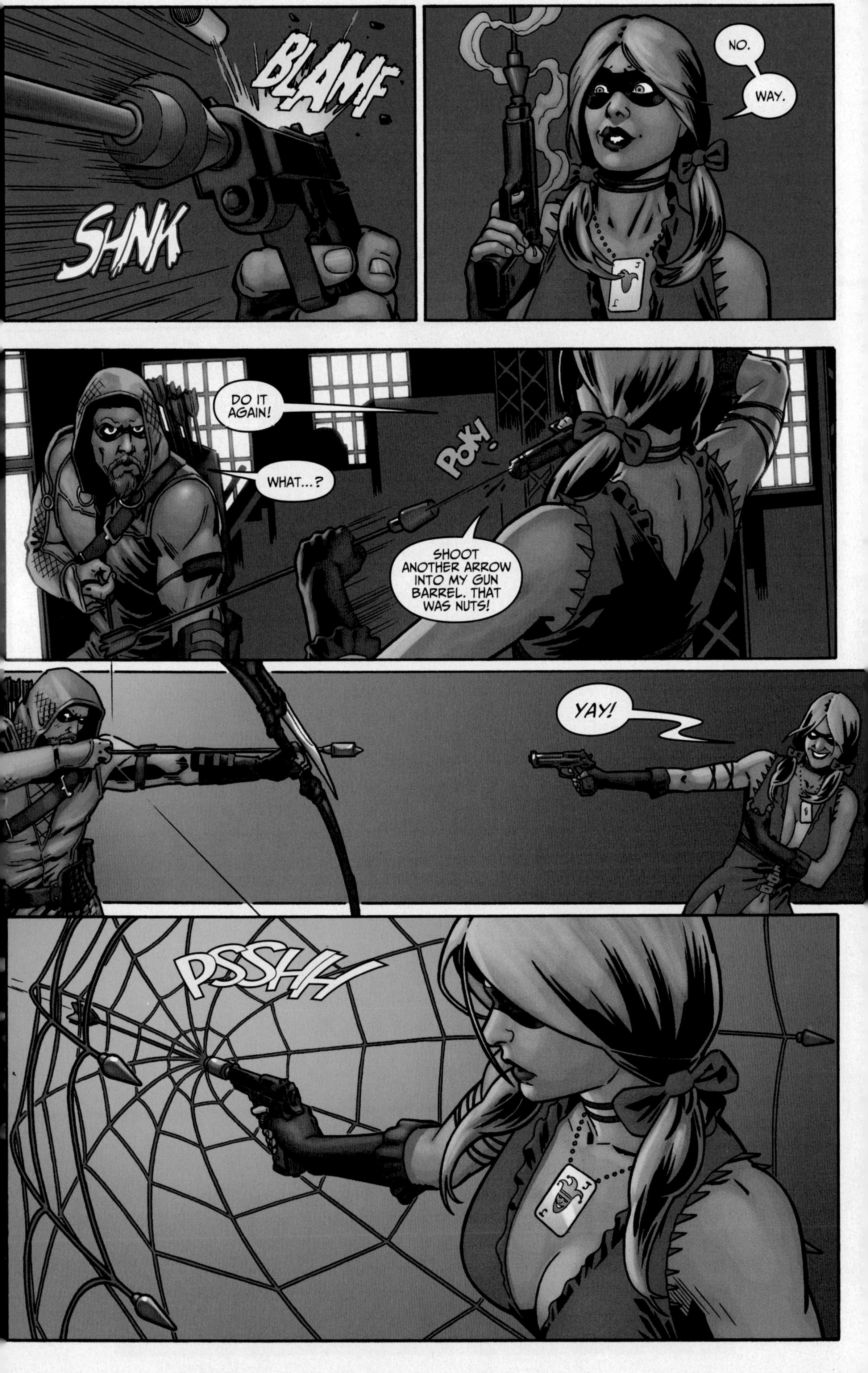
BLAMF
SHNK
NO.
WAY.
DO IT AGAIN!
WHAT...?
POK!
SHOOT ANOTHER ARROW INTO MY GUN BARREL. THAT WAS NUTS!
YAY!
PSSHH

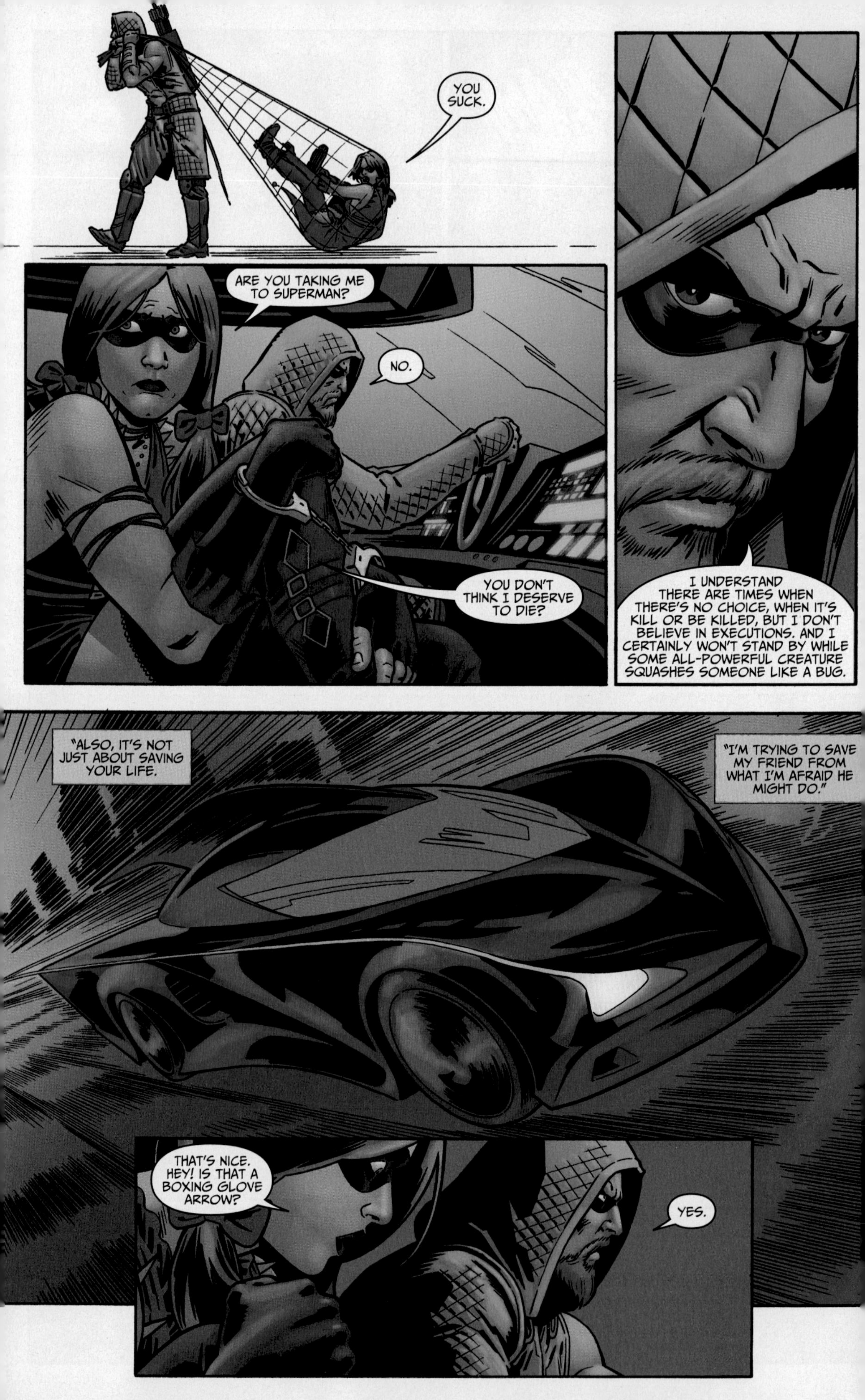

YOU SUCK.
ARE YOU TAKING ME TO SUPERMAN?
NO.
YOU DON'T THINK I DESERVE TO DIE?
I UNDERSTAND THERE ARE TIMES WHEN THERE'S NO CHOICE, WHEN IT'S KILL OR BE KILLED, BUT I DON'T BELIEVE IN EXECUTIONS. AND I CERTAINLY WON'T STAND BY WHILE SOME ALL-POWERFUL CREATURE SQUASHES SOMEONE LIKE A BUG.
"ALSO, IT'S NOT JUST ABOUT SAVING YOUR LIFE.
"I'M TRYING TO SAVE MY FRIEND FROM WHAT I'M AFRAID HE MIGHT DO."
THAT'S NICE. HEY! IS THAT A BOXING GLOVE ARROW?
YES.

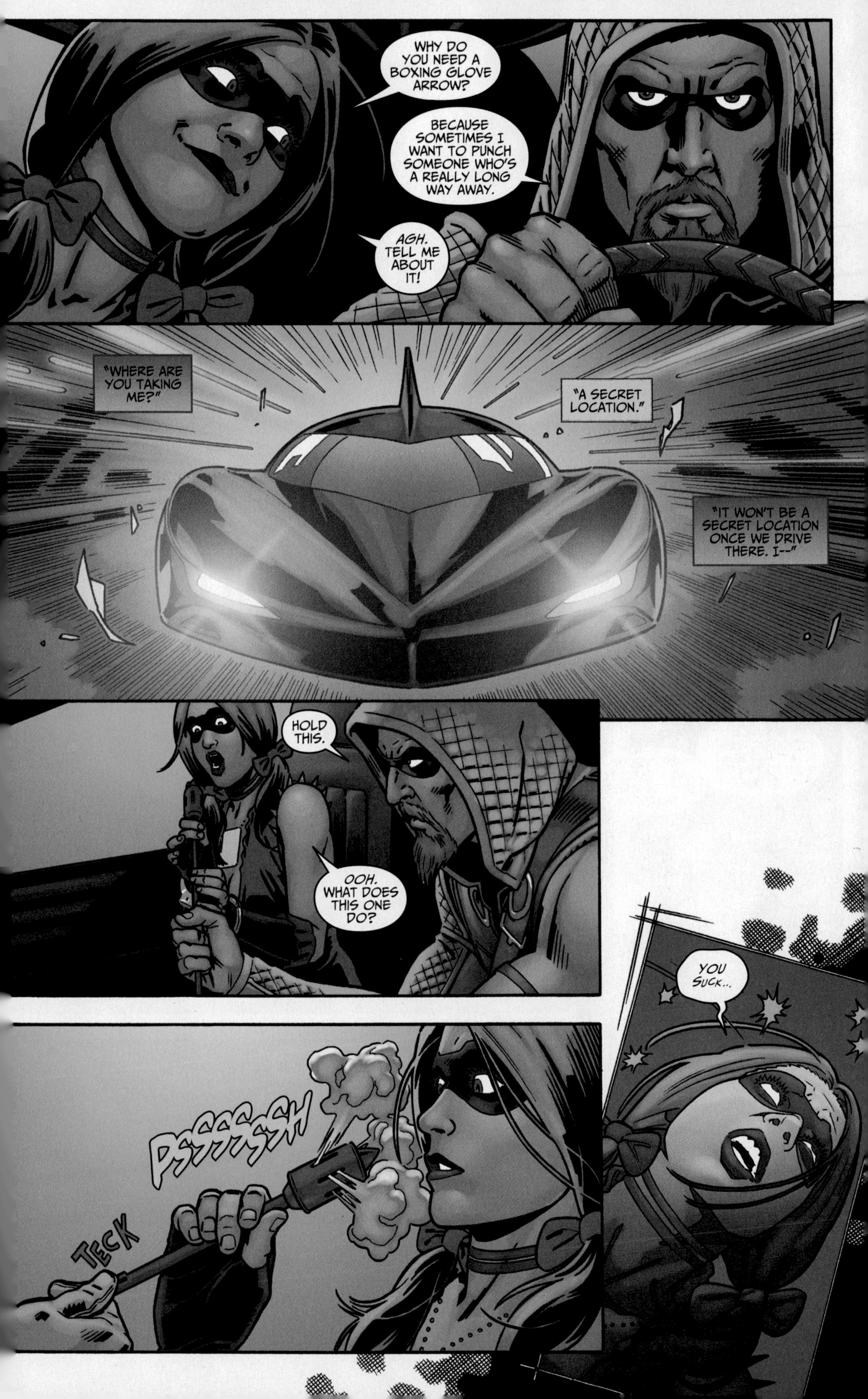

WHY DO YOU NEED A BOXING GLOVE ARROW?
BECAUSE SOMETIMES I WANT TO PUNCH SOMEONE WHO'S A REALLY LONG WAY AWAY.
AGH. TELL ME ABOUT IT!
"WHERE ARE YOU TAKING ME?"
"A SECRET LOCATION."
"IT WON'T BE A SECRET LOCATION ONCE WE DRIVE THERE. I--"
HOLD THIS.
OOH. WHAT DOES THIS ONE DO?
DSSSSSSH
TECK
YOU SUCK...

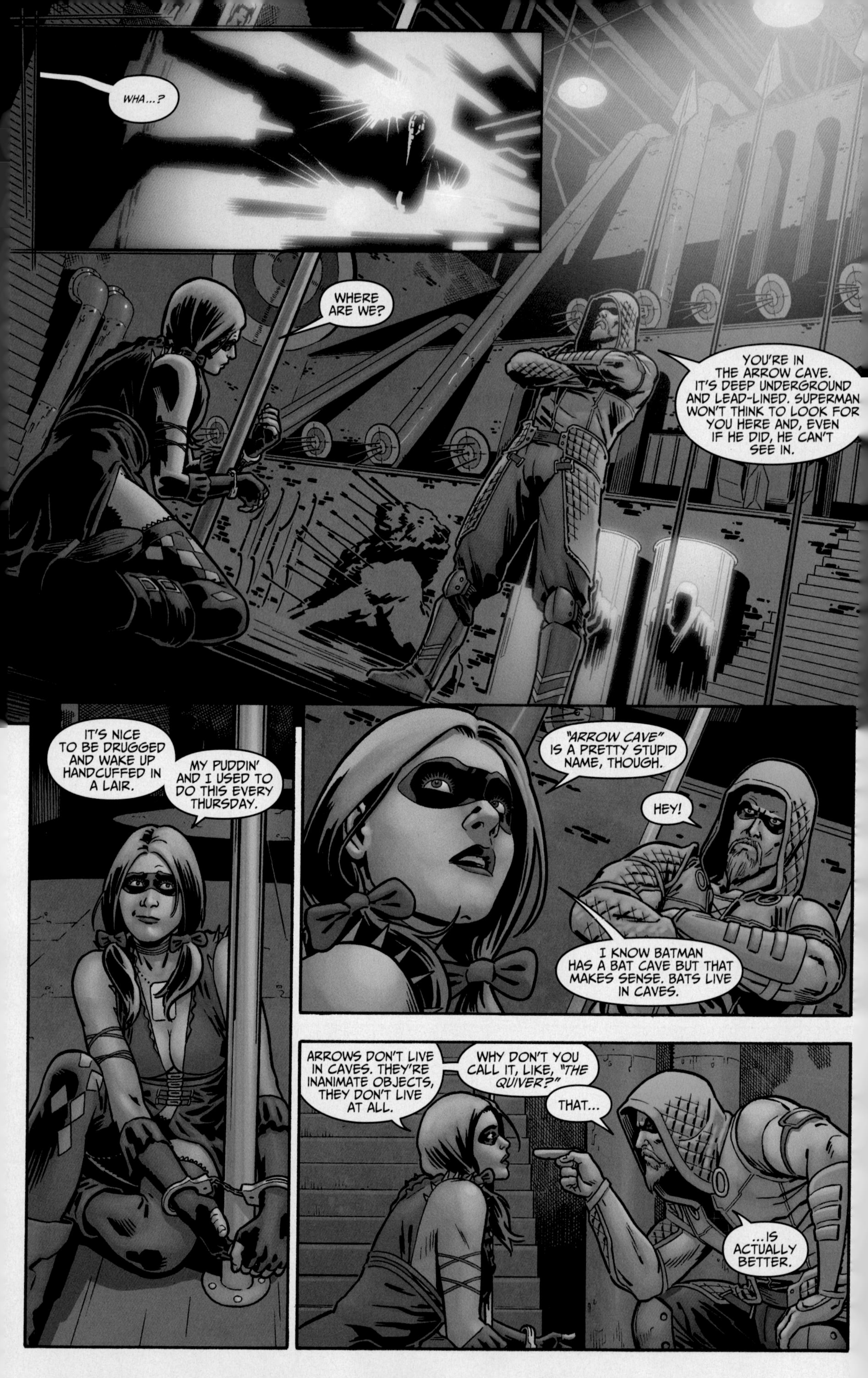
WHA...?
WHERE ARE WE?
YOU'RE IN THE ARROW CAVE. IT'S DEEP UNDERGROUND AND LEAD-LINED. SUPERMAN WON'T THINK TO LOOK FOR YOU HERE AND, EVEN IF HE DID, HE CAN'T SEE IN.
IT'S NICE TO BE DRUGGED AND WAKE UP HANDCUFFED IN A LAIR.
MY PUDDIN' AND I USED TO DO THIS EVERY THURSDAY.
"ARROW CAVE" IS A PRETTY STUPID NAME, THOUGH.
HEY!
I KNOW BATMAN HAS A BAT CAVE BUT THAT MAKES SENSE. BATS LIVE IN CAVES.
ARROWS DON'T LIVE IN CAVES. THEY'RE INANIMATE OBJECTS, THEY DON'T LIVE AT ALL.
WHY DON'T YOU CALL IT, LIKE, "THE QUIVER?"
THAT...
...IS ACTUALLY BETTER.

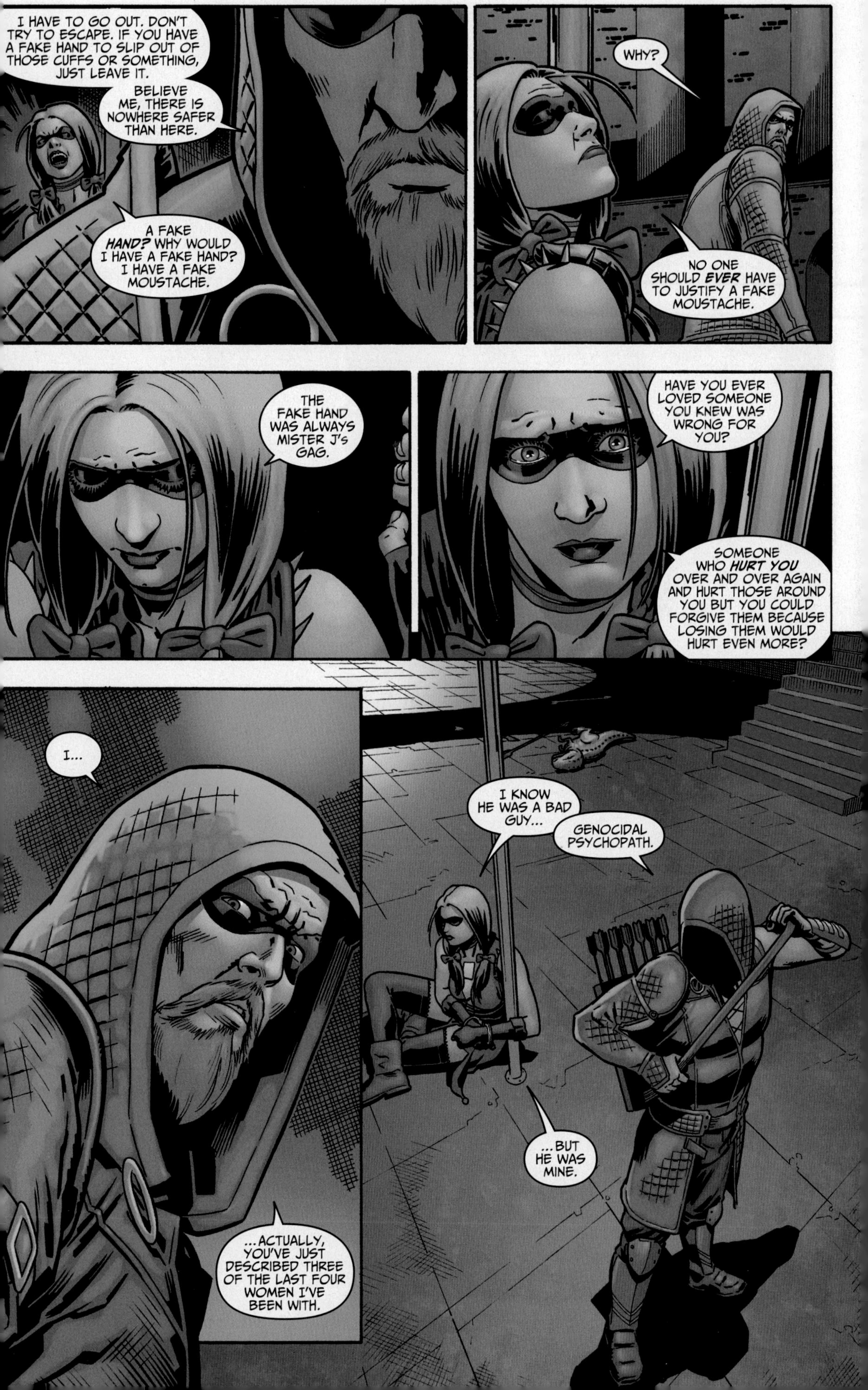
I HAVE TO GO OUT. DON'T TRY TO ESCAPE. IF YOU HAVE A FAKE HAND TO SLIP OUT OF THOSE CUFFS OR SOMETHING, JUST LEAVE IT.
BELIEVE ME, THERE IS NOWHERE SAFER THAN HERE.
A FAKE HAND? WHY WOULD I HAVE A FAKE HAND? I HAVE A FAKE MOUSTACHE.
WHY?
NO ONE SHOULD EVER HAVE TO JUSTIFY A FAKE MOUSTACHE.
THE FAKE HAND WAS ALWAYS MISTER J's GAG.
HAVE YOU EVER LOVED SOMEONE YOU KNEW WAS WRONG FOR YOU?
SOMEONE WHO HURT YOU OVER AND OVER AGAIN AND HURT THOSE AROUND YOU BUT YOU COULD FORGIVE THEM BECAUSE LOSING THEM WOULD HURT EVEN MORE?
I...
...ACTUALLY, YOU'VE JUST DESCRIBED THREE OF THE LAST FOUR WOMEN I'VE BEEN WITH.
I KNOW HE WAS A BAD GUY...
GENOCIDAL PSYCHOPATH.
...BUT HE WAS MINE.

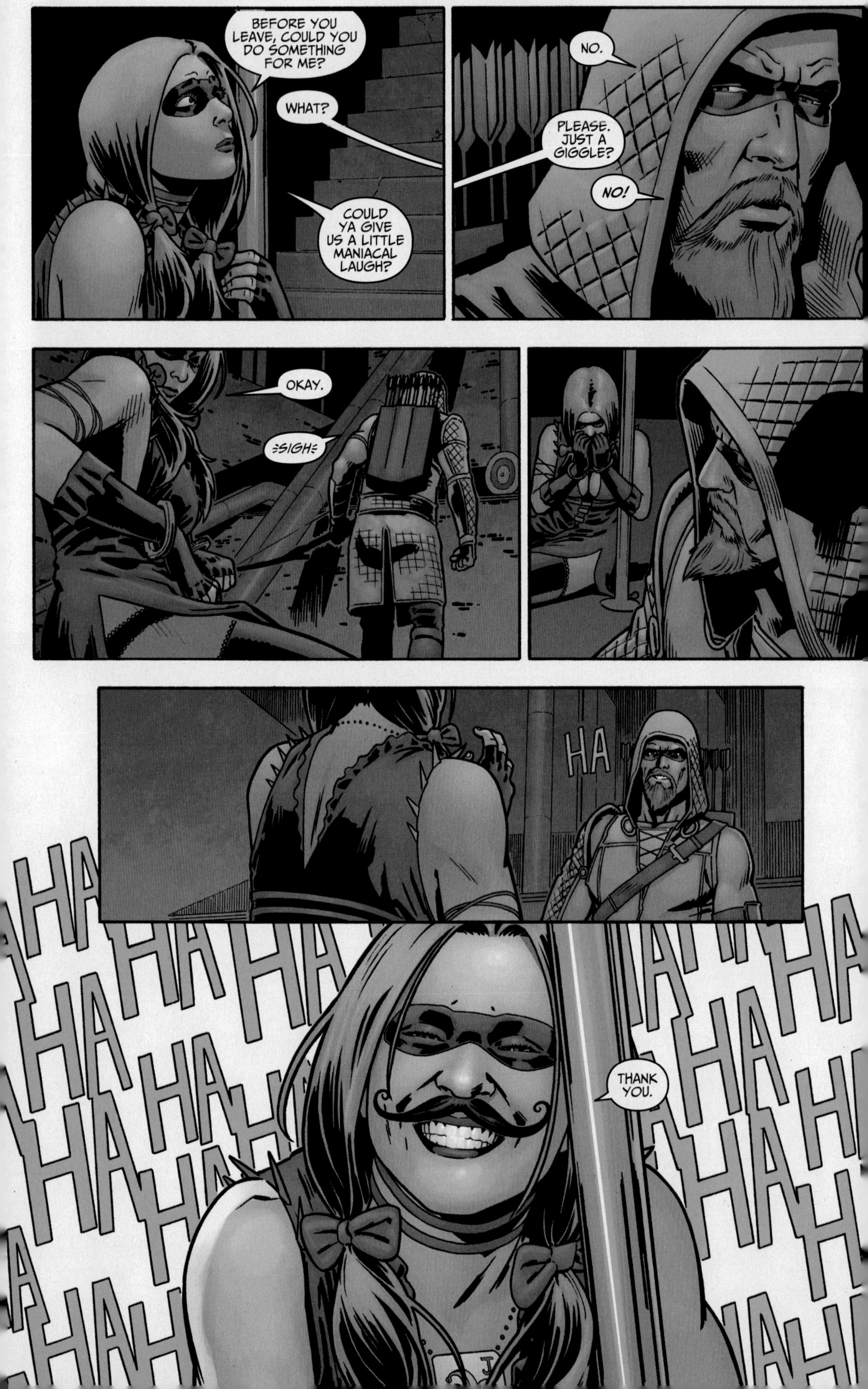
BEFORE YOU LEAVE, COULD YOU DO SOMETHING FOR ME?
WHAT?
COULD YA GIVE US A LITTLE MANIACAL LAUGH?
NO.
PLEASE. JUST A GIGGLE?
NO!
OKAY.
SIGH
HA
HA HA HA HA HA HA HA HA HA HA HA HA HA HA HA
THANK YOU.

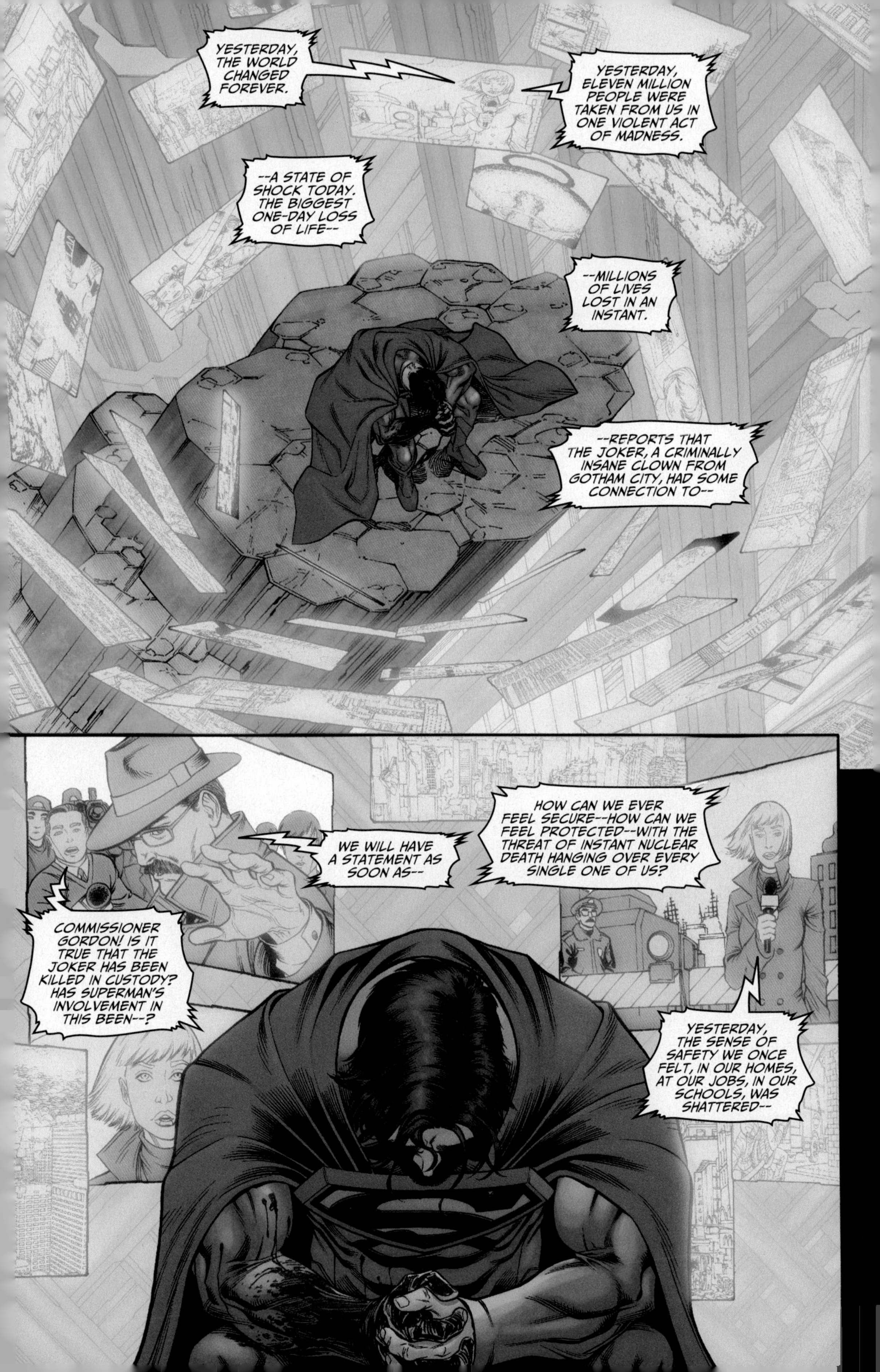
YESTERDAY, THE WORLD CHANGED FOREVER.
YESTERDAY, ELEVEN MILLION PEOPLE WERE TAKEN FROM US IN ONE VIOLENT ACT OF MADNESS.
--A STATE OF SHOCK TODAY. THE BIGGEST ONE-DAY LOSS OF LIFE--
--MILLIONS OF LIVES LOST IN AN INSTANT.
--REPORTS THAT THE JOKER, A CRIMINALLY INSANE CLOWN FROM GOTHAM CITY, HAD SOME CONNECTION TO--
WE WILL HAVE A STATEMENT AS SOON AS--
HOW CAN WE EVER FEEL SECURE--HOW CAN WE FEEL PROTECTED--WITH THE THREAT OF INSTANT NUCLEAR DEATH HANGING OVER EVERY SINGLE ONE OF US?
COMMISSIONER GORDON! IS IT TRUE THAT THE JOKER HAS BEEN KILLED IN CUSTODY? HAS SUPERMAN'S INVOLVEMENT IN THIS BEEN--?
YESTERDAY, THE SENSE OF SAFETY WE ONCE FELT, IN OUR HOMES, AT OUR JOBS, IN OUR SCHOOLS, WAS SHATTERED--

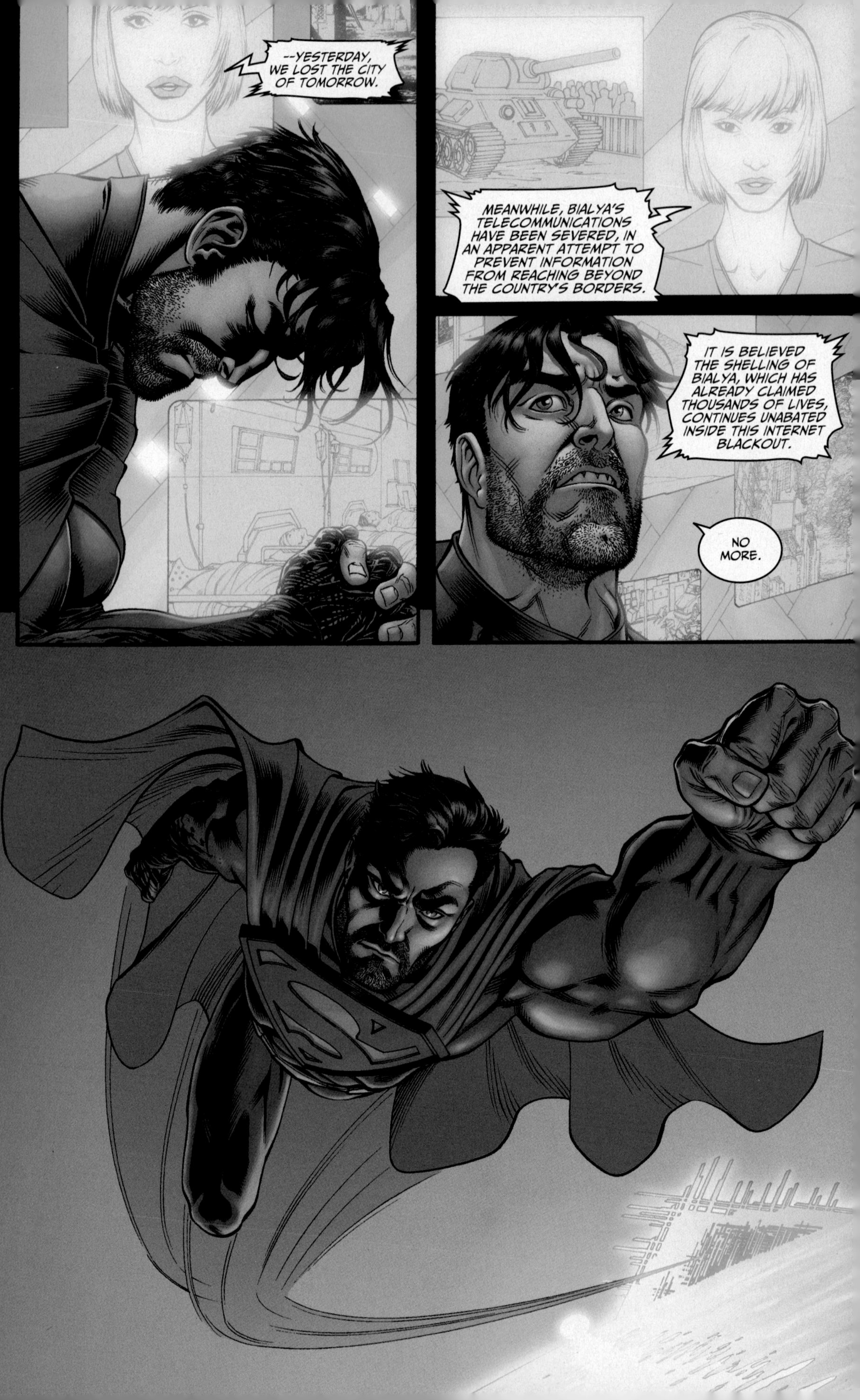
--YESTERDAY, WE LOST THE CITY OF TOMORROW.
MEANWHILE, BIALYA'S TELECOMMUNICATIONS HAVE BEEN SEVERED, IN AN APPARENT ATTEMPT TO PREVENT INFORMATION FROM REACHING BEYOND THE COUNTRY'S BORDERS.
IT IS BELIEVED THE SHELLING OF BIALYA, WHICH HAS ALREADY CLAIMED THOUSANDS OF LIVES, CONTINUES UNABATED INSIDE THIS INTERNET BLACKOUT.
NO MORE.

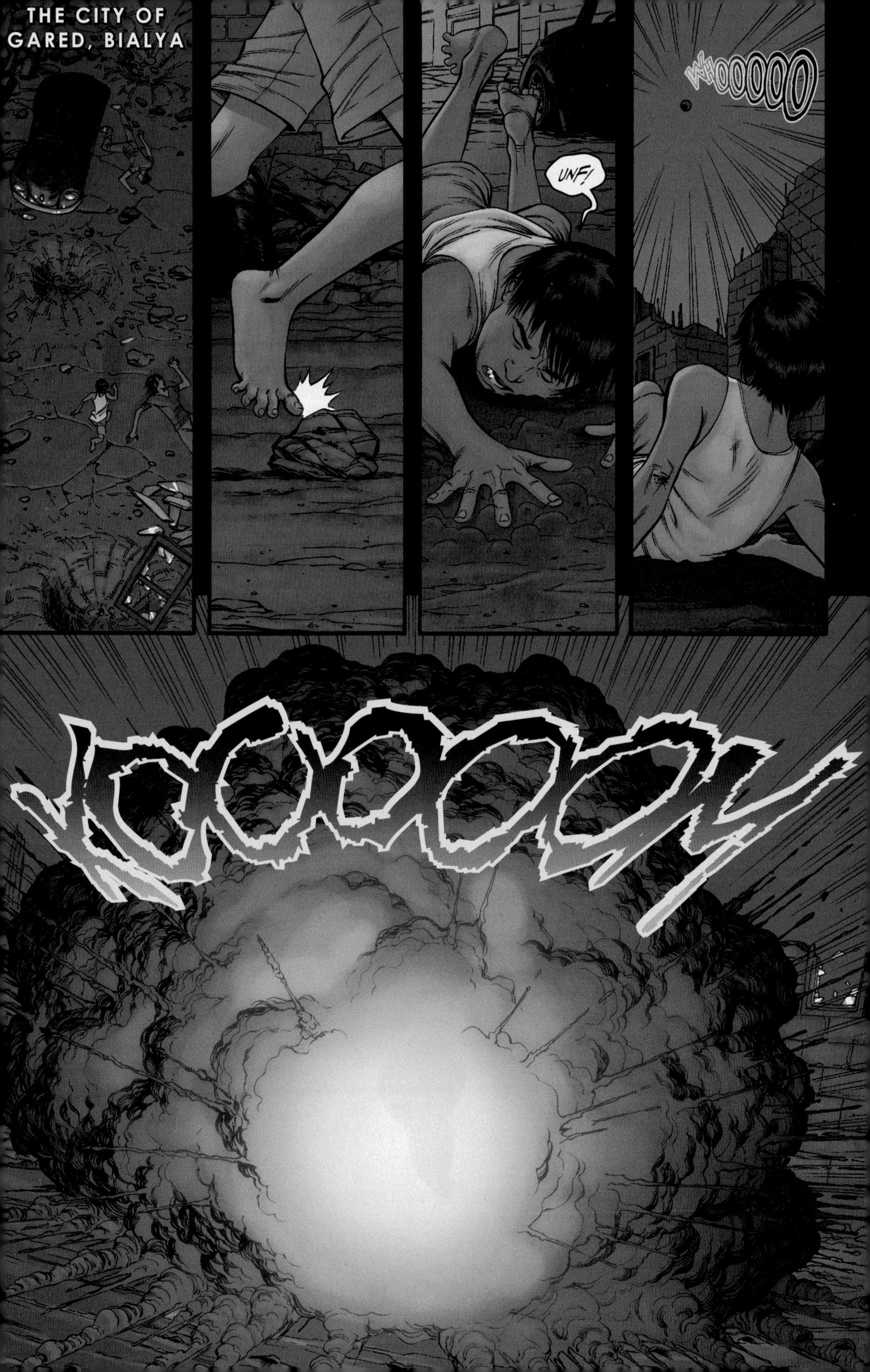
THE CITY OF GARED, BIALYA
UNF!
WHOOOOO

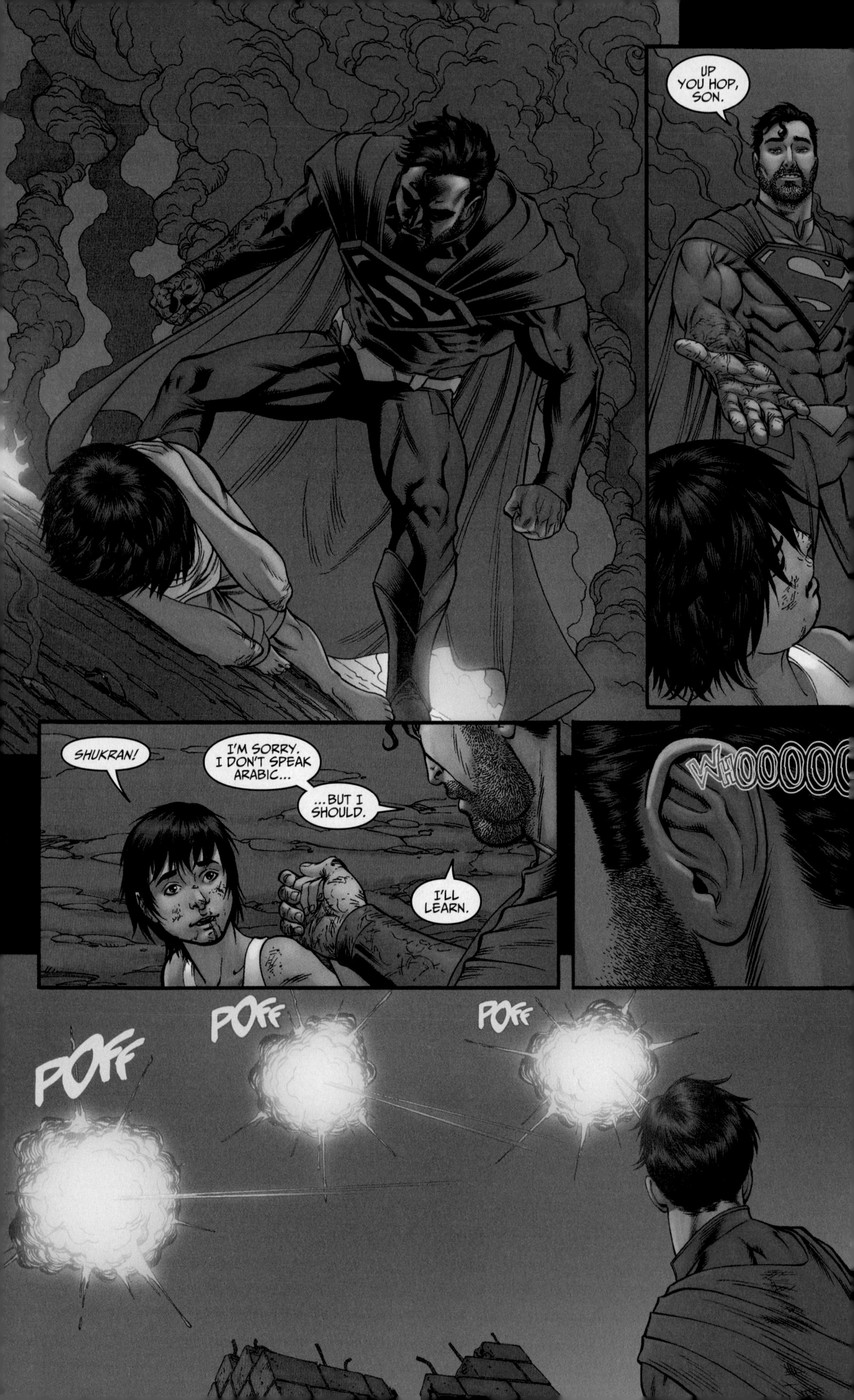
UP YOU HOP, SON.
SHUKRAN!
I'M SORRY. I DON'T SPEAK ARABIC...
...BUT I SHOULD.
I'LL LEARN.
WHOOOOO
POFF
POFF
POFF

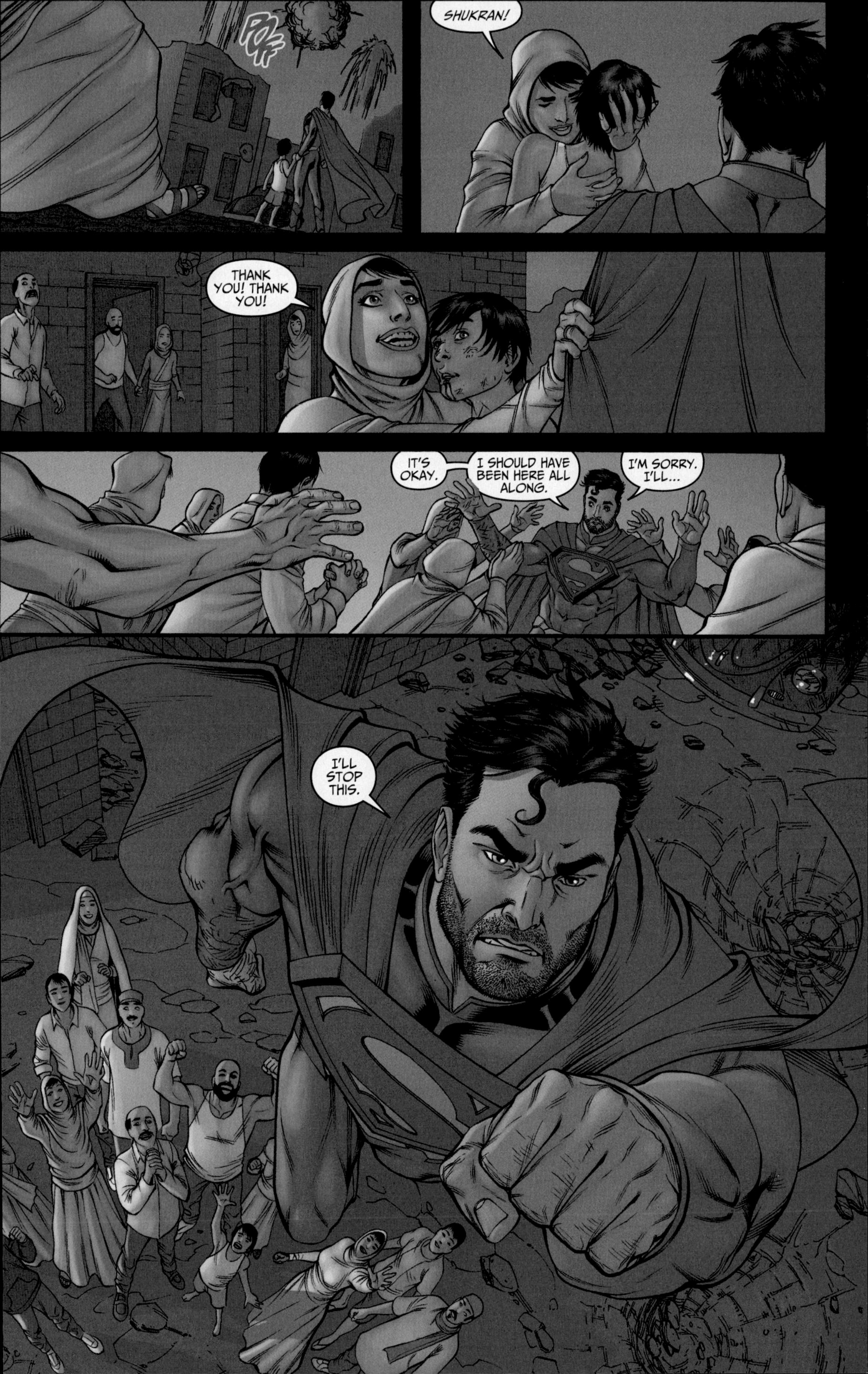
POFF
SHUKRAN!
THANK YOU! THANK YOU!
IT'S OKAY.
I SHOULD HAVE BEEN HERE ALL ALONG.
I'M SORRY. I'LL...
I'LL STOP THIS.

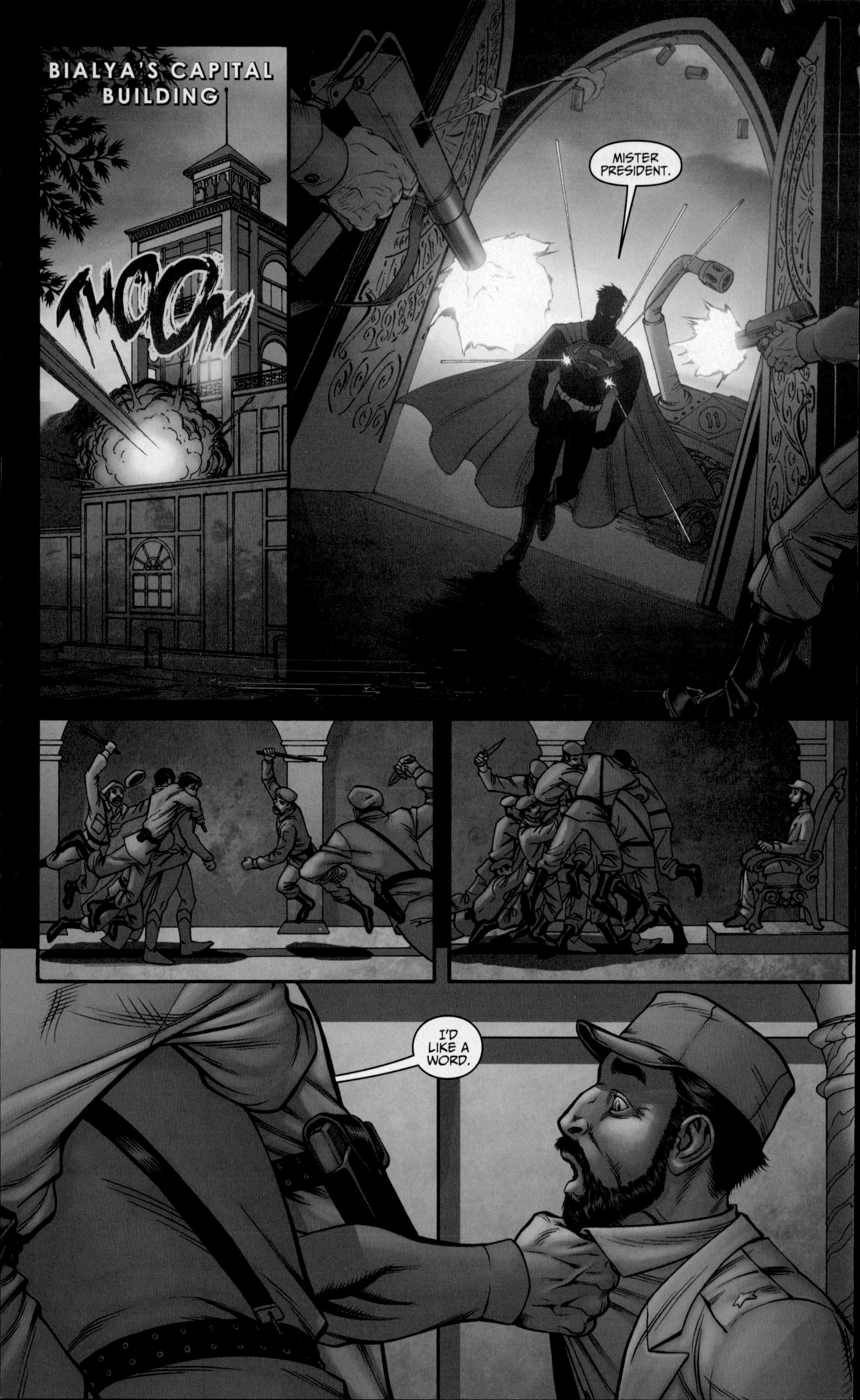
BIALYA'S CAPITAL BUILDING
THOOM
MISTER PRESIDENT.
I'D LIKE A WORD.

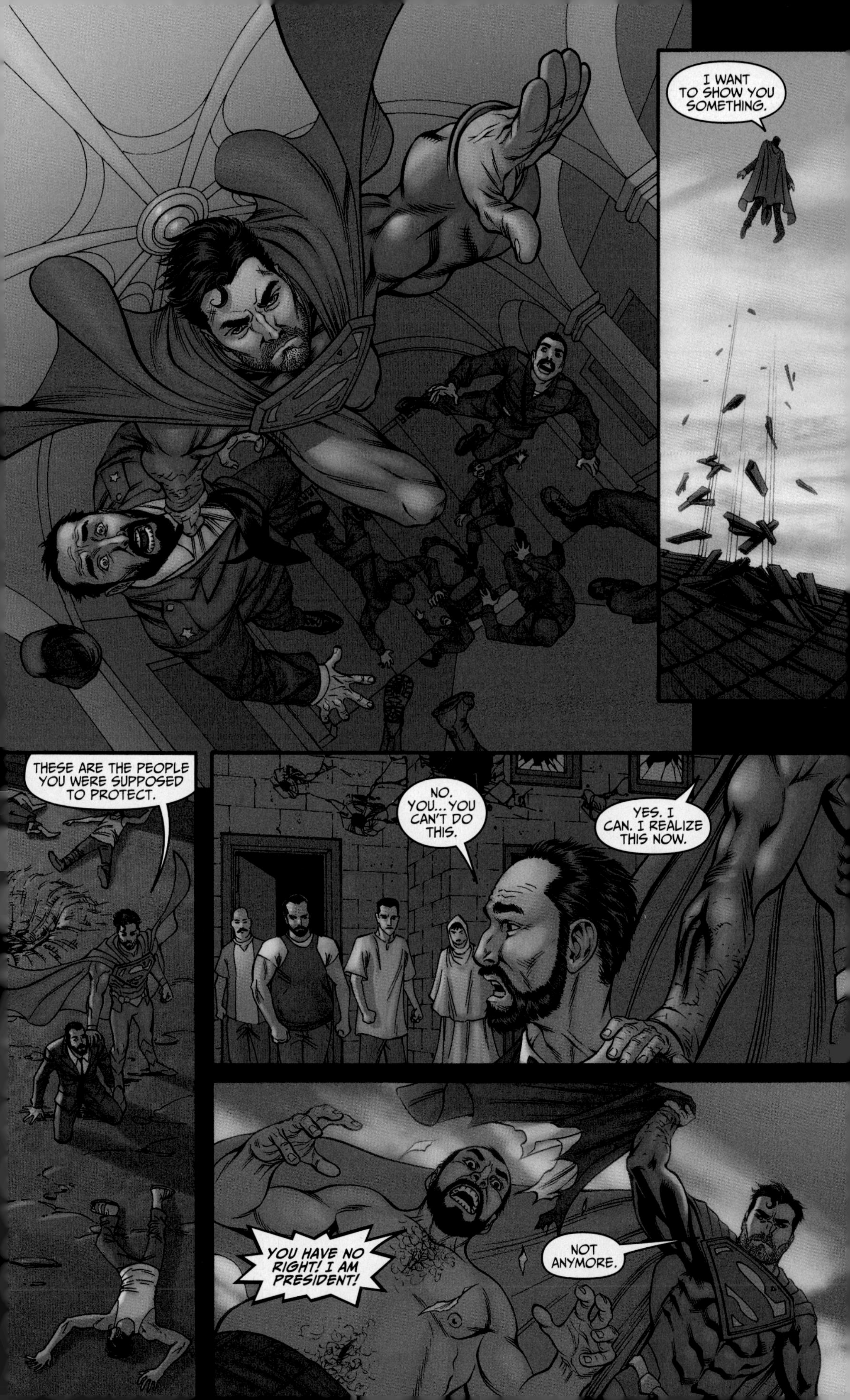
I WANT TO SHOW YOU SOMETHING.
THESE ARE THE PEOPLE YOU WERE SUPPOSED TO PROTECT.
NO. YOU...YOU CAN'T DO THIS.
YES. I CAN. I REALIZE THIS NOW.
YOU HAVE NO RIGHT! I AM PRESIDENT!
NOT ANYMORE.

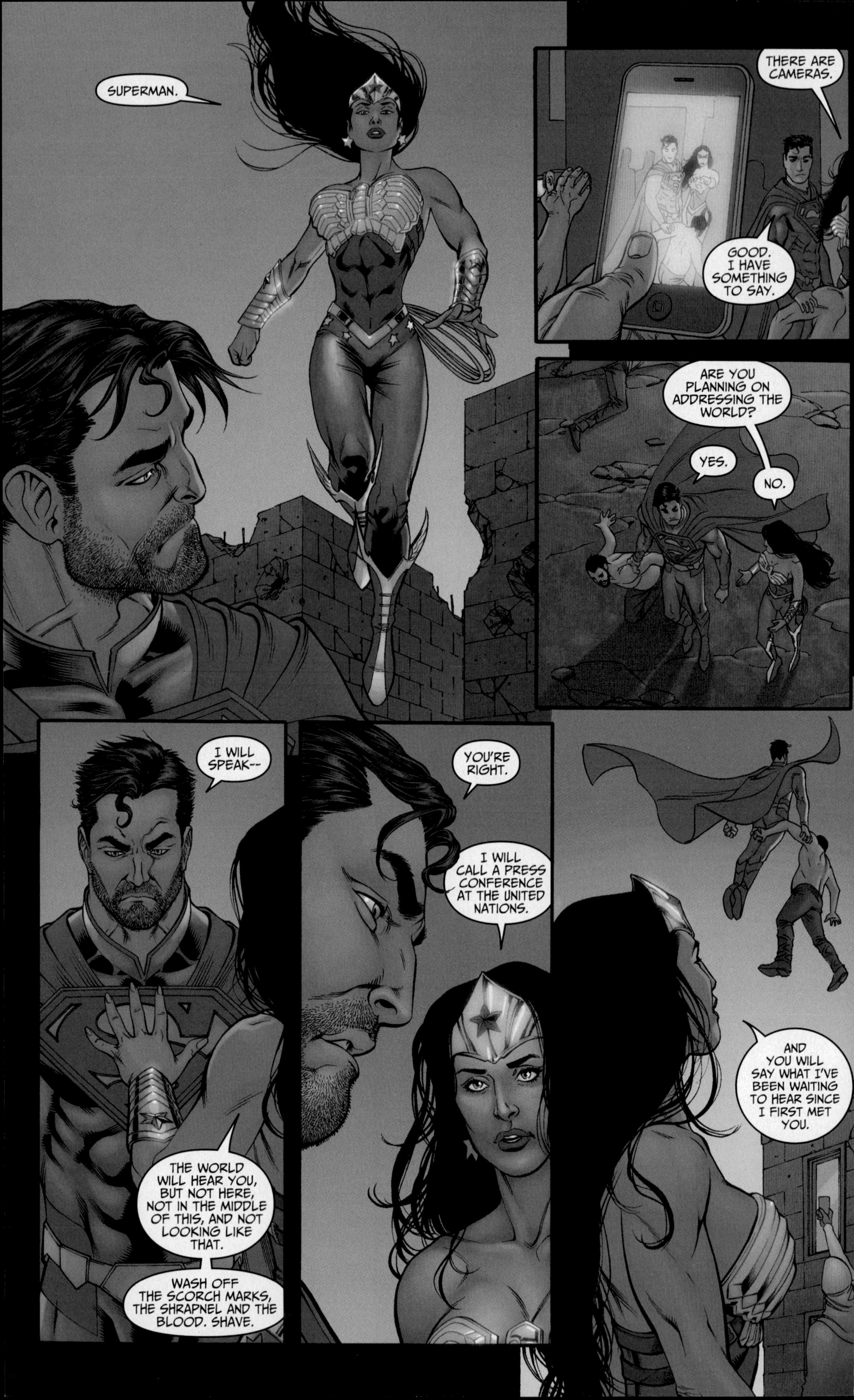
SUPERMAN.
THERE ARE CAMERAS.
GOOD. I HAVE SOMETHING TO SAY.
ARE YOU PLANNING ON ADDRESSING THE WORLD?
YES.
NO.
I WILL SPEAK--
THE WORLD WILL HEAR YOU, BUT NOT HERE, NOT IN THE MIDDLE OF THIS, AND NOT LOOKING LIKE THAT.
WASH OFF THE SCORCH MARKS, THE SHRAPNEL AND THE BLOOD. SHAVE.
YOU'RE RIGHT.
I WILL CALL A PRESS CONFERENCE AT THE UNITED NATIONS.
AND YOU WILL SAY WHAT I'VE BEEN WAITING TO HEAR SINCE I FIRST MET YOU.

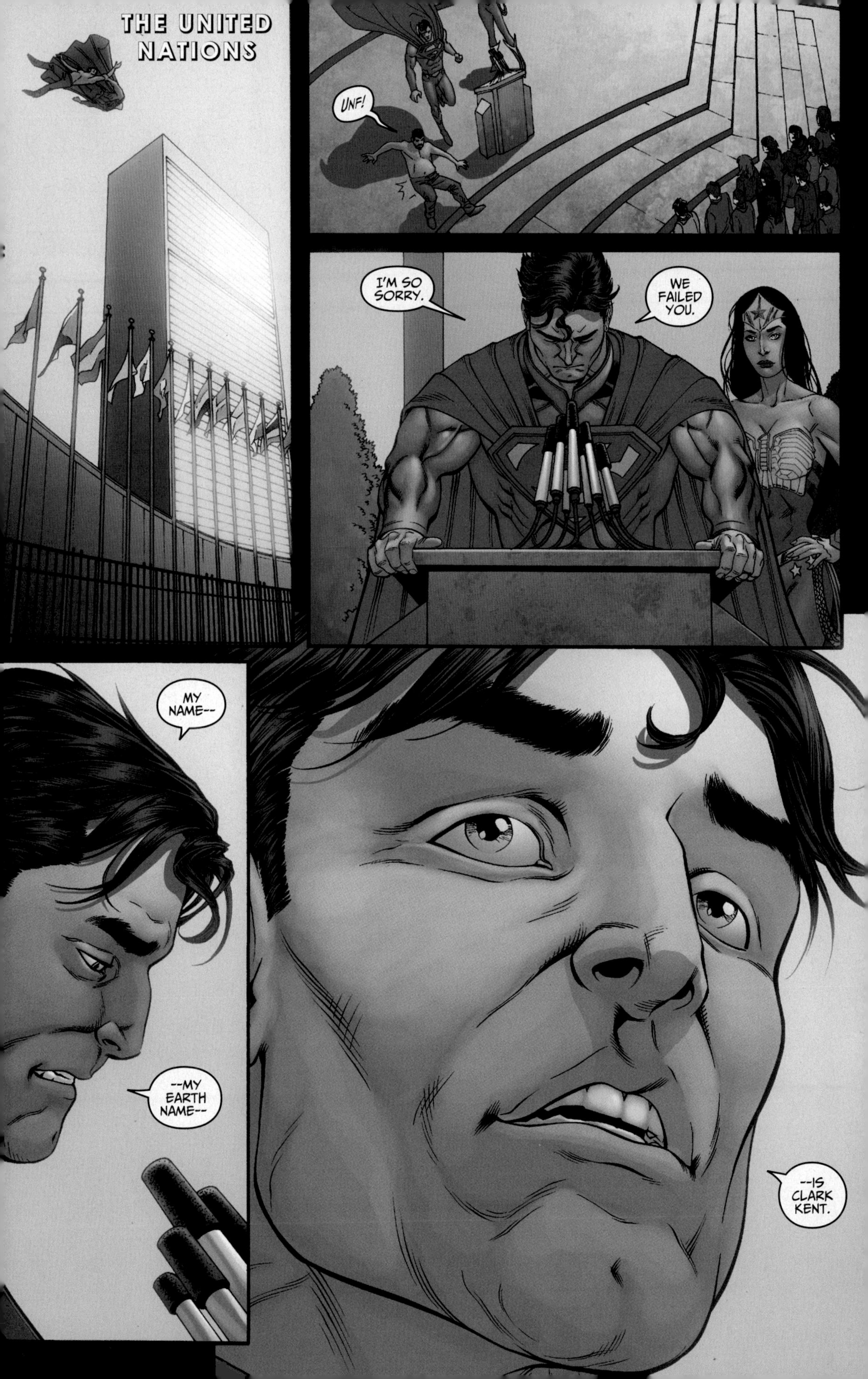
THE UNITED NATIONS
UNF!
I'M SO SORRY.
WE FAILED YOU.
MY NAME--
--MY EARTH NAME--
--IS CLARK KENT.

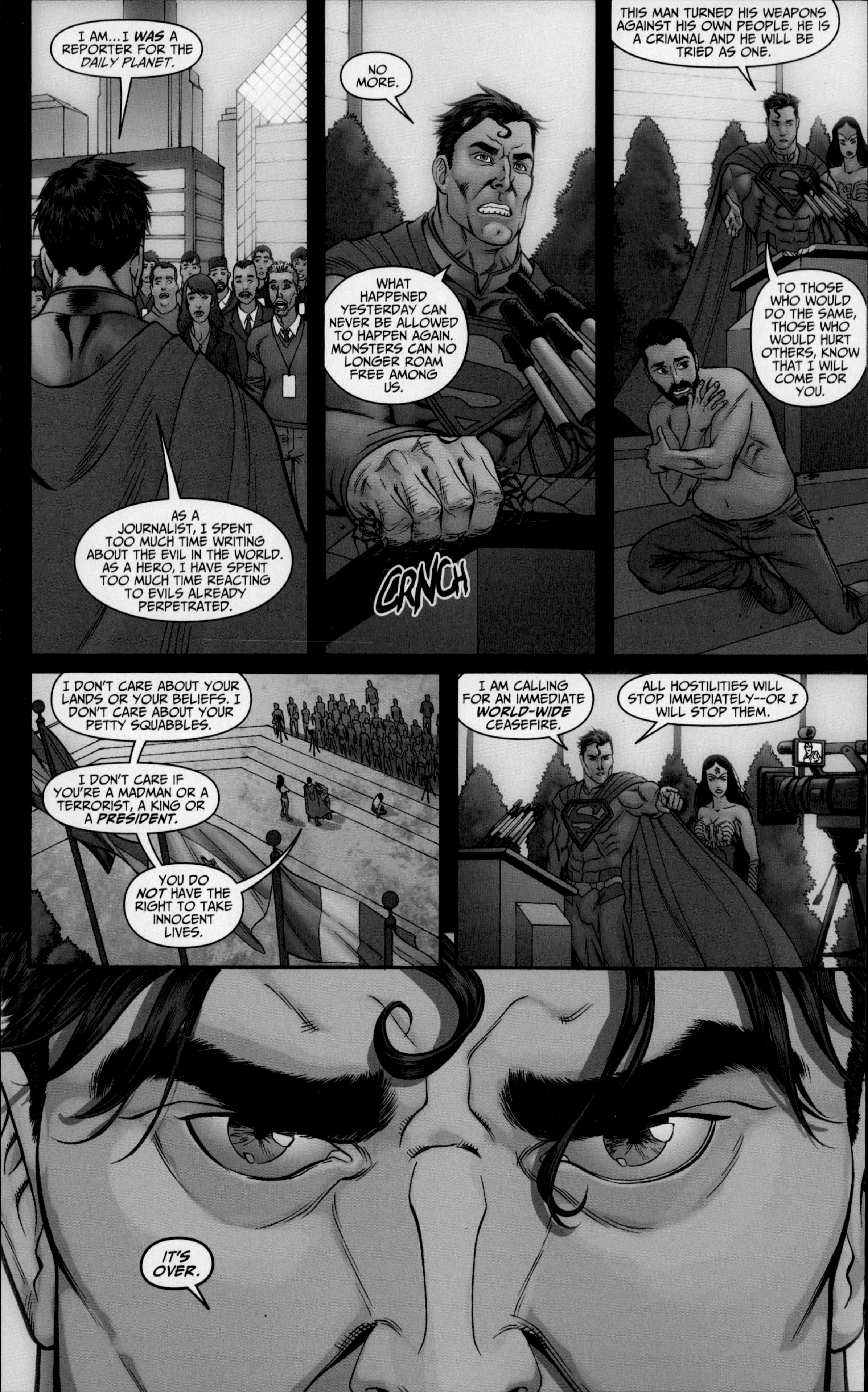
I AM...I *WAS* A REPORTER FOR THE *DAILY PLANET.*
AS A JOURNALIST, I SPENT TOO MUCH TIME WRITING ABOUT THE EVIL IN THE WORLD. AS A HERO, I HAVE SPENT TOO MUCH TIME REACTING TO EVILS ALREADY PERPETRATED.
NO MORE.
WHAT HAPPENED YESTERDAY CAN NEVER BE ALLOWED TO HAPPEN AGAIN. MONSTERS CAN NO LONGER ROAM FREE AMONG US.
CRNCH
THIS MAN TURNED HIS WEAPONS AGAINST HIS OWN PEOPLE. HE IS A CRIMINAL AND HE WILL BE TRIED AS ONE.
TO THOSE WHO WOULD DO THE SAME, THOSE WHO WOULD HURT OTHERS, KNOW THAT I WILL COME FOR YOU.
I DON'T CARE ABOUT YOUR LANDS OR YOUR BELIEFS. I DON'T CARE ABOUT YOUR PETTY SQUABBLES.
I DON'T CARE IF YOU'RE A MADMAN OR A TERRORIST, A KING OR A *PRESIDENT.*
YOU DO *NOT* HAVE THE RIGHT TO TAKE INNOCENT LIVES.
I AM CALLING FOR AN IMMEDIATE *WORLD-WIDE* CEASEFIRE.
ALL HOSTILITIES WILL STOP IMMEDIATELY--OR *I* WILL STOP THEM.
IT'S OVER.

PART THREE

Jheremy Raapack David Yardin Artists

Cover Art by Jheremy Raapack & Andrew Elder

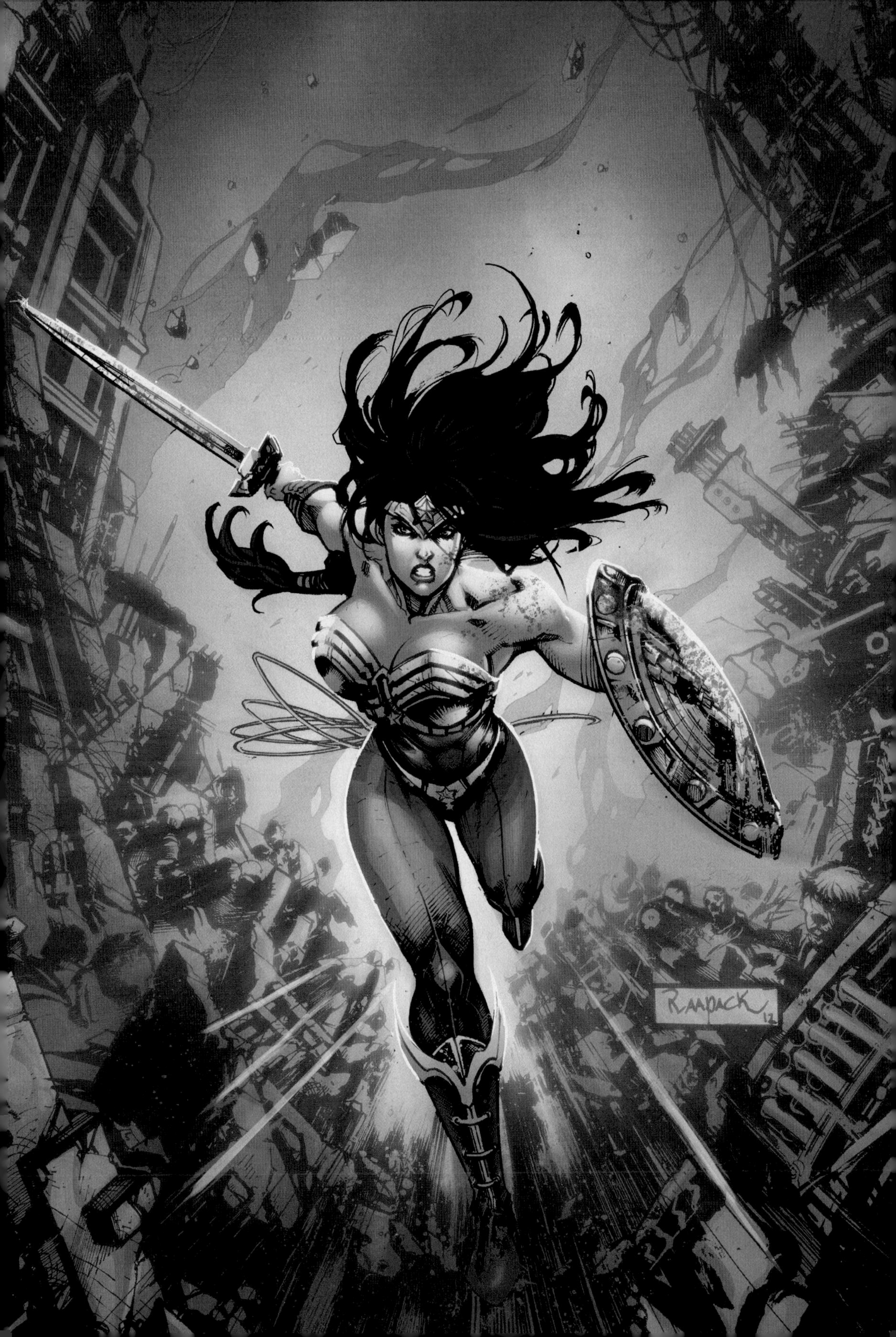

RAAPACK 12

THERMAL CONFIRMED. TARGET IS STATIC.

"ARMING MISSILE."

CLICK

MISSILE AWAY.

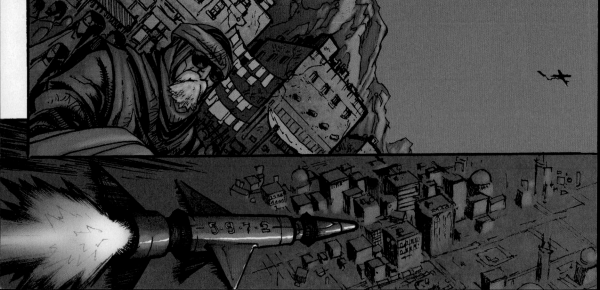

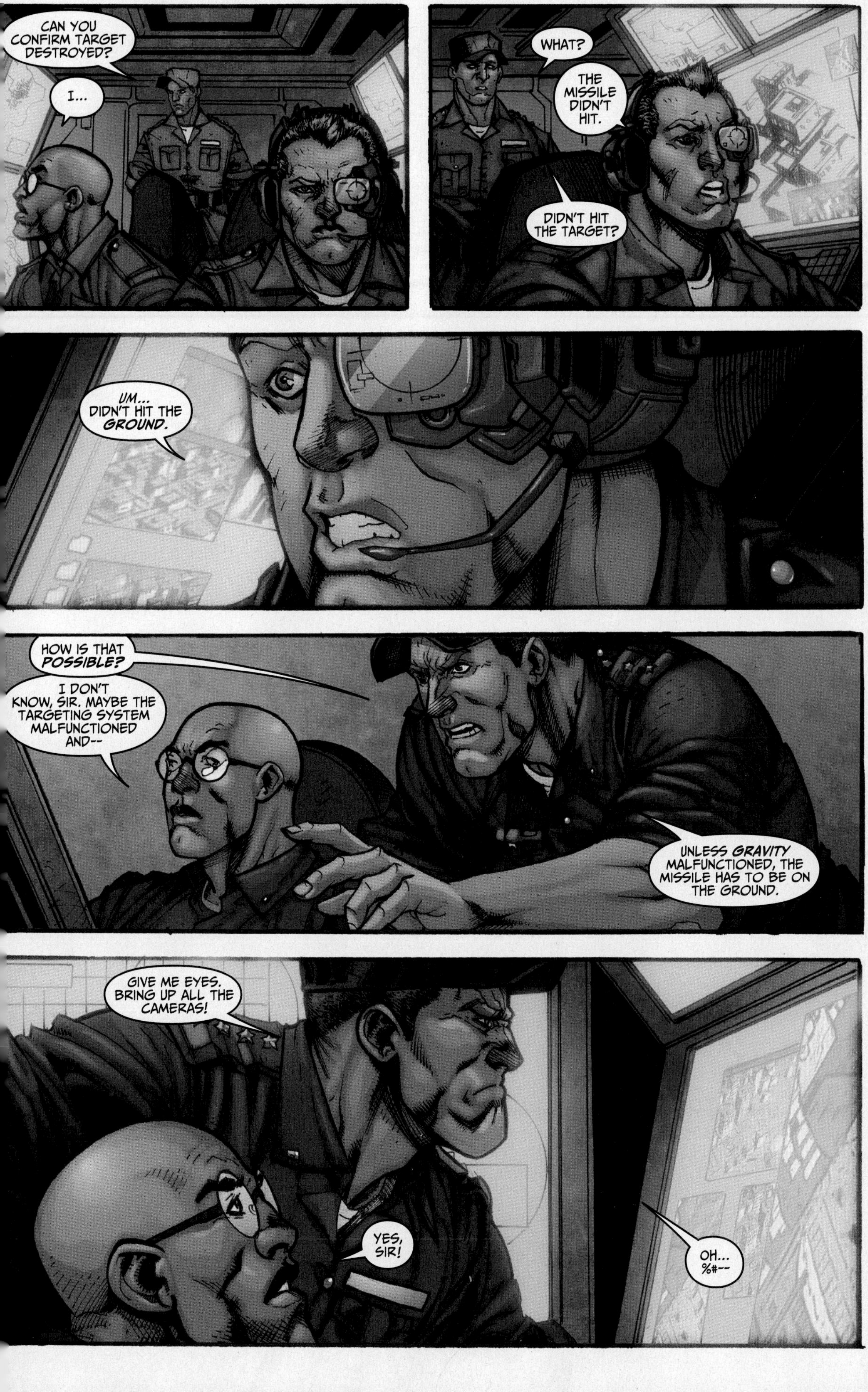
CAN YOU CONFIRM TARGET DESTROYED?
I...
WHAT?
THE MISSILE DIDN'T HIT.
DIDN'T HIT THE TARGET?
UM... DIDN'T HIT THE GROUND.
HOW IS THAT POSSIBLE?
I DON'T KNOW, SIR. MAYBE THE TARGETING SYSTEM MALFUNCTIONED AND--
UNLESS GRAVITY MALFUNCTIONED, THE MISSILE HAS TO BE ON THE GROUND.
GIVE ME EYES. BRING UP ALL THE CAMERAS!
YES, SIR!
OH... %#--

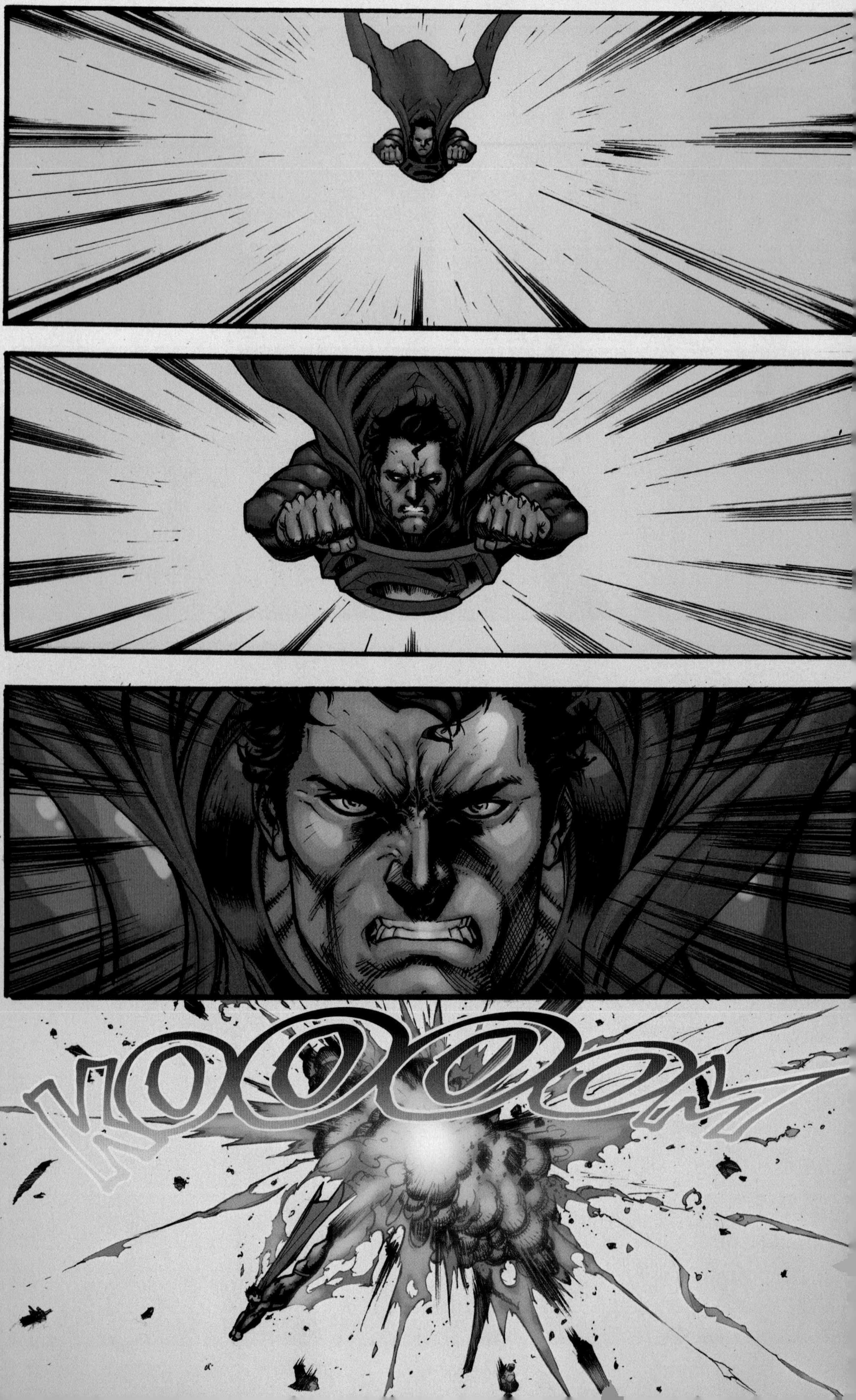
KOOOOOM

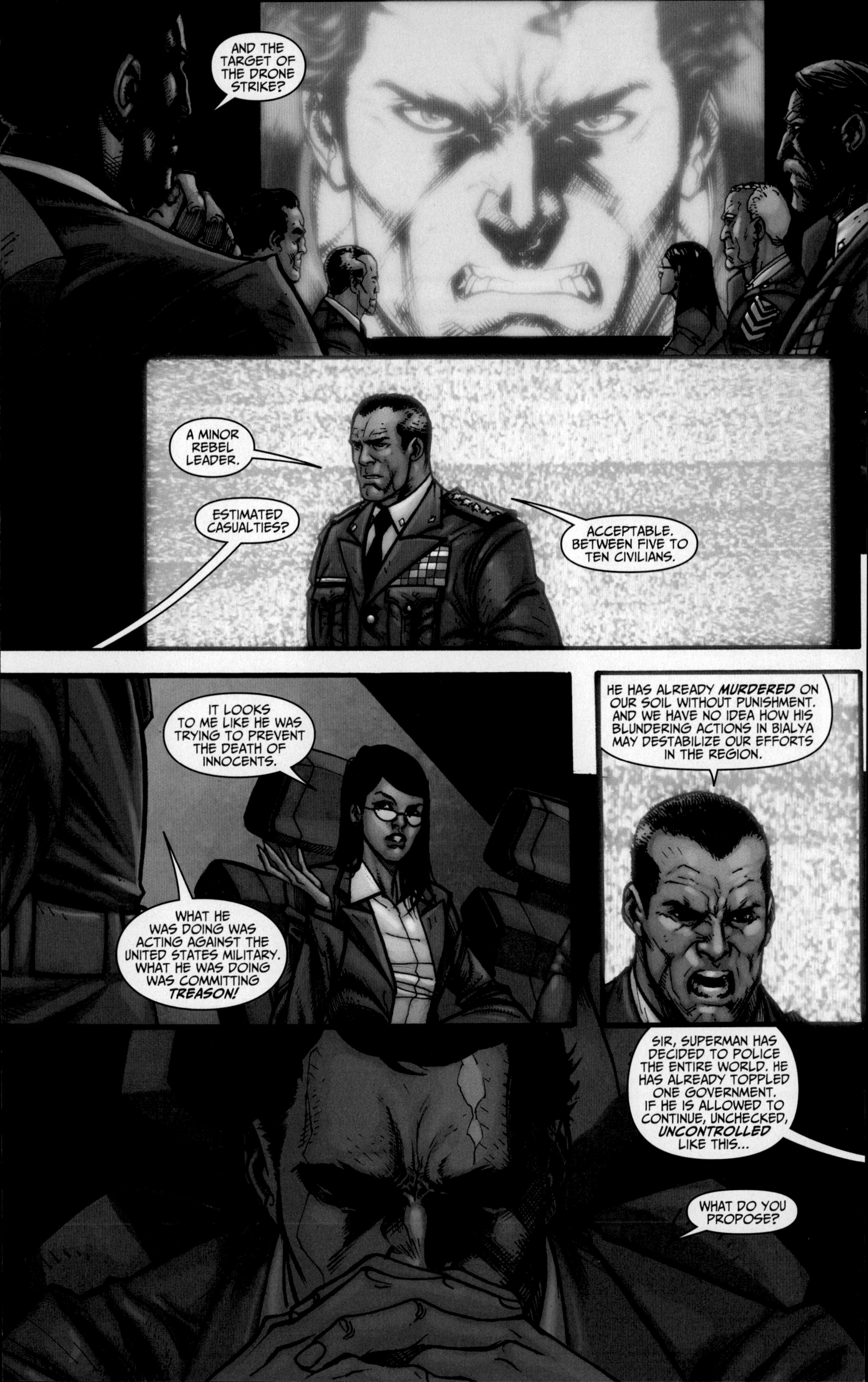
AND THE TARGET OF THE DRONE STRIKE?
A MINOR REBEL LEADER.
ESTIMATED CASUALTIES?
ACCEPTABLE. BETWEEN FIVE TO TEN CIVILIANS.
IT LOOKS TO ME LIKE HE WAS TRYING TO PREVENT THE DEATH OF INNOCENTS.
WHAT HE WAS DOING WAS ACTING AGAINST THE UNITED STATES MILITARY. WHAT HE WAS DOING WAS COMMITTING ***TREASON!***
HE HAS ALREADY ***MURDERED*** ON OUR SOIL WITHOUT PUNISHMENT. AND WE HAVE NO IDEA HOW HIS BLUNDERING ACTIONS IN BIALYA MAY DESTABILIZE OUR EFFORTS IN THE REGION.
SIR, SUPERMAN HAS DECIDED TO POLICE THE ENTIRE WORLD. HE HAS ALREADY TOPPLED ONE GOVERNMENT. IF HE IS ALLOWED TO CONTINUE, UNCHECKED, ***UNCONTROLLED*** LIKE THIS...
WHAT DO YOU PROPOSE?

"WE HAVE ONE CHANCE AT THIS. WE HAVE ONE CARD WE CAN PLAY."

"HAVE YOU THOUGHT ABOUT THE CONSEQUENCES, GENERAL? IF WE MOVE AGAINST HIM AND *FAIL...?*"

"THERE WILL BE ABSOLUTELY NO SIGN OF YOUR INVOLVEMENT IN THIS, SIR. THESE WILL BE INDEPENDENT CONTRACTORS HIRED THROUGH A SERIES OF SHELL COMPANIES.

"AND WE WON'T FAIL. WE'VE PLANNED THIS."

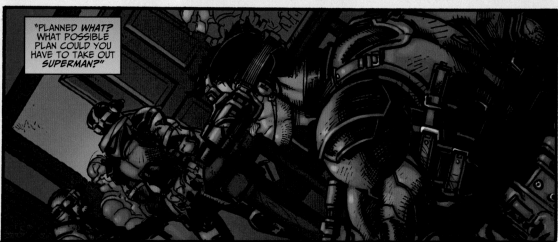

"PLANNED *WHAT?* WHAT POSSIBLE PLAN COULD YOU HAVE TO TAKE OUT *SUPERMAN?*"

"I'M NOT SUGGESTING WE TAKE OUT *SUPERMAN.*"

CRRRACK

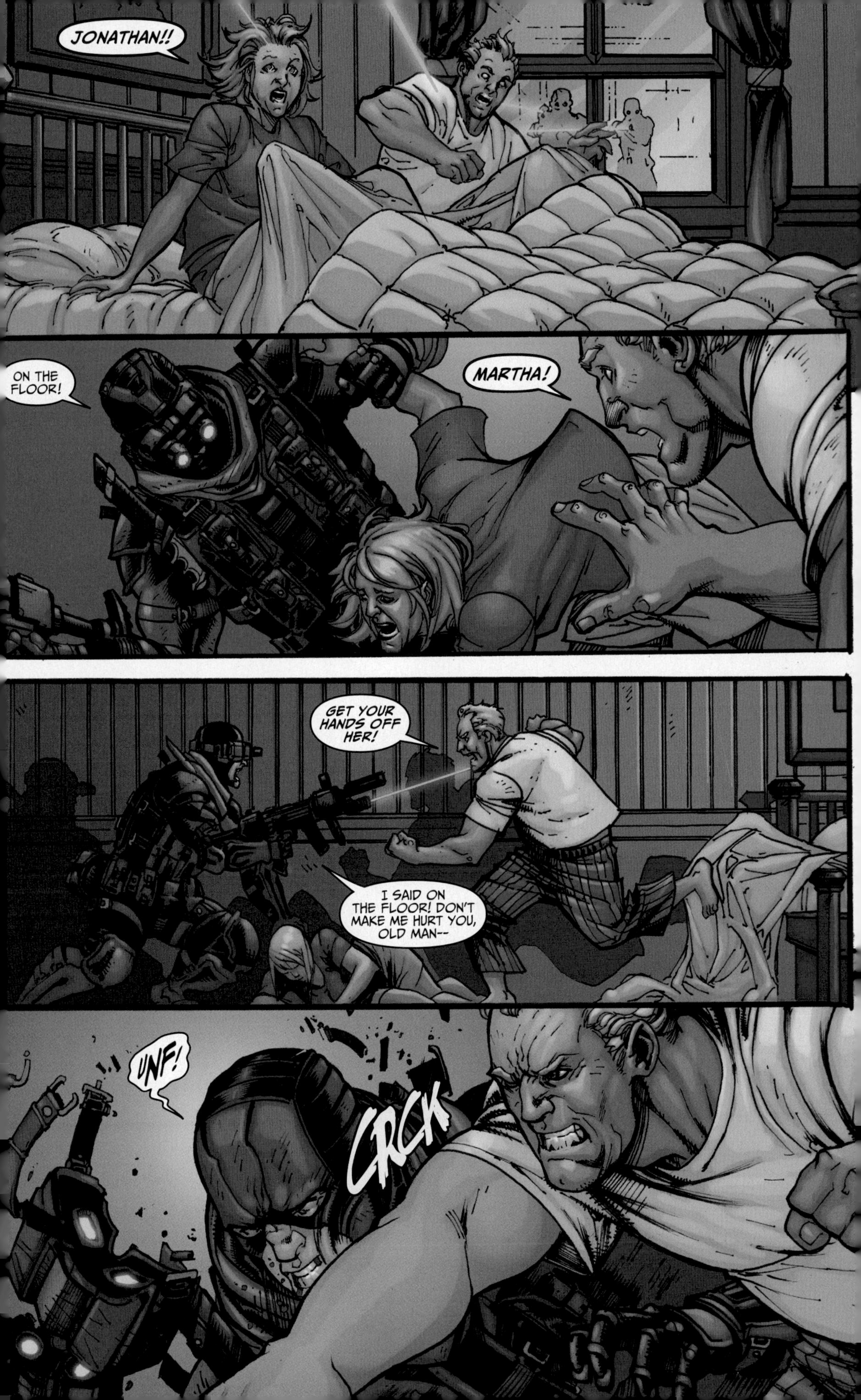
JONATHAN!!
ON THE FLOOR!
MARTHA!
GET YOUR HANDS OFF HER!
I SAID ON THE FLOOR! DON'T MAKE ME HURT YOU, OLD MAN--
UNF!
CRCK

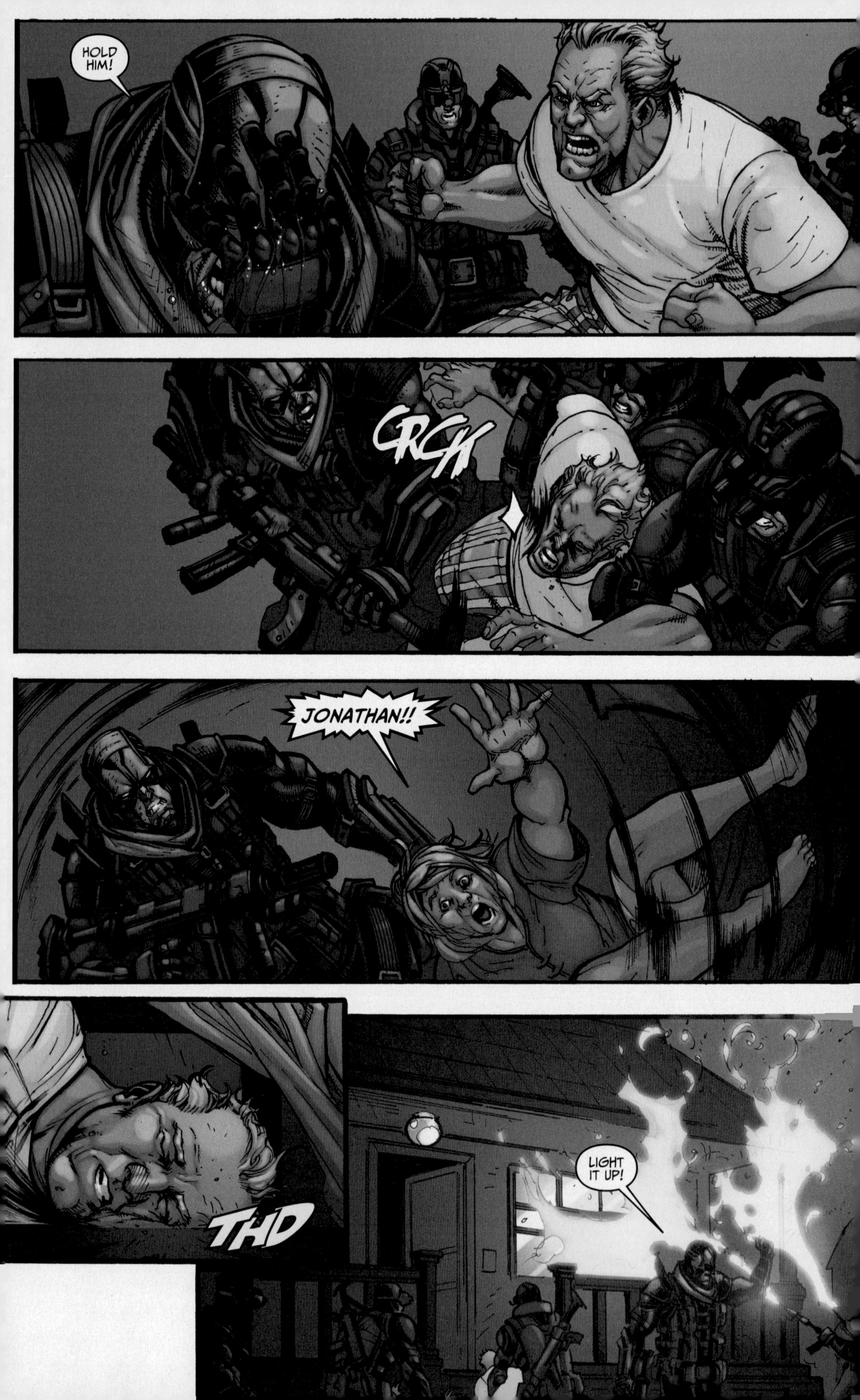
HOLD HIM!
CRCK
JONATHAN!!
THD
LIGHT IT UP!

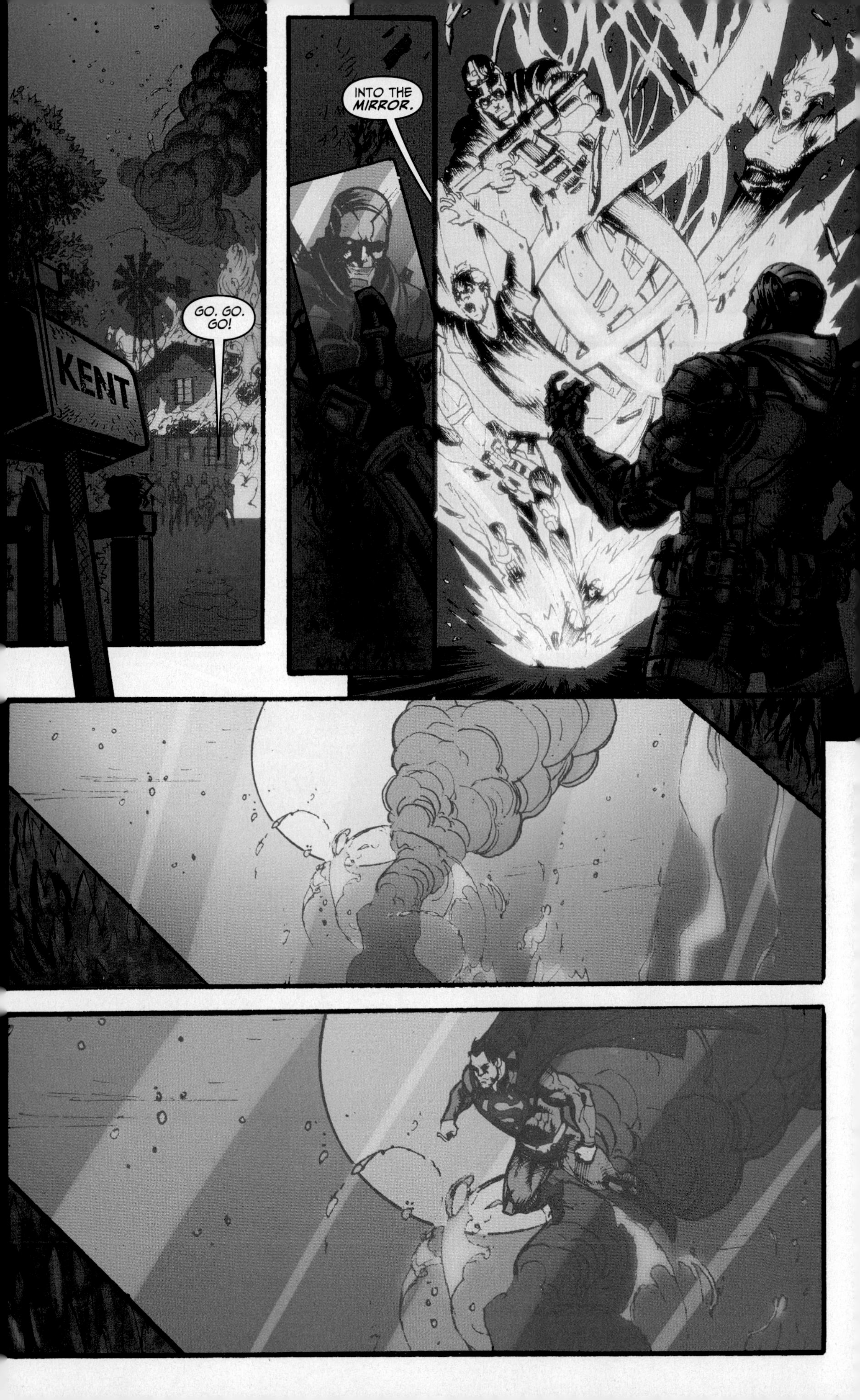
KENT
GO. GO. GO!
INTO THE MIRROR.

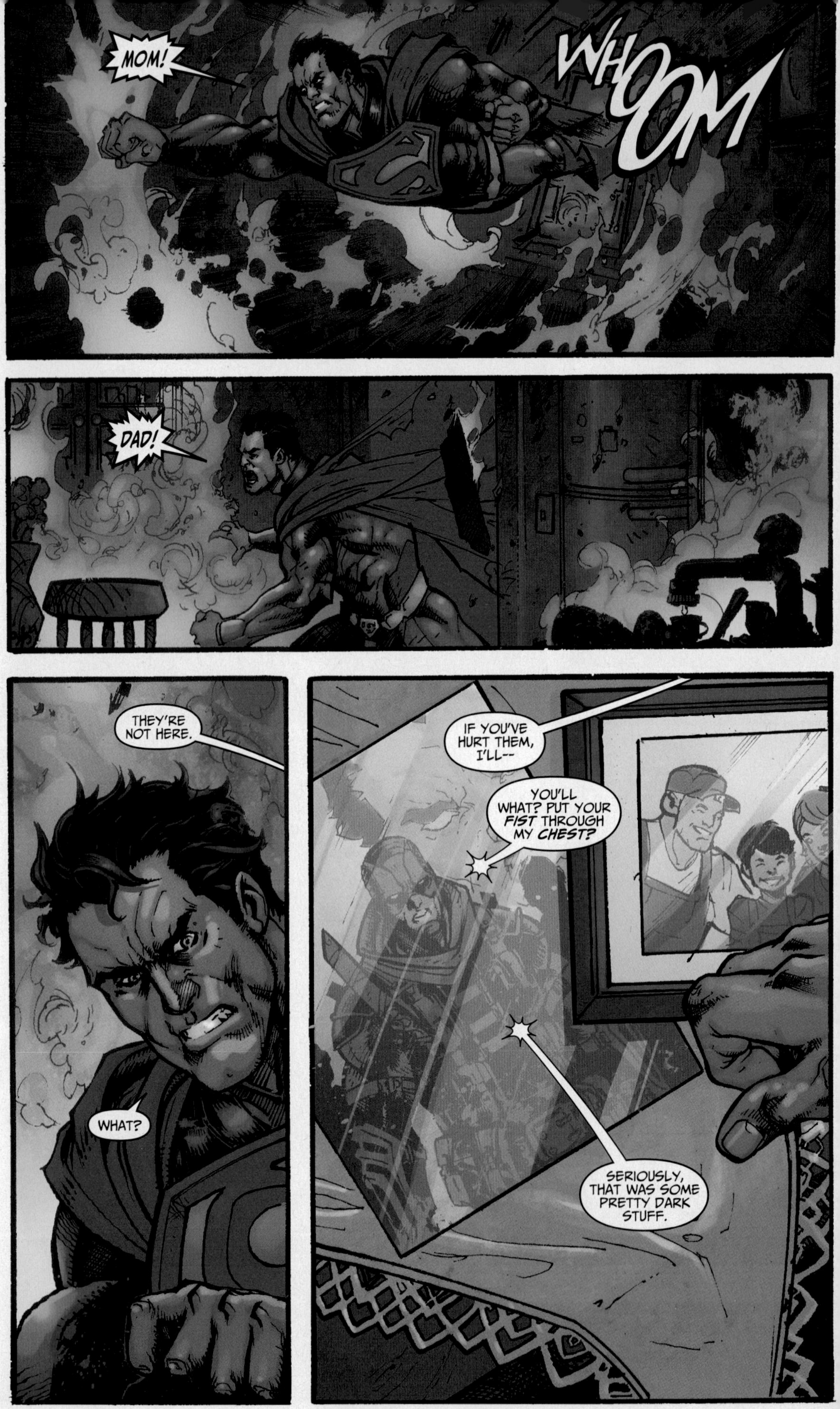
MOM!
WHOOM
DAD!
THEY'RE NOT HERE.
WHAT?
IF YOU'VE HURT THEM, I'LL--
YOU'LL WHAT? PUT YOUR FIST THROUGH MY CHEST?
SERIOUSLY, THAT WAS SOME PRETTY DARK STUFF.

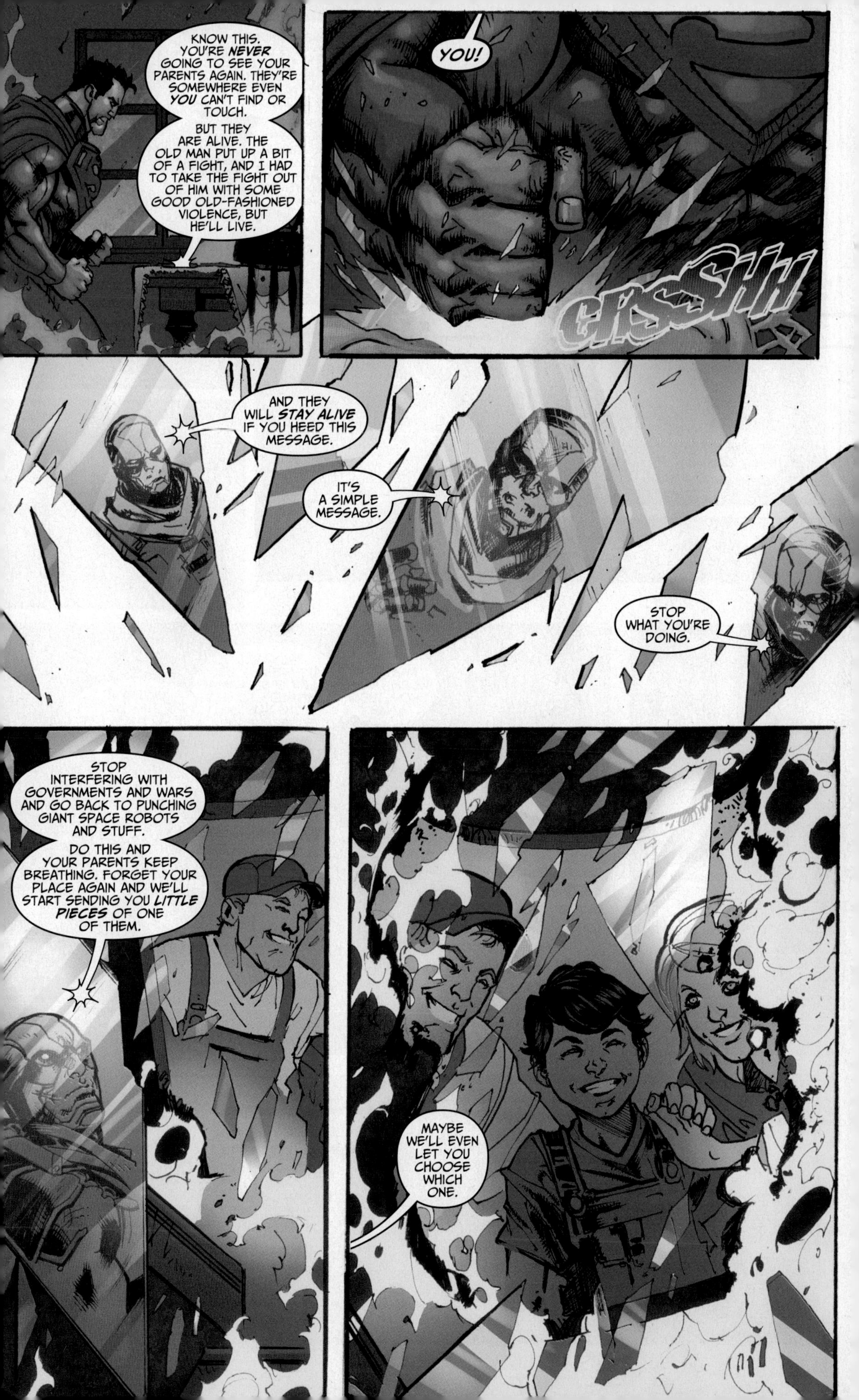

KNOW THIS. YOU'RE NEVER GOING TO SEE YOUR PARENTS AGAIN. THEY'RE SOMEWHERE EVEN YOU CAN'T FIND OR TOUCH.
BUT THEY ARE ALIVE. THE OLD MAN PUT UP A BIT OF A FIGHT, AND I HAD TO TAKE THE FIGHT OUT OF HIM WITH SOME GOOD OLD-FASHIONED VIOLENCE, BUT HE'LL LIVE.
YOU!
CRSSHH
AND THEY WILL STAY ALIVE IF YOU HEED THIS MESSAGE.
IT'S A SIMPLE MESSAGE.
STOP WHAT YOU'RE DOING.
STOP INTERFERING WITH GOVERNMENTS AND WARS AND GO BACK TO PUNCHING GIANT SPACE ROBOTS AND STUFF.
DO THIS AND YOUR PARENTS KEEP BREATHING. FORGET YOUR PLACE AGAIN AND WE'LL START SENDING YOU LITTLE PIECES OF ONE OF THEM.
MAYBE WE'LL EVEN LET YOU CHOOSE WHICH ONE.

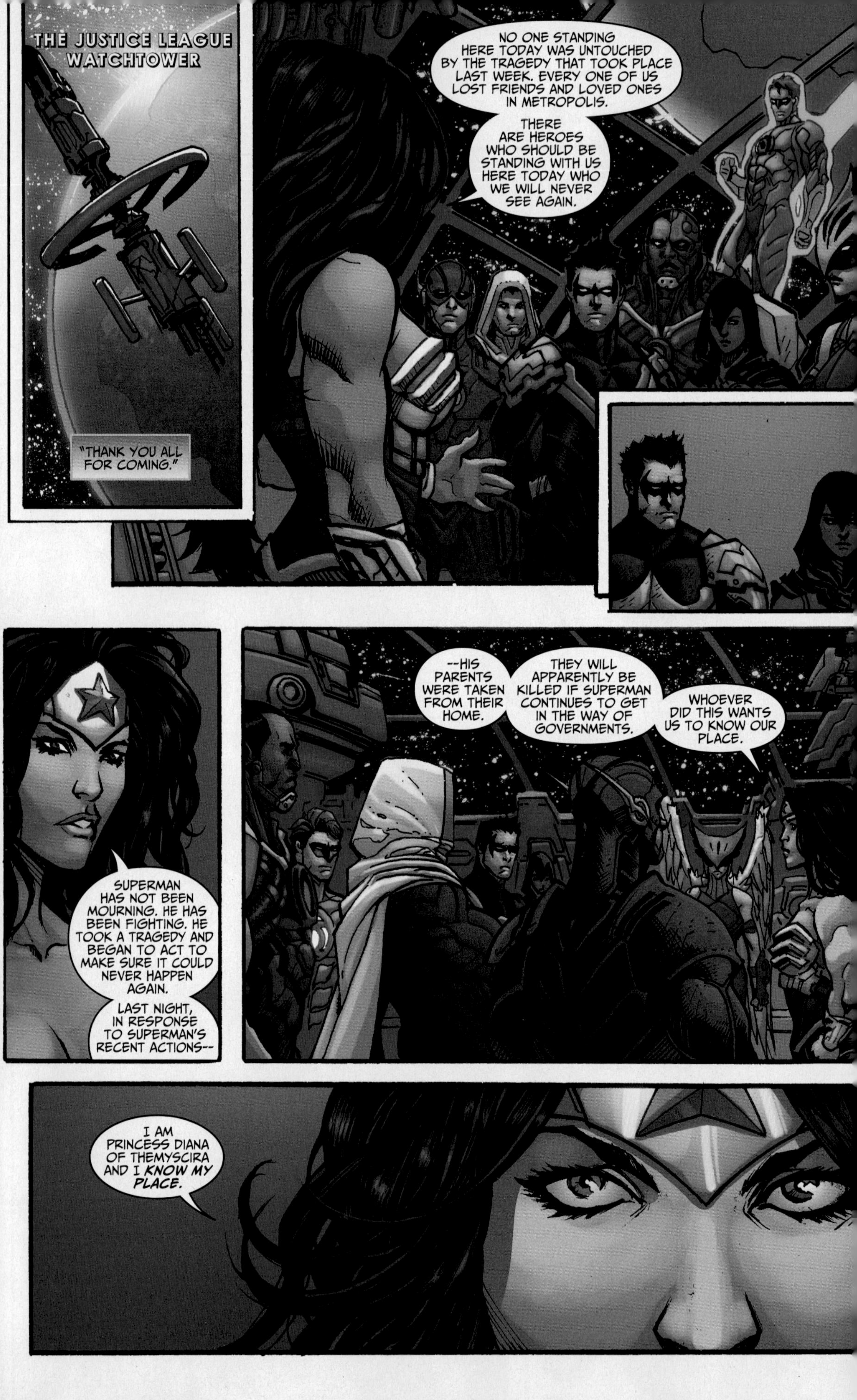
THE JUSTICE LEAGUE WATCHTOWER
"THANK YOU ALL FOR COMING."
NO ONE STANDING HERE TODAY WAS UNTOUCHED BY THE TRAGEDY THAT TOOK PLACE LAST WEEK. EVERY ONE OF US LOST FRIENDS AND LOVED ONES IN METROPOLIS.
THERE ARE HEROES WHO SHOULD BE STANDING WITH US HERE TODAY WHO WE WILL NEVER SEE AGAIN.
SUPERMAN HAS NOT BEEN MOURNING. HE HAS BEEN FIGHTING. HE TOOK A TRAGEDY AND BEGAN TO ACT TO MAKE SURE IT COULD NEVER HAPPEN AGAIN.
LAST NIGHT, IN RESPONSE TO SUPERMAN'S RECENT ACTIONS--
--HIS PARENTS WERE TAKEN FROM THEIR HOME.
THEY WILL APPARENTLY BE KILLED IF SUPERMAN CONTINUES TO GET IN THE WAY OF GOVERNMENTS.
WHOEVER DID THIS WANTS US TO KNOW OUR PLACE.
I AM PRINCESS DIANA OF THEMYSCIRA AND I *KNOW MY PLACE*.

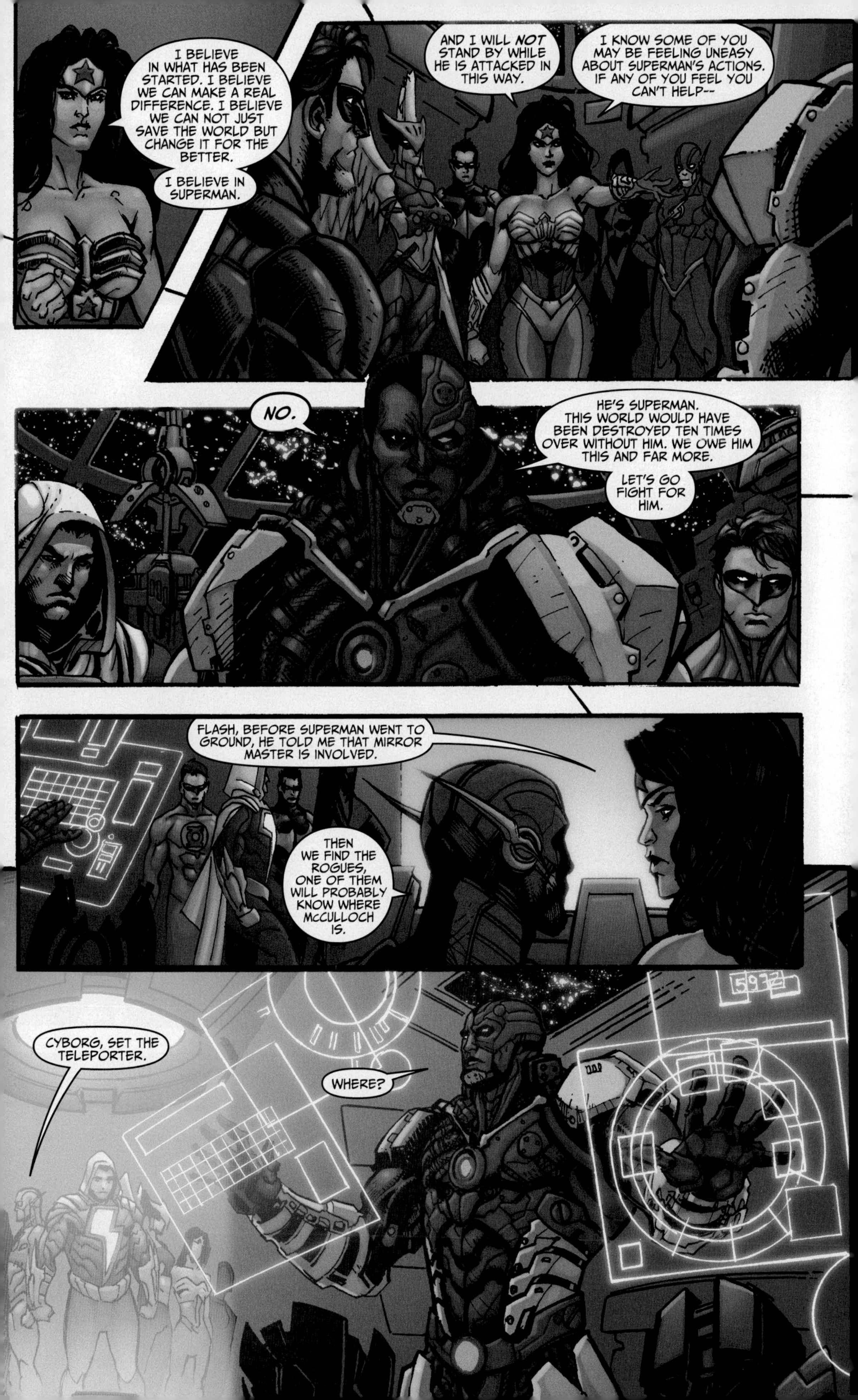
I BELIEVE IN WHAT HAS BEEN STARTED. I BELIEVE WE CAN MAKE A REAL DIFFERENCE. I BELIEVE WE CAN NOT JUST SAVE THE WORLD BUT CHANGE IT FOR THE BETTER.
I BELIEVE IN SUPERMAN.
AND I WILL *NOT* STAND BY WHILE HE IS ATTACKED IN THIS WAY.
I KNOW SOME OF YOU MAY BE FEELING UNEASY ABOUT SUPERMAN'S ACTIONS. IF ANY OF YOU FEEL YOU CAN'T HELP--
NO.
HE'S SUPERMAN. THIS WORLD WOULD HAVE BEEN DESTROYED TEN TIMES OVER WITHOUT HIM. WE OWE HIM THIS AND FAR MORE.
LET'S GO FIGHT FOR HIM.
FLASH, BEFORE SUPERMAN WENT TO GROUND, HE TOLD ME THAT MIRROR MASTER IS INVOLVED.
THEN WE FIND THE ROGUES, ONE OF THEM WILL PROBABLY KNOW WHERE McCULLOCH IS.
CYBORG, SET THE TELEPORTER.
WHERE?

"CENTRAL CITY."

WHERE--

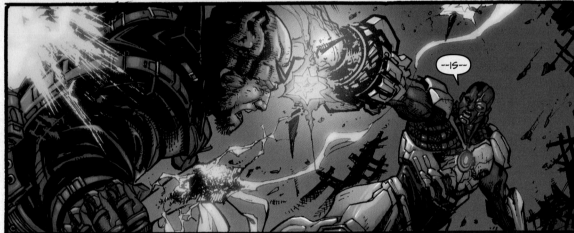

--IS--

--HE?

WHERE'S MIRROR MASTER?

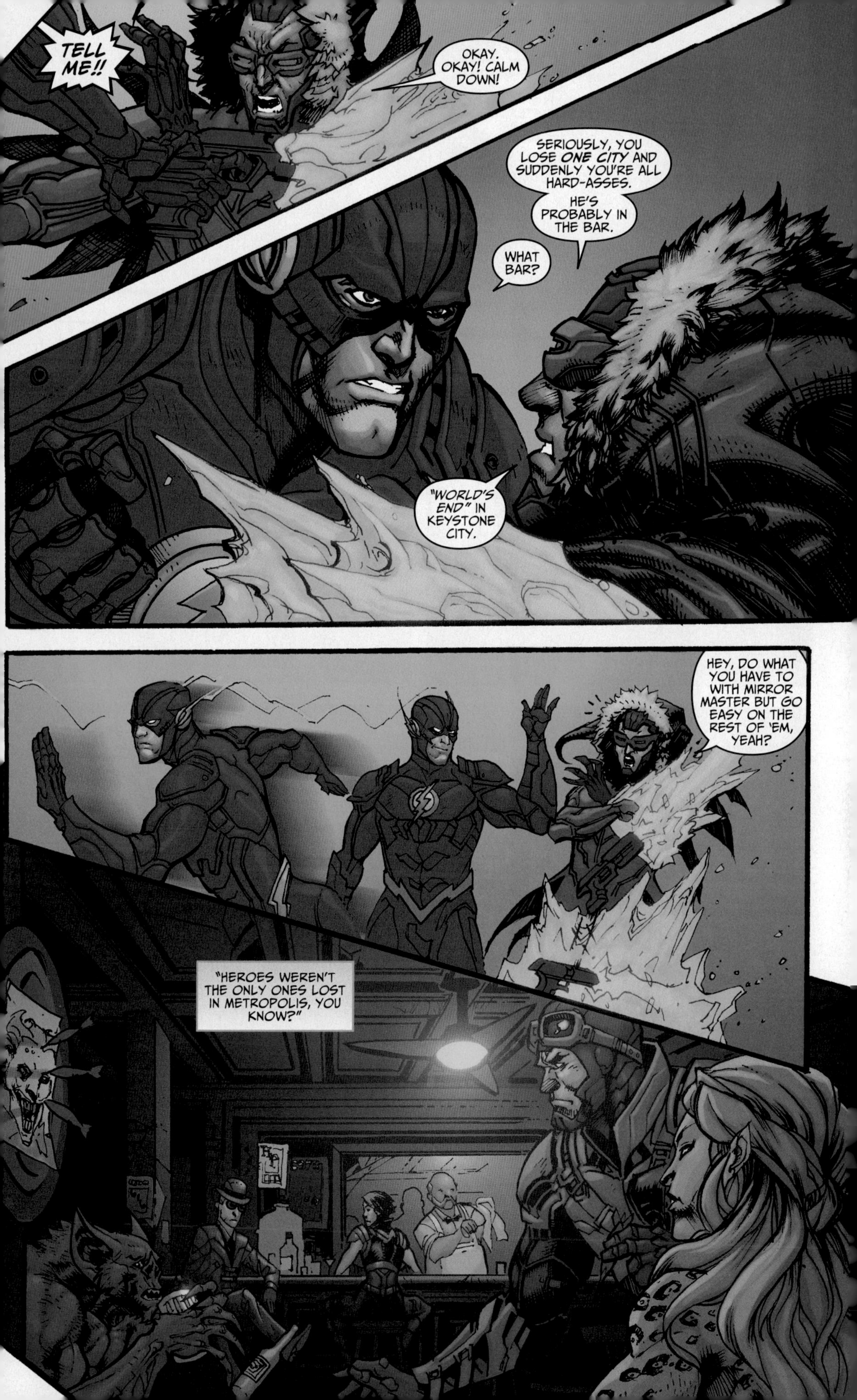
TELL ME!!
OKAY. OKAY! CALM DOWN!
SERIOUSLY, YOU LOSE ONE CITY AND SUDDENLY YOU'RE ALL HARD-ASSES.
HE'S PROBABLY IN THE BAR.
WHAT BAR?
"WORLD'S END" IN KEYSTONE CITY.
HEY, DO WHAT YOU HAVE TO WITH MIRROR MASTER BUT GO EASY ON THE REST OF 'EM, YEAH?
"HEROES WEREN'T THE ONLY ONES LOST IN METROPOLIS, YOU KNOW?"

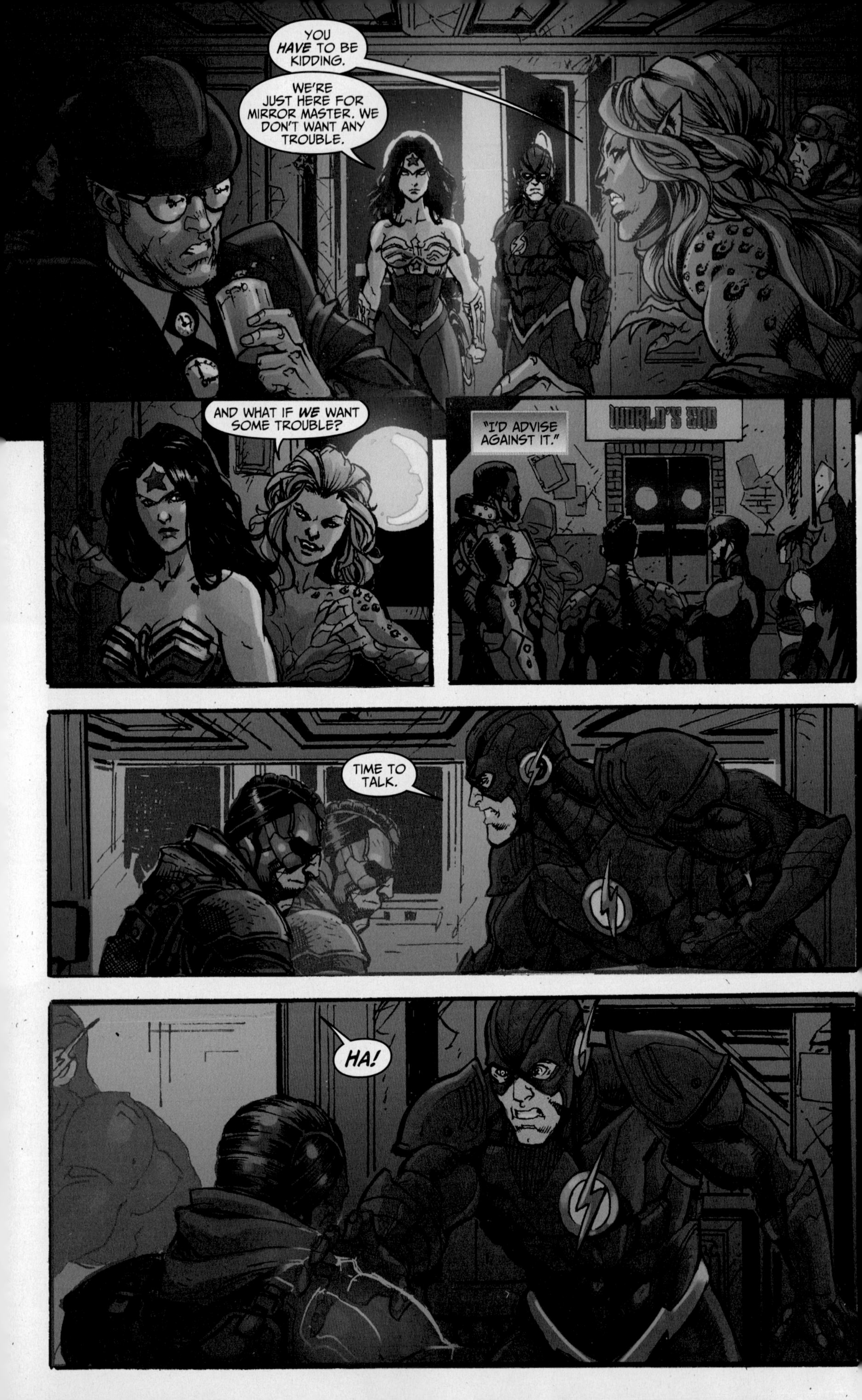
YOU *HAVE* TO BE KIDDING.
WE'RE JUST HERE FOR MIRROR MASTER. WE DON'T WANT ANY TROUBLE.
AND WHAT IF *WE* WANT SOME TROUBLE?
"I'D ADVISE AGAINST IT."
WORLD'S END
TIME TO TALK.
HA!

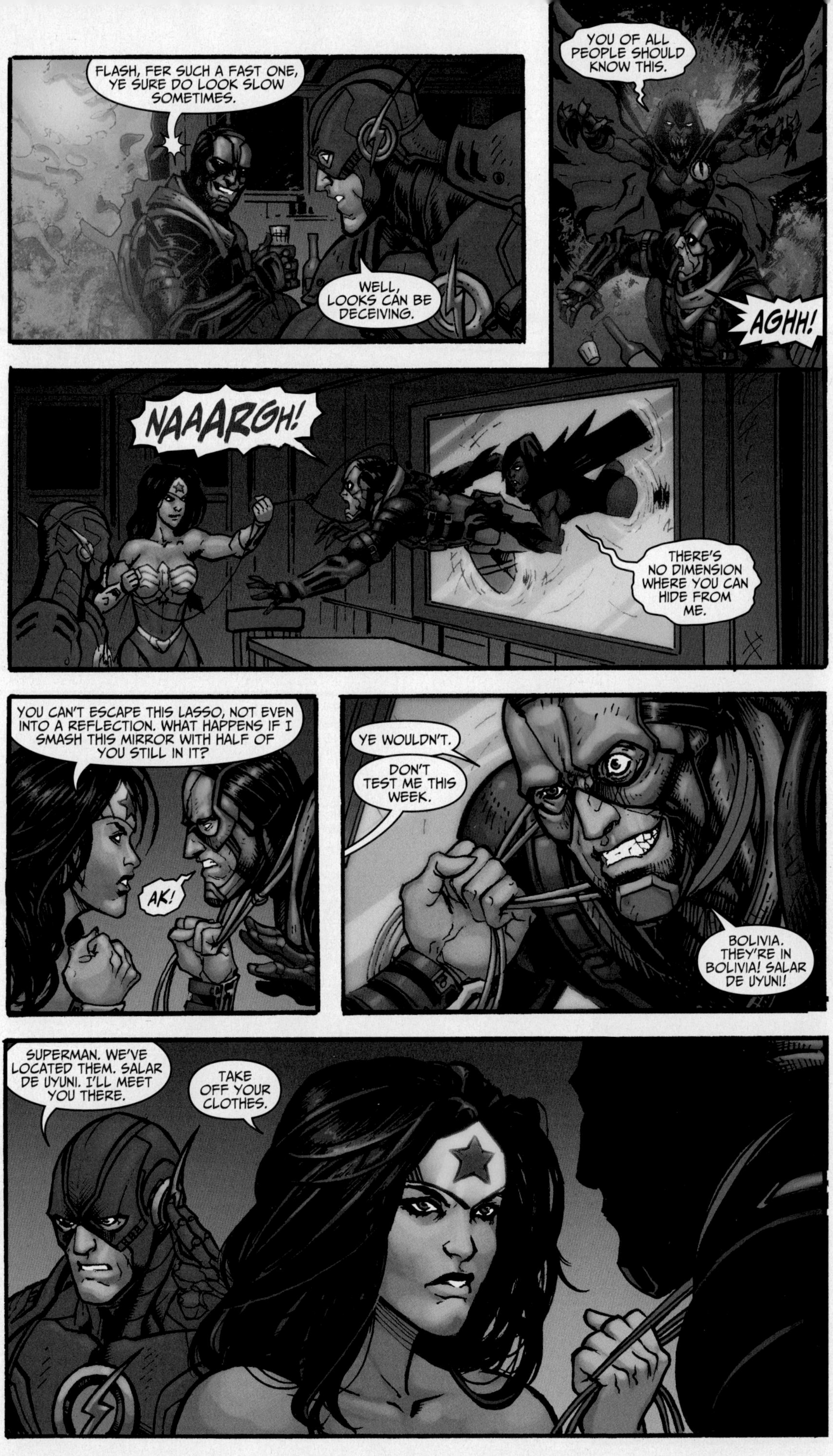
FLASH, FER SUCH A FAST ONE, YE SURE DO LOOK SLOW SOMETIMES.
WELL, LOOKS CAN BE DECEIVING.
YOU OF ALL PEOPLE SHOULD KNOW THIS.
AGHH!
NAAARGH!
THERE'S NO DIMENSION WHERE YOU CAN HIDE FROM ME.
YOU CAN'T ESCAPE THIS LASSO, NOT EVEN INTO A REFLECTION. WHAT HAPPENS IF I SMASH THIS MIRROR WITH HALF OF YOU STILL IN IT?
AK!
YE WOULDN'T.
DON'T TEST ME THIS WEEK.
BOLIVIA. THEY'RE IN BOLIVIA! SALAR DE UYUNI!
SUPERMAN. WE'VE LOCATED THEM. SALAR DE UYUNI. I'LL MEET YOU THERE.
TAKE OFF YOUR CLOTHES.

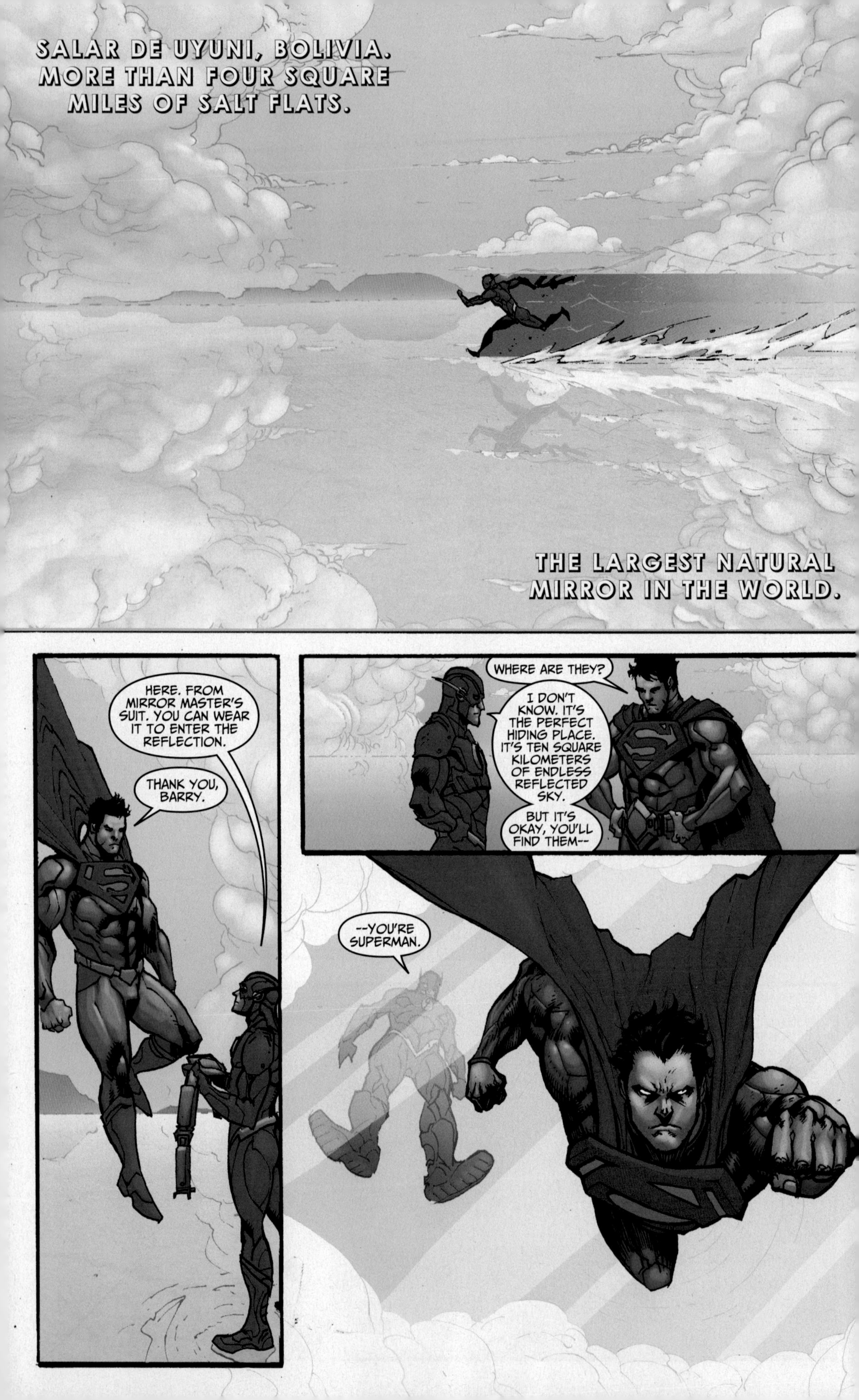
SALAR DE UYUNI, BOLIVIA. MORE THAN FOUR SQUARE MILES OF SALT FLATS.
THE LARGEST NATURAL MIRROR IN THE WORLD.
HERE. FROM MIRROR MASTER'S SUIT. YOU CAN WEAR IT TO ENTER THE REFLECTION.
THANK YOU, BARRY.
WHERE ARE THEY?
I DON'T KNOW. IT'S THE PERFECT HIDING PLACE. IT'S TEN SQUARE KILOMETERS OF ENDLESS REFLECTED SKY.
BUT IT'S OKAY, YOU'LL FIND THEM--
--YOU'RE SUPERMAN.

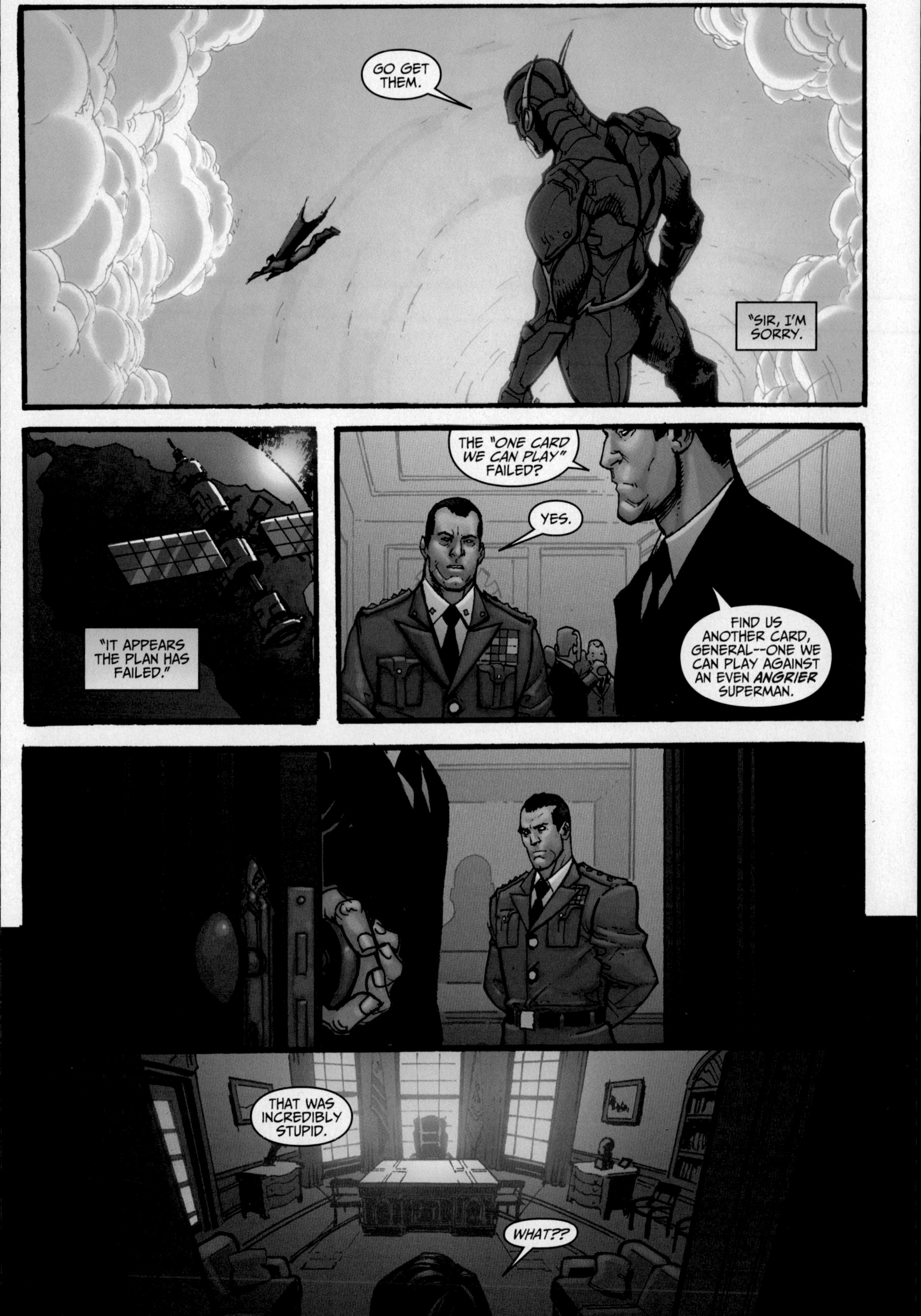
GO GET THEM.
"SIR, I'M SORRY.
"IT APPEARS THE PLAN HAS FAILED."
THE "ONE CARD WE CAN PLAY" FAILED?
YES.
FIND US ANOTHER CARD, GENERAL--ONE WE CAN PLAY AGAINST AN EVEN ANGRIER SUPERMAN.
THAT WAS INCREDIBLY STUPID.
WHAT??

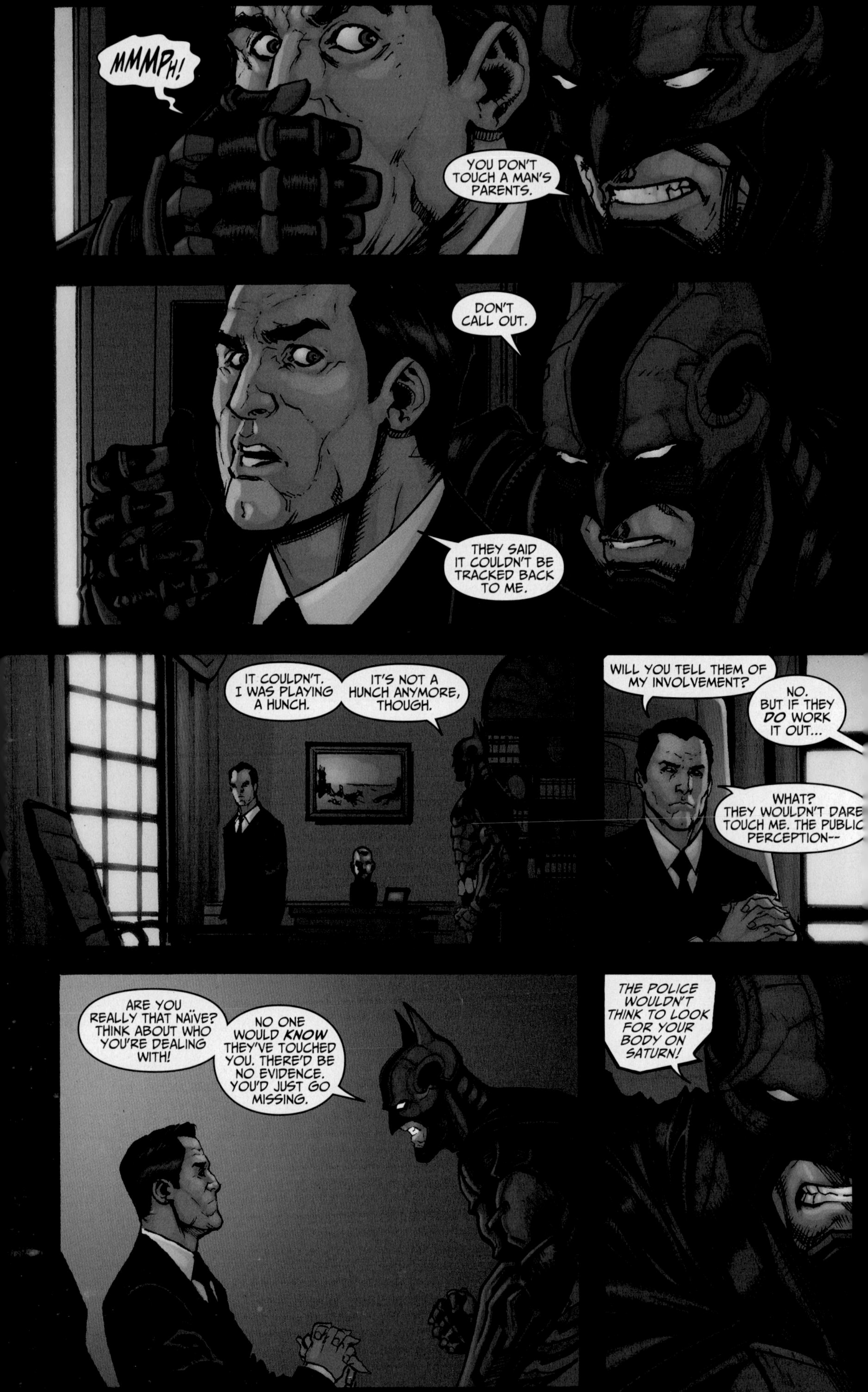
MMMPH!
YOU DON'T TOUCH A MAN'S PARENTS.
DON'T CALL OUT.
THEY SAID IT COULDN'T BE TRACKED BACK TO ME.
IT COULDN'T. I WAS PLAYING A HUNCH.
IT'S NOT A HUNCH ANYMORE, THOUGH.
WILL YOU TELL THEM OF MY INVOLVEMENT?
NO. BUT IF THEY DO WORK IT OUT...
WHAT? THEY WOULDN'T DARE TOUCH ME. THE PUBLIC PERCEPTION--
ARE YOU REALLY THAT NAÏVE? THINK ABOUT WHO YOU'RE DEALING WITH!
NO ONE WOULD KNOW THEY'VE TOUCHED YOU. THERE'D BE NO EVIDENCE. YOU'D JUST GO MISSING.
THE POLICE WOULDN'T THINK TO LOOK FOR YOUR BODY ON SATURN!

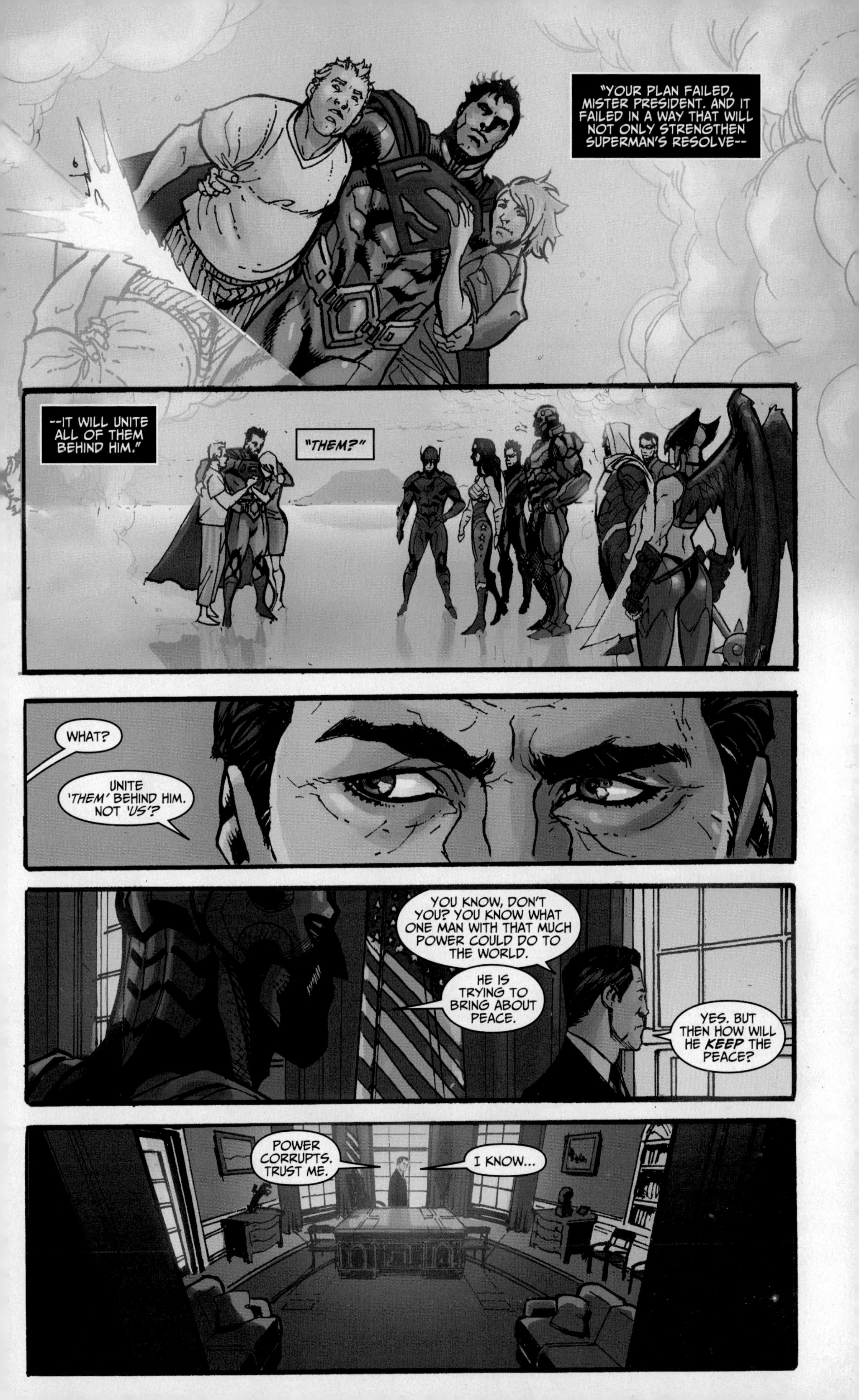
"YOUR PLAN FAILED, MISTER PRESIDENT. AND IT FAILED IN A WAY THAT WILL NOT ONLY STRENGTHEN SUPERMAN'S RESOLVE--
--IT WILL UNITE ALL OF THEM BEHIND HIM."
"THEM?"
WHAT?
UNITE 'THEM' BEHIND HIM. NOT 'US'?
YOU KNOW, DON'T YOU? YOU KNOW WHAT ONE MAN WITH THAT MUCH POWER COULD DO TO THE WORLD.
HE IS TRYING TO BRING ABOUT PEACE.
YES. BUT THEN HOW WILL HE KEEP THE PEACE?
POWER CORRUPTS. TRUST ME.
I KNOW...

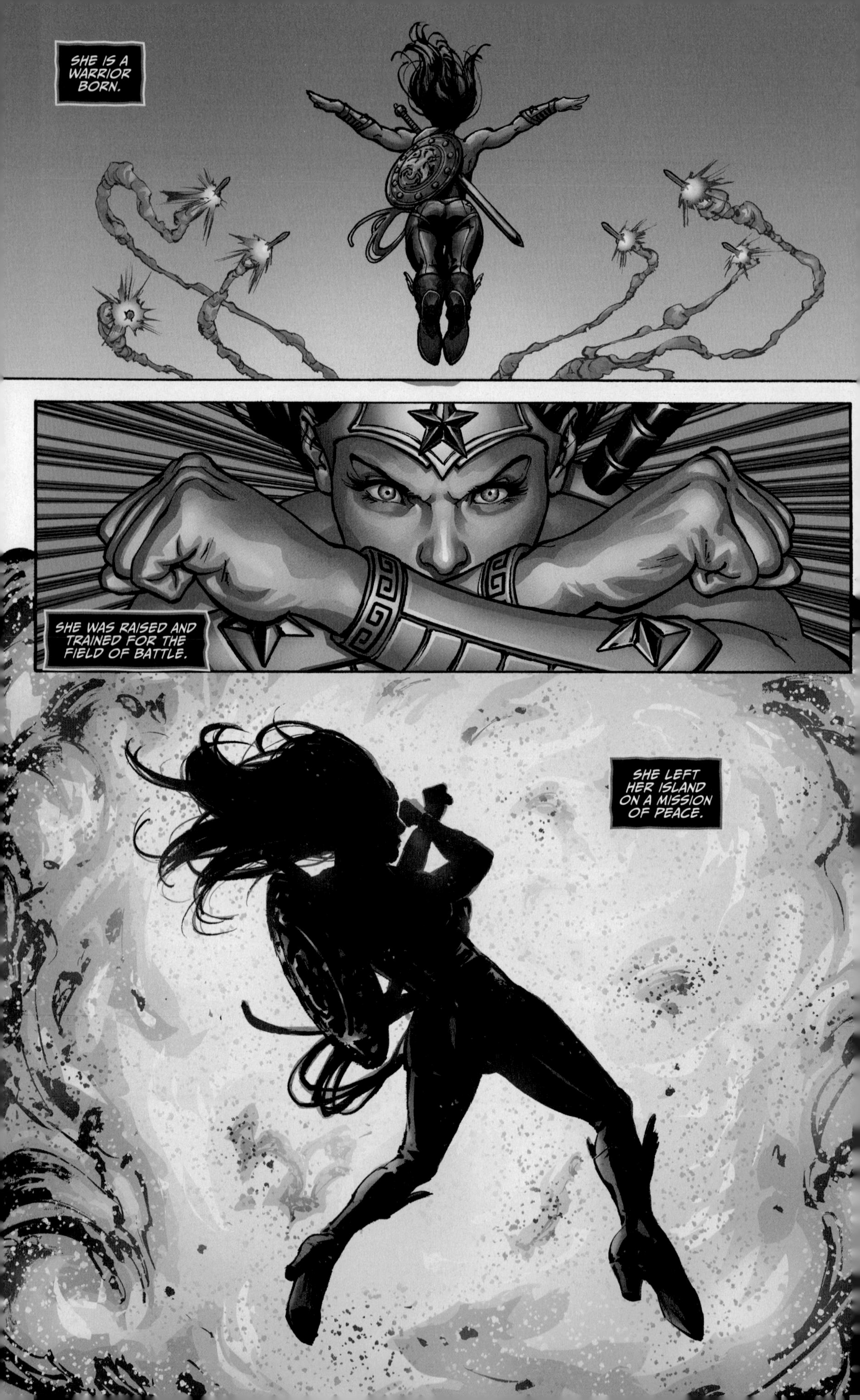
SHE IS A WARRIOR BORN.
SHE WAS RAISED AND TRAINED FOR THE FIELD OF BATTLE.
SHE LEFT HER ISLAND ON A MISSION OF PEACE.

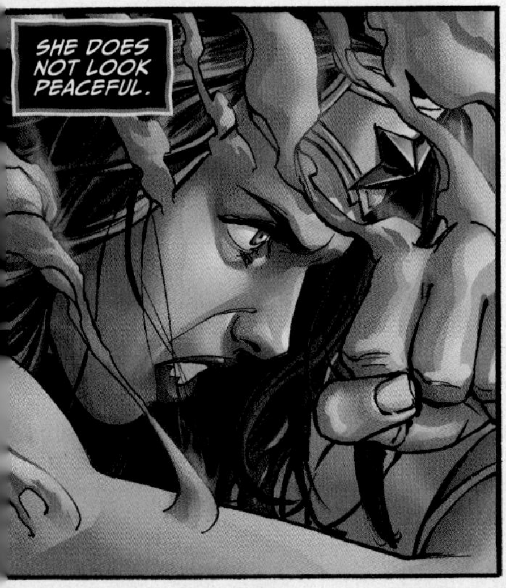
SHE DOES NOT LOOK PEACEFUL.

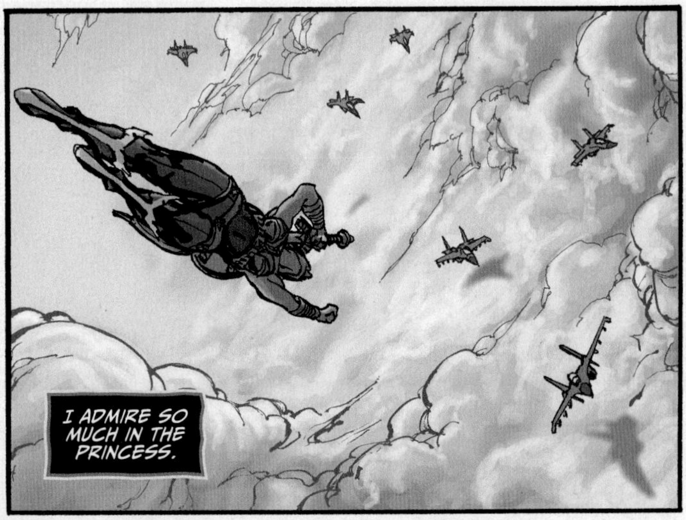
I ADMIRE SO MUCH IN THE PRINCESS.

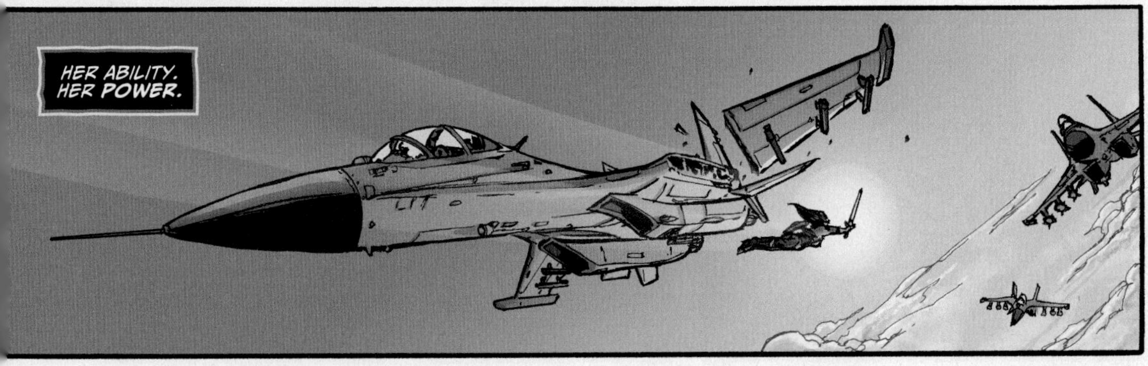
HER ABILITY. HER POWER.

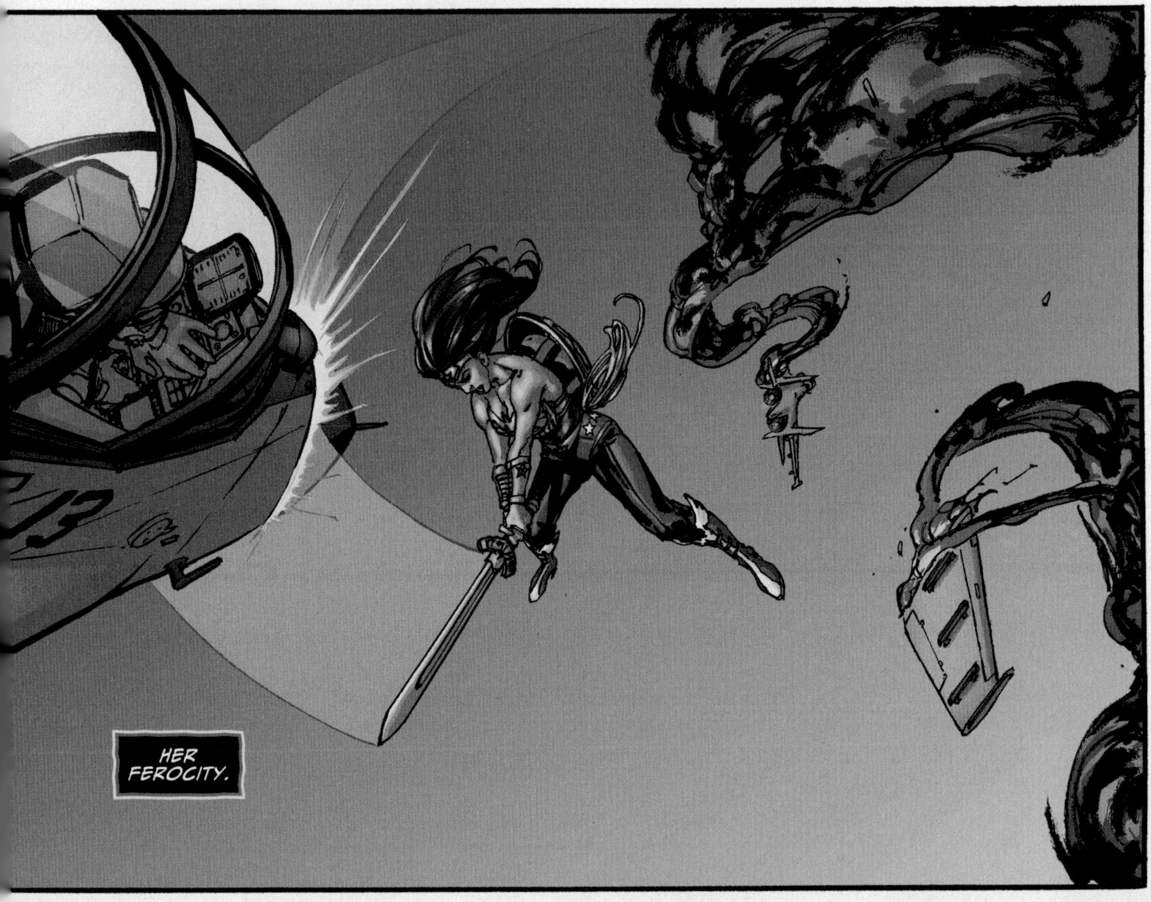
HER FEROCITY.

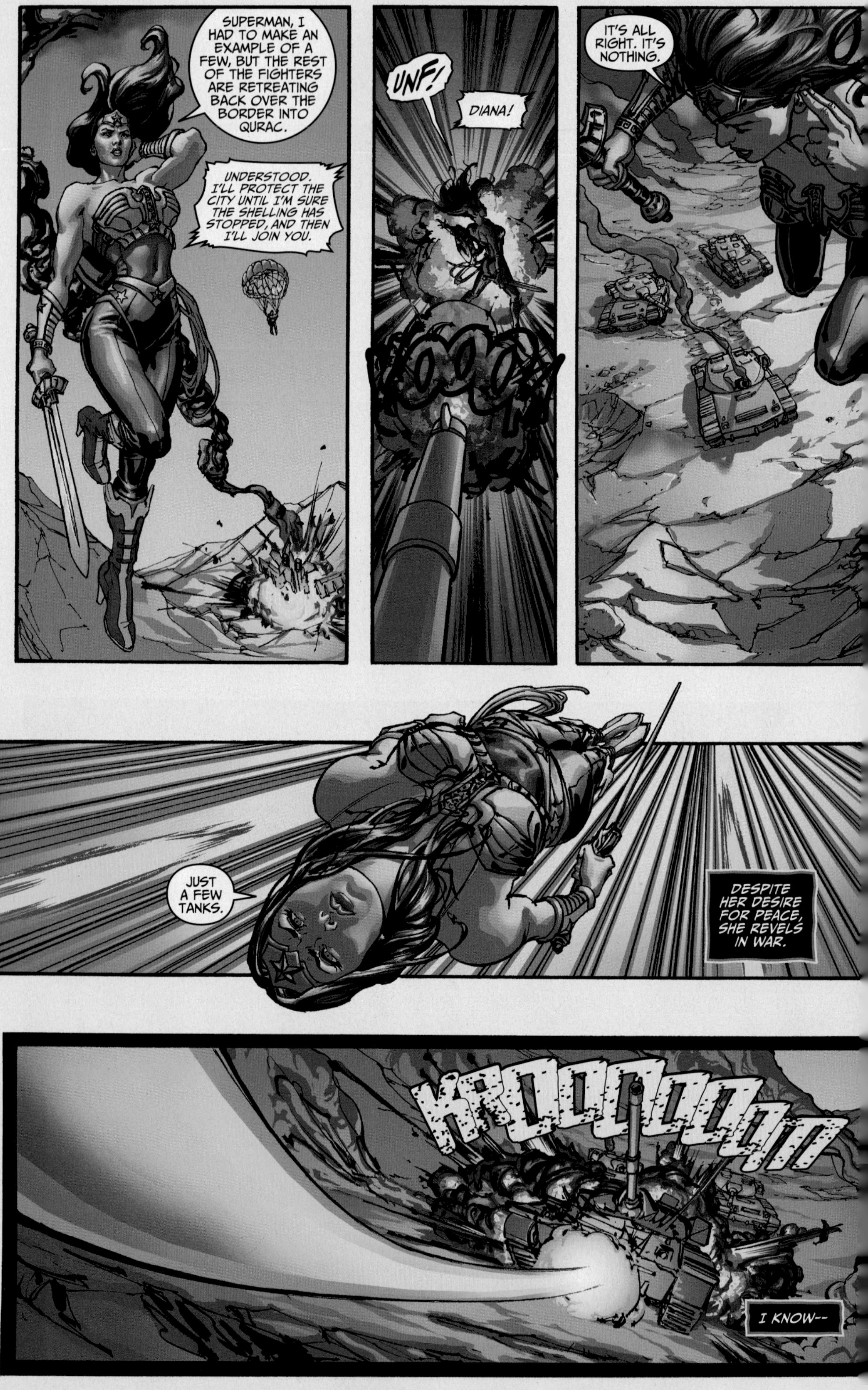
SUPERMAN, I HAD TO MAKE AN EXAMPLE OF A FEW, BUT THE REST OF THE FIGHTERS ARE RETREATING BACK OVER THE BORDER INTO QURAC.
UNDERSTOOD. I'LL PROTECT THE CITY UNTIL I'M SURE THE SHELLING HAS STOPPED, AND THEN I'LL JOIN YOU.
UNF!
DIANA!
IT'S ALL RIGHT. IT'S NOTHING.
JUST A FEW TANKS.
DESPITE HER DESIRE FOR PEACE, SHE REVELS IN WAR.
KROOOOOOM
I KNOW--

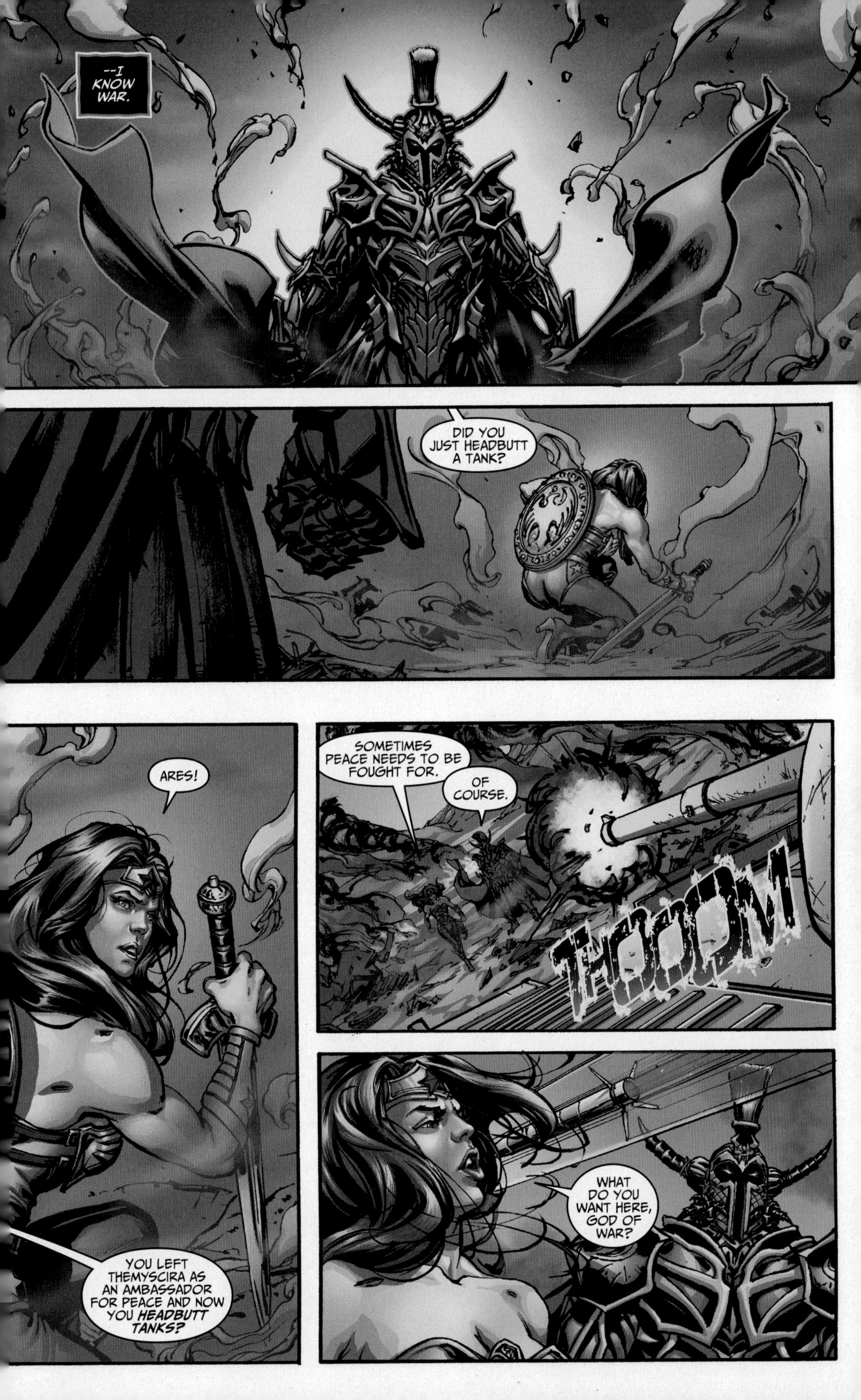
--I KNOW WAR.
DID YOU JUST HEADBUTT A TANK?
ARES!
YOU LEFT THEMYSCIRA AS AN AMBASSADOR FOR PEACE AND NOW YOU *HEADBUTT TANKS?*
SOMETIMES PEACE NEEDS TO BE FOUGHT FOR.
OF COURSE.
THOOM
WHAT DO YOU WANT HERE, GOD OF WAR?

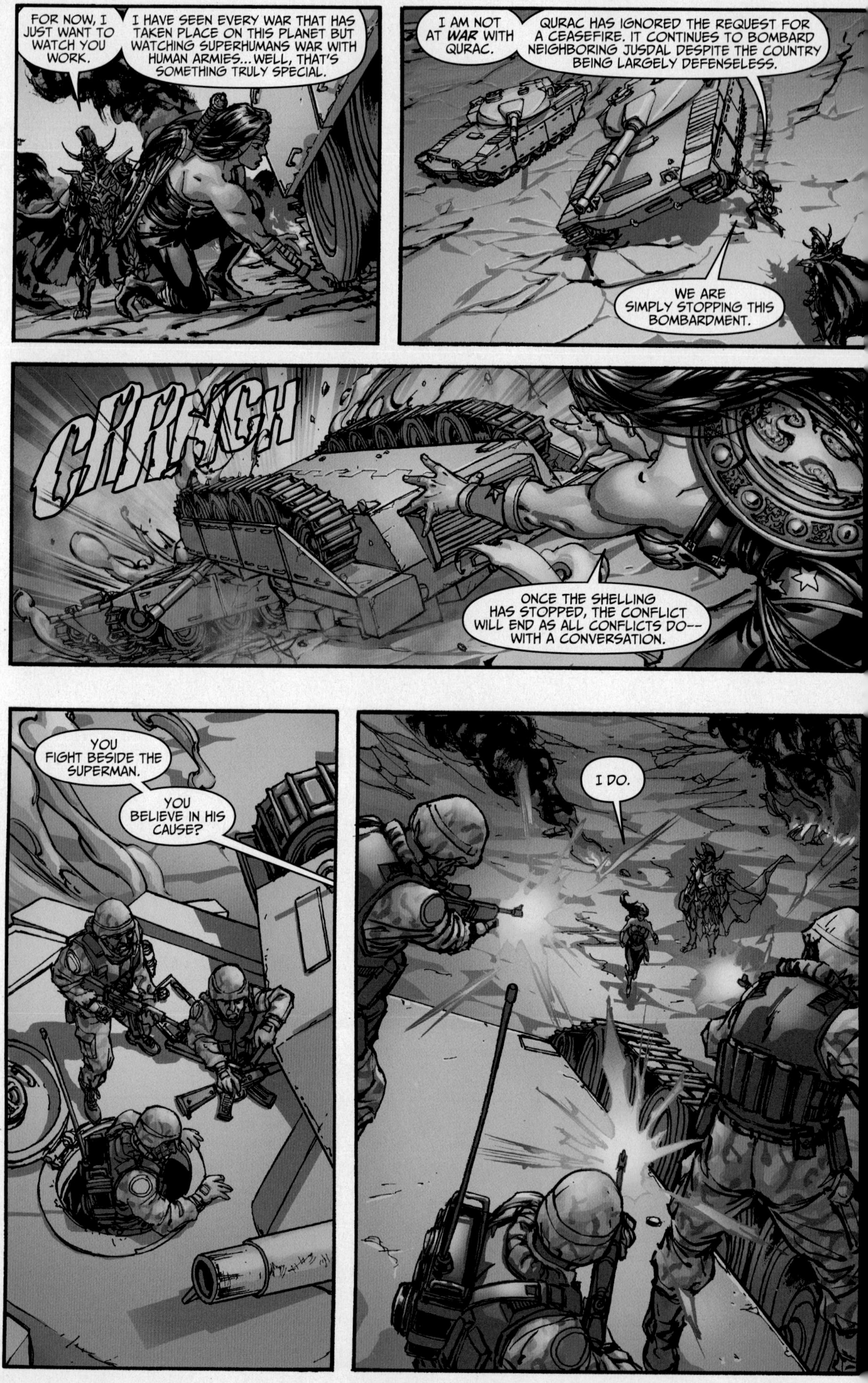
FOR NOW, I JUST WANT TO WATCH YOU WORK.
I HAVE SEEN EVERY WAR THAT HAS TAKEN PLACE ON THIS PLANET BUT WATCHING SUPERHUMANS WAR WITH HUMAN ARMIES...WELL, THAT'S SOMETHING TRULY SPECIAL.
I AM NOT AT WAR WITH QURAC.
QURAC HAS IGNORED THE REQUEST FOR A CEASEFIRE. IT CONTINUES TO BOMBARD NEIGHBORING JUSDAL DESPITE THE COUNTRY BEING LARGELY DEFENSELESS.
WE ARE SIMPLY STOPPING THIS BOMBARDMENT.
CRRSCH
ONCE THE SHELLING HAS STOPPED, THE CONFLICT WILL END AS ALL CONFLICTS DO-- WITH A CONVERSATION.
YOU FIGHT BESIDE THE SUPERMAN.
YOU BELIEVE IN HIS CAUSE?
I DO.

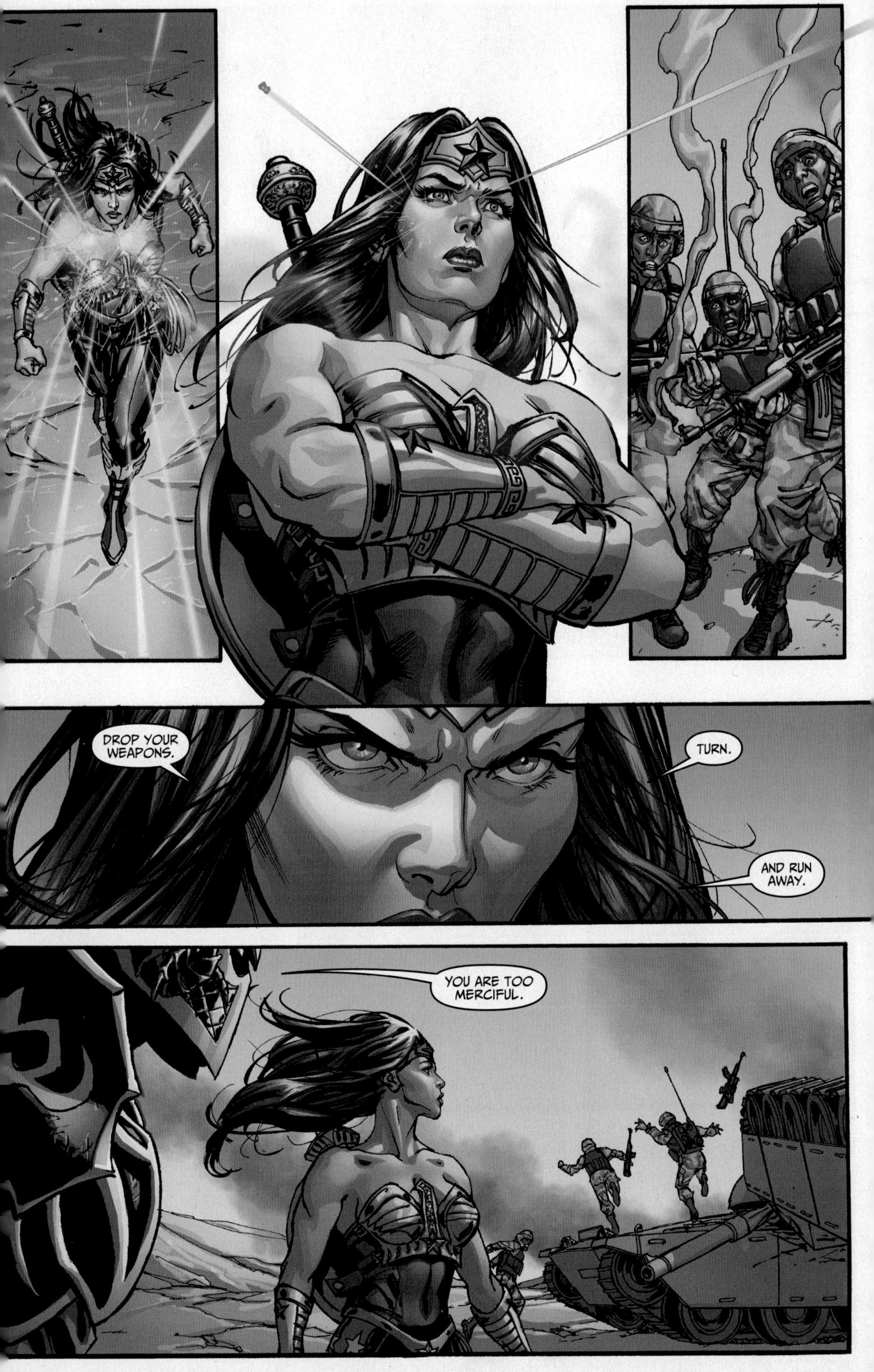
DROP YOUR WEAPONS.
TURN.
AND RUN AWAY.
YOU ARE TOO MERCIFUL.

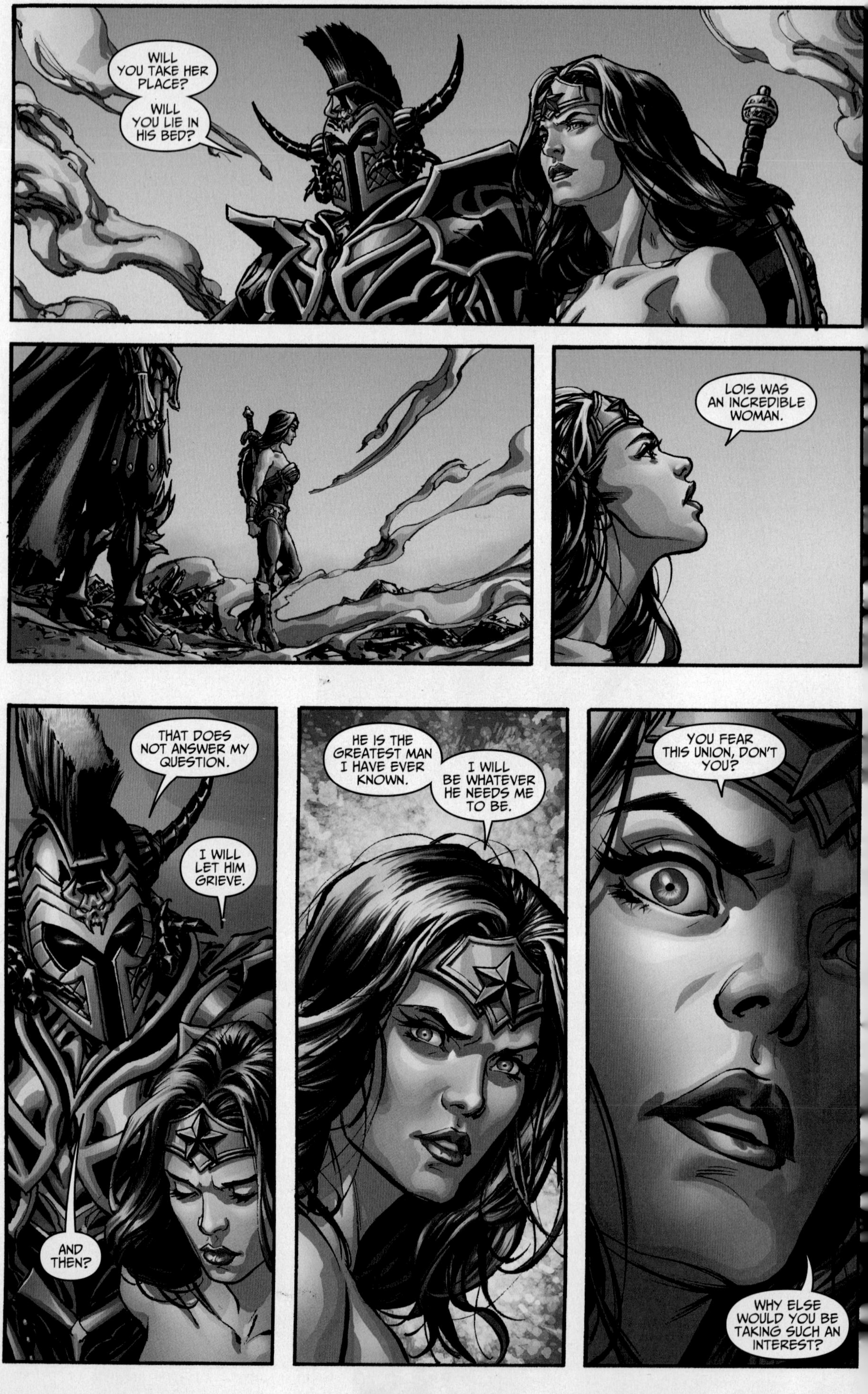
WILL YOU TAKE HER PLACE?
WILL YOU LIE IN HIS BED?
LOIS WAS AN INCREDIBLE WOMAN.
THAT DOES NOT ANSWER MY QUESTION.
I WILL LET HIM GRIEVE.
AND THEN?
HE IS THE GREATEST MAN I HAVE EVER KNOWN.
I WILL BE WHATEVER HE NEEDS ME TO BE.
YOU FEAR THIS UNION, DON'T YOU?
WHY ELSE WOULD YOU BE TAKING SUCH AN INTEREST?

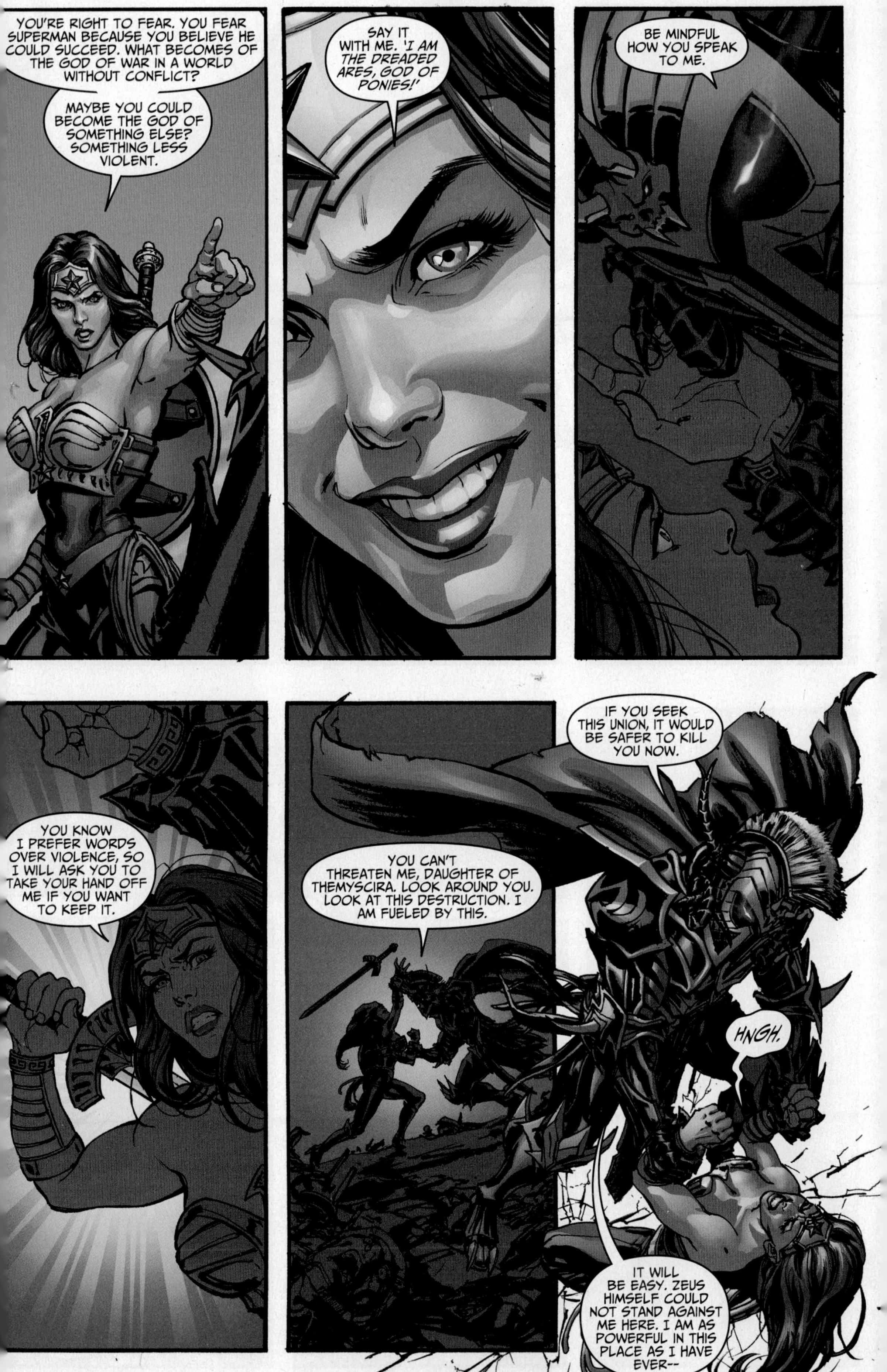
YOU'RE RIGHT TO FEAR. YOU FEAR SUPERMAN BECAUSE YOU BELIEVE HE COULD SUCCEED. WHAT BECOMES OF THE GOD OF WAR IN A WORLD WITHOUT CONFLICT?
MAYBE YOU COULD BECOME THE GOD OF SOMETHING ELSE? SOMETHING LESS VIOLENT.
SAY IT WITH ME. 'I AM THE DREADED ARES, GOD OF PONIES!'
BE MINDFUL HOW YOU SPEAK TO ME.
YOU KNOW I PREFER WORDS OVER VIOLENCE, SO I WILL ASK YOU TO TAKE YOUR HAND OFF ME IF YOU WANT TO KEEP IT.
YOU CAN'T THREATEN ME, DAUGHTER OF THEMYSCIRA. LOOK AROUND YOU. LOOK AT THIS DESTRUCTION. I AM FUELED BY THIS.
IF YOU SEEK THIS UNION, IT WOULD BE SAFER TO KILL YOU NOW.
HNGH.
IT WILL BE EASY. ZEUS HIMSELF COULD NOT STAND AGAINST ME HERE. I AM AS POWERFUL IN THIS PLACE AS I HAVE EVER--

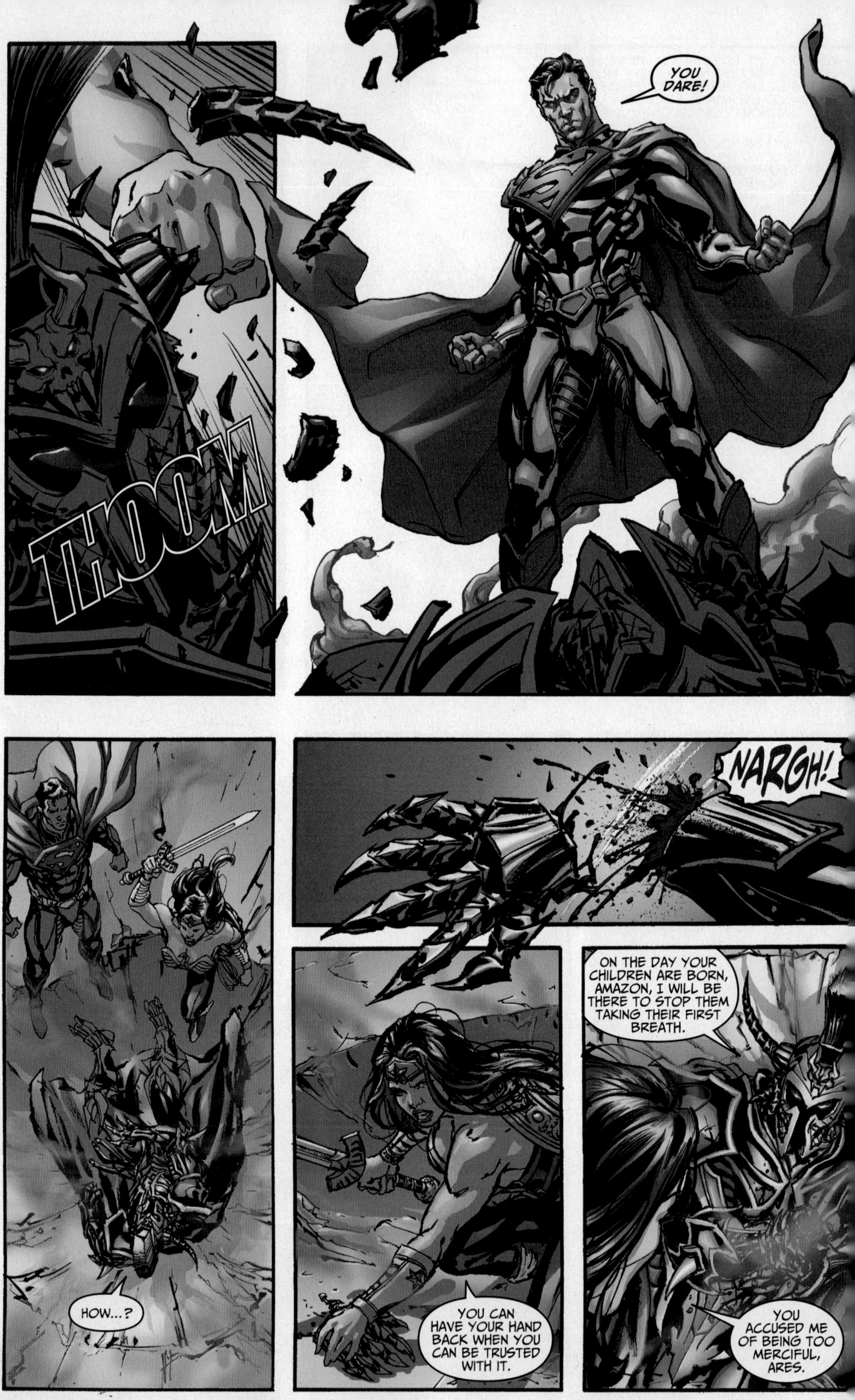
THOOM
YOU DARE!
NARGH!
HOW...?
YOU CAN HAVE YOUR HAND BACK WHEN YOU CAN BE TRUSTED WITH IT.
ON THE DAY YOUR CHILDREN ARE BORN, AMAZON, I WILL BE THERE TO STOP THEM TAKING THEIR FIRST BREATH.
YOU ACCUSED ME OF BEING TOO MERCIFUL, ARES.

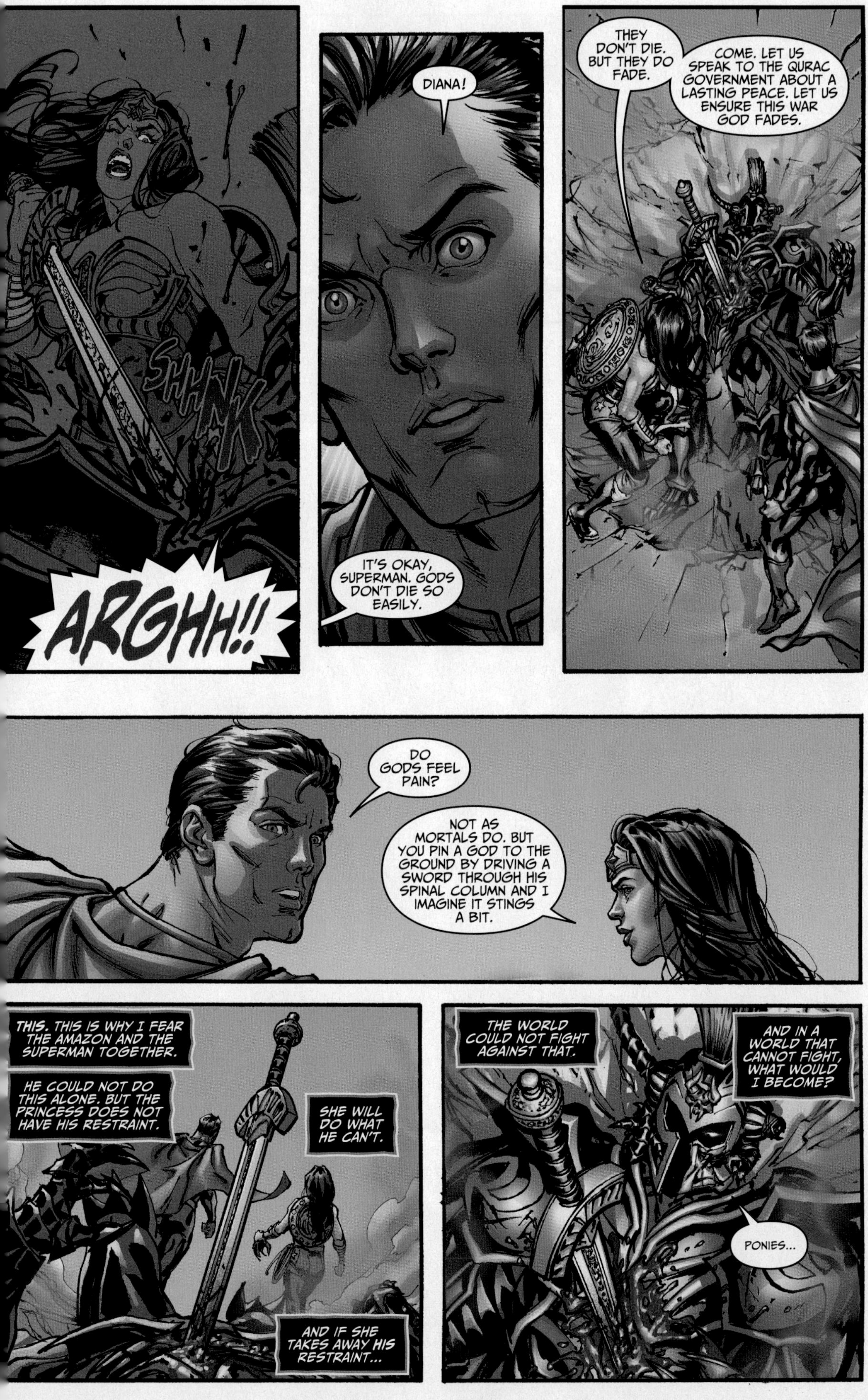
SHHHNK
ARGHH!!
DIANA!
IT'S OKAY, SUPERMAN. GODS DON'T DIE SO EASILY.
THEY DON'T DIE. BUT THEY DO FADE.
COME. LET US SPEAK TO THE QURAC GOVERNMENT ABOUT A LASTING PEACE. LET US ENSURE THIS WAR GOD FADES.
DO GODS FEEL PAIN?
NOT AS MORTALS DO. BUT YOU PIN A GOD TO THE GROUND BY DRIVING A SWORD THROUGH HIS SPINAL COLUMN AND I IMAGINE IT STINGS A BIT.
THIS. THIS IS WHY I FEAR THE AMAZON AND THE SUPERMAN TOGETHER.
HE COULD NOT DO THIS ALONE. BUT THE PRINCESS DOES NOT HAVE HIS RESTRAINT.
SHE WILL DO WHAT HE CAN'T.
AND IF SHE TAKES AWAY HIS RESTRAINT...
THE WORLD COULD NOT FIGHT AGAINST THAT.
AND IN A WORLD THAT CANNOT FIGHT, WHAT WOULD I BECOME?
PONIES...

PART FOUR

Mike S. Miller Tom Derenick Artists

Cover Art by Mico Suayan & David López and Santi Casas of Ikari Studio

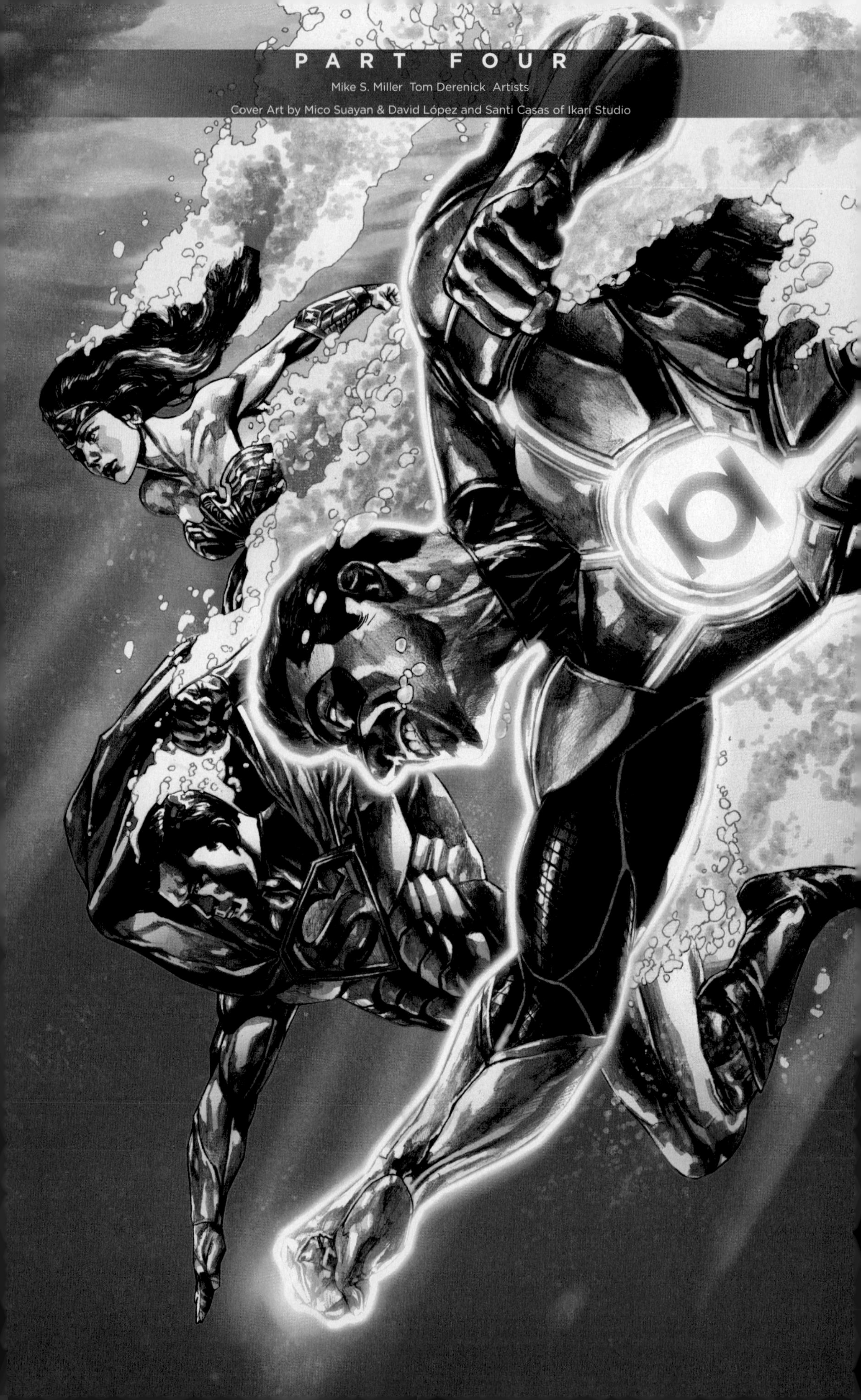

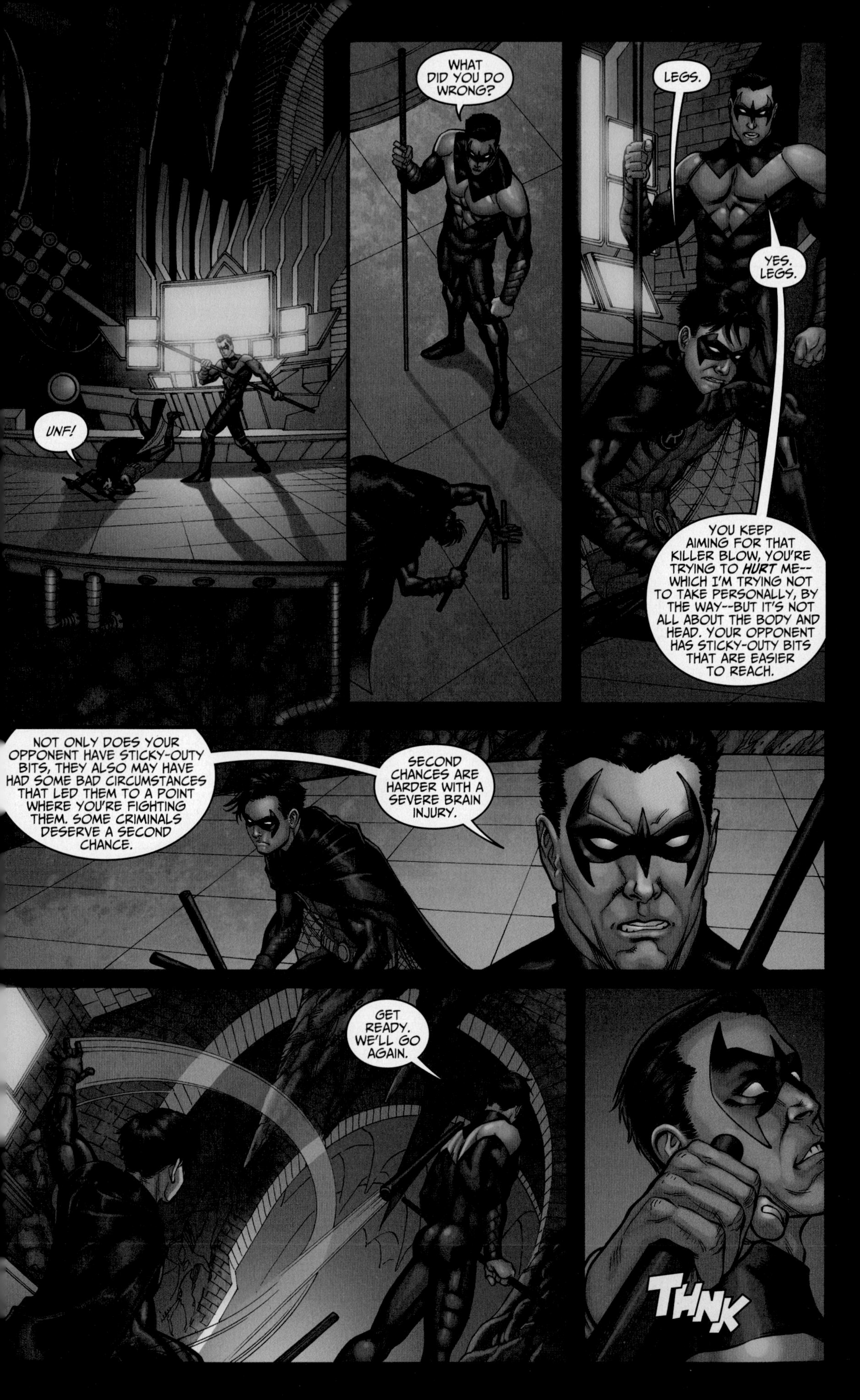
UNF!
WHAT DID YOU DO WRONG?
LEGS.
YES. LEGS.
YOU KEEP AIMING FOR THAT KILLER BLOW, YOU'RE TRYING TO *HURT* ME--WHICH I'M TRYING NOT TO TAKE PERSONALLY, BY THE WAY--BUT IT'S NOT ALL ABOUT THE BODY AND HEAD. YOUR OPPONENT HAS STICKY-OUTY BITS THAT ARE EASIER TO REACH.
NOT ONLY DOES YOUR OPPONENT HAVE STICKY-OUTY BITS, THEY ALSO MAY HAVE HAD SOME BAD CIRCUMSTANCES THAT LED THEM TO A POINT WHERE YOU'RE FIGHTING THEM. SOME CRIMINALS DESERVE A SECOND CHANCE.
SECOND CHANCES ARE HARDER WITH A SEVERE BRAIN INJURY.
GET READY. WE'LL GO AGAIN.
THNK

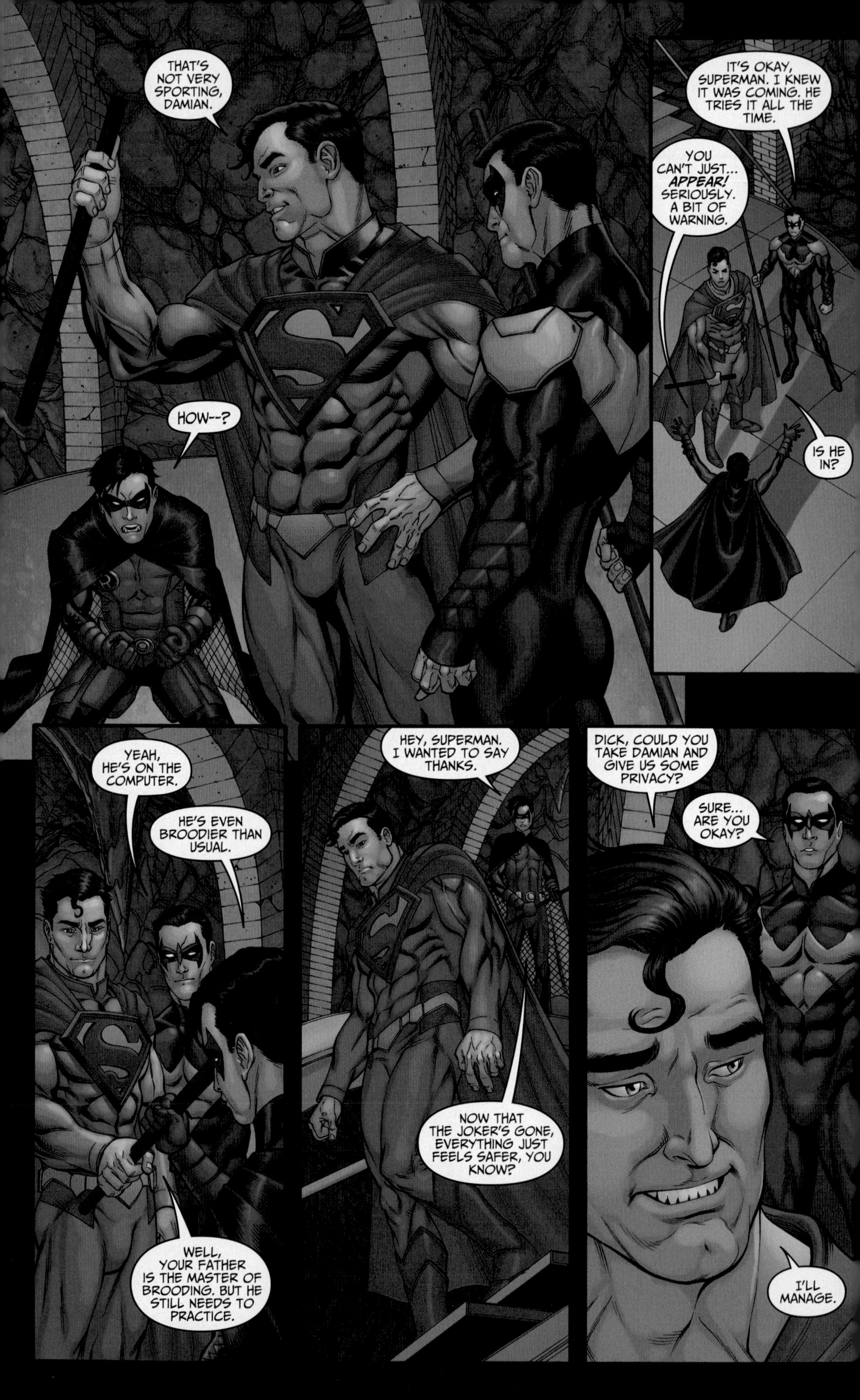
THAT'S NOT VERY SPORTING, DAMIAN.
HOW--?
IT'S OKAY, SUPERMAN. I KNEW IT WAS COMING. HE TRIES IT ALL THE TIME.
YOU CAN'T JUST... APPEAR! SERIOUSLY. A BIT OF WARNING.
IS HE IN?
YEAH, HE'S ON THE COMPUTER.
HE'S EVEN BROODIER THAN USUAL.
WELL, YOUR FATHER IS THE MASTER OF BROODING. BUT HE STILL NEEDS TO PRACTICE.
HEY, SUPERMAN. I WANTED TO SAY THANKS.
NOW THAT THE JOKER'S GONE, EVERYTHING JUST FEELS SAFER, YOU KNOW?
DICK, COULD YOU TAKE DAMIAN AND GIVE US SOME PRIVACY?
SURE... ARE YOU OKAY?
I'LL MANAGE.

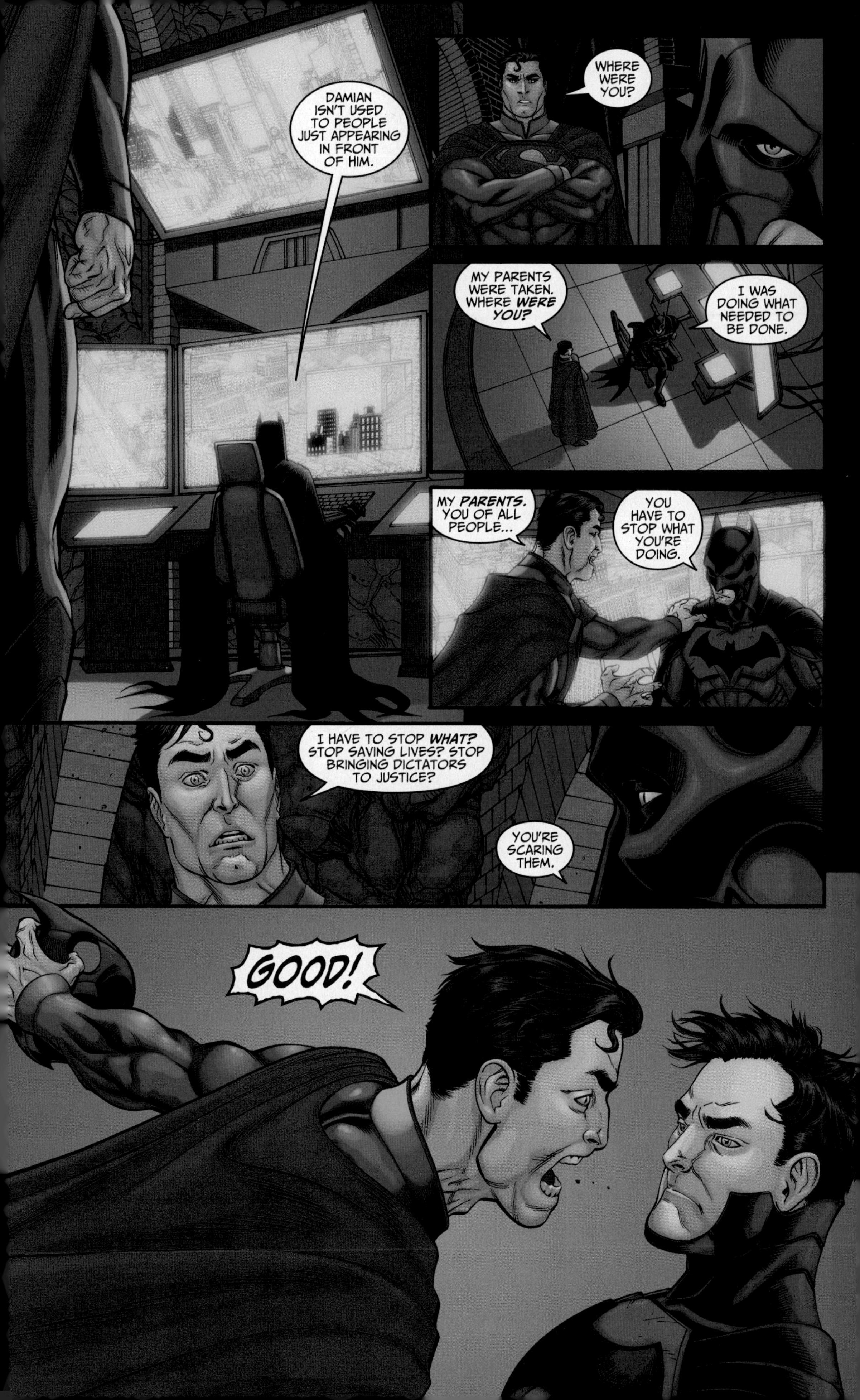
DAMIAN ISN'T USED TO PEOPLE JUST APPEARING IN FRONT OF HIM.
WHERE WERE YOU?
MY PARENTS WERE TAKEN. WHERE *WERE YOU?*
I WAS DOING WHAT NEEDED TO BE DONE.
MY *PARENTS*. YOU OF ALL PEOPLE...
YOU HAVE TO STOP WHAT YOU'RE DOING.
I HAVE TO STOP *WHAT?* STOP SAVING LIVES? STOP BRINGING DICTATORS TO JUSTICE?
YOU'RE SCARING THEM.
GOOD!

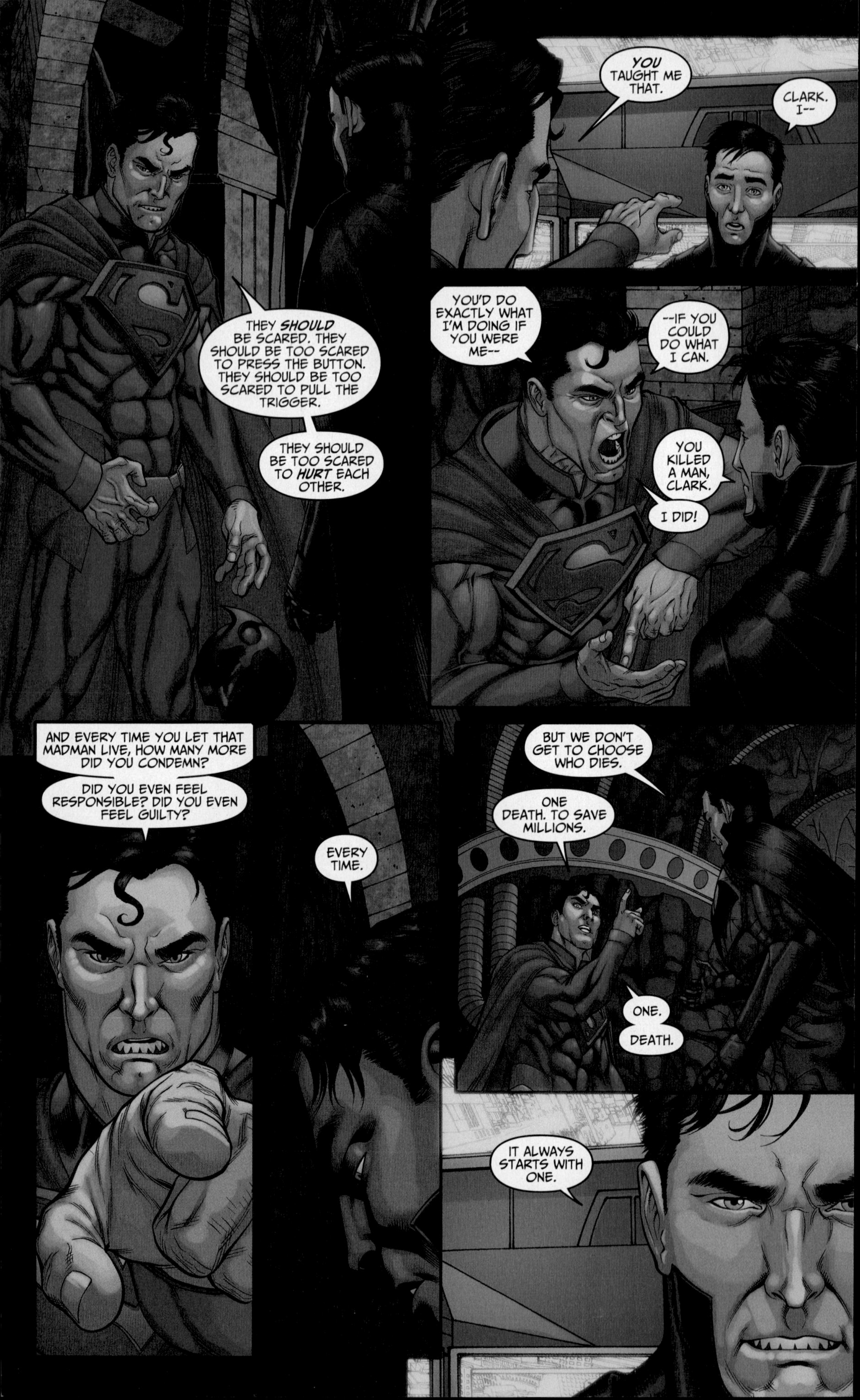
YOU TAUGHT ME THAT.
CLARK. I--
THEY SHOULD BE SCARED. THEY SHOULD BE TOO SCARED TO PRESS THE BUTTON. THEY SHOULD BE TOO SCARED TO PULL THE TRIGGER.
THEY SHOULD BE TOO SCARED TO HURT EACH OTHER.
YOU'D DO EXACTLY WHAT I'M DOING IF YOU WERE ME--
--IF YOU COULD DO WHAT I CAN.
YOU KILLED A MAN, CLARK.
I DID!
AND EVERY TIME YOU LET THAT MADMAN LIVE, HOW MANY MORE DID YOU CONDEMN?
DID YOU EVEN FEEL RESPONSIBLE? DID YOU EVEN FEEL GUILTY?
EVERY TIME.
BUT WE DON'T GET TO CHOOSE WHO DIES.
ONE DEATH. TO SAVE MILLIONS.
ONE.
DEATH.
IT ALWAYS STARTS WITH ONE.

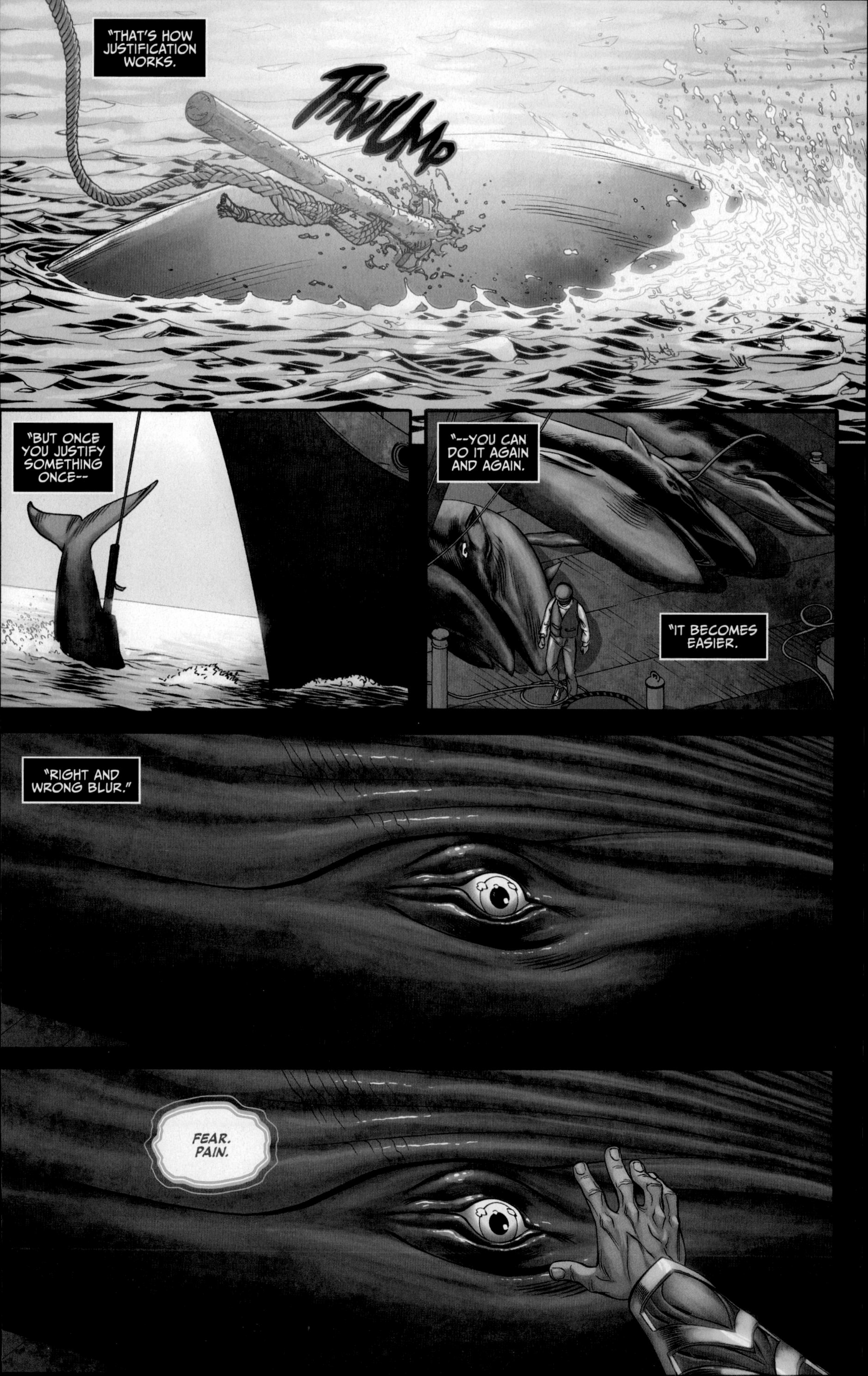
"THAT'S HOW JUSTIFICATION WORKS.
THWUMP
"BUT ONCE YOU JUSTIFY SOMETHING ONCE--
"--YOU CAN DO IT AGAIN AND AGAIN.
"IT BECOMES EASIER.
"RIGHT AND WRONG BLUR."
FEAR. PAIN.

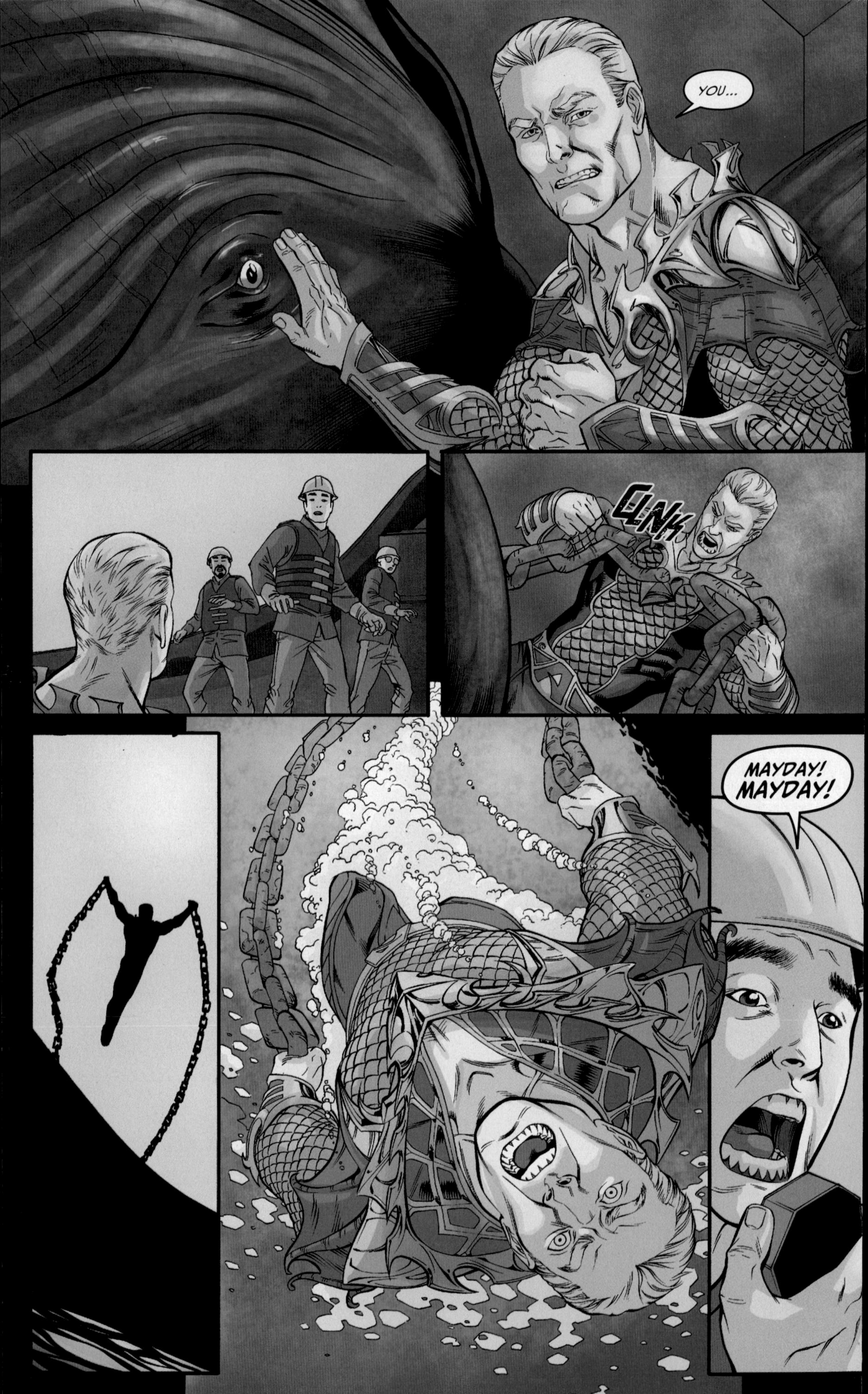
YOU...
CLNK
MAYDAY! MAYDAY!

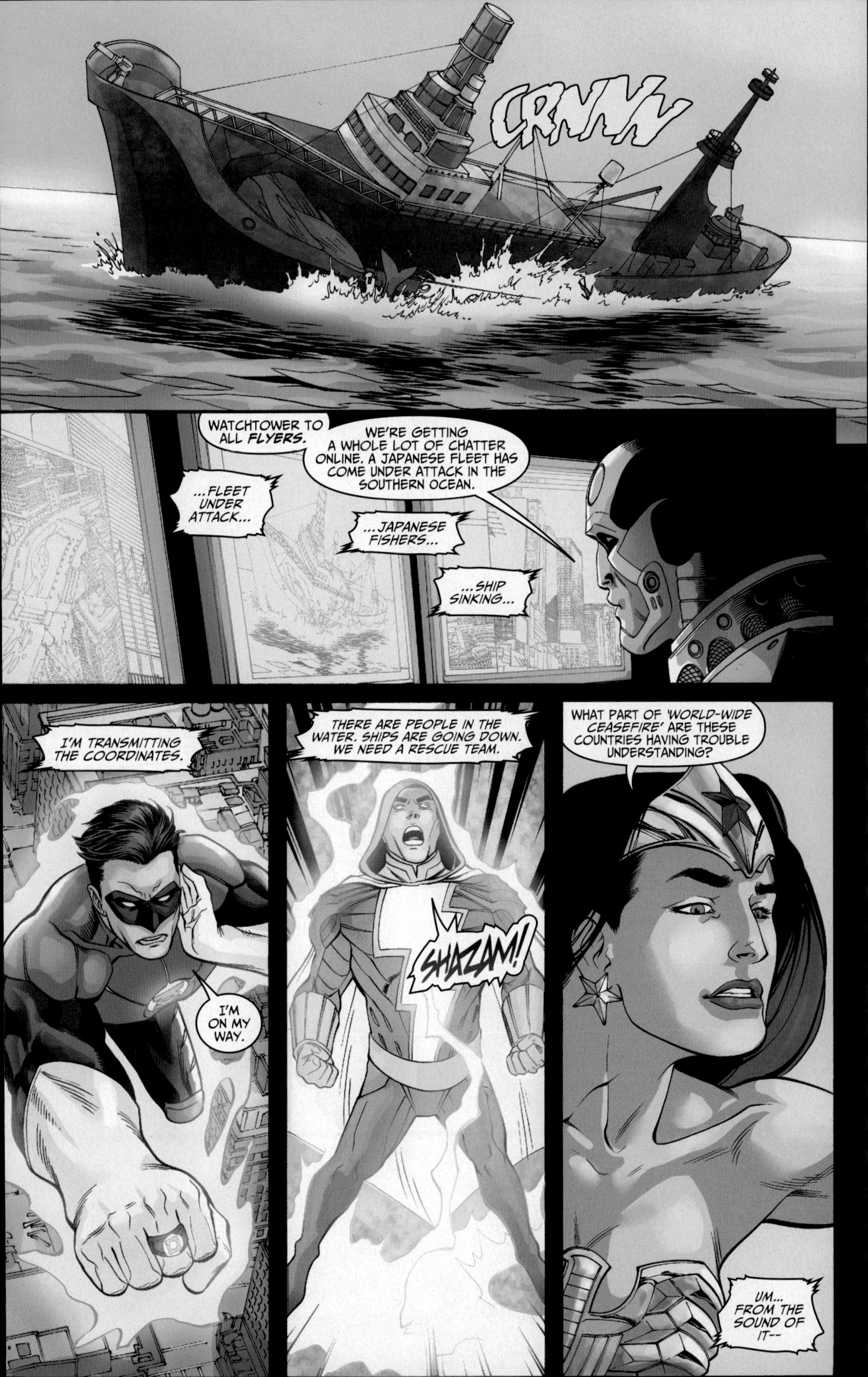
CRNNN
WATCHTOWER TO ALL FLYERS.
WE'RE GETTING A WHOLE LOT OF CHATTER ONLINE. A JAPANESE FLEET HAS COME UNDER ATTACK IN THE SOUTHERN OCEAN.
...FLEET UNDER ATTACK...
...JAPANESE FISHERS...
...SHIP SINKING...
I'M TRANSMITTING THE COORDINATES.
I'M ON MY WAY.
THERE ARE PEOPLE IN THE WATER. SHIPS ARE GOING DOWN. WE NEED A RESCUE TEAM.
SHAZAM!
WHAT PART OF 'WORLD-WIDE CEASEFIRE' ARE THESE COUNTRIES HAVING TROUBLE UNDERSTANDING?
UM... FROM THE SOUND OF IT--

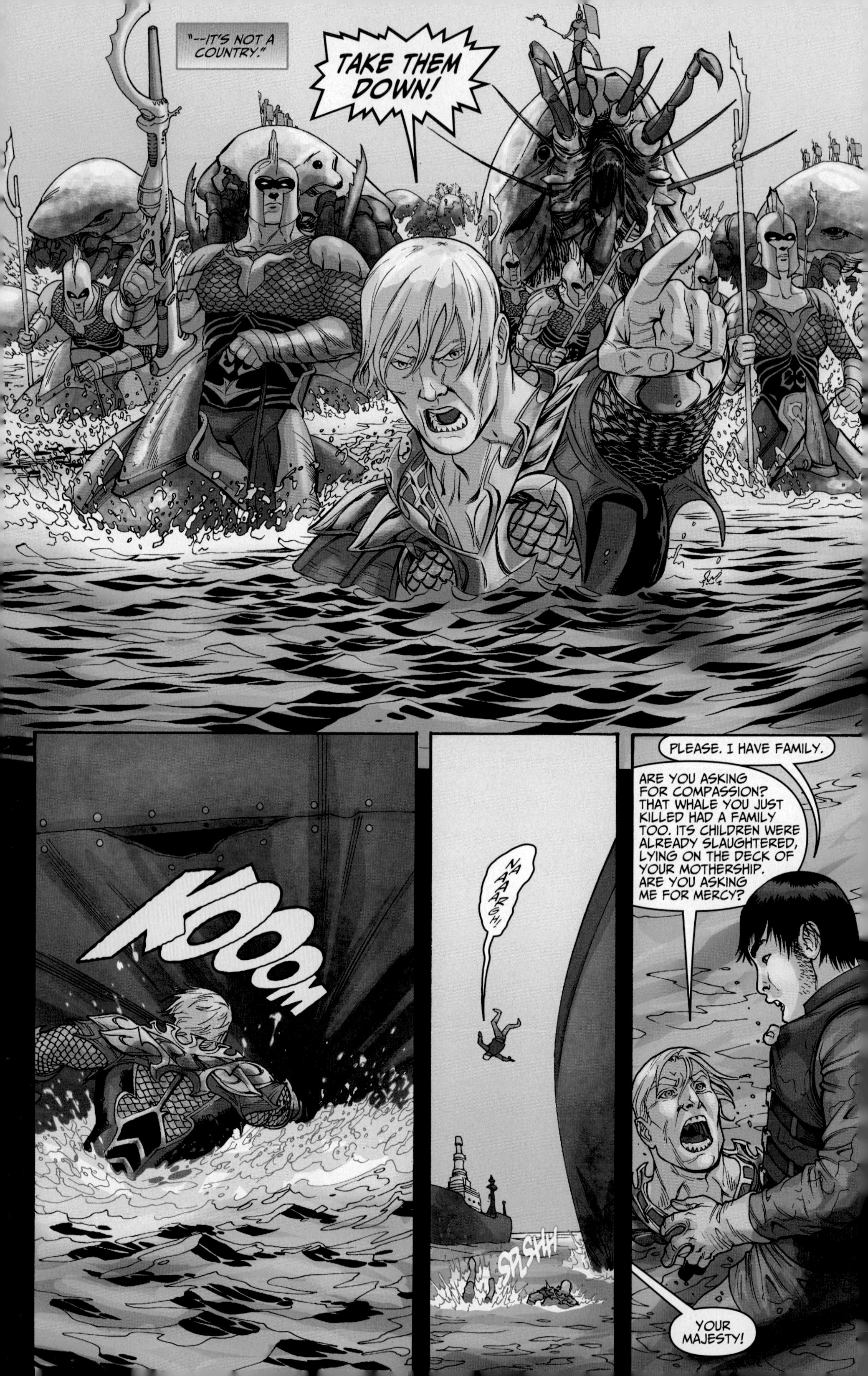
"--IT'S NOT A COUNTRY."
TAKE THEM DOWN!
KOOOM
NAAAARGH!
SPLSHH
PLEASE. I HAVE FAMILY.
ARE YOU ASKING FOR COMPASSION? THAT WHALE YOU JUST KILLED HAD A FAMILY TOO. ITS CHILDREN WERE ALREADY SLAUGHTERED, LYING ON THE DECK OF YOUR MOTHERSHIP. ARE YOU ASKING ME FOR MERCY?
YOUR MAJESTY!

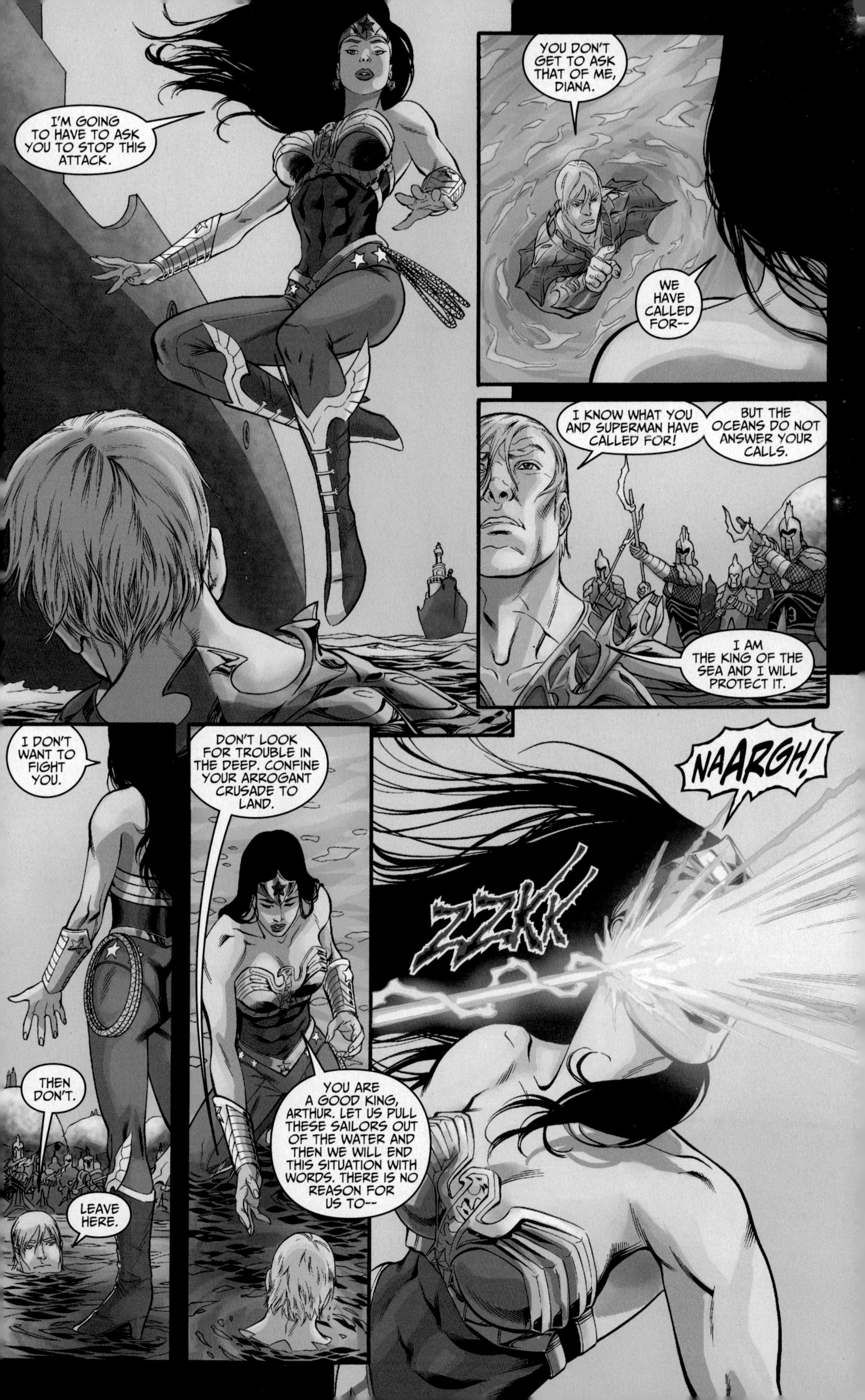

I'M GOING TO HAVE TO ASK YOU TO STOP THIS ATTACK.
YOU DON'T GET TO ASK THAT OF ME, DIANA.
WE HAVE CALLED FOR--
I KNOW WHAT YOU AND SUPERMAN HAVE CALLED FOR!
BUT THE OCEANS DO NOT ANSWER YOUR CALLS.
I AM THE KING OF THE SEA AND I WILL PROTECT IT.
I DON'T WANT TO FIGHT YOU.
THEN DON'T.
LEAVE HERE.
DON'T LOOK FOR TROUBLE IN THE DEEP. CONFINE YOUR ARROGANT CRUSADE TO LAND.
YOU ARE A GOOD KING, ARTHUR. LET US PULL THESE SAILORS OUT OF THE WATER AND THEN WE WILL END THIS SITUATION WITH WORDS. THERE IS NO REASON FOR US TO--
NAARGH!
ZZKK

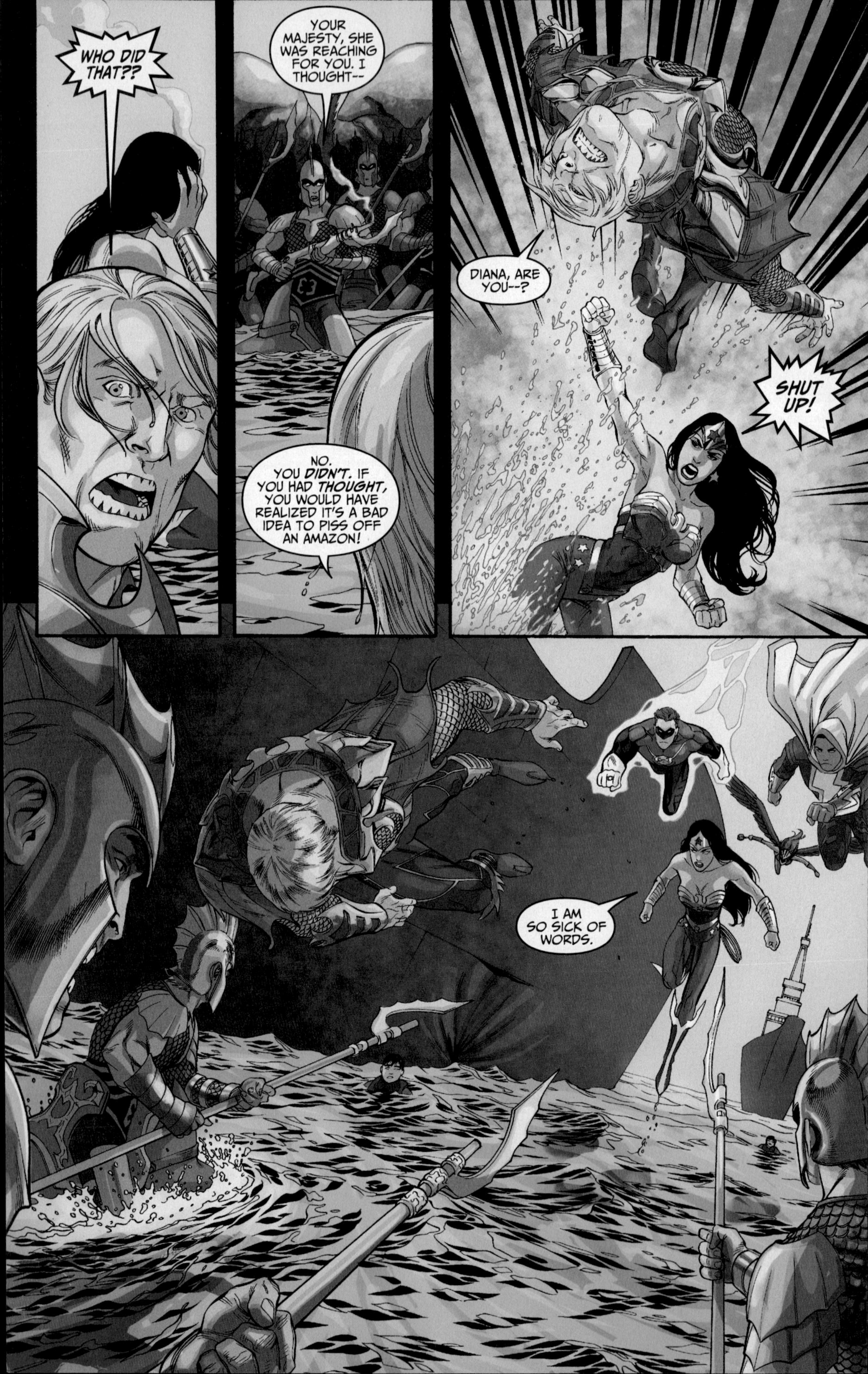
WHO DID THAT??
YOUR MAJESTY, SHE WAS REACHING FOR YOU. I THOUGHT--
NO. YOU DIDN'T. IF YOU HAD THOUGHT, YOU WOULD HAVE REALIZED IT'S A BAD IDEA TO PISS OFF AN AMAZON!
DIANA, ARE YOU--?
SHUT UP!
I AM SO SICK OF WORDS.

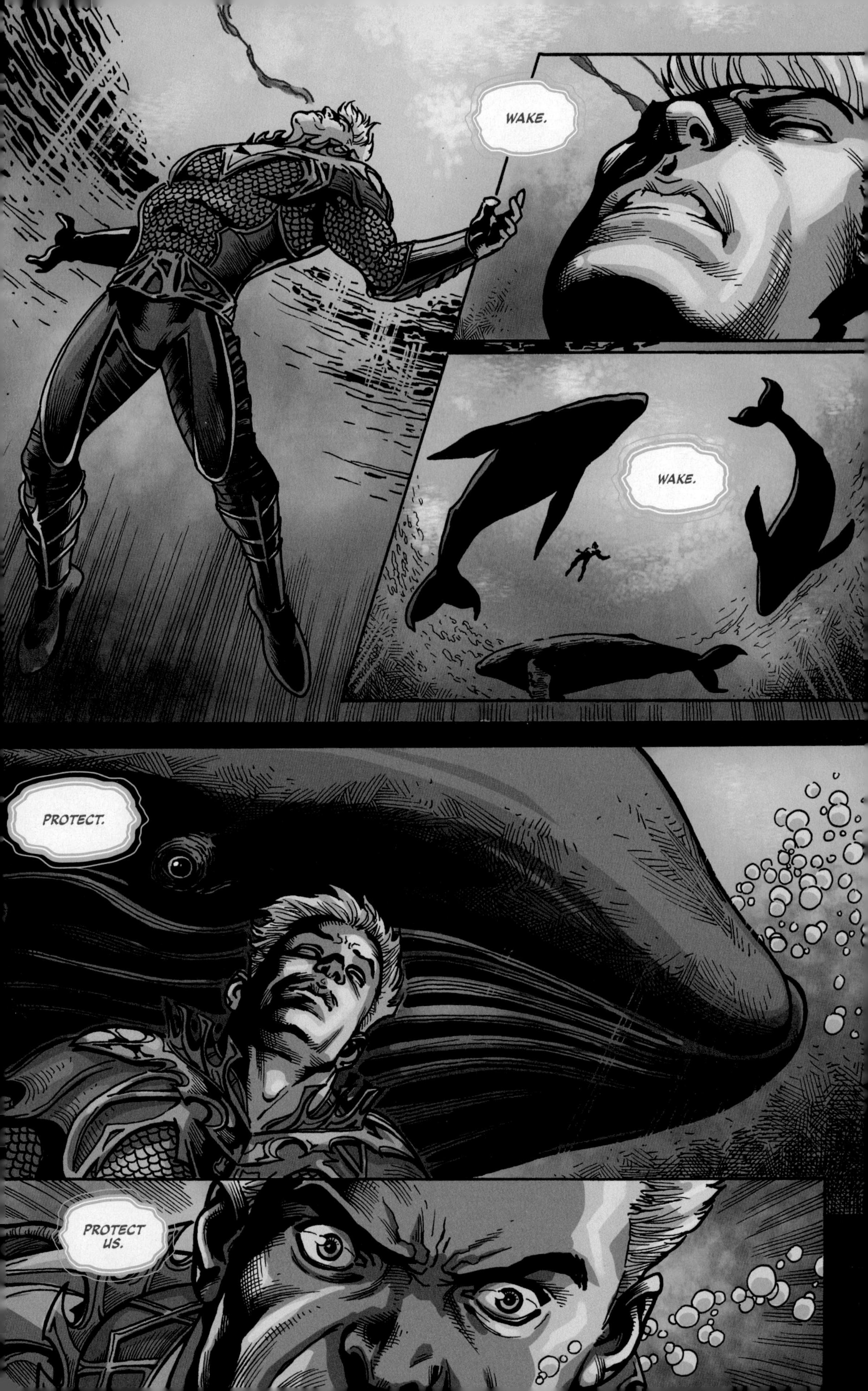
WAKE.
WAKE.
PROTECT.
PROTECT US.

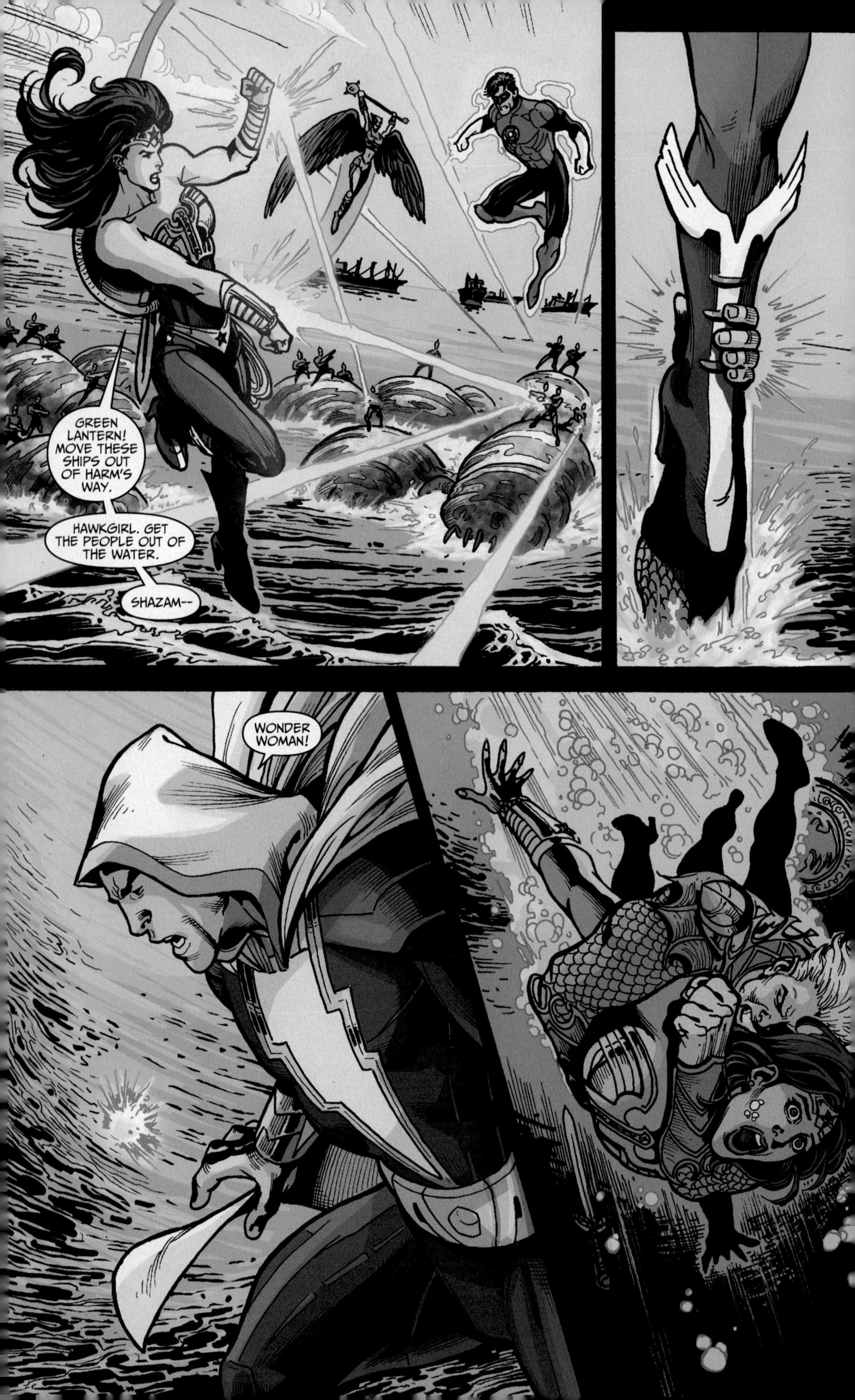
GREEN LANTERN! MOVE THESE SHIPS OUT OF HARM'S WAY.
HAWKGIRL. GET THE PEOPLE OUT OF THE WATER.
SHAZAM--
WONDER WOMAN!

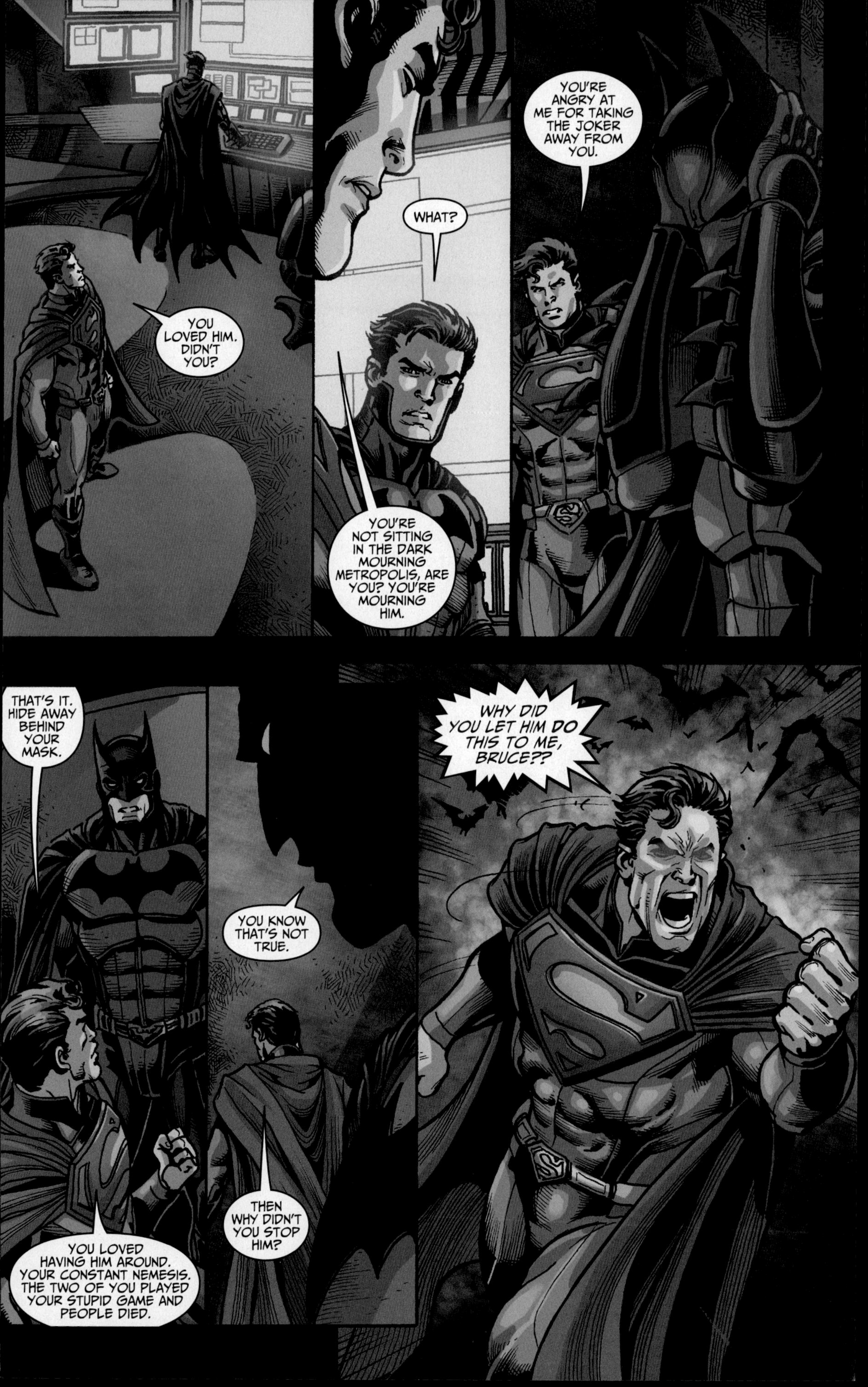
YOU LOVED HIM. DIDN'T YOU?
WHAT?
YOU'RE NOT SITTING IN THE DARK MOURNING METROPOLIS, ARE YOU? YOU'RE MOURNING HIM.
YOU'RE ANGRY AT ME FOR TAKING THE JOKER AWAY FROM YOU.
THAT'S IT. HIDE AWAY BEHIND YOUR MASK.
YOU LOVED HAVING HIM AROUND. YOUR CONSTANT NEMESIS. THE TWO OF YOU PLAYED YOUR STUPID GAME AND PEOPLE DIED.
YOU KNOW THAT'S NOT TRUE.
THEN WHY DIDN'T YOU STOP HIM?
WHY DID YOU LET HIM DO THIS TO ME, BRUCE??

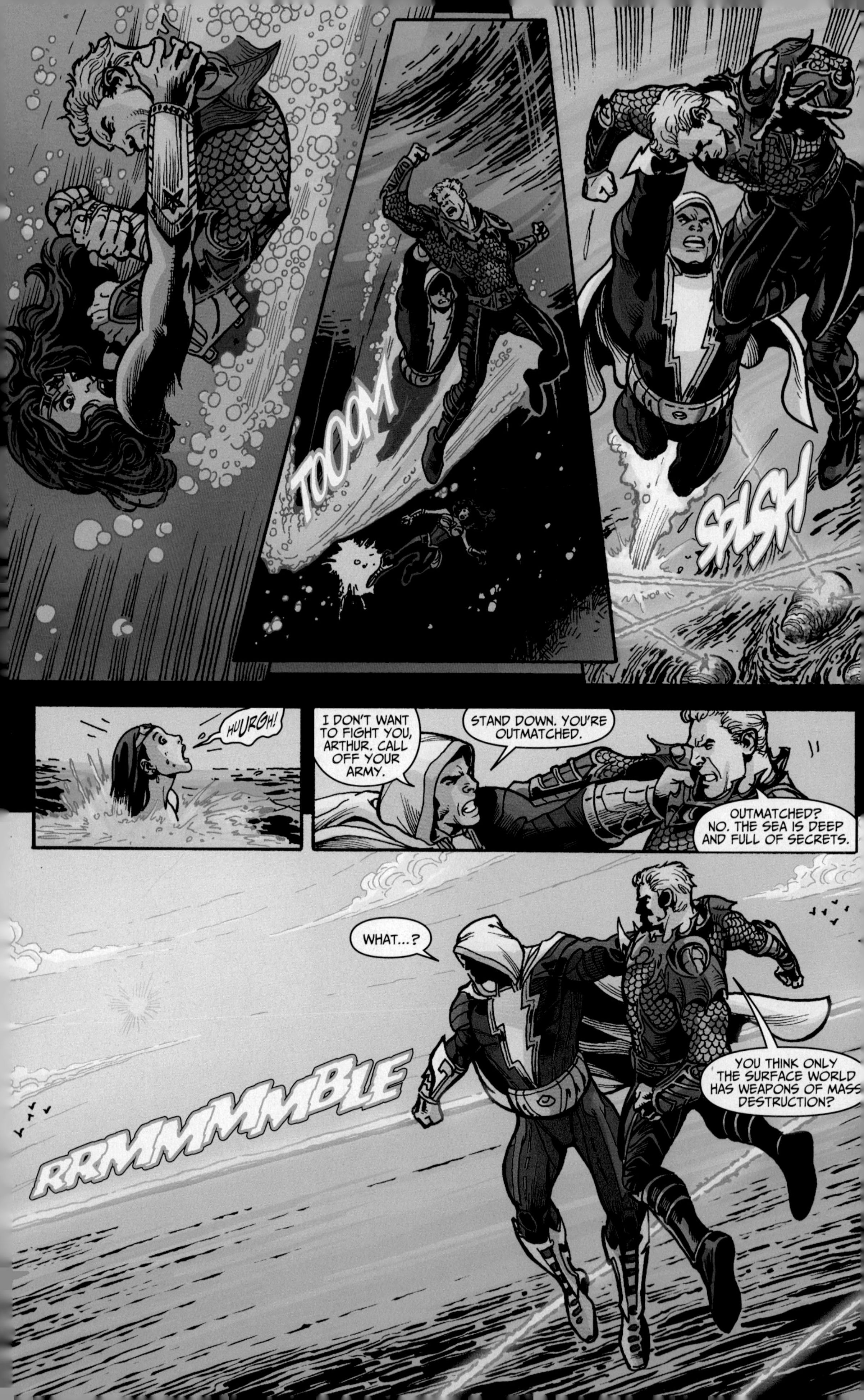
TOOOM
SPLSH
HUURGH!
I DON'T WANT TO FIGHT YOU, ARTHUR. CALL OFF YOUR ARMY.
STAND DOWN. YOU'RE OUTMATCHED.
OUTMATCHED? NO. THE SEA IS DEEP AND FULL OF SECRETS.
WHAT...?
RRMMMMMBLE
YOU THINK ONLY THE SURFACE WORLD HAS WEAPONS OF MASS DESTRUCTION?

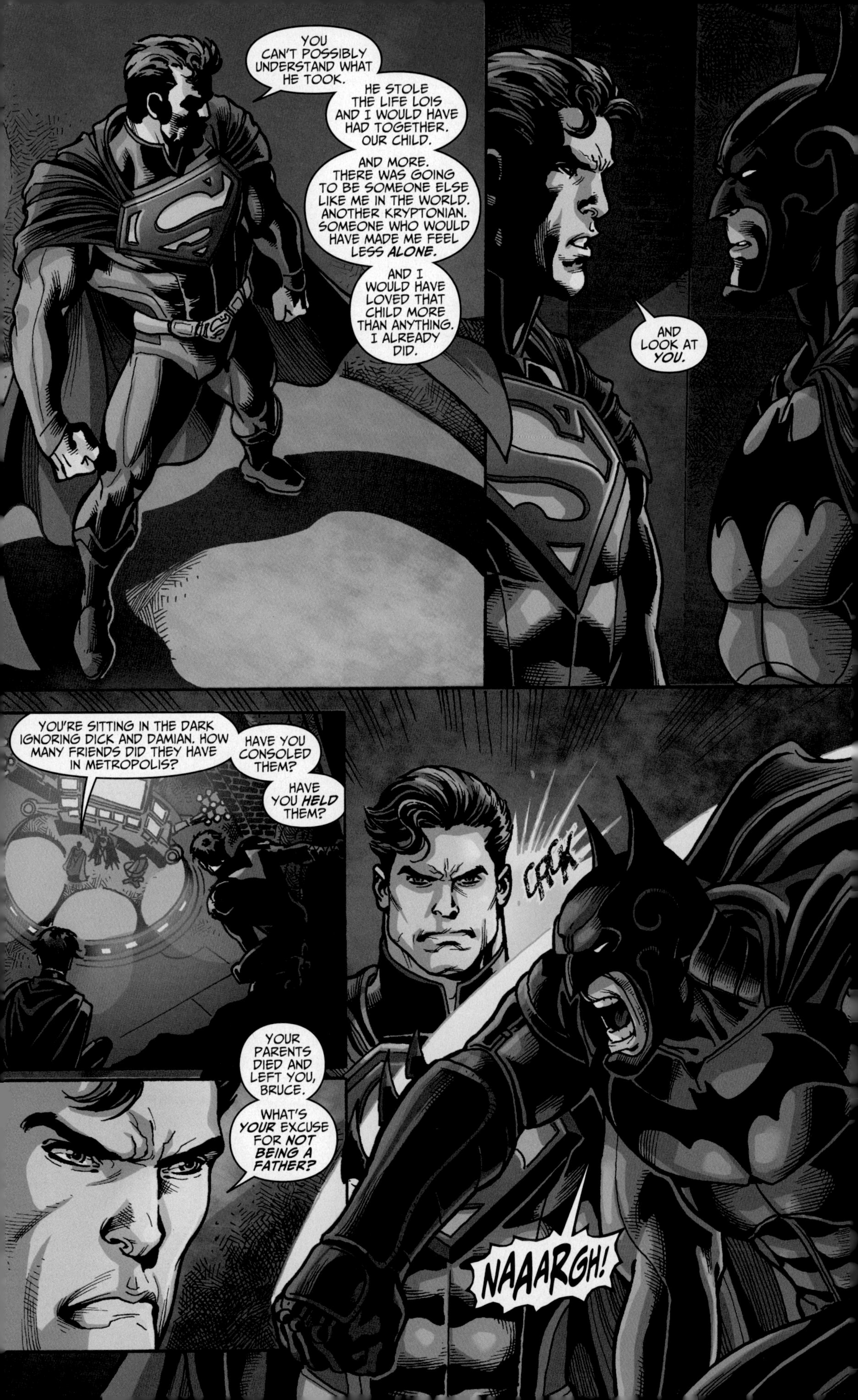
YOU CAN'T POSSIBLY UNDERSTAND WHAT HE TOOK.
HE STOLE THE LIFE LOIS AND I WOULD HAVE HAD TOGETHER. OUR CHILD.
AND MORE. THERE WAS GOING TO BE SOMEONE ELSE LIKE ME IN THE WORLD. ANOTHER KRYPTONIAN. SOMEONE WHO WOULD HAVE MADE ME FEEL LESS ALONE.
AND I WOULD HAVE LOVED THAT CHILD MORE THAN ANYTHING. I ALREADY DID.
AND LOOK AT YOU.
YOU'RE SITTING IN THE DARK IGNORING DICK AND DAMIAN. HOW MANY FRIENDS DID THEY HAVE IN METROPOLIS?
HAVE YOU CONSOLED THEM?
HAVE YOU HELD THEM?
YOUR PARENTS DIED AND LEFT YOU, BRUCE.
WHAT'S YOUR EXCUSE FOR NOT BEING A FATHER?
CRCK
NAAARGH!

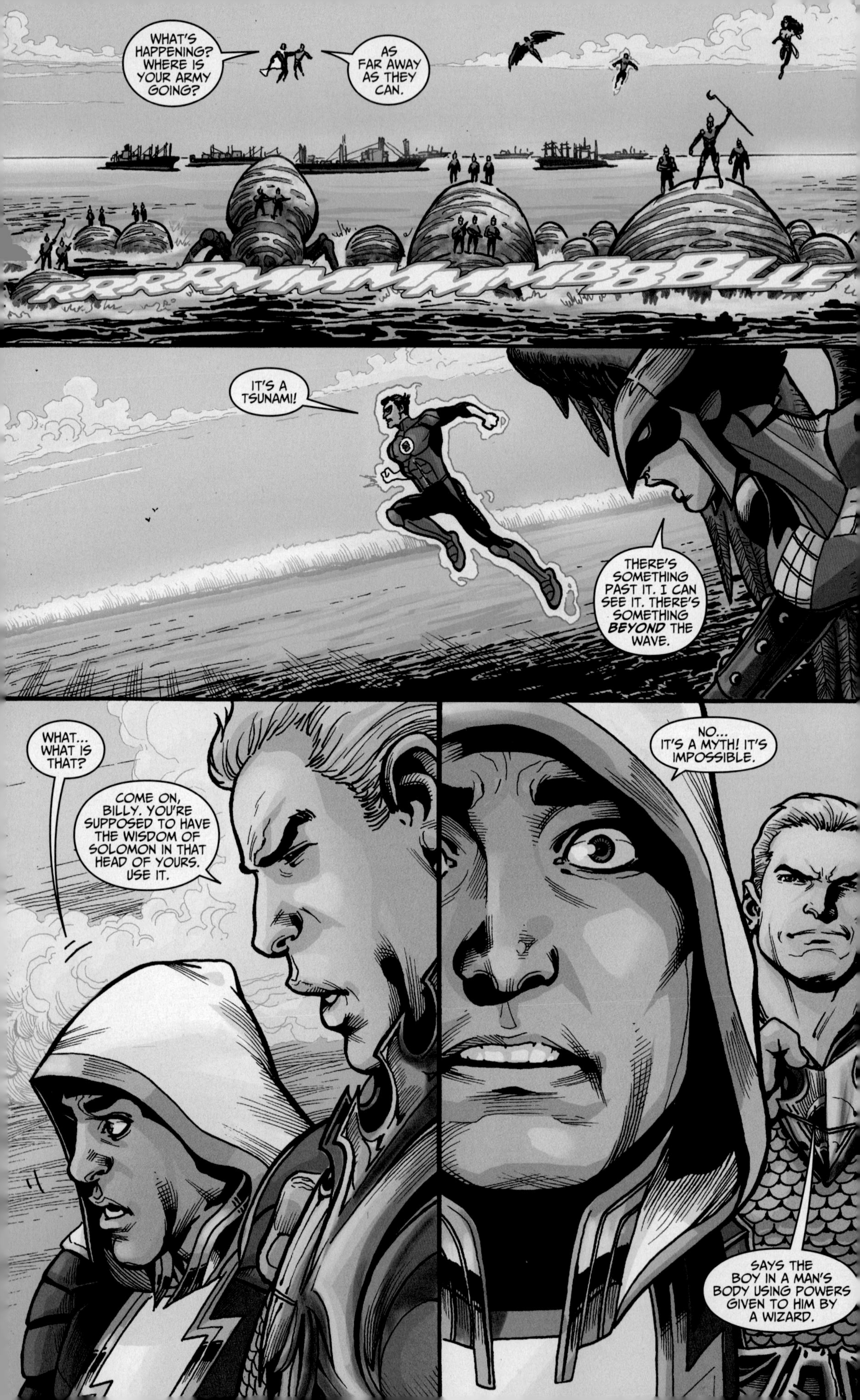
WHAT'S HAPPENING? WHERE IS YOUR ARMY GOING?
AS FAR AWAY AS THEY CAN.
RRRRMMMMMBBBLLE
IT'S A TSUNAMI!
THERE'S SOMETHING PAST IT. I CAN SEE IT. THERE'S SOMETHING BEYOND THE WAVE.
WHAT... WHAT IS THAT?
COME ON, BILLY. YOU'RE SUPPOSED TO HAVE THE WISDOM OF SOLOMON IN THAT HEAD OF YOURS. USE IT.
NO... IT'S A MYTH! IT'S IMPOSSIBLE.
SAYS THE BOY IN A MAN'S BODY USING POWERS GIVEN TO HIM BY A WIZARD.

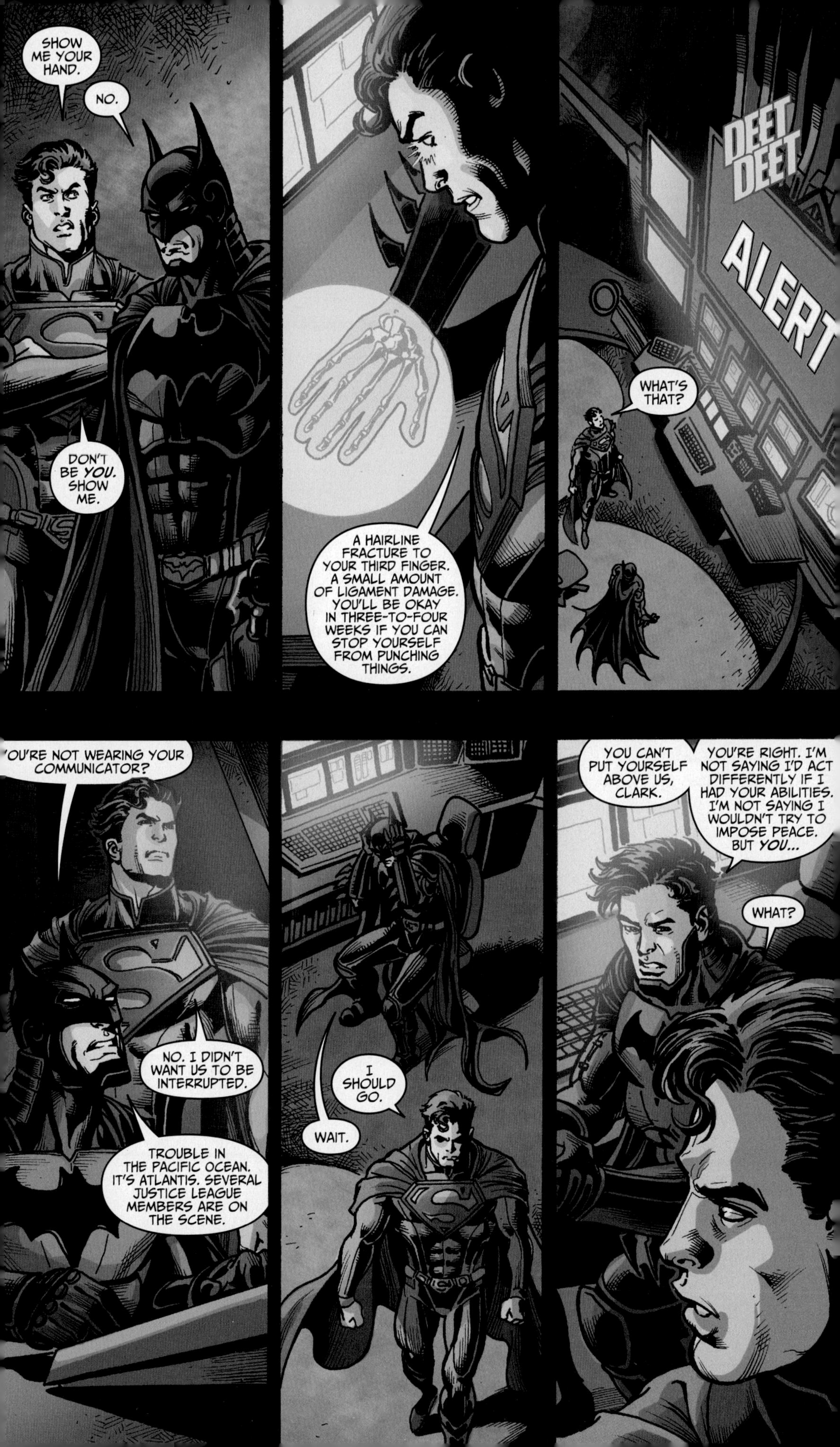
SHOW ME YOUR HAND.
NO.
DON'T BE *YOU.* SHOW ME.
A HAIRLINE FRACTURE TO YOUR THIRD FINGER. A SMALL AMOUNT OF LIGAMENT DAMAGE. YOU'LL BE OKAY IN THREE-TO-FOUR WEEKS IF YOU CAN STOP YOURSELF FROM PUNCHING THINGS.
DEET DEET
ALERT
WHAT'S THAT?
YOU'RE NOT WEARING YOUR COMMUNICATOR?
NO. I DIDN'T WANT US TO BE INTERRUPTED.
TROUBLE IN THE PACIFIC OCEAN. IT'S ATLANTIS. SEVERAL JUSTICE LEAGUE MEMBERS ARE ON THE SCENE.
I SHOULD GO.
WAIT.
YOU CAN'T PUT YOURSELF ABOVE US, CLARK.
YOU'RE RIGHT. I'M NOT SAYING I'D ACT DIFFERENTLY IF I HAD YOUR ABILITIES. I'M NOT SAYING I WOULDN'T TRY TO IMPOSE PEACE. BUT *YOU...*
WHAT?

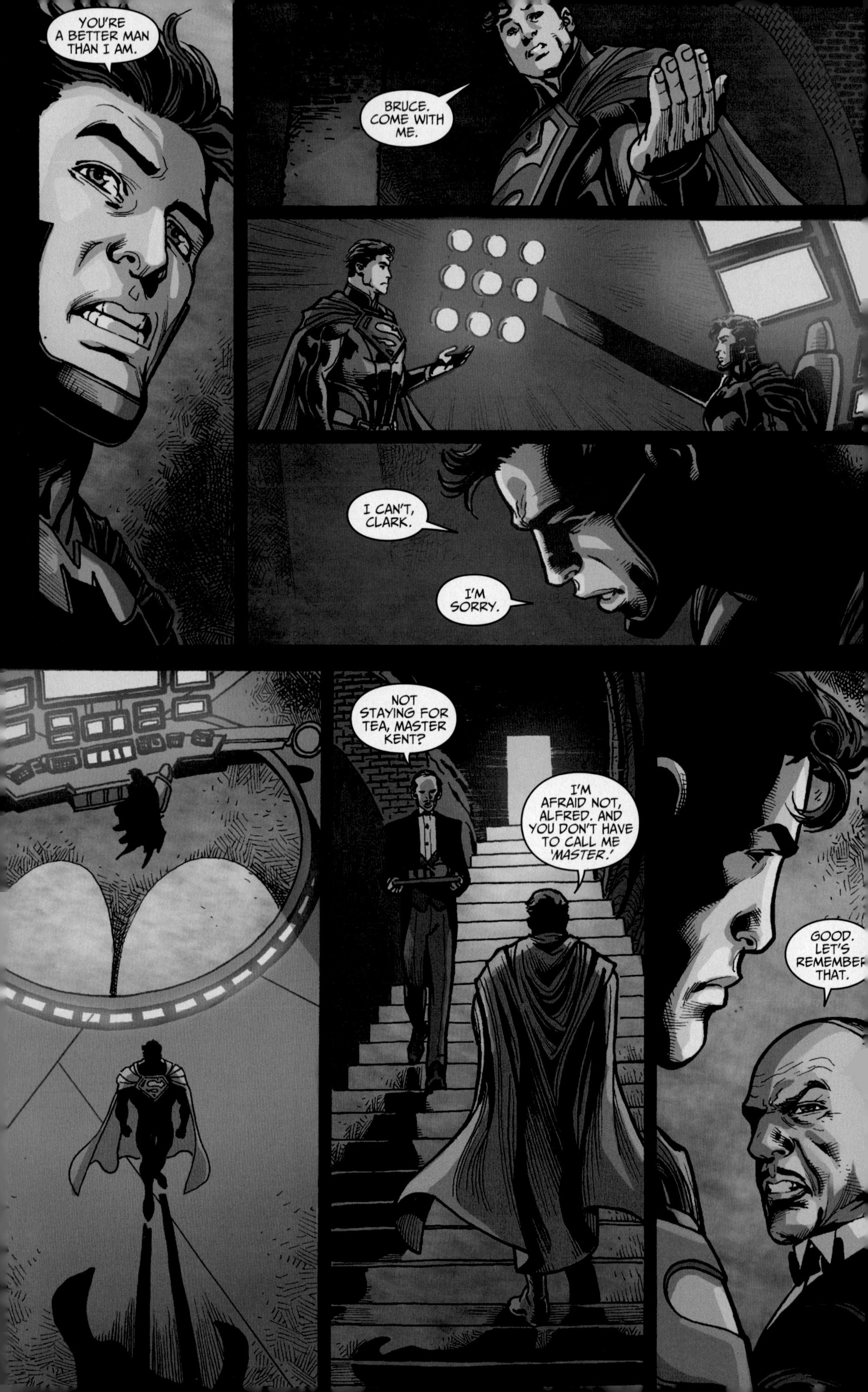
YOU'RE A BETTER MAN THAN I AM.
BRUCE. COME WITH ME.
I CAN'T, CLARK.
I'M SORRY.
NOT STAYING FOR TEA, MASTER KENT?
I'M AFRAID NOT, ALFRED. AND YOU DON'T HAVE TO CALL ME 'MASTER.'
GOOD. LET'S REMEMBER THAT.

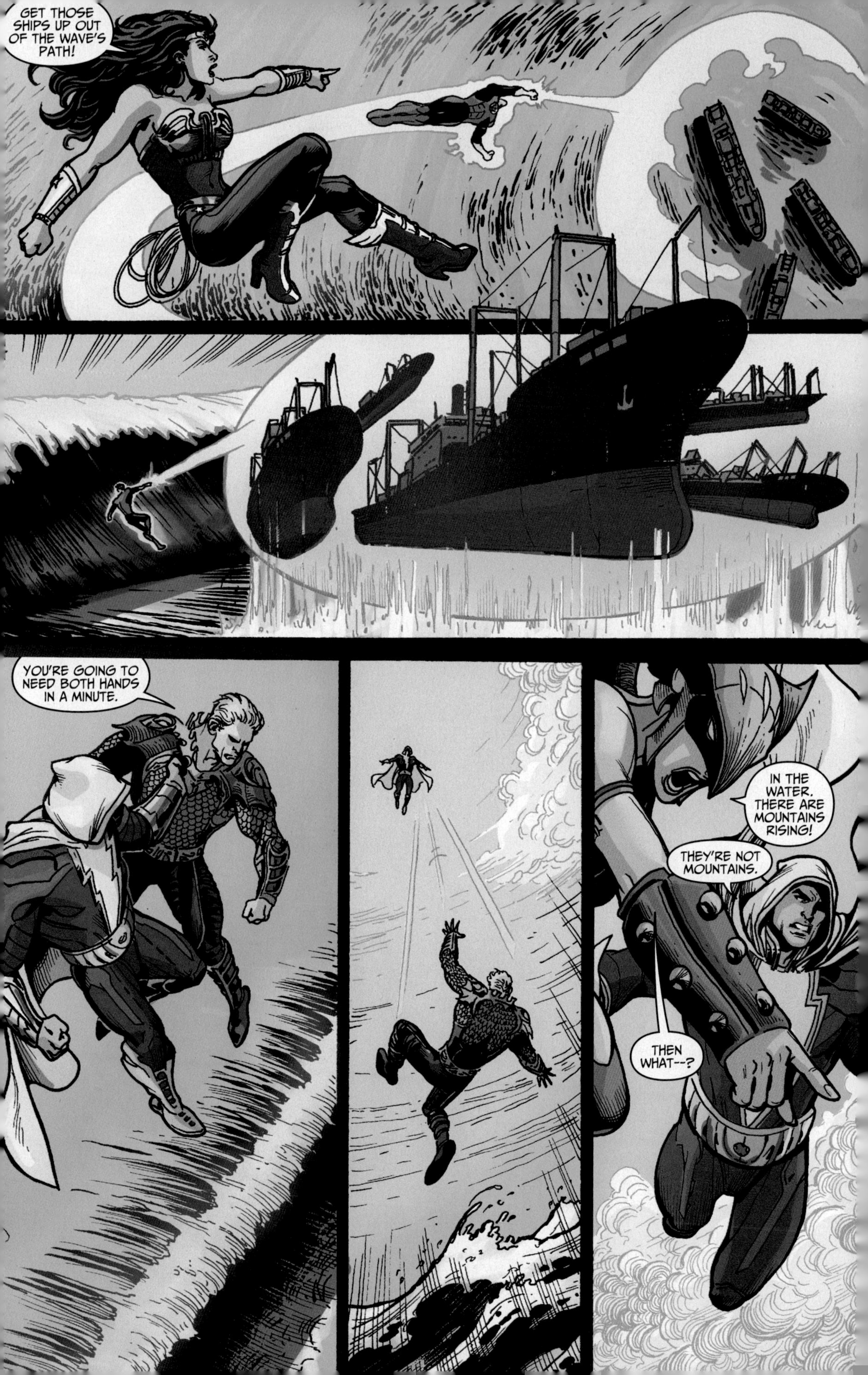
GET THOSE SHIPS UP OUT OF THE WAVE'S PATH!
YOU'RE GOING TO NEED BOTH HANDS IN A MINUTE.
IN THE WATER. THERE ARE MOUNTAINS RISING!
THEY'RE NOT MOUNTAINS.
THEN WHAT--?

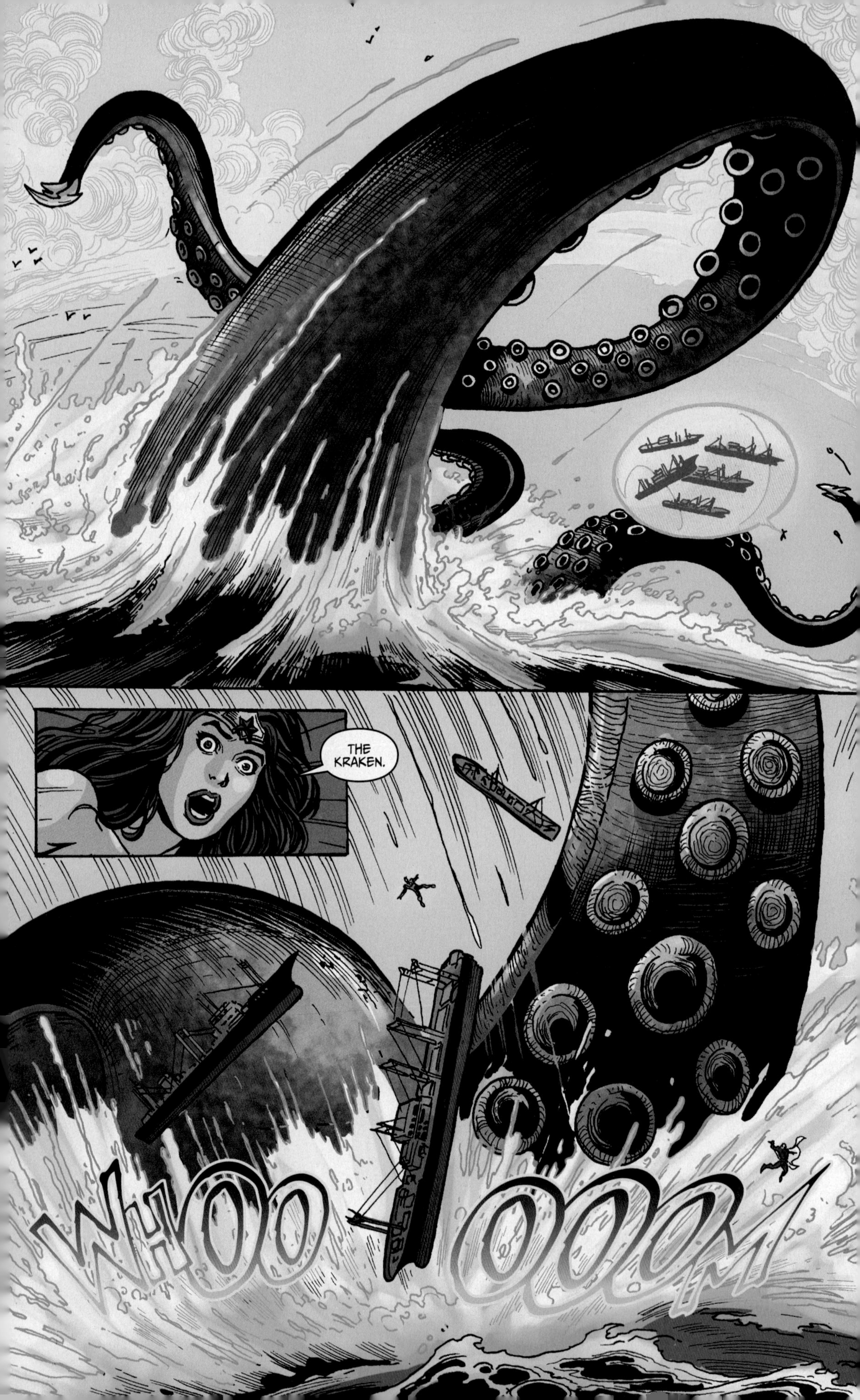
THE KRAKEN.
WHOOOOOOM

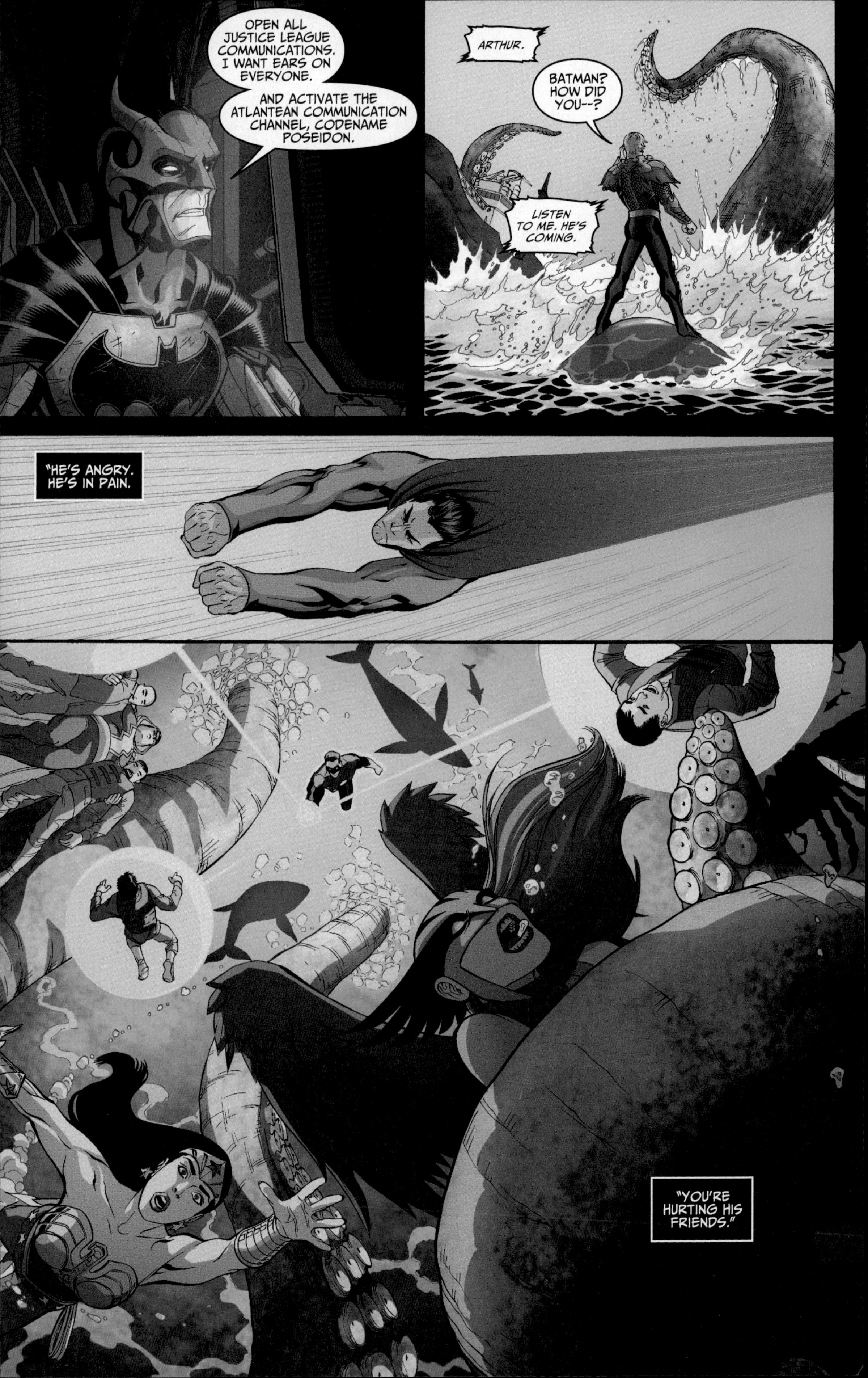
OPEN ALL JUSTICE LEAGUE COMMUNICATIONS. I WANT EARS ON EVERYONE.
AND ACTIVATE THE ATLANTEAN COMMUNICATION CHANNEL, CODENAME POSEIDON.
ARTHUR.
BATMAN? HOW DID YOU--?
LISTEN TO ME. HE'S COMING.
"HE'S ANGRY. HE'S IN PAIN.
"YOU'RE HURTING HIS FRIENDS."

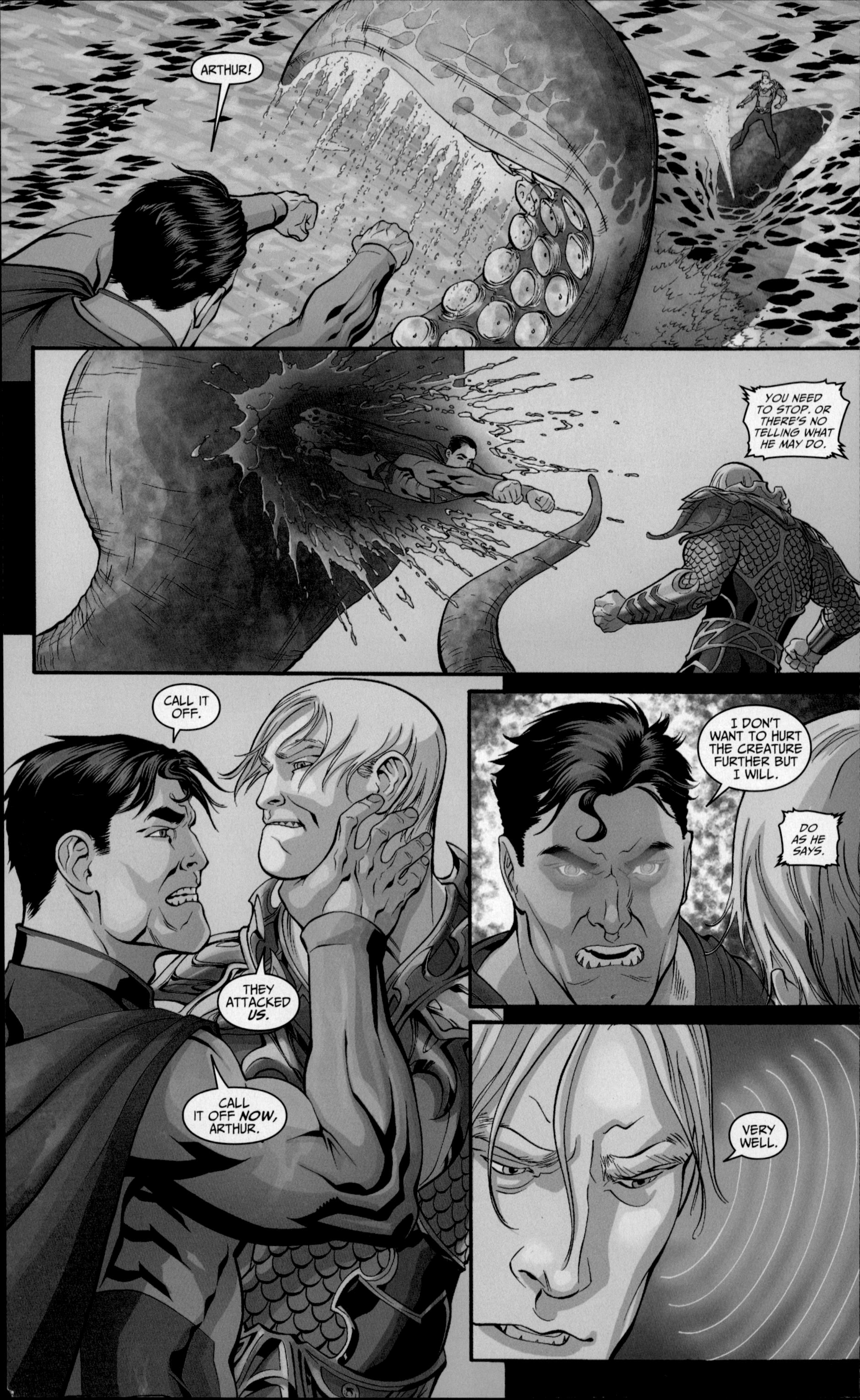
ARTHUR!
YOU NEED TO STOP. OR THERE'S NO TELLING WHAT HE MAY DO.
CALL IT OFF.
THEY ATTACKED *US.*
CALL IT OFF *NOW,* ARTHUR.
I DON'T WANT TO HURT THE CREATURE FURTHER BUT I WILL.
DO AS HE SAYS.
VERY WELL.

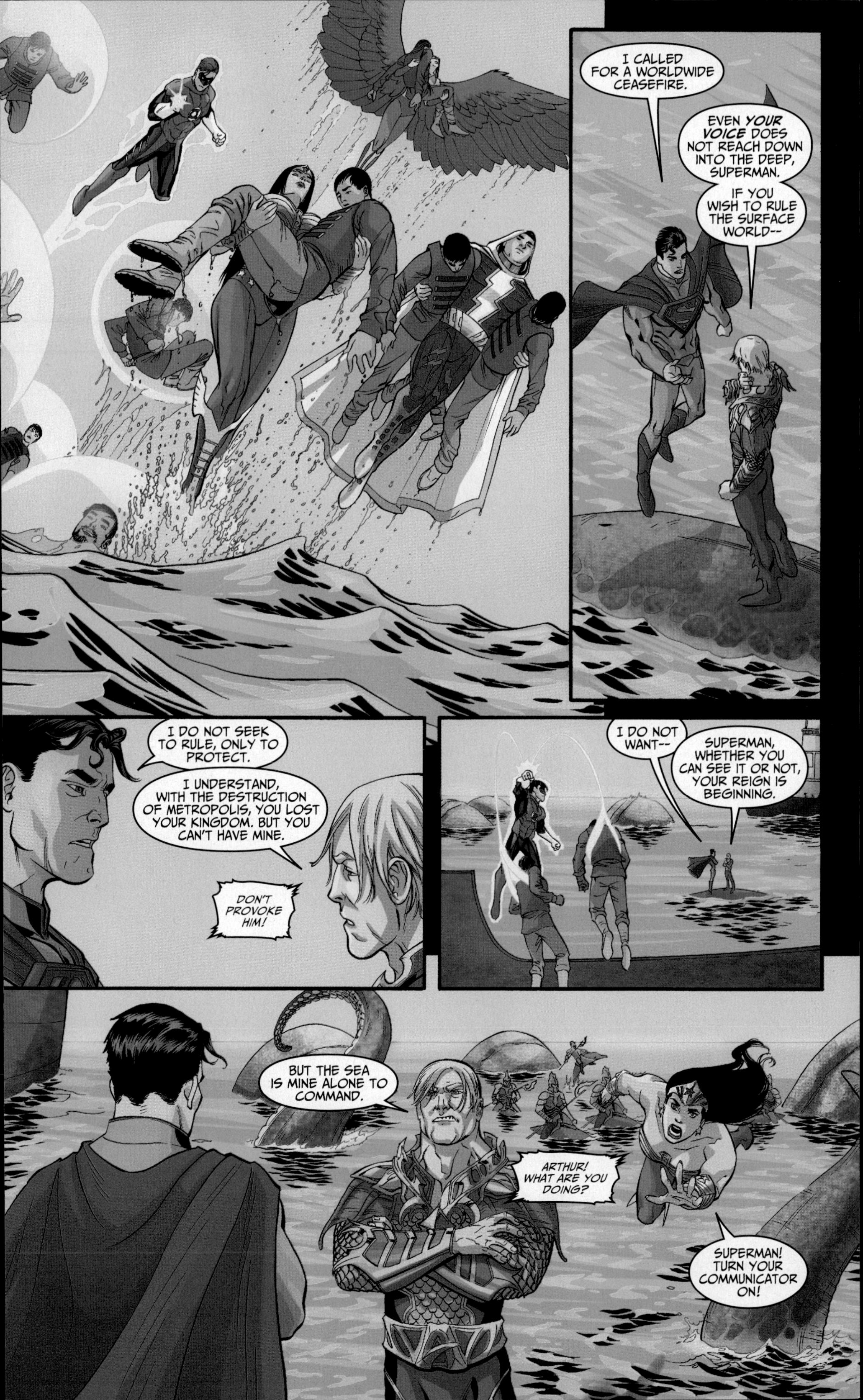
I CALLED FOR A WORLDWIDE CEASEFIRE.
EVEN *YOUR VOICE* DOES NOT REACH DOWN INTO THE DEEP, SUPERMAN.
IF YOU WISH TO RULE THE SURFACE WORLD--
I DO NOT SEEK TO RULE, ONLY TO PROTECT.
I UNDERSTAND, WITH THE DESTRUCTION OF METROPOLIS, YOU LOST YOUR KINGDOM. BUT YOU CAN'T HAVE MINE.
DON'T PROVOKE HIM!
I DO NOT WANT--
SUPERMAN, WHETHER YOU CAN SEE IT OR NOT, YOUR REIGN IS BEGINNING.
BUT THE SEA IS MINE ALONE TO COMMAND.
ARTHUR! WHAT ARE YOU DOING?
SUPERMAN! TURN YOUR COMMUNICATOR ON!

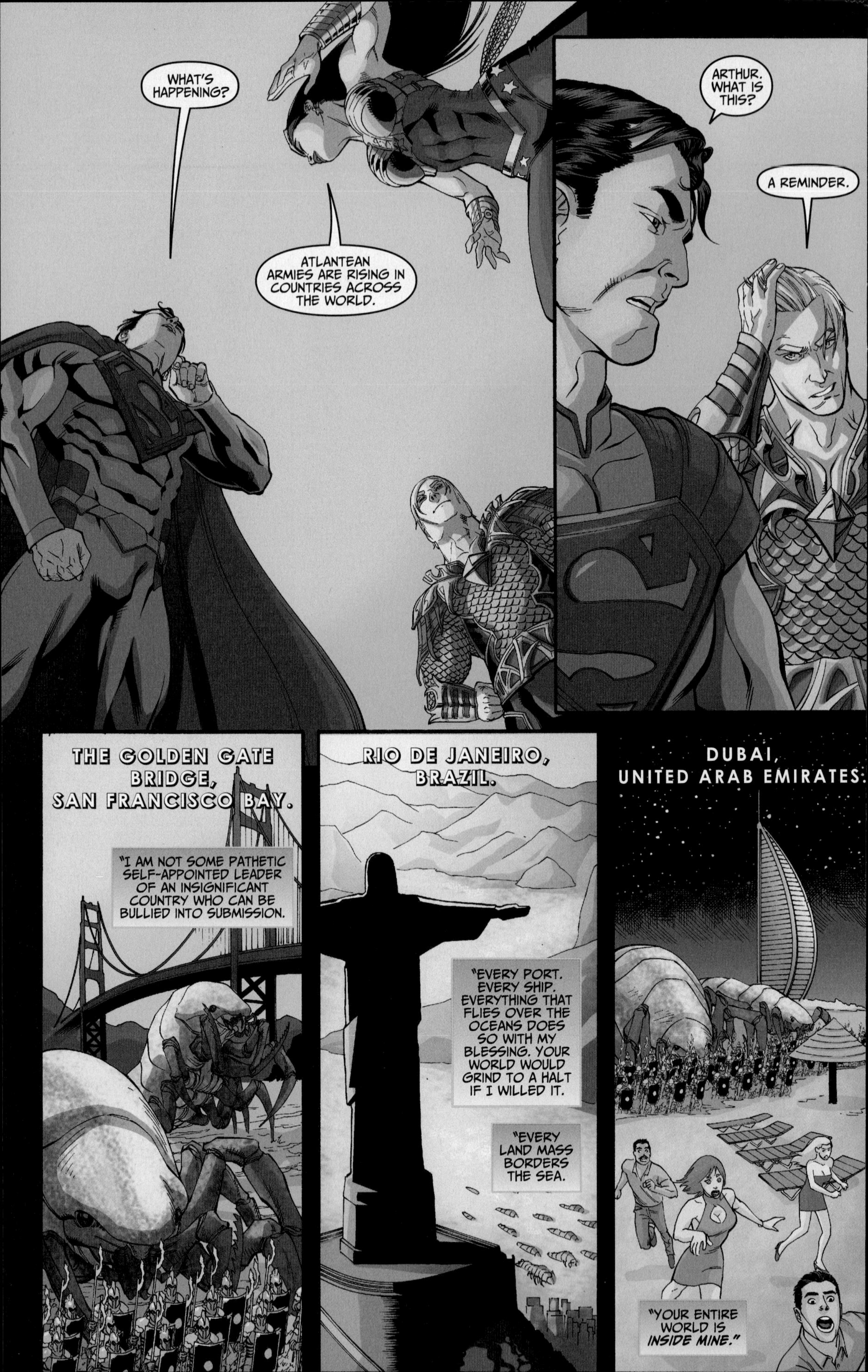

WHAT'S HAPPENING?
ATLANTEAN ARMIES ARE RISING IN COUNTRIES ACROSS THE WORLD.
ARTHUR. WHAT IS THIS?
A REMINDER.
THE GOLDEN GATE BRIDGE, SAN FRANCISCO BAY.
"I AM NOT SOME PATHETIC SELF-APPOINTED LEADER OF AN INSIGNIFICANT COUNTRY WHO CAN BE BULLIED INTO SUBMISSION.
RIO DE JANEIRO, BRAZIL.
"EVERY PORT. EVERY SHIP. EVERYTHING THAT FLIES OVER THE OCEANS DOES SO WITH MY BLESSING. YOUR WORLD WOULD GRIND TO A HALT IF I WILLED IT.
"EVERY LAND MASS BORDERS THE SEA.
DUBAI, UNITED ARAB EMIRATES.
"YOUR ENTIRE WORLD IS *INSIDE MINE.*"

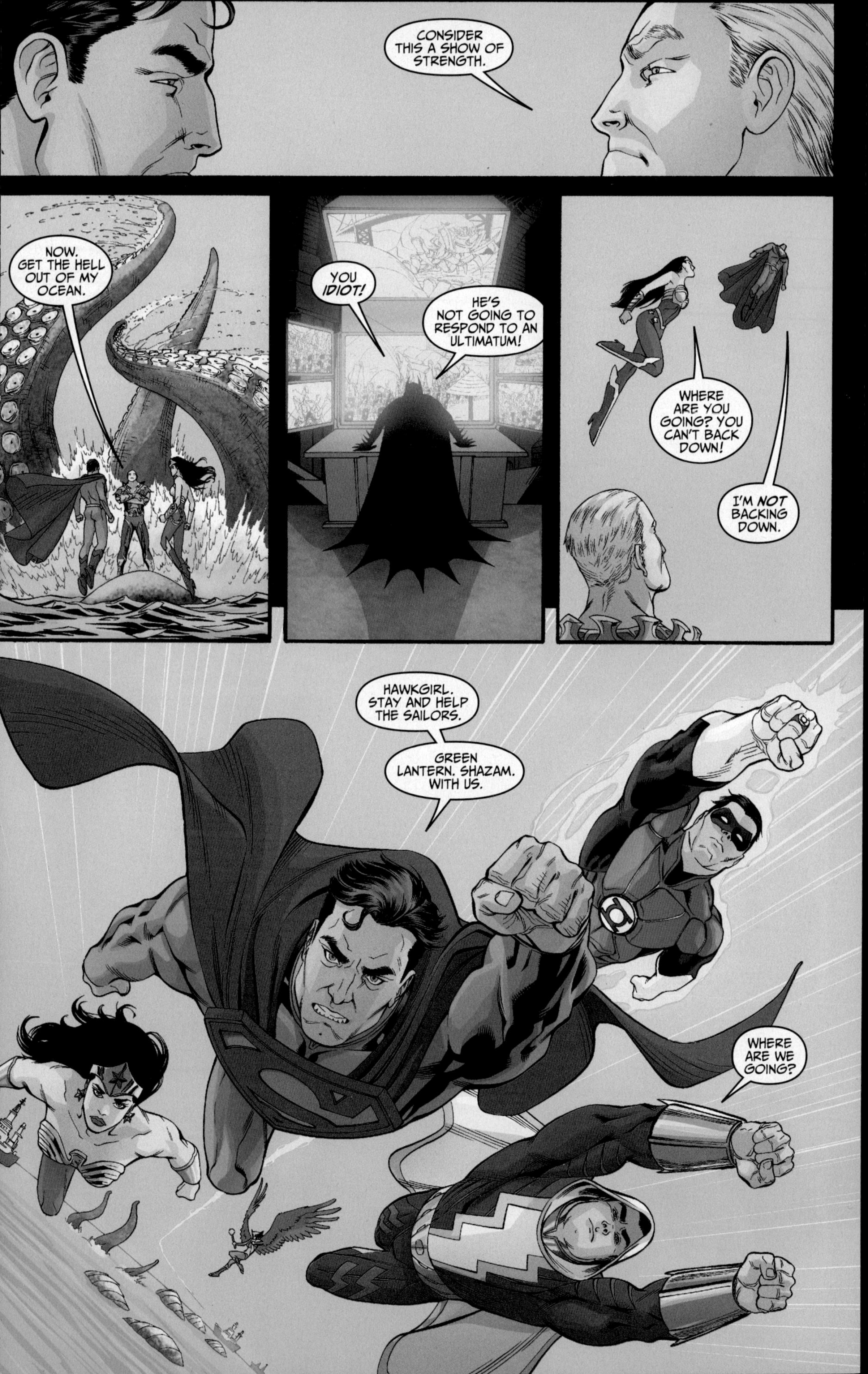
CONSIDER THIS A SHOW OF STRENGTH.
NOW. GET THE HELL OUT OF MY OCEAN.
YOU *IDIOT!*
HE'S NOT GOING TO RESPOND TO AN ULTIMATUM!
WHERE ARE YOU GOING? YOU CAN'T BACK DOWN!
I'M *NOT* BACKING DOWN.
HAWKGIRL. STAY AND HELP THE SAILORS.
GREEN LANTERN. SHAZAM. WITH US.
WHERE ARE WE GOING?

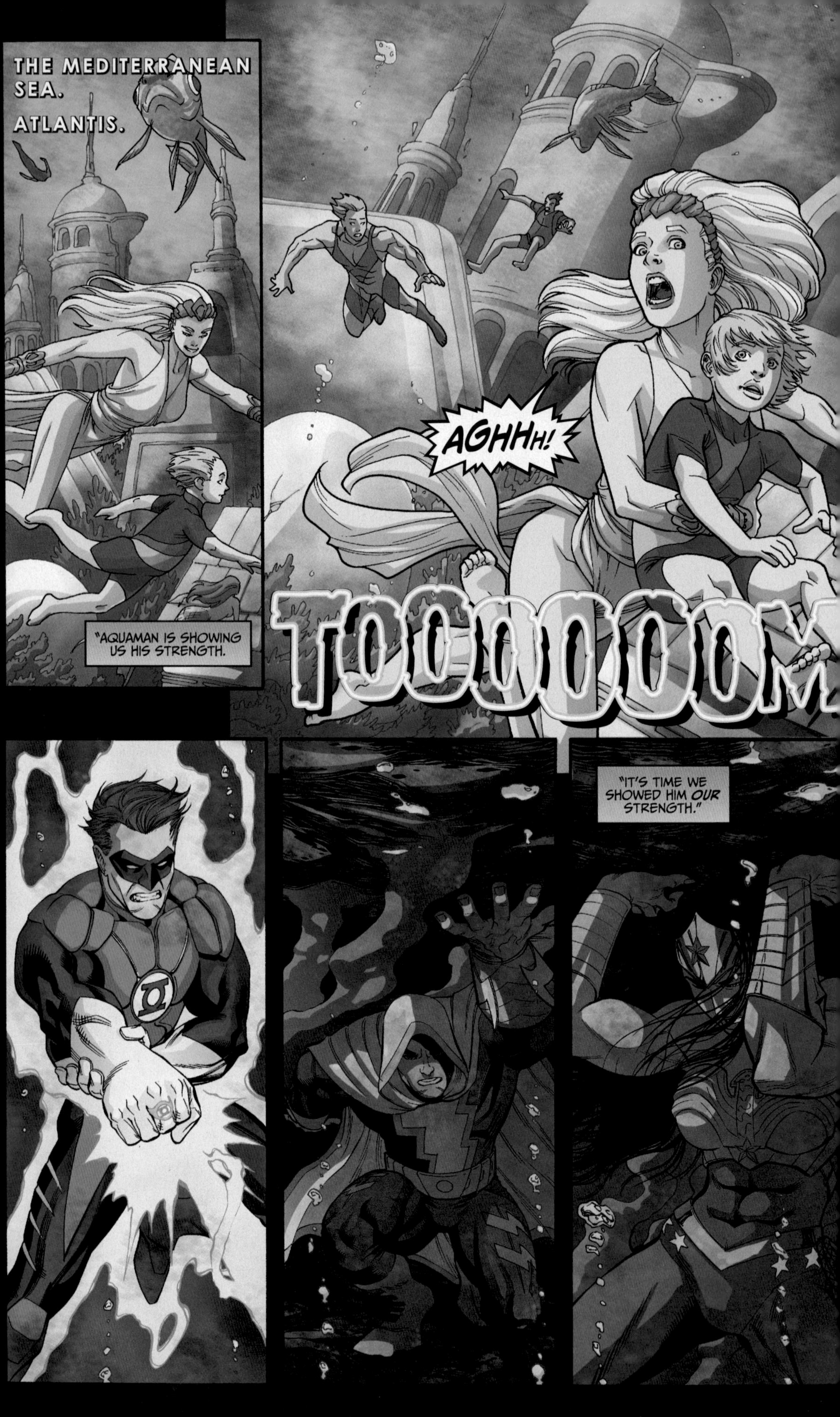
THE MEDITERRANEAN SEA.
ATLANTIS.
"AQUAMAN IS SHOWING US HIS STRENGTH.
AGHHH!
TOOOOOOM
"IT'S TIME WE SHOWED HIM OUR STRENGTH."

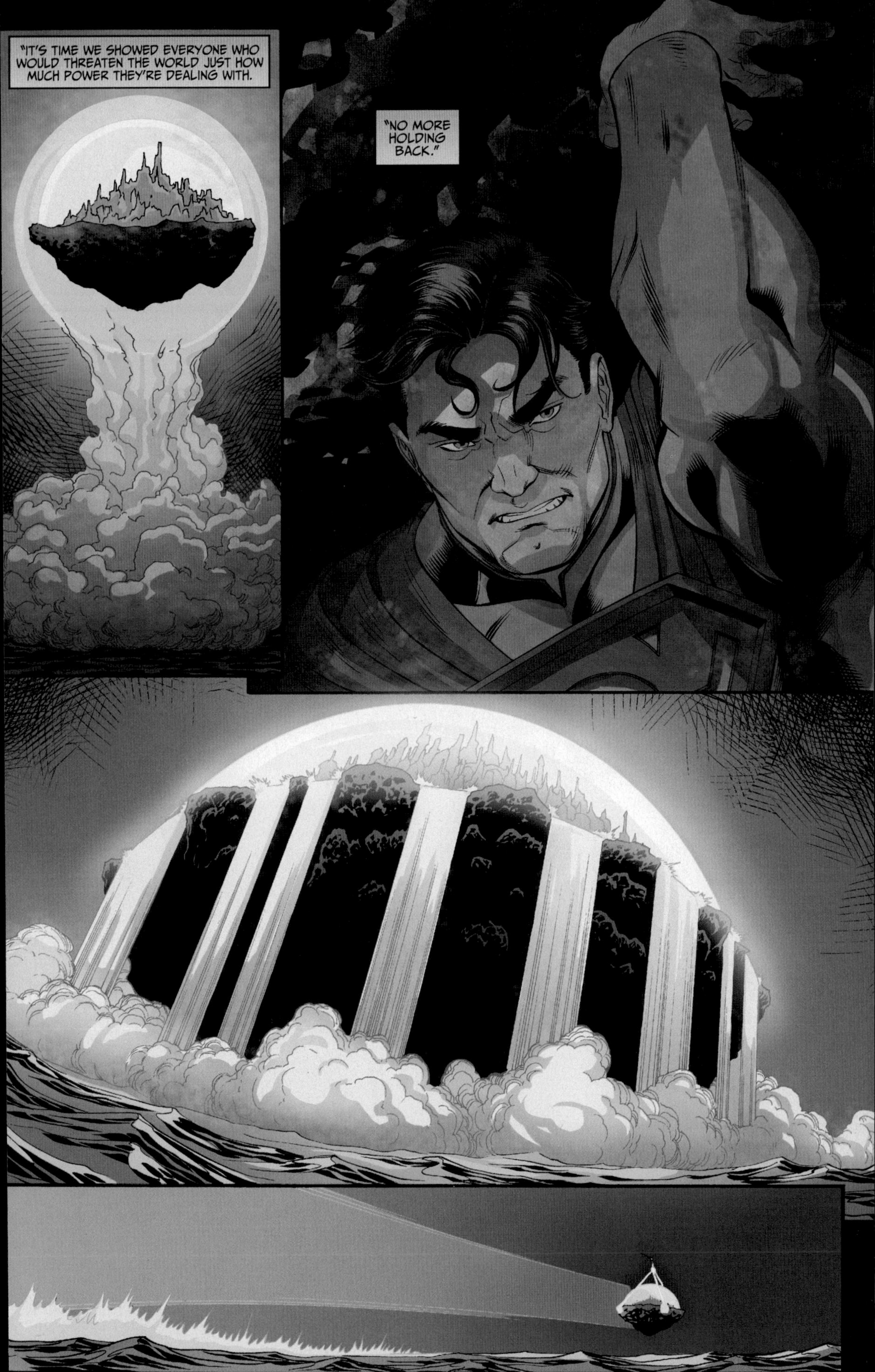
"IT'S TIME WE SHOWED EVERYONE WHO WOULD THREATEN THE WORLD JUST HOW MUCH POWER THEY'RE DEALING WITH.
"NO MORE HOLDING BACK."

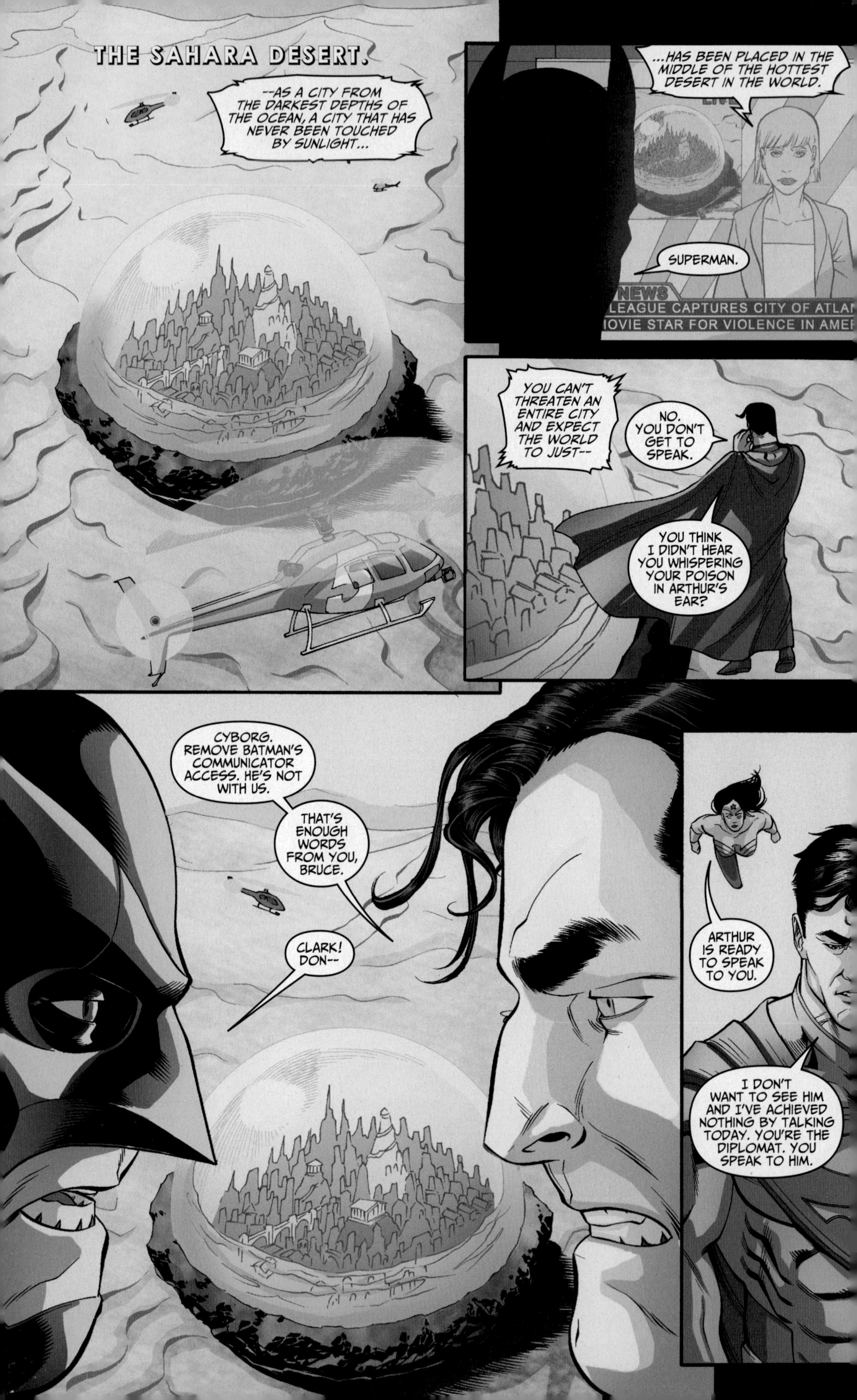
THE SAHARA DESERT.
--AS A CITY FROM THE DARKEST DEPTHS OF THE OCEAN, A CITY THAT HAS NEVER BEEN TOUCHED BY SUNLIGHT...
...HAS BEEN PLACED IN THE MIDDLE OF THE HOTTEST DESERT IN THE WORLD.
SUPERMAN.
NEWS
LEAGUE CAPTURES CITY OF ATLAN
MOVIE STAR FOR VIOLENCE IN AMER
YOU CAN'T THREATEN AN ENTIRE CITY AND EXPECT THE WORLD TO JUST--
NO. YOU DON'T GET TO SPEAK.
YOU THINK I DIDN'T HEAR YOU WHISPERING YOUR POISON IN ARTHUR'S EAR?
CYBORG. REMOVE BATMAN'S COMMUNICATOR ACCESS. HE'S NOT WITH US.
THAT'S ENOUGH WORDS FROM YOU, BRUCE.
CLARK! DON--
ARTHUR IS READY TO SPEAK TO YOU.
I DON'T WANT TO SEE HIM AND I'VE ACHIEVED NOTHING BY TALKING TODAY. YOU'RE THE DIPLOMAT. YOU SPEAK TO HIM.

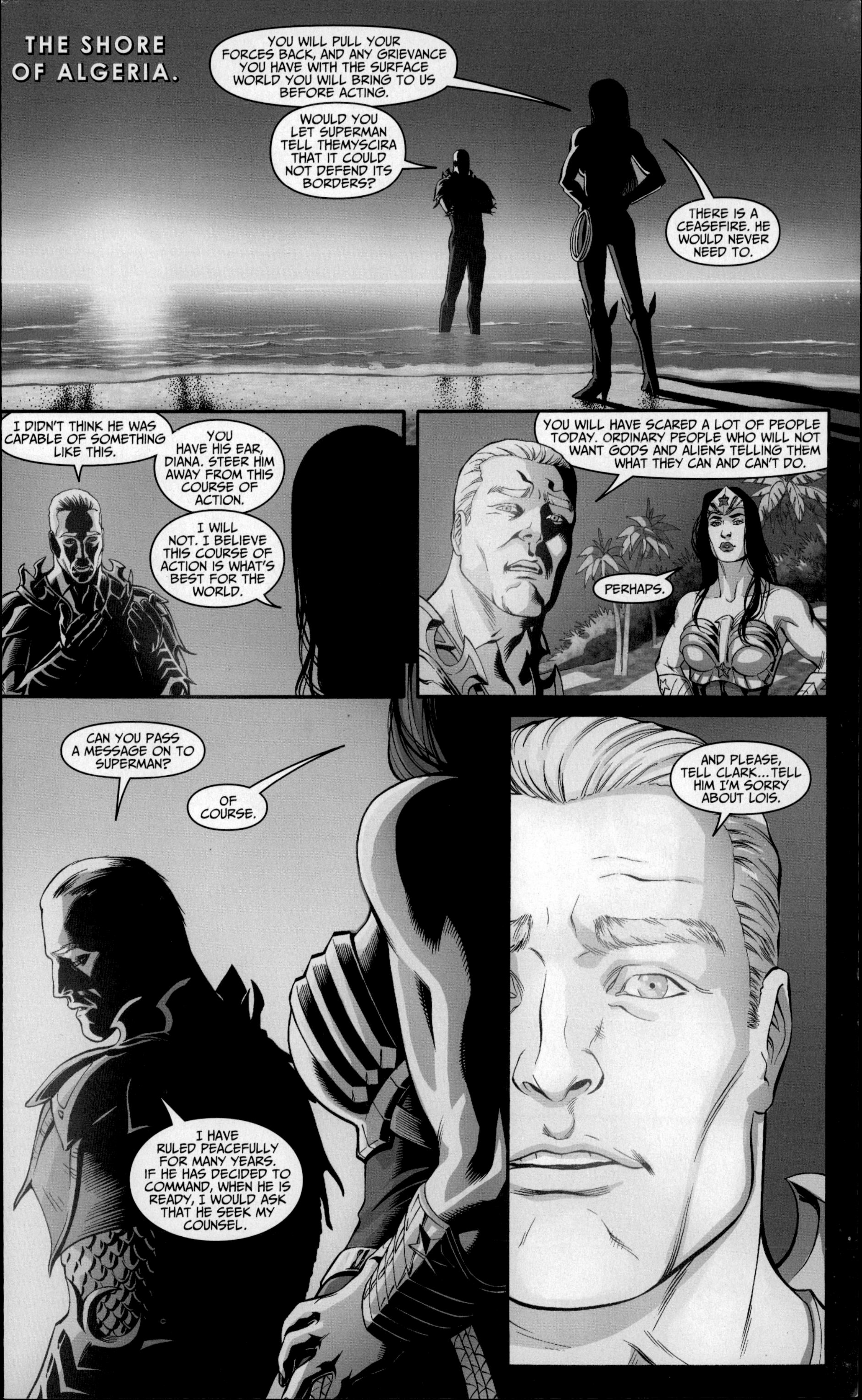
THE SHORE OF ALGERIA.
YOU WILL PULL YOUR FORCES BACK, AND ANY GRIEVANCE YOU HAVE WITH THE SURFACE WORLD YOU WILL BRING TO US BEFORE ACTING.
WOULD YOU LET SUPERMAN TELL THEMYSCIRA THAT IT COULD NOT DEFEND ITS BORDERS?
THERE IS A CEASEFIRE. HE WOULD NEVER NEED TO.
I DIDN'T THINK HE WAS CAPABLE OF SOMETHING LIKE THIS.
YOU HAVE HIS EAR, DIANA. STEER HIM AWAY FROM THIS COURSE OF ACTION.
I WILL NOT. I BELIEVE THIS COURSE OF ACTION IS WHAT'S BEST FOR THE WORLD.
YOU WILL HAVE SCARED A LOT OF PEOPLE TODAY. ORDINARY PEOPLE WHO WILL NOT WANT GODS AND ALIENS TELLING THEM WHAT THEY CAN AND CAN'T DO.
PERHAPS.
CAN YOU PASS A MESSAGE ON TO SUPERMAN?
OF COURSE.
I HAVE RULED PEACEFULLY FOR MANY YEARS. IF HE HAS DECIDED TO COMMAND, WHEN HE IS READY, I WOULD ASK THAT HE SEEK MY COUNSEL.
AND PLEASE, TELL CLARK... TELL HIM I'M SORRY ABOUT LOIS.

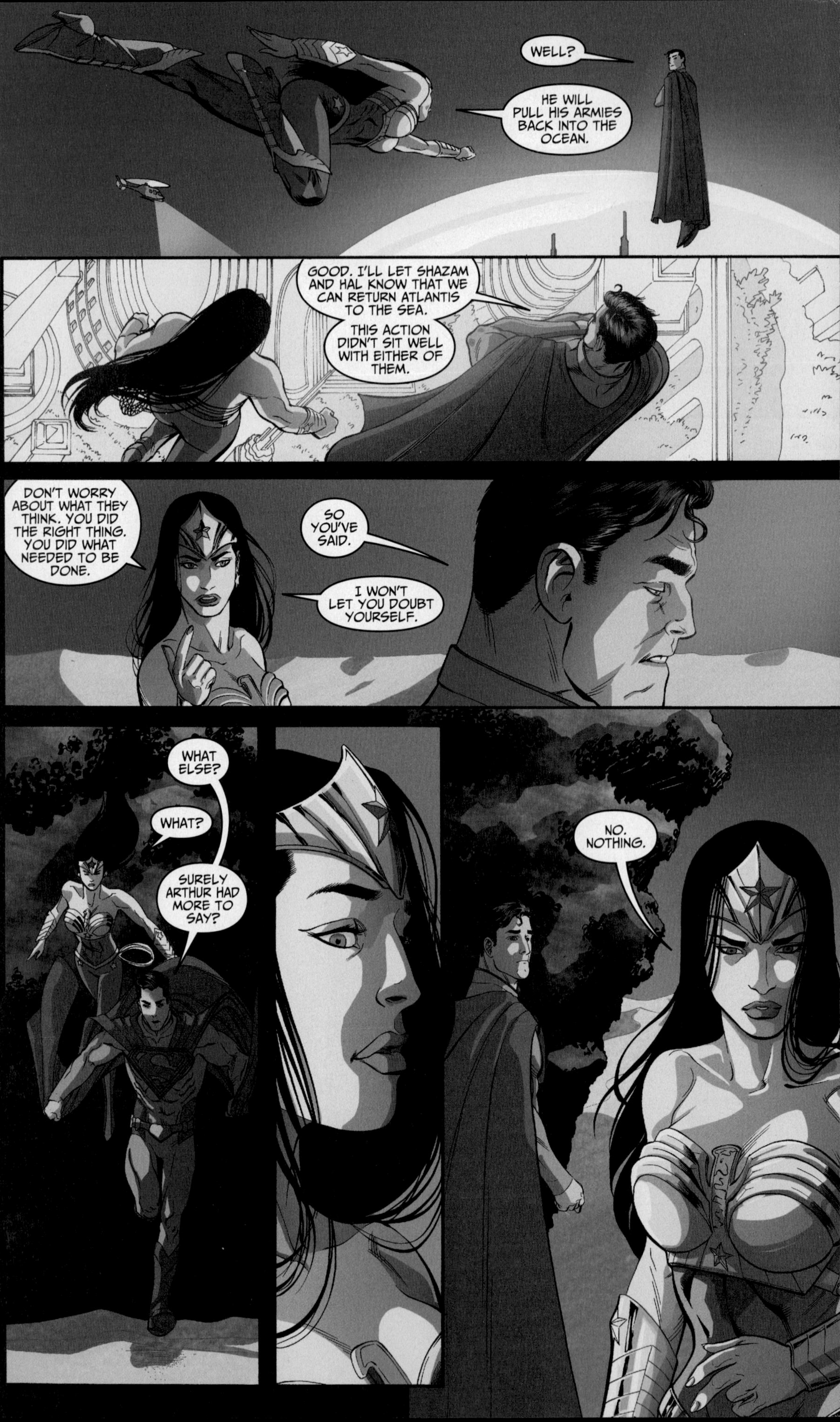
WELL?
HE WILL PULL HIS ARMIES BACK INTO THE OCEAN.
GOOD. I'LL LET SHAZAM AND HAL KNOW THAT WE CAN RETURN ATLANTIS TO THE SEA.
THIS ACTION DIDN'T SIT WELL WITH EITHER OF THEM.
DON'T WORRY ABOUT WHAT THEY THINK. YOU DID THE RIGHT THING. YOU DID WHAT NEEDED TO BE DONE.
SO YOU'VE SAID.
I WON'T LET YOU DOUBT YOURSELF.
WHAT ELSE?
WHAT?
SURELY ARTHUR HAD MORE TO SAY?
NO. NOTHING.

PART FIVE

Tom Derenick Jheremy Raapack Artists

Cover Art by Drew Johnson, Ray Snyder, and Kathryn Layno

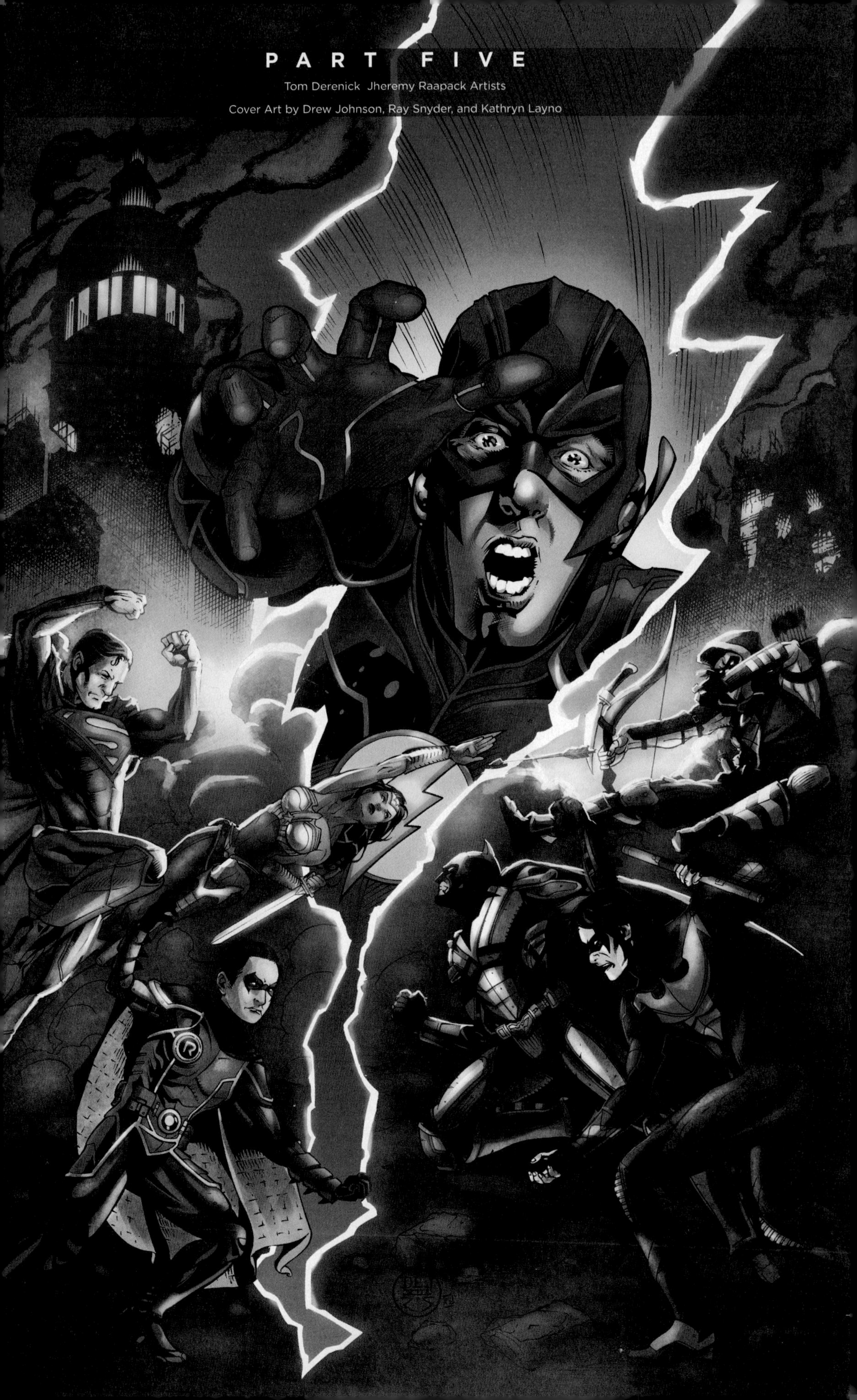

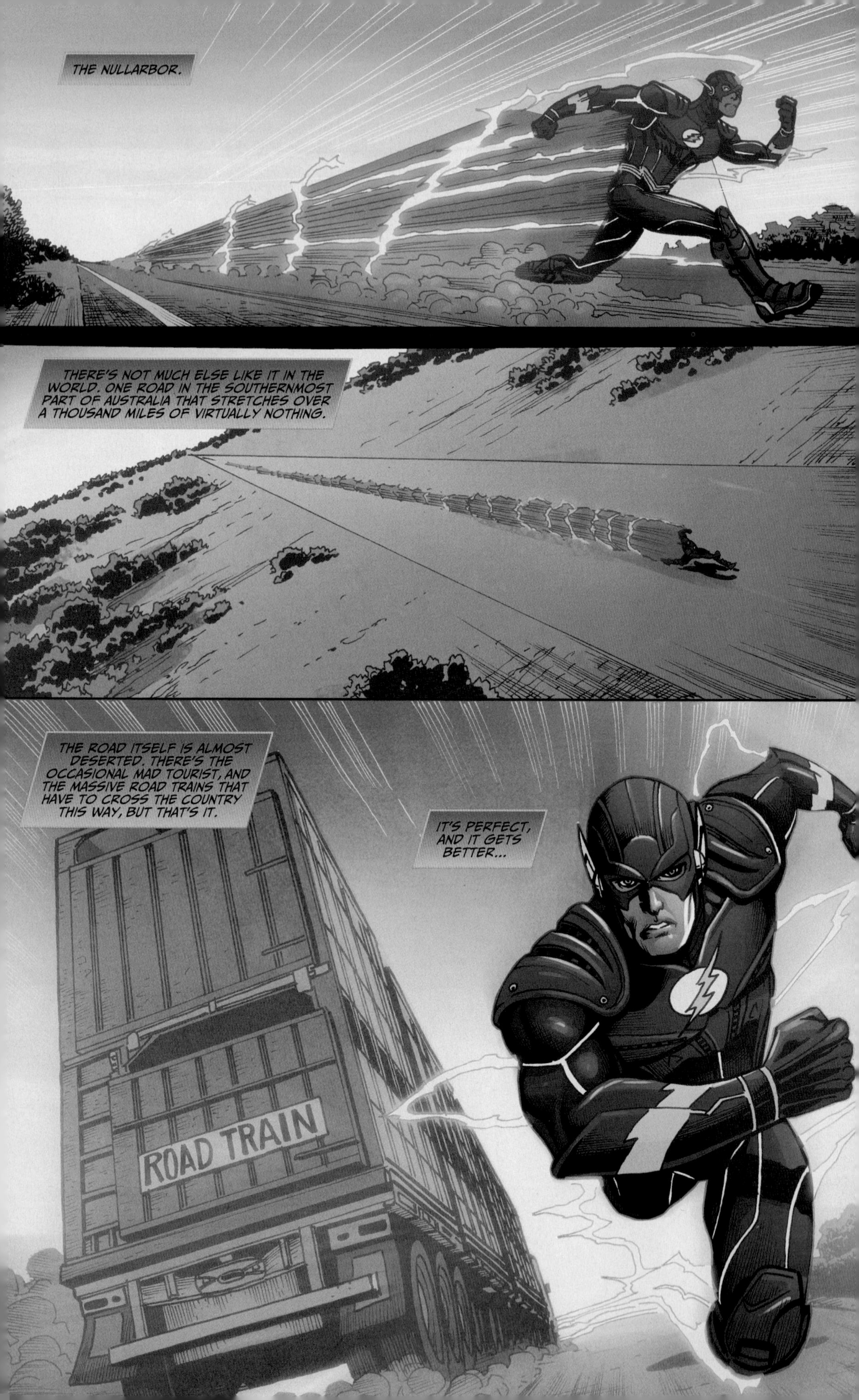
THE NULLARBOR.
THERE'S NOT MUCH ELSE LIKE IT IN THE WORLD. ONE ROAD IN THE SOUTHERNMOST PART OF AUSTRALIA THAT STRETCHES OVER A THOUSAND MILES OF VIRTUALLY NOTHING.
THE ROAD ITSELF IS ALMOST DESERTED. THERE'S THE OCCASIONAL MAD TOURIST, AND THE MASSIVE ROAD TRAINS THAT HAVE TO CROSS THE COUNTRY THIS WAY, BUT THAT'S IT.
IT'S PERFECT, AND IT GETS BETTER...
ROAD TRAIN

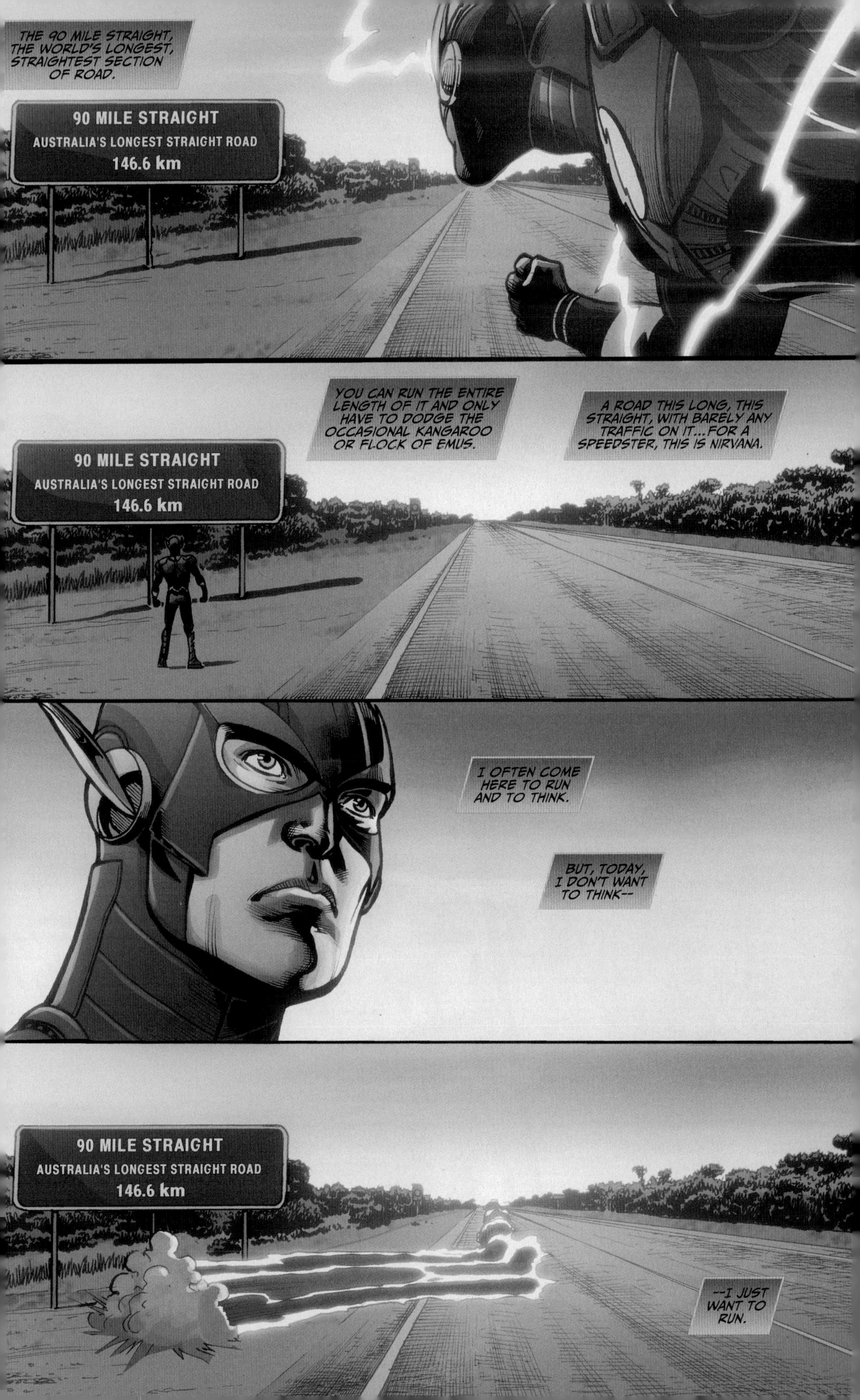
THE 90 MILE STRAIGHT, THE WORLD'S LONGEST, STRAIGHTEST SECTION OF ROAD.
90 MILE STRAIGHT
AUSTRALIA'S LONGEST STRAIGHT ROAD
146.6 km
YOU CAN RUN THE ENTIRE LENGTH OF IT AND ONLY HAVE TO DODGE THE OCCASIONAL KANGAROO OR FLOCK OF EMUS.
A ROAD THIS LONG, THIS STRAIGHT, WITH BARELY ANY TRAFFIC ON IT...FOR A SPEEDSTER, THIS IS NIRVANA.
90 MILE STRAIGHT
AUSTRALIA'S LONGEST STRAIGHT ROAD
146.6 km
I OFTEN COME HERE TO RUN AND TO THINK.
BUT, TODAY, I DON'T WANT TO THINK--
90 MILE STRAIGHT
AUSTRALIA'S LONGEST STRAIGHT ROAD
146.6 km
--I JUST WANT TO RUN.

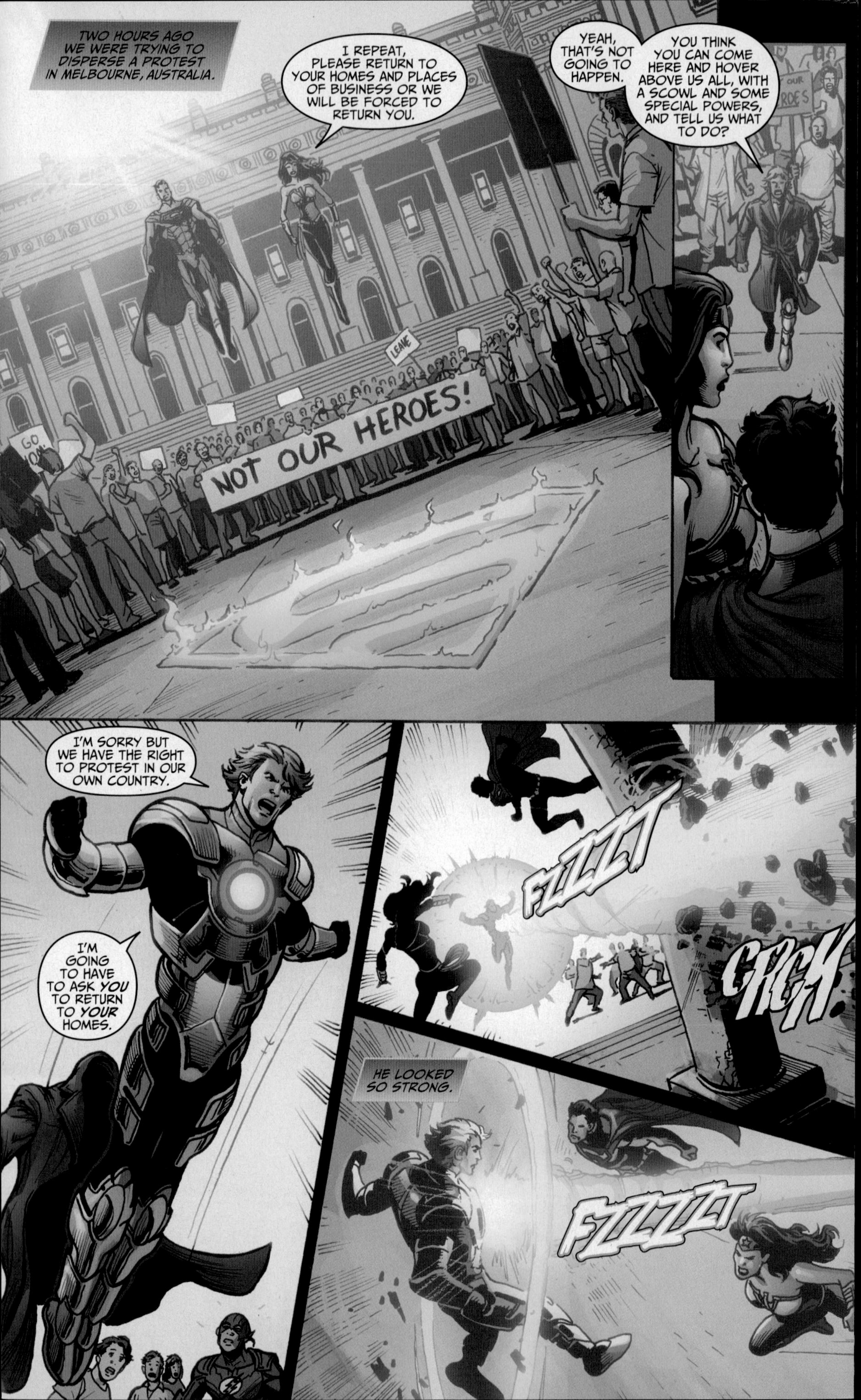
TWO HOURS AGO WE WERE TRYING TO DISPERSE A PROTEST IN MELBOURNE, AUSTRALIA.
I REPEAT, PLEASE RETURN TO YOUR HOMES AND PLACES OF BUSINESS OR WE WILL BE FORCED TO RETURN YOU.
YEAH, THAT'S NOT GOING TO HAPPEN.
YOU THINK YOU CAN COME HERE AND HOVER ABOVE US ALL, WITH A SCOWL AND SOME SPECIAL POWERS, AND TELL US WHAT TO DO?
LEAVE
NOT OUR HEROES!
I'M SORRY BUT WE HAVE THE RIGHT TO PROTEST IN OUR OWN COUNTRY.
I'M GOING TO HAVE TO ASK *YOU* TO RETURN TO *YOUR* HOMES.
FZZZT
CRCH
HE LOOKED SO STRONG.
FZZZZT

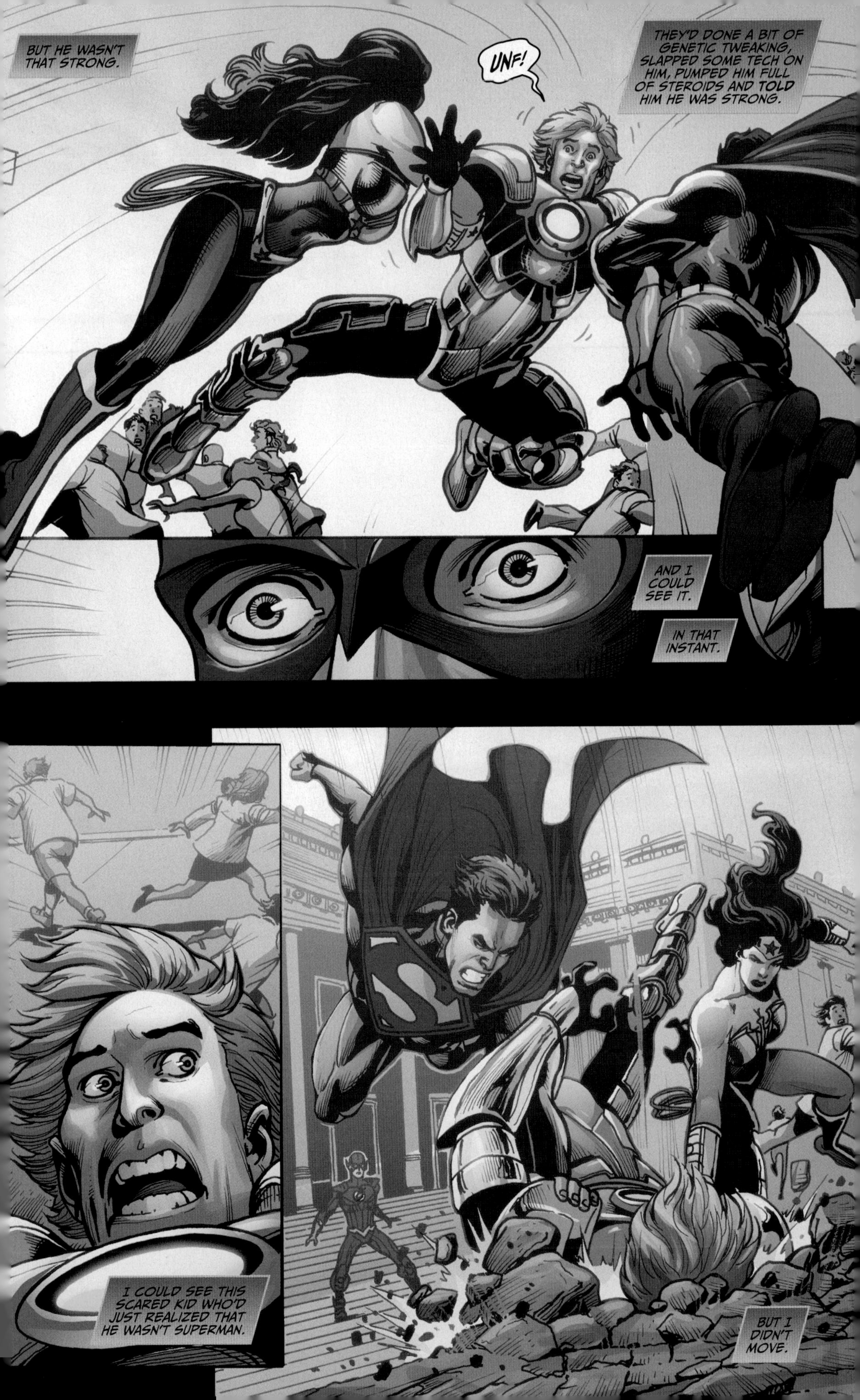
BUT HE WASN'T THAT STRONG.
UNF!
THEY'D DONE A BIT OF GENETIC TWEAKING, SLAPPED SOME TECH ON HIM, PUMPED HIM FULL OF STEROIDS AND TOLD HIM HE WAS STRONG.
AND I COULD SEE IT.
IN THAT INSTANT.
I COULD SEE THIS SCARED KID WHO'D JUST REALIZED THAT HE WASN'T SUPERMAN.
BUT I DIDN'T MOVE.

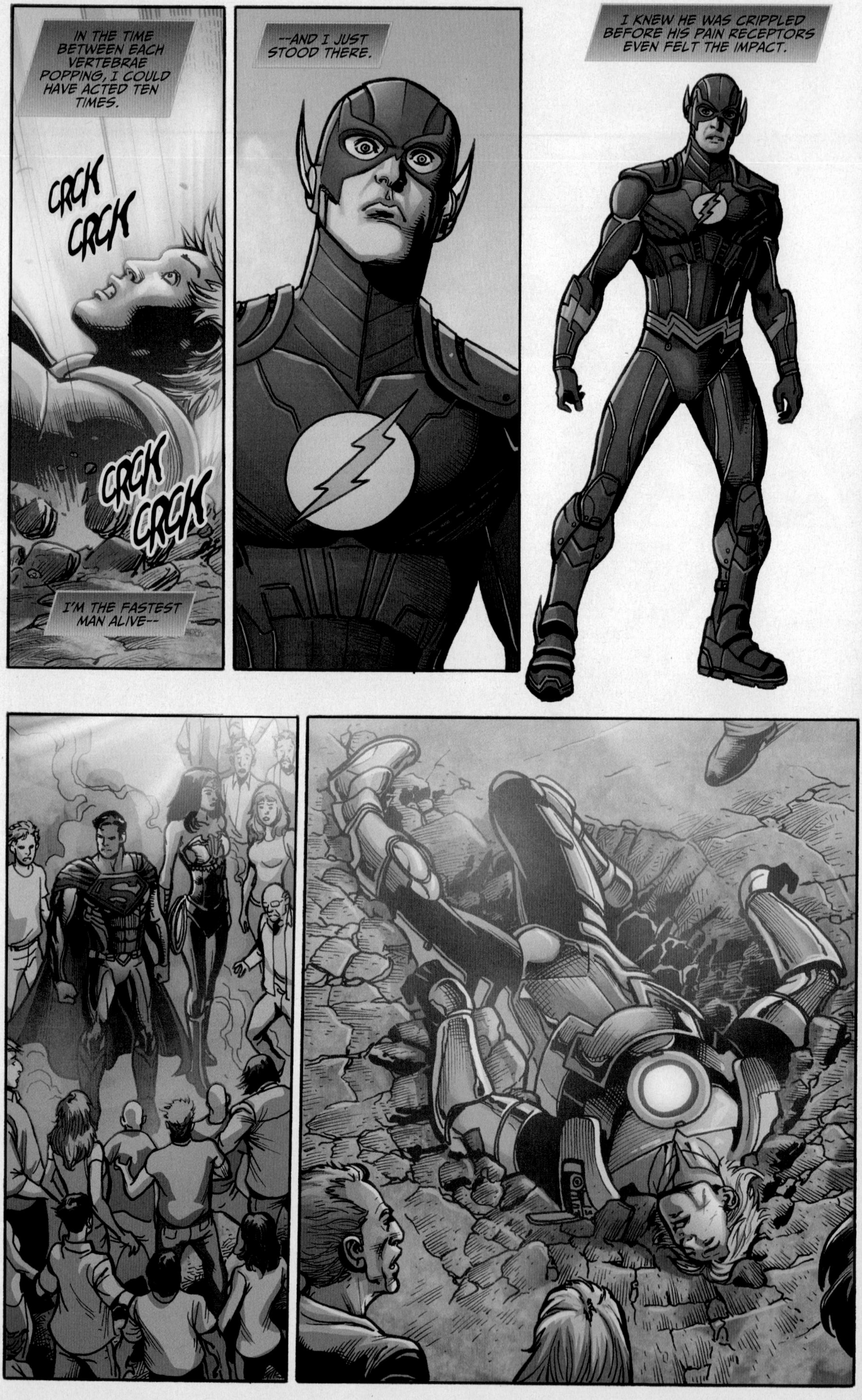

IN THE TIME BETWEEN EACH VERTEBRAE POPPING, I COULD HAVE ACTED TEN TIMES.
CRCK CRCK
CRCK CRCK
I'M THE FASTEST MAN ALIVE--
--AND I JUST STOOD THERE.
I KNEW HE WAS CRIPPLED BEFORE HIS PAIN RECEPTORS EVEN FELT THE IMPACT.

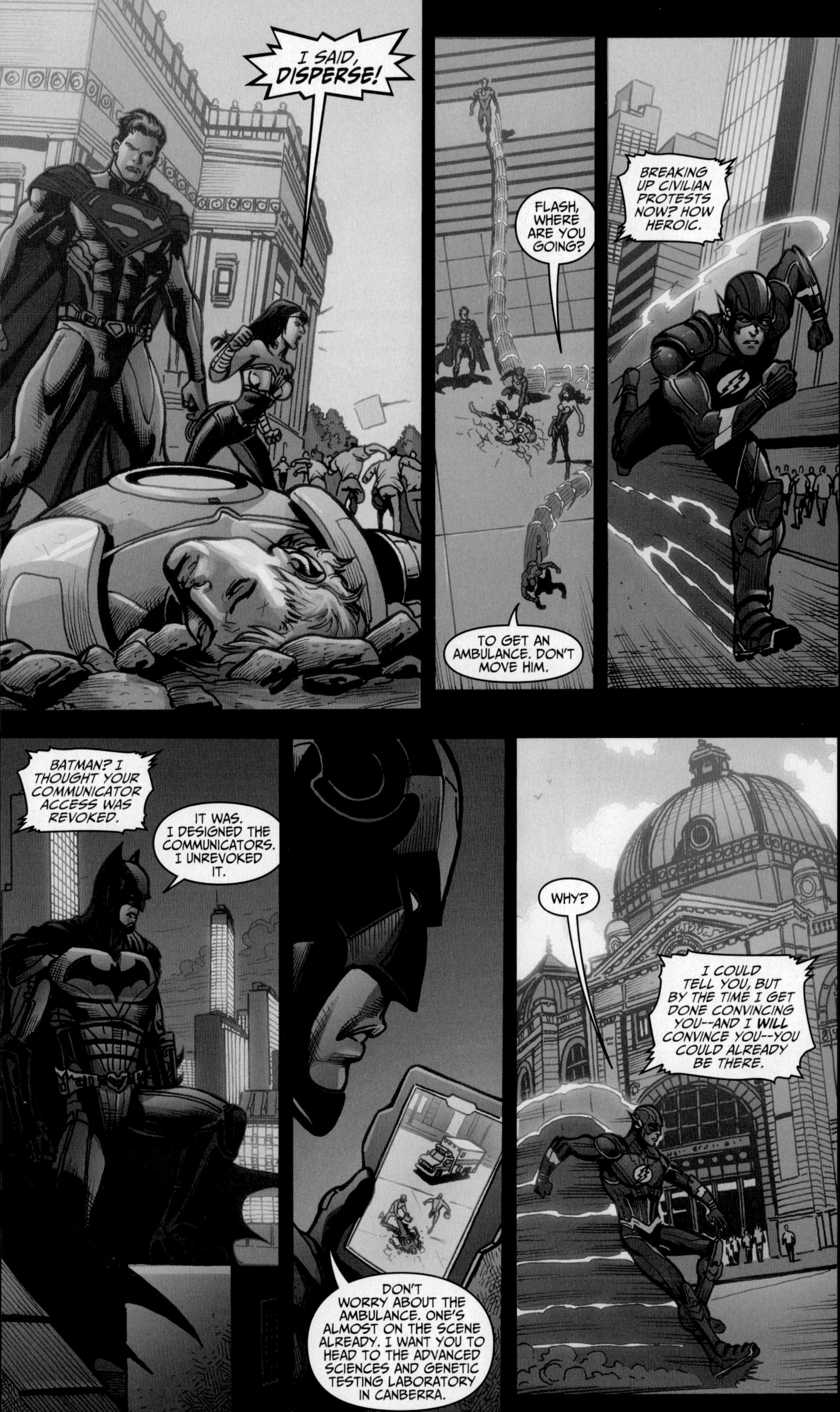
I SAID, DISPERSE!
FLASH, WHERE ARE YOU GOING?
TO GET AN AMBULANCE. DON'T MOVE HIM.
BREAKING UP CIVILIAN PROTESTS NOW? HOW HEROIC.
BATMAN? I THOUGHT YOUR COMMUNICATOR ACCESS WAS REVOKED.
IT WAS. I DESIGNED THE COMMUNICATORS. I UNREVOKED IT.
DON'T WORRY ABOUT THE AMBULANCE. ONE'S ALMOST ON THE SCENE ALREADY. I WANT YOU TO HEAD TO THE ADVANCED SCIENCES AND GENETIC TESTING LABORATORY IN CANBERRA.
WHY?
I COULD TELL YOU, BUT BY THE TIME I GET DONE CONVINCING YOU--AND I WILL CONVINCE YOU--YOU COULD ALREADY BE THERE.

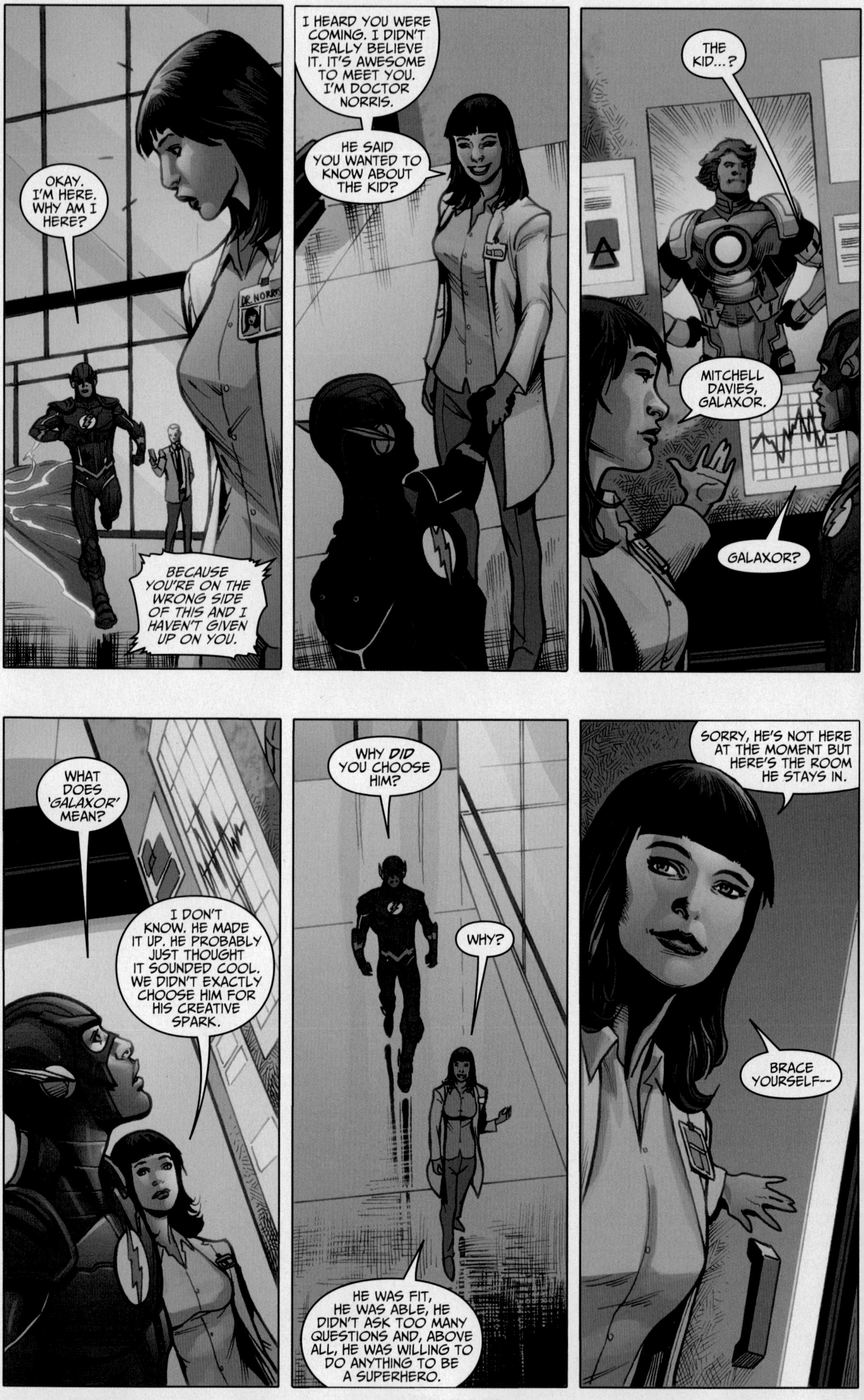
OKAY. I'M HERE. WHY AM I HERE?
BECAUSE YOU'RE ON THE WRONG SIDE OF THIS AND I HAVEN'T GIVEN UP ON YOU.
I HEARD YOU WERE COMING. I DIDN'T REALLY BELIEVE IT. IT'S AWESOME TO MEET YOU. I'M DOCTOR NORRIS.
HE SAID YOU WANTED TO KNOW ABOUT THE KID?
THE KID...?
MITCHELL DAVIES, GALAXOR.
GALAXOR?
WHAT DOES 'GALAXOR' MEAN?
I DON'T KNOW. HE MADE IT UP. HE PROBABLY JUST THOUGHT IT SOUNDED COOL. WE DIDN'T EXACTLY CHOOSE HIM FOR HIS CREATIVE SPARK.
WHY DID YOU CHOOSE HIM?
WHY?
HE WAS FIT, HE WAS ABLE, HE DIDN'T ASK TOO MANY QUESTIONS AND, ABOVE ALL, HE WAS WILLING TO DO ANYTHING TO BE A SUPERHERO.
SORRY, HE'S NOT HERE AT THE MOMENT BUT HERE'S THE ROOM HE STAYS IN.
BRACE YOURSELF--

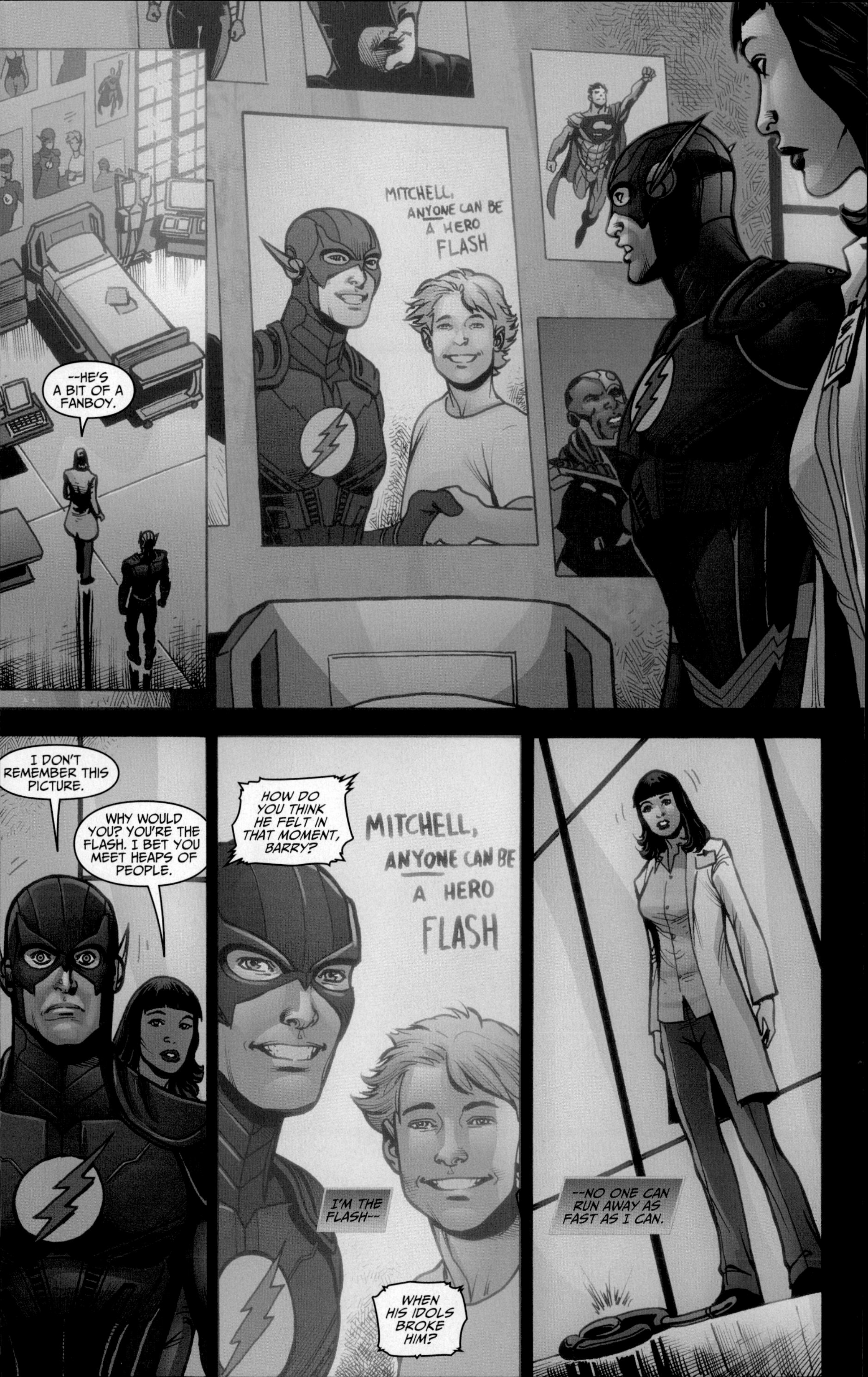
--HE'S A BIT OF A FANBOY.
MITCHELL, ANYONE CAN BE A HERO FLASH
I DON'T REMEMBER THIS PICTURE.
WHY WOULD YOU? YOU'RE THE FLASH. I BET YOU MEET HEAPS OF PEOPLE.
HOW DO YOU THINK HE FELT IN THAT MOMENT, BARRY?
MITCHELL, ANYONE CAN BE A HERO FLASH
I'M THE FLASH--
WHEN HIS IDOLS BROKE HIM?
--NO ONE CAN RUN AWAY AS FAST AS I CAN.

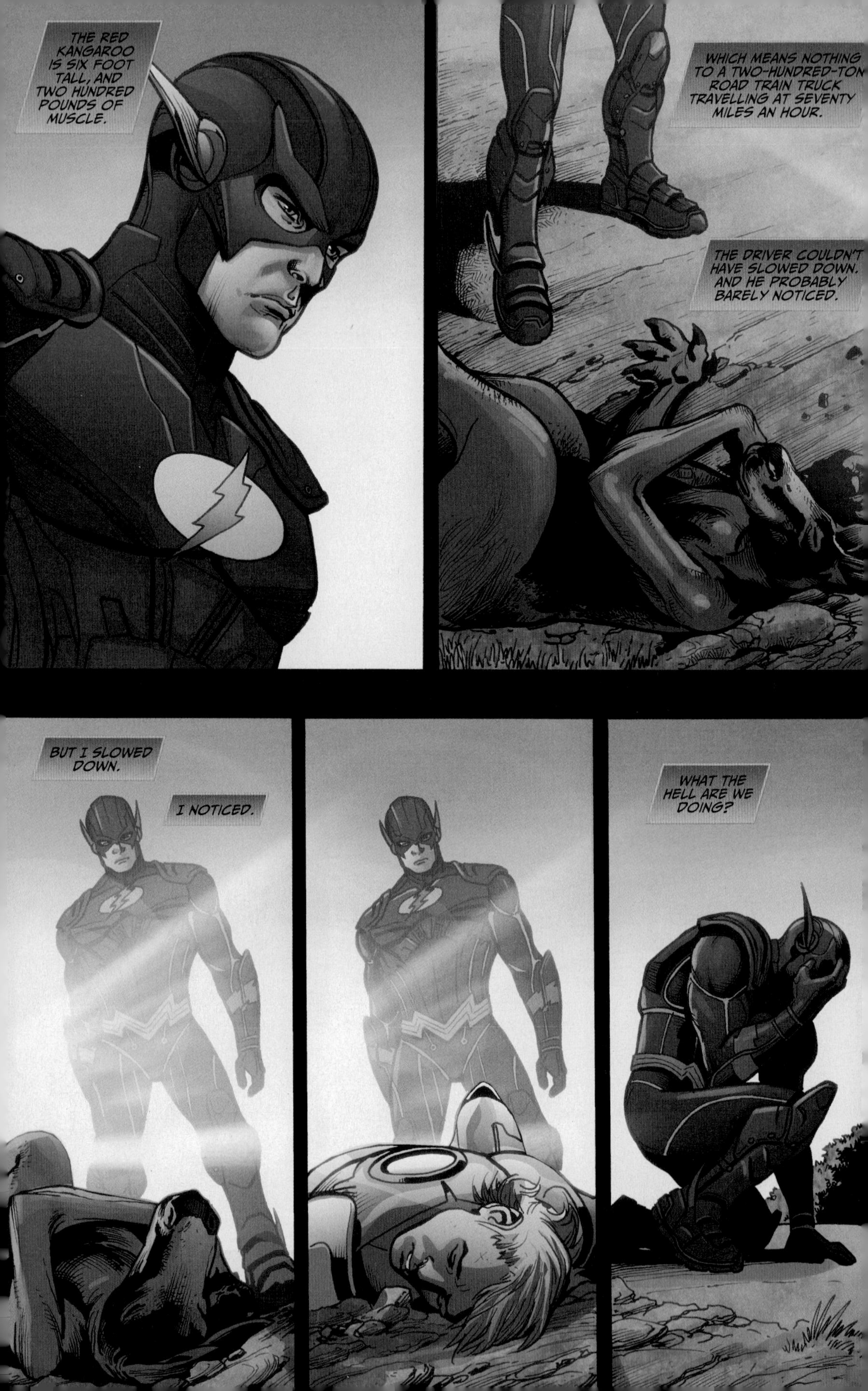
THE RED KANGAROO IS SIX FOOT TALL, AND TWO HUNDRED POUNDS OF MUSCLE.
WHICH MEANS NOTHING TO A TWO-HUNDRED-TON ROAD TRAIN TRUCK TRAVELLING AT SEVENTY MILES AN HOUR.
THE DRIVER COULDN'T HAVE SLOWED DOWN. AND HE PROBABLY BARELY NOTICED.
BUT I SLOWED DOWN.
I NOTICED.
WHAT THE HELL ARE WE DOING?

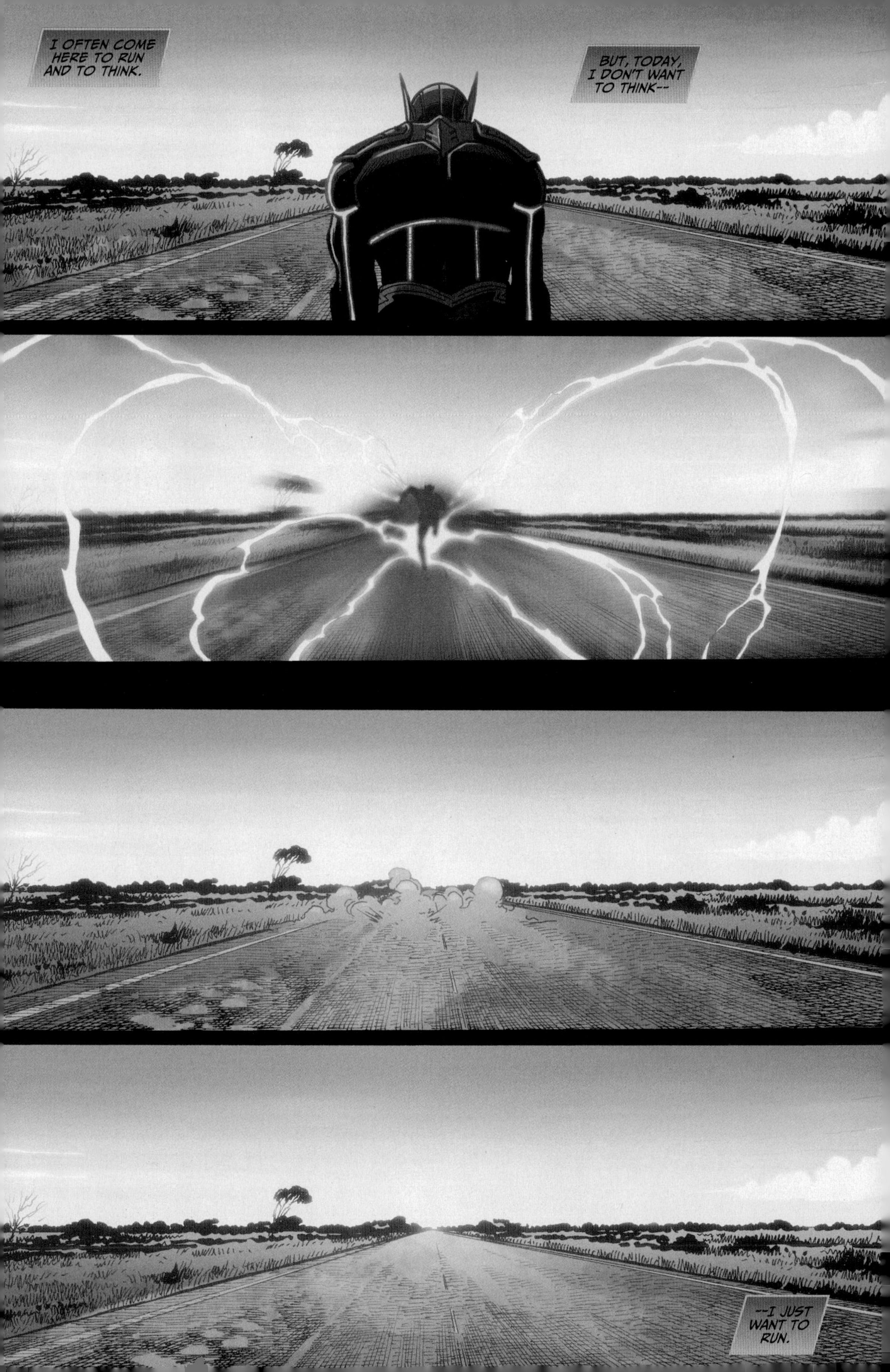
I OFTEN COME HERE TO RUN AND TO THINK.
BUT, TODAY, I DON'T WANT TO THINK--
--I JUST WANT TO RUN.

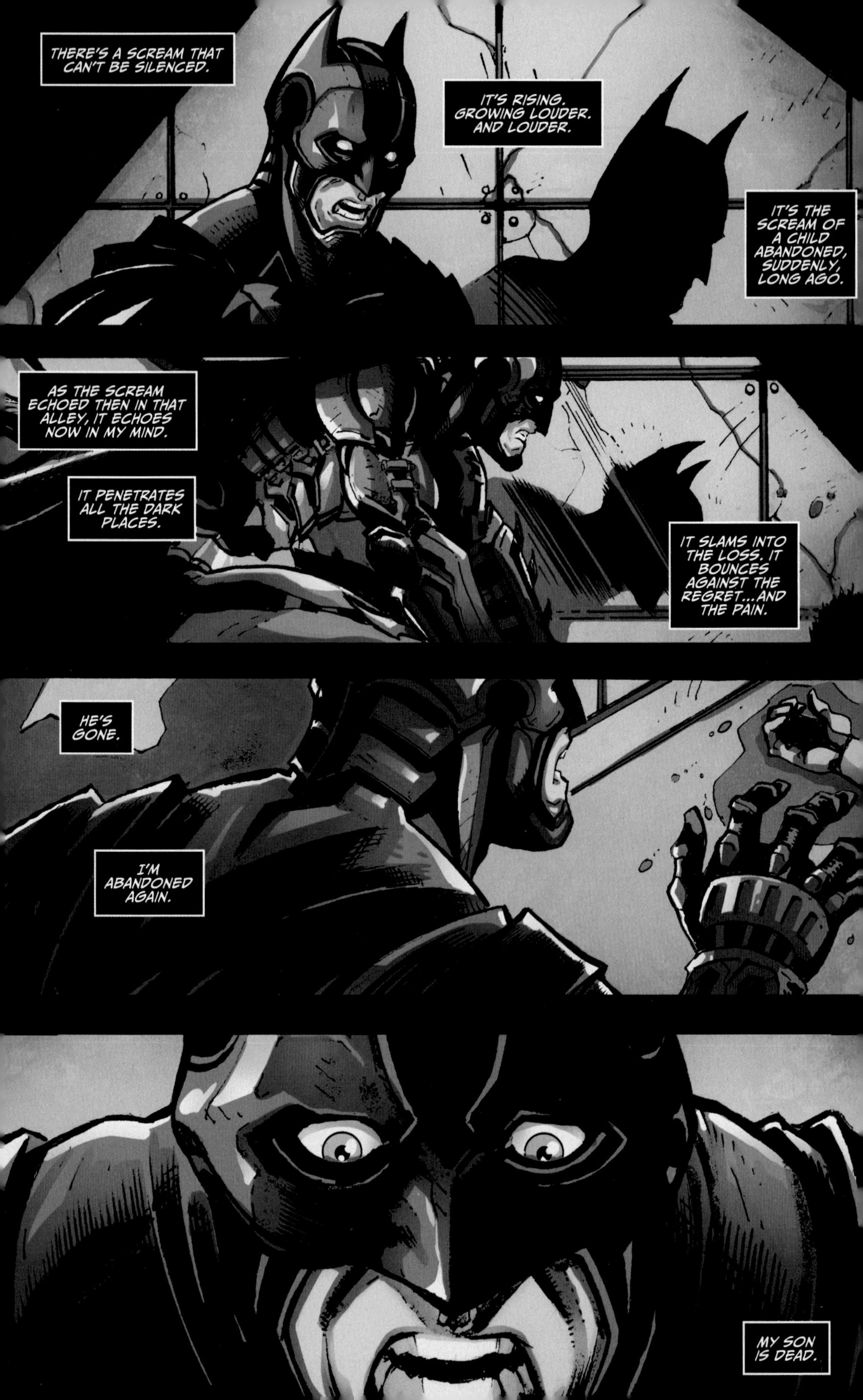
THERE'S A SCREAM THAT CAN'T BE SILENCED.
IT'S RISING. GROWING LOUDER. AND LOUDER.
IT'S THE SCREAM OF A CHILD ABANDONED, SUDDENLY, LONG AGO.
AS THE SCREAM ECHOED THEN IN THAT ALLEY, IT ECHOES NOW IN MY MIND.
IT PENETRATES ALL THE DARK PLACES.
IT SLAMS INTO THE LOSS. IT BOUNCES AGAINST THE REGRET...AND THE PAIN.
HE'S GONE.
I'M ABANDONED AGAIN.
MY SON IS DEAD.

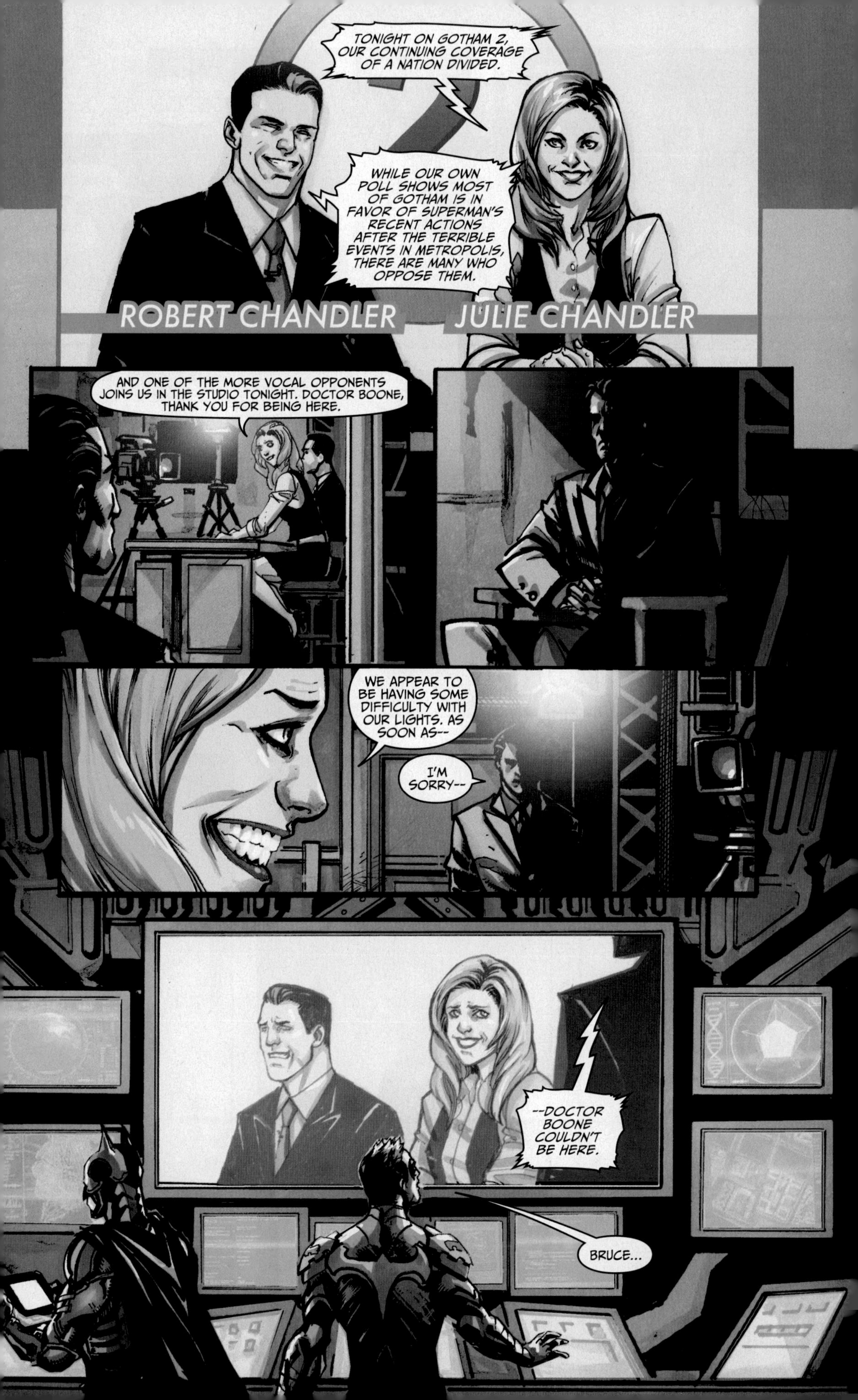
TONIGHT ON GOTHAM 2, OUR CONTINUING COVERAGE OF A NATION DIVIDED.
WHILE OUR OWN POLL SHOWS MOST OF GOTHAM IS IN FAVOR OF SUPERMAN'S RECENT ACTIONS AFTER THE TERRIBLE EVENTS IN METROPOLIS, THERE ARE MANY WHO OPPOSE THEM.
ROBERT CHANDLER
JULIE CHANDLER
AND ONE OF THE MORE VOCAL OPPONENTS JOINS US IN THE STUDIO TONIGHT. DOCTOR BOONE, THANK YOU FOR BEING HERE.
WE APPEAR TO BE HAVING SOME DIFFICULTY WITH OUR LIGHTS. AS SOON AS--
I'M SORRY--
--DOCTOR BOONE COULDN'T BE HERE.
BRUCE...

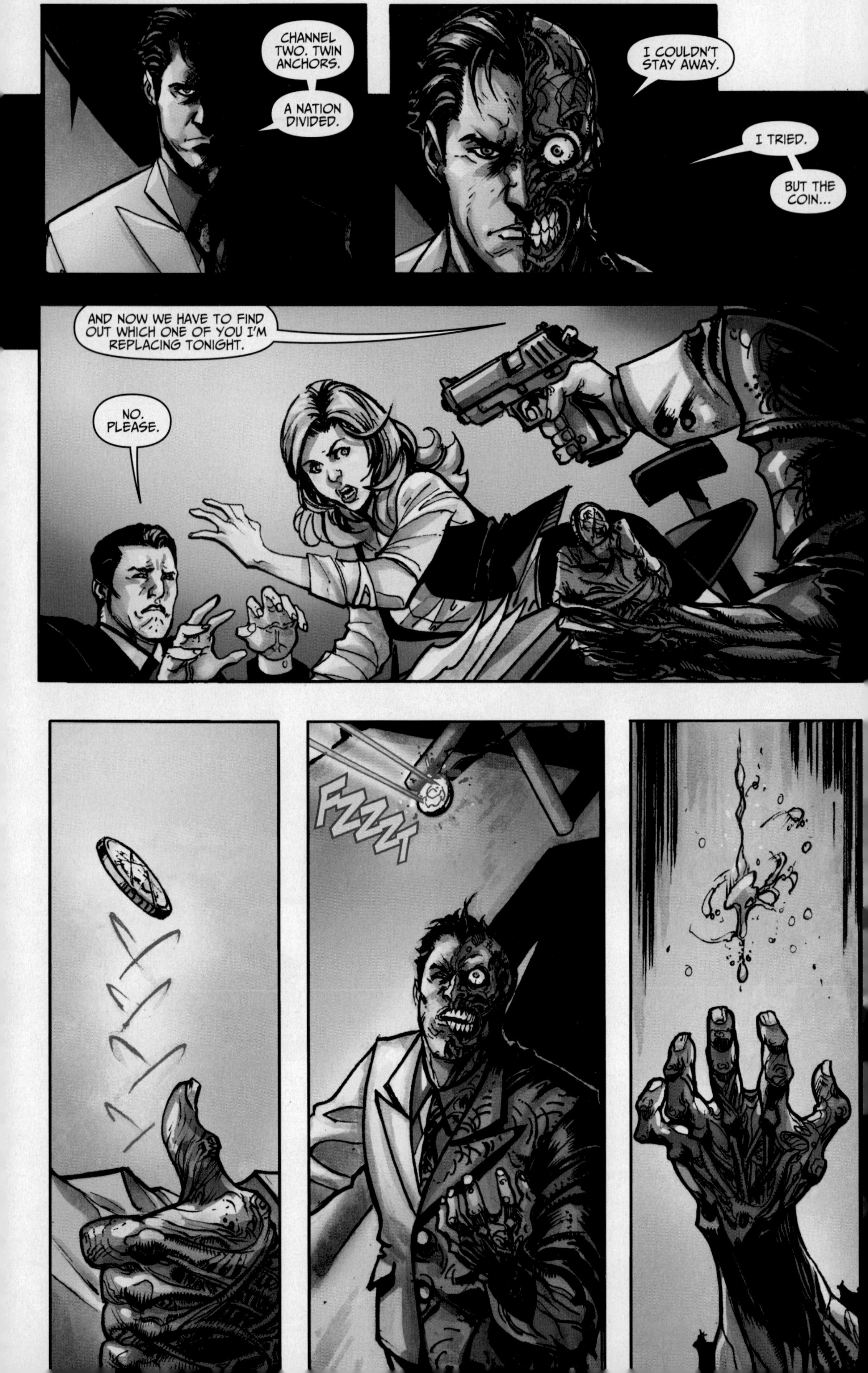
CHANNEL TWO. TWIN ANCHORS.
A NATION DIVIDED.
I COULDN'T STAY AWAY.
I TRIED.
BUT THE COIN...
AND NOW WE HAVE TO FIND OUT WHICH ONE OF YOU I'M REPLACING TONIGHT.
NO. PLEASE.
FZZZT

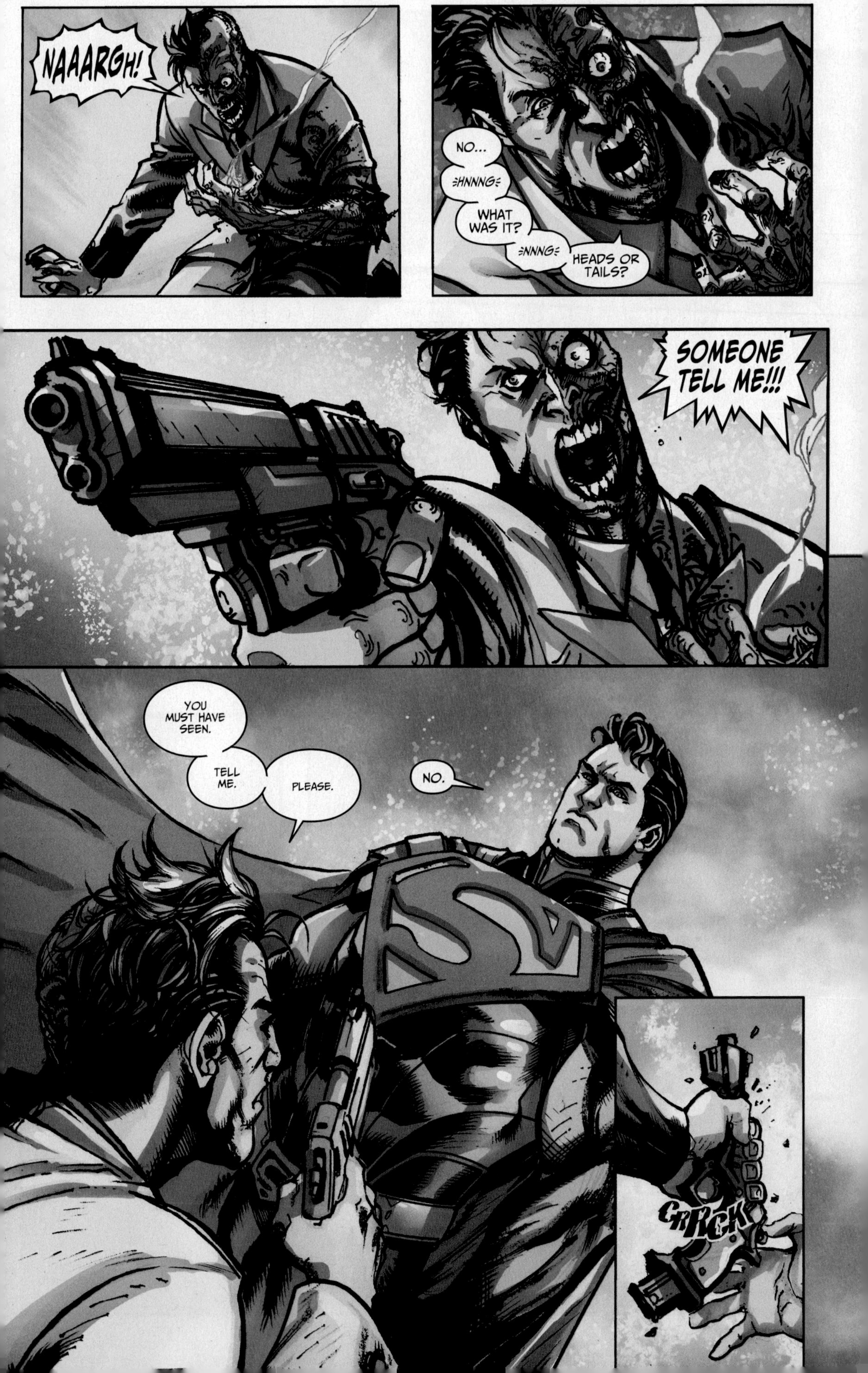
NAAARGH!
NO...
HNNNG
WHAT WAS IT?
NNNG
HEADS OR TAILS?
SOMEONE TELL ME!!!
YOU MUST HAVE SEEN.
TELL ME.
PLEASE.
NO.
CRRCK

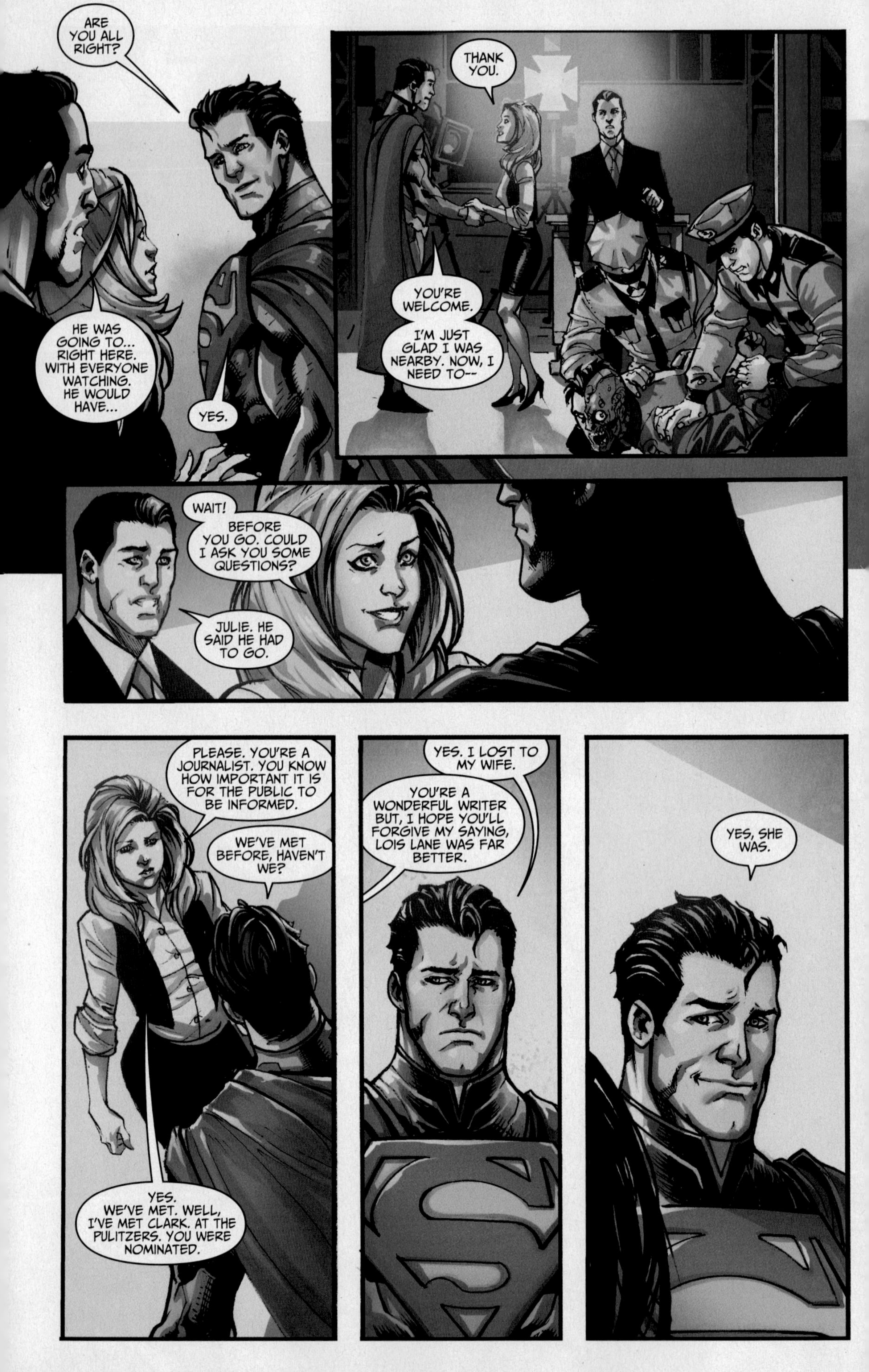
ARE YOU ALL RIGHT?
HE WAS GOING TO... RIGHT HERE. WITH EVERYONE WATCHING. HE WOULD HAVE...
YES.
THANK YOU.
YOU'RE WELCOME.
I'M JUST GLAD I WAS NEARBY. NOW, I NEED TO--
WAIT!
BEFORE YOU GO. COULD I ASK YOU SOME QUESTIONS?
JULIE. HE SAID HE HAD TO GO.
PLEASE. YOU'RE A JOURNALIST. YOU KNOW HOW IMPORTANT IT IS FOR THE PUBLIC TO BE INFORMED.
WE'VE MET BEFORE, HAVEN'T WE?
YES. WE'VE MET. WELL, I'VE MET CLARK. AT THE PULITZERS. YOU WERE NOMINATED.
YES. I LOST TO MY WIFE.
YOU'RE A WONDERFUL WRITER BUT, I HOPE YOU'LL FORGIVE MY SAYING, LOIS LANE WAS FAR BETTER.
YES, SHE WAS.

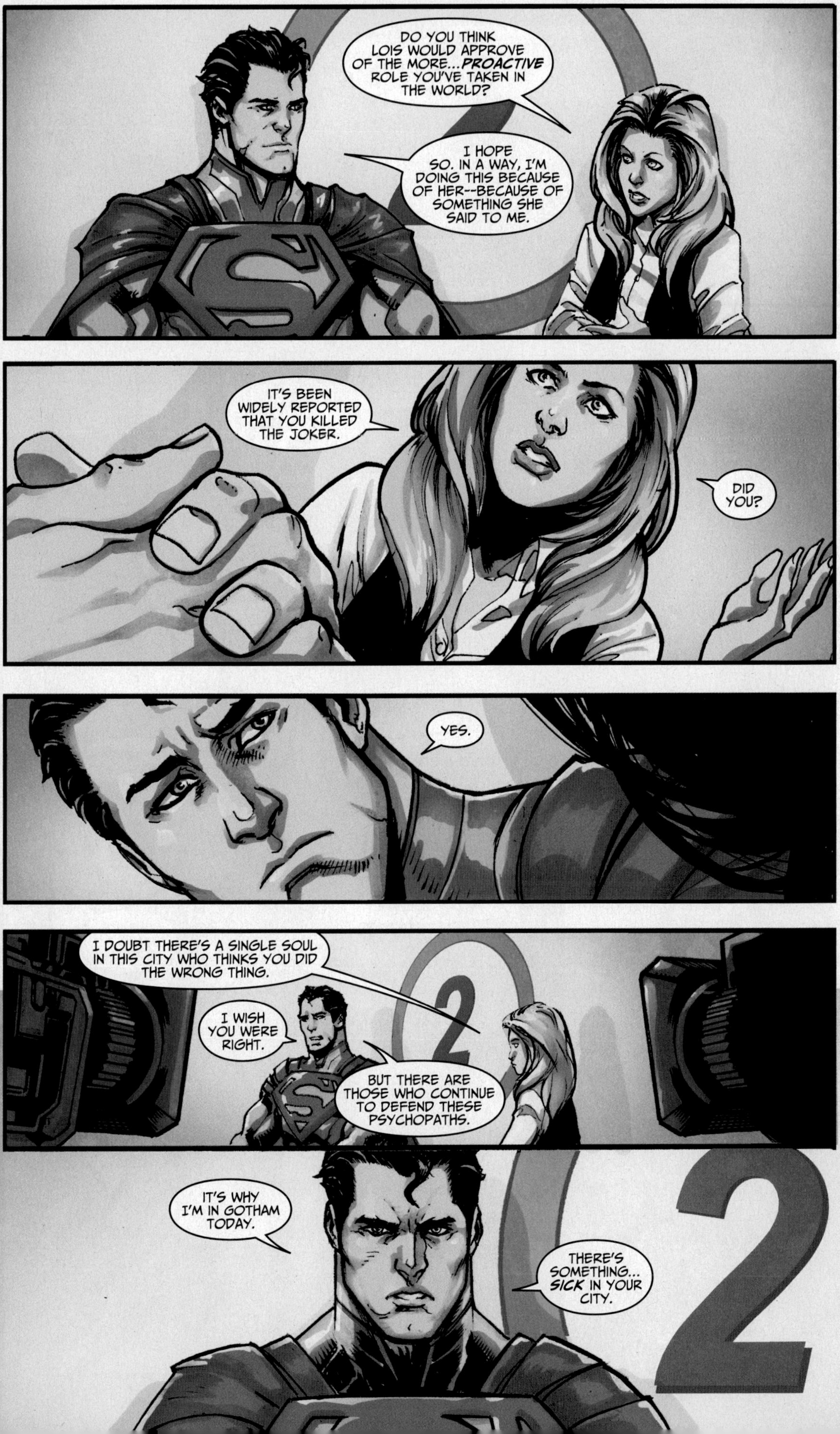
DO YOU THINK LOIS WOULD APPROVE OF THE MORE...*PROACTIVE* ROLE YOU'VE TAKEN IN THE WORLD?
I HOPE SO. IN A WAY, I'M DOING THIS BECAUSE OF HER--BECAUSE OF SOMETHING SHE SAID TO ME.
IT'S BEEN WIDELY REPORTED THAT YOU KILLED THE JOKER.
DID YOU?
YES.
I DOUBT THERE'S A SINGLE SOUL IN THIS CITY WHO THINKS YOU DID THE WRONG THING.
I WISH YOU WERE RIGHT.
BUT THERE ARE THOSE WHO CONTINUE TO DEFEND THESE PSYCHOPATHS.
IT'S WHY I'M IN GOTHAM TODAY.
THERE'S SOMETHING... *SICK* IN YOUR CITY.

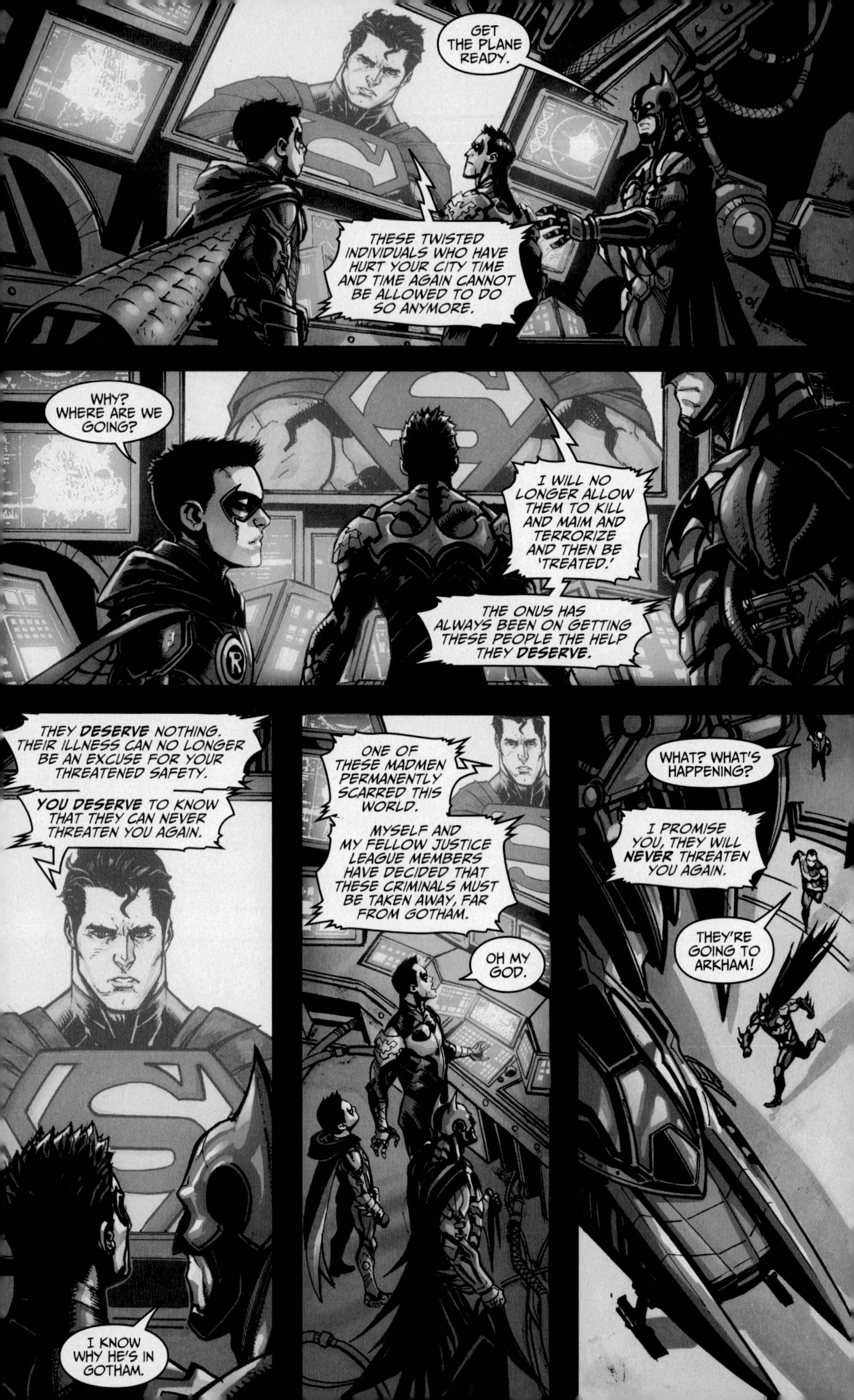
GET THE PLANE READY.
THESE TWISTED INDIVIDUALS WHO HAVE HURT YOUR CITY TIME AND TIME AGAIN CANNOT BE ALLOWED TO DO SO ANYMORE.
WHY? WHERE ARE WE GOING?
I WILL NO LONGER ALLOW THEM TO KILL AND MAIM AND TERRORIZE AND THEN BE 'TREATED.'
THE ONUS HAS ALWAYS BEEN ON GETTING THESE PEOPLE THE HELP THEY DESERVE.
THEY DESERVE NOTHING. THEIR ILLNESS CAN NO LONGER BE AN EXCUSE FOR YOUR THREATENED SAFETY.
YOU DESERVE TO KNOW THAT THEY CAN NEVER THREATEN YOU AGAIN.
I KNOW WHY HE'S IN GOTHAM.
ONE OF THESE MADMEN PERMANENTLY SCARRED THIS WORLD.
MYSELF AND MY FELLOW JUSTICE LEAGUE MEMBERS HAVE DECIDED THAT THESE CRIMINALS MUST BE TAKEN AWAY, FAR FROM GOTHAM.
OH MY GOD.
WHAT? WHAT'S HAPPENING?
I PROMISE YOU, THEY WILL NEVER THREATEN YOU AGAIN.
THEY'RE GOING TO ARKHAM!

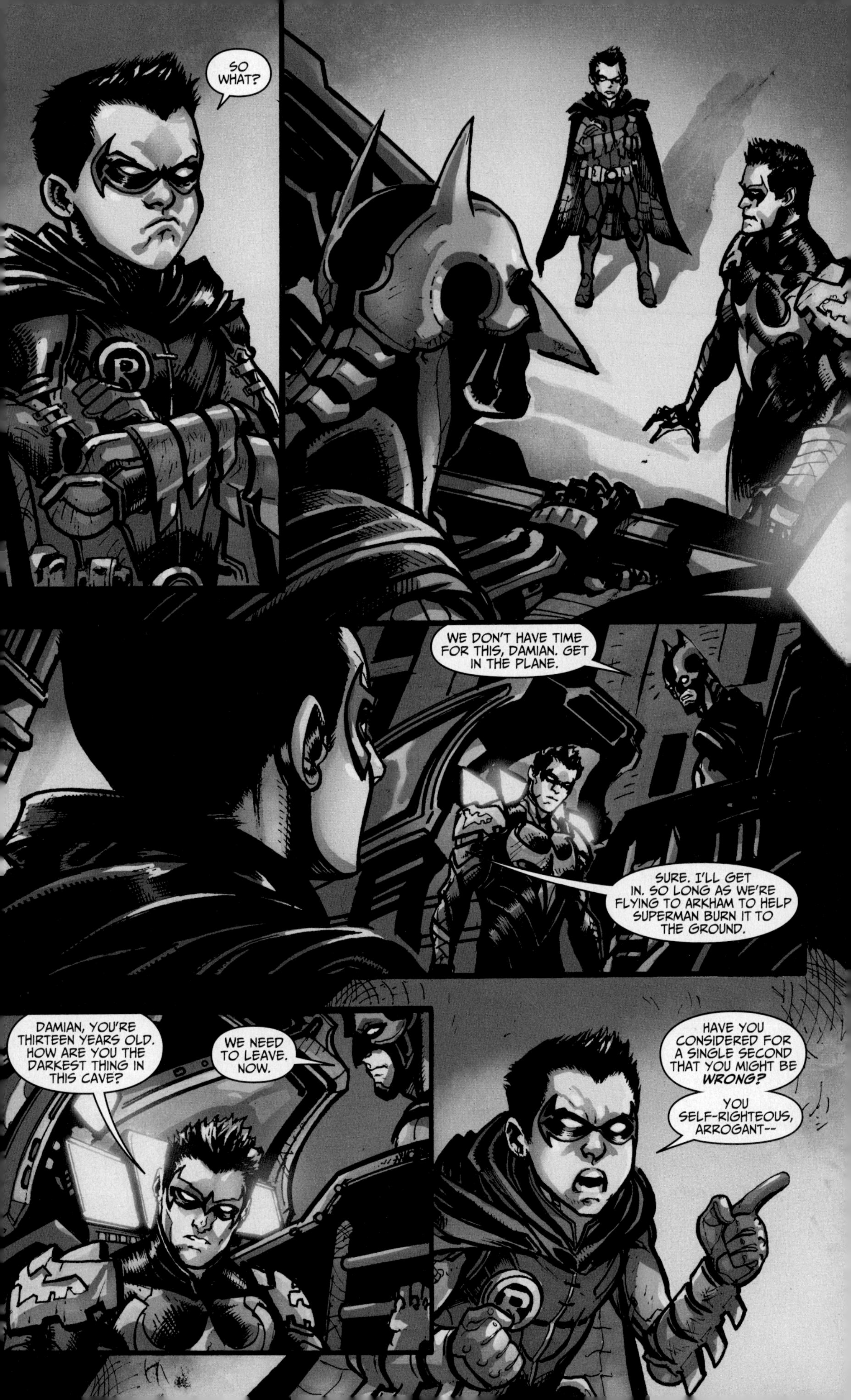
SO WHAT?
WE DON'T HAVE TIME FOR THIS, DAMIAN. GET IN THE PLANE.
SURE. I'LL GET IN. SO LONG AS WE'RE FLYING TO ARKHAM TO HELP SUPERMAN BURN IT TO THE GROUND.
DAMIAN, YOU'RE THIRTEEN YEARS OLD. HOW ARE YOU THE DARKEST THING IN THIS CAVE?
WE NEED TO LEAVE. NOW.
HAVE YOU CONSIDERED FOR A SINGLE SECOND THAT YOU MIGHT BE WRONG?
YOU SELF-RIGHTEOUS, ARROGANT--

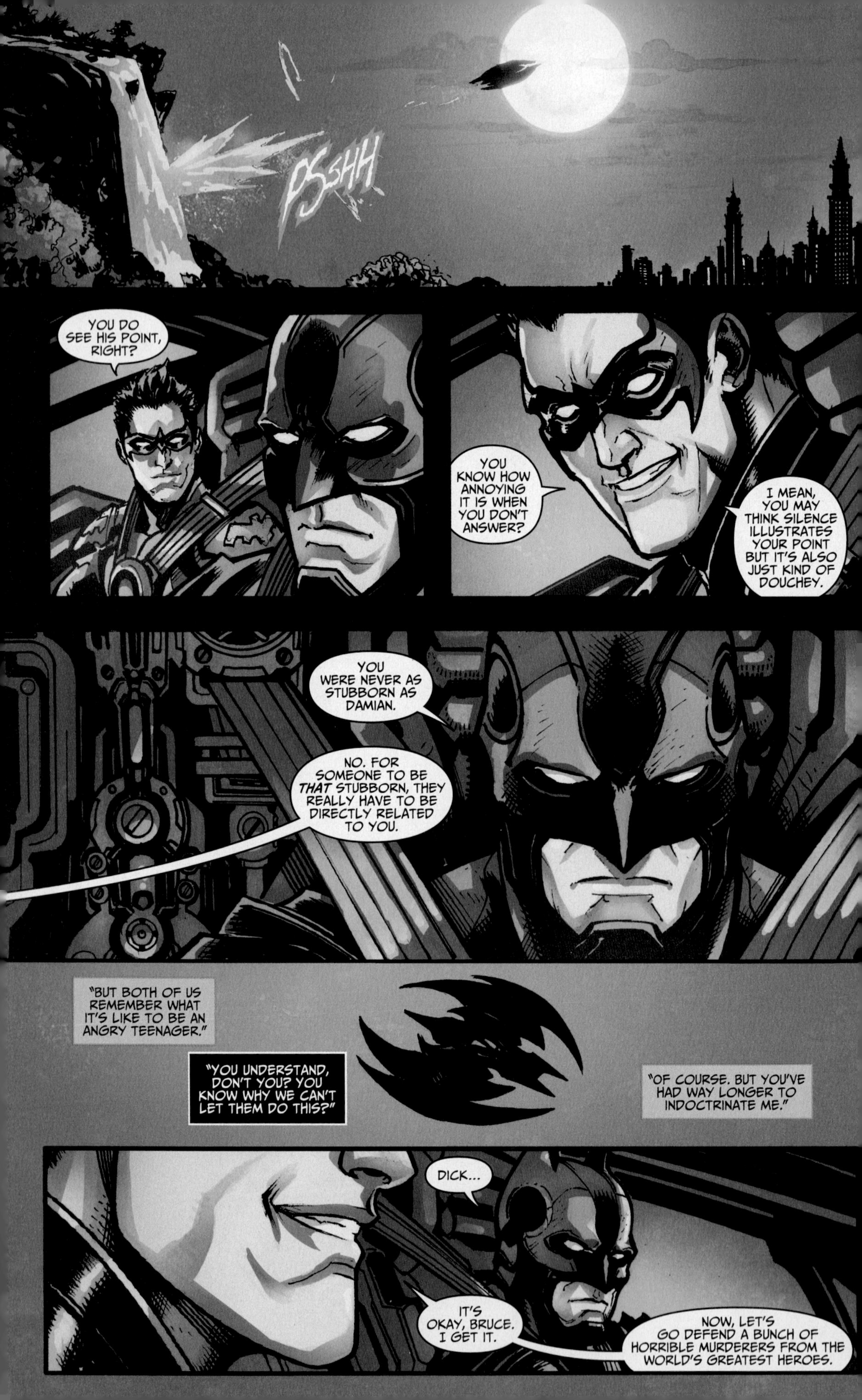
PSSHH
YOU DO SEE HIS POINT, RIGHT?
YOU KNOW HOW ANNOYING IT IS WHEN YOU DON'T ANSWER?
I MEAN, YOU MAY THINK SILENCE ILLUSTRATES YOUR POINT BUT IT'S ALSO JUST KIND OF DOUCHEY.
YOU WERE NEVER AS STUBBORN AS DAMIAN.
NO. FOR SOMEONE TO BE *THAT* STUBBORN, THEY REALLY HAVE TO BE DIRECTLY RELATED TO YOU.
"BUT BOTH OF US REMEMBER WHAT IT'S LIKE TO BE AN ANGRY TEENAGER."
"YOU UNDERSTAND, DON'T YOU? YOU KNOW WHY WE CAN'T LET THEM DO THIS?"
"OF COURSE. BUT YOU'VE HAD WAY LONGER TO INDOCTRINATE ME."
DICK...
IT'S OKAY, BRUCE. I GET IT.
NOW, LET'S GO DEFEND A BUNCH OF HORRIBLE MURDERERS FROM THE WORLD'S GREATEST HEROES.

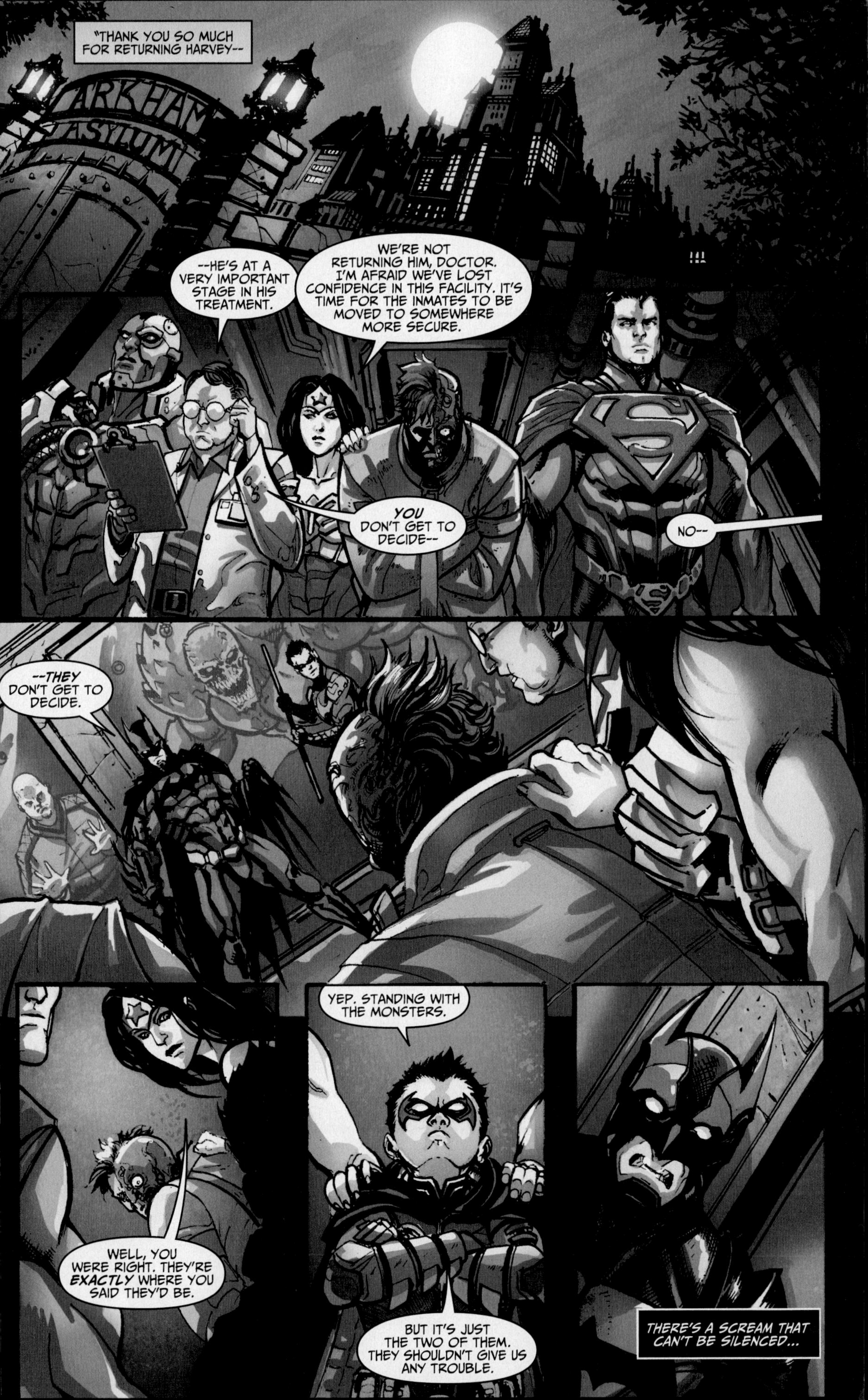
"THANK YOU SO MUCH FOR RETURNING HARVEY--
ARKHAM ASYLUM
--HE'S AT A VERY IMPORTANT STAGE IN HIS TREATMENT.
WE'RE NOT RETURNING HIM, DOCTOR. I'M AFRAID WE'VE LOST CONFIDENCE IN THIS FACILITY. IT'S TIME FOR THE INMATES TO BE MOVED TO SOMEWHERE MORE SECURE.
YOU DON'T GET TO DECIDE--
NO--
--THEY DON'T GET TO DECIDE.
WELL, YOU WERE RIGHT. THEY'RE *EXACTLY* WHERE YOU SAID THEY'D BE.
YEP. STANDING WITH THE MONSTERS.
BUT IT'S JUST THE TWO OF THEM. THEY SHOULDN'T GIVE US ANY TROUBLE.
THERE'S A SCREAM THAT CAN'T BE SILENCED...

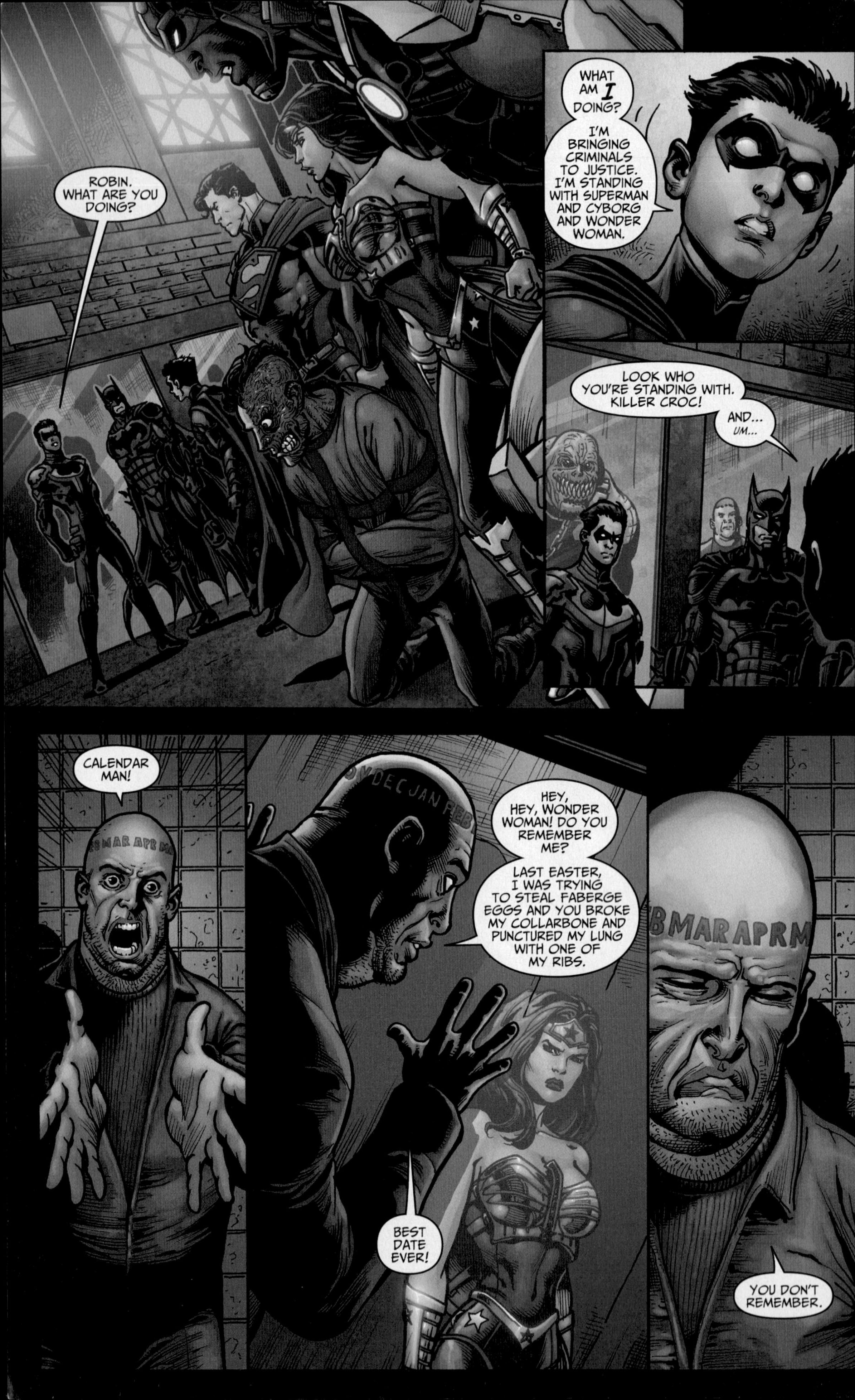
ROBIN. WHAT ARE YOU DOING?
WHAT AM I DOING?
I'M BRINGING CRIMINALS TO JUSTICE. I'M STANDING WITH SUPERMAN AND CYBORG AND WONDER WOMAN.
LOOK WHO YOU'RE STANDING WITH. KILLER CROC!
AND... UM...
CALENDAR MAN!
HEY, HEY, WONDER WOMAN! DO YOU REMEMBER ME?
LAST EASTER, I WAS TRYING TO STEAL FABERGE EGGS AND YOU BROKE MY COLLARBONE AND PUNCTURED MY LUNG WITH ONE OF MY RIBS.
BEST DATE EVER!
YOU DON'T REMEMBER.

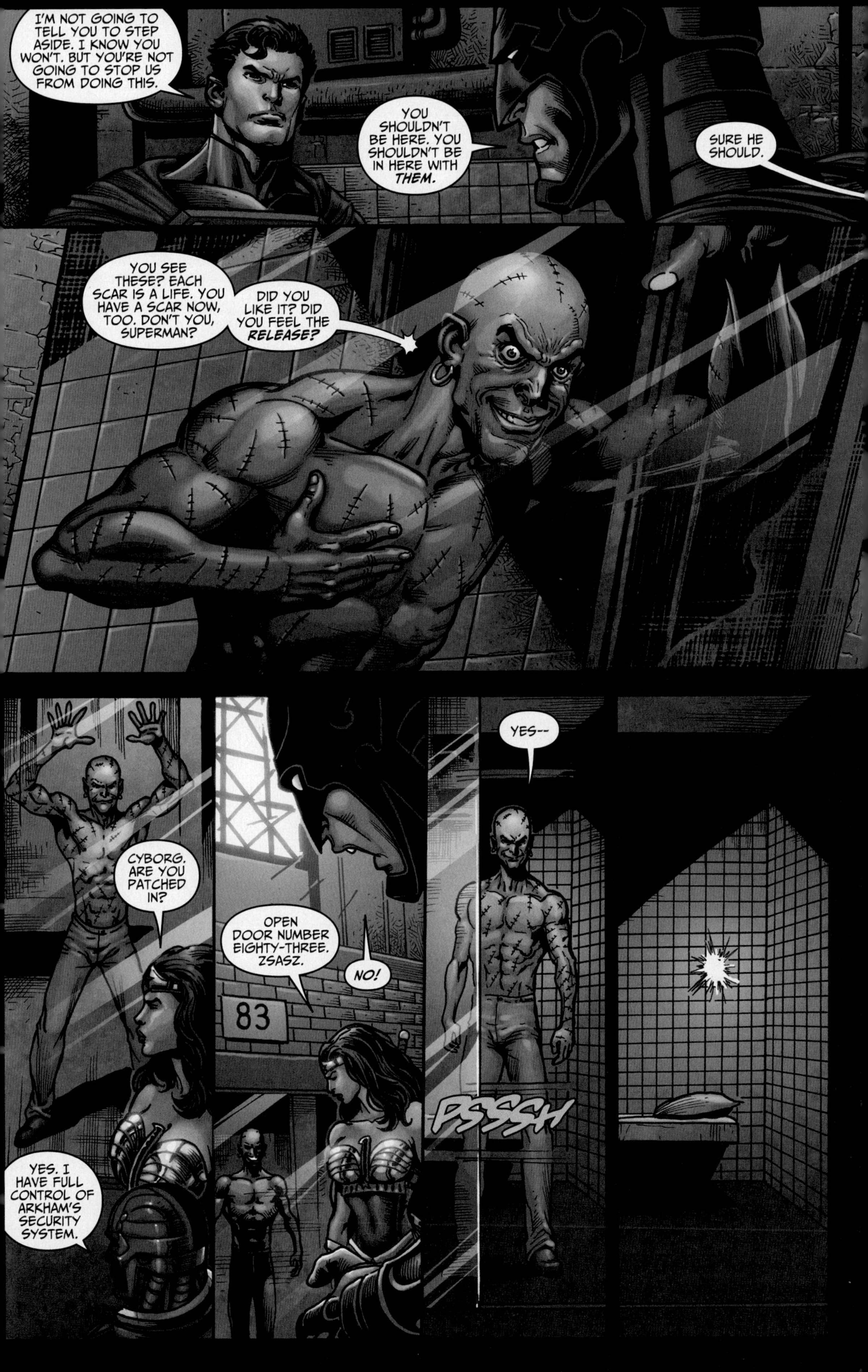
I'M NOT GOING TO TELL YOU TO STEP ASIDE. I KNOW YOU WON'T. BUT YOU'RE NOT GOING TO STOP US FROM DOING THIS.
YOU SHOULDN'T BE HERE. YOU SHOULDN'T BE IN HERE WITH *THEM.*
SURE HE SHOULD.
YOU SEE THESE? EACH SCAR IS A LIFE. YOU HAVE A SCAR NOW, TOO. DON'T YOU, SUPERMAN?
DID YOU LIKE IT? DID YOU FEEL THE *RELEASE?*
CYBORG. ARE YOU PATCHED IN?
YES. I HAVE FULL CONTROL OF ARKHAM'S SECURITY SYSTEM.
OPEN DOOR NUMBER EIGHTY-THREE. ZSASZ.
NO!
83
PSSSH
YES--

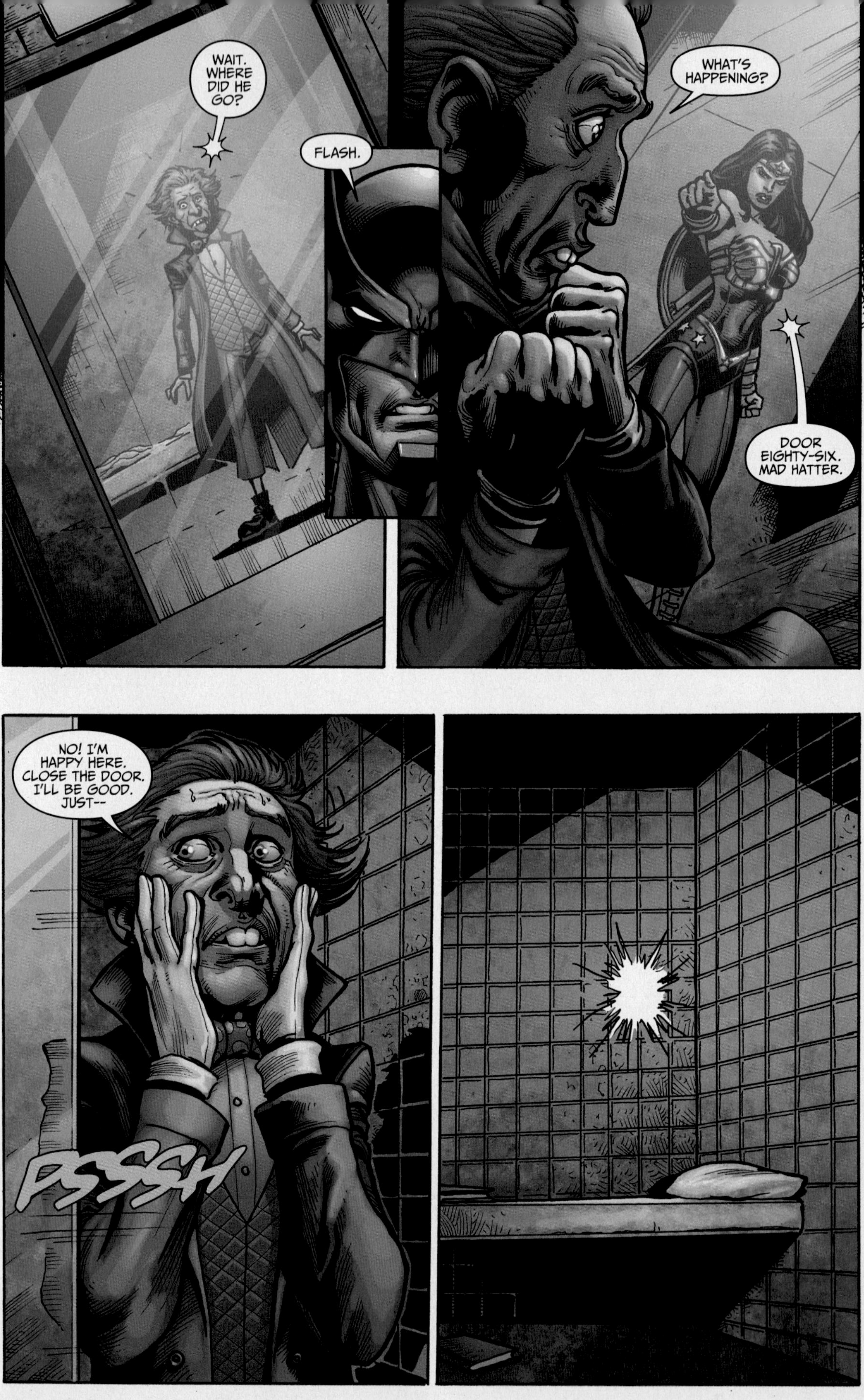
WAIT. WHERE DID HE GO?
FLASH.
WHAT'S HAPPENING?
DOOR EIGHTY-SIX. MAD HATTER.
NO! I'M HAPPY HERE. CLOSE THE DOOR. I'LL BE GOOD. JUST--
PSSSH

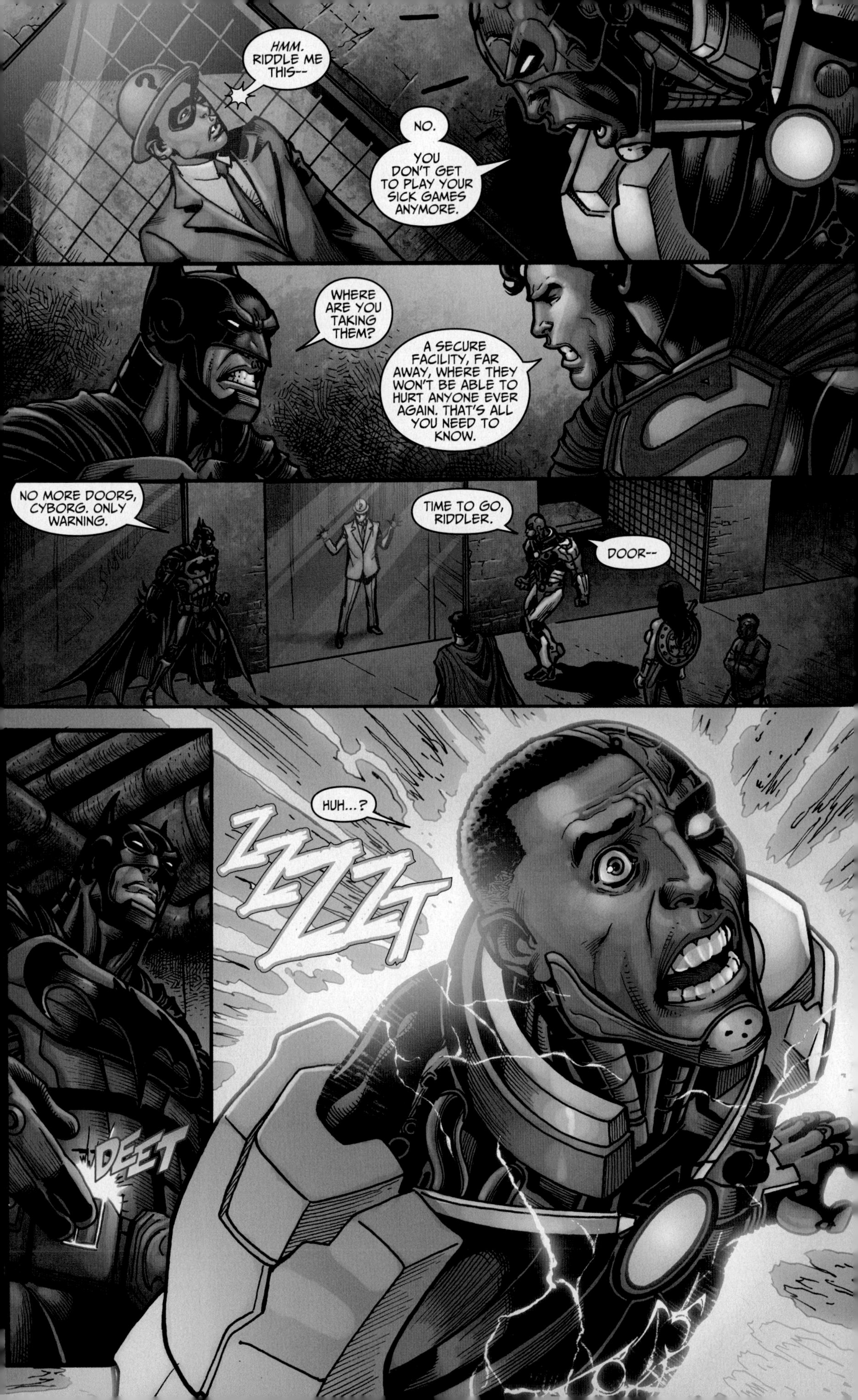
HMM. RIDDLE ME THIS--
NO.
YOU DON'T GET TO PLAY YOUR SICK GAMES ANYMORE.
WHERE ARE YOU TAKING THEM?
A SECURE FACILITY, FAR AWAY, WHERE THEY WON'T BE ABLE TO HURT ANYONE EVER AGAIN. THAT'S ALL YOU NEED TO KNOW.
NO MORE DOORS, CYBORG. ONLY WARNING.
TIME TO GO, RIDDLER.
DOOR--
HUH...?
ZZZZT
DEET

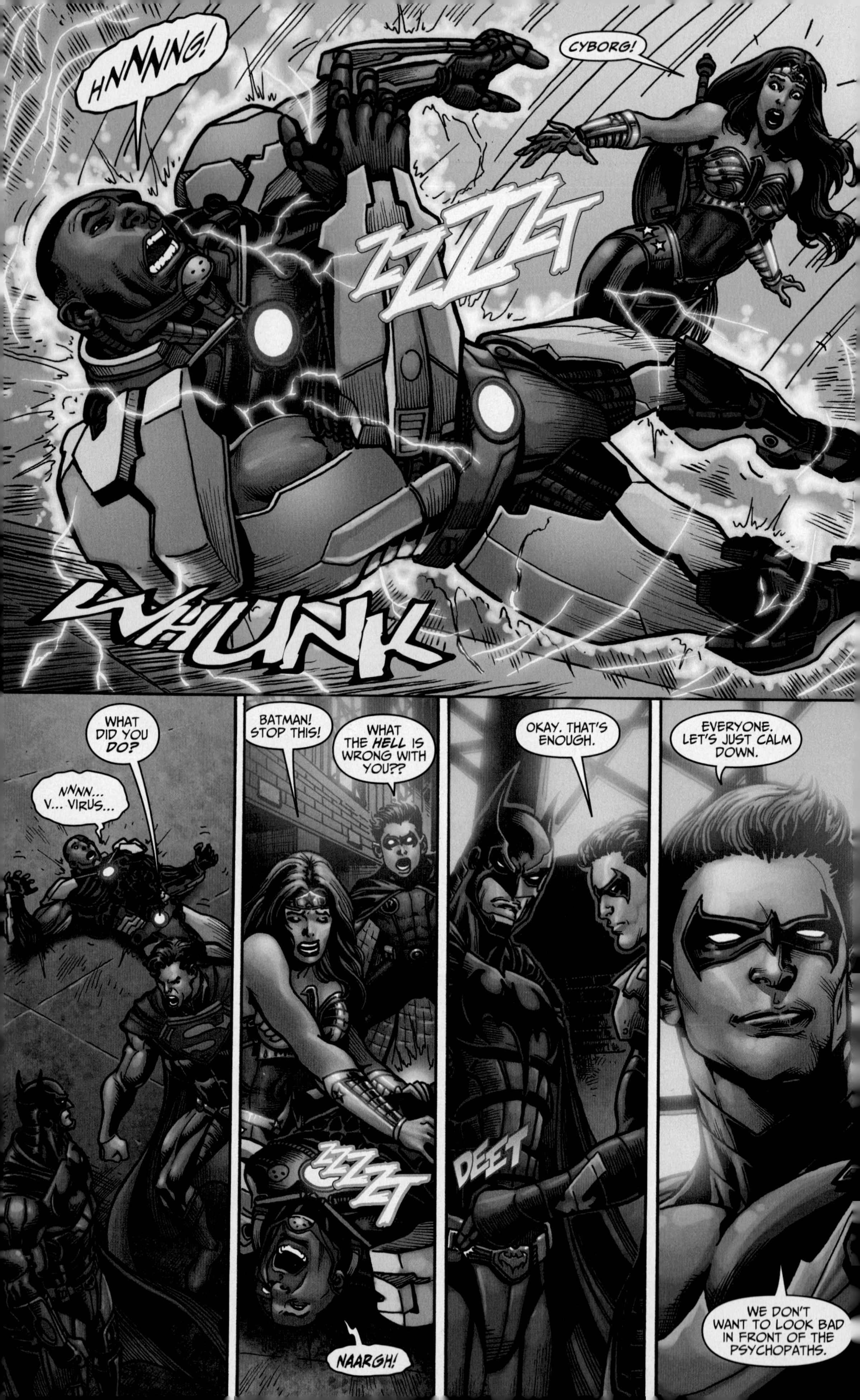

HNNNNG!
CYBORG!
ZZZZT
WHUNK
WHAT DID YOU DO?
NNNN... V... VIRUS...
BATMAN! STOP THIS!
WHAT THE HELL IS WRONG WITH YOU??
ZZZZT
NAARGH!
OKAY. THAT'S ENOUGH.
DEET
EVERYONE. LET'S JUST CALM DOWN.
WE DON'T WANT TO LOOK BAD IN FRONT OF THE PSYCHOPATHS.

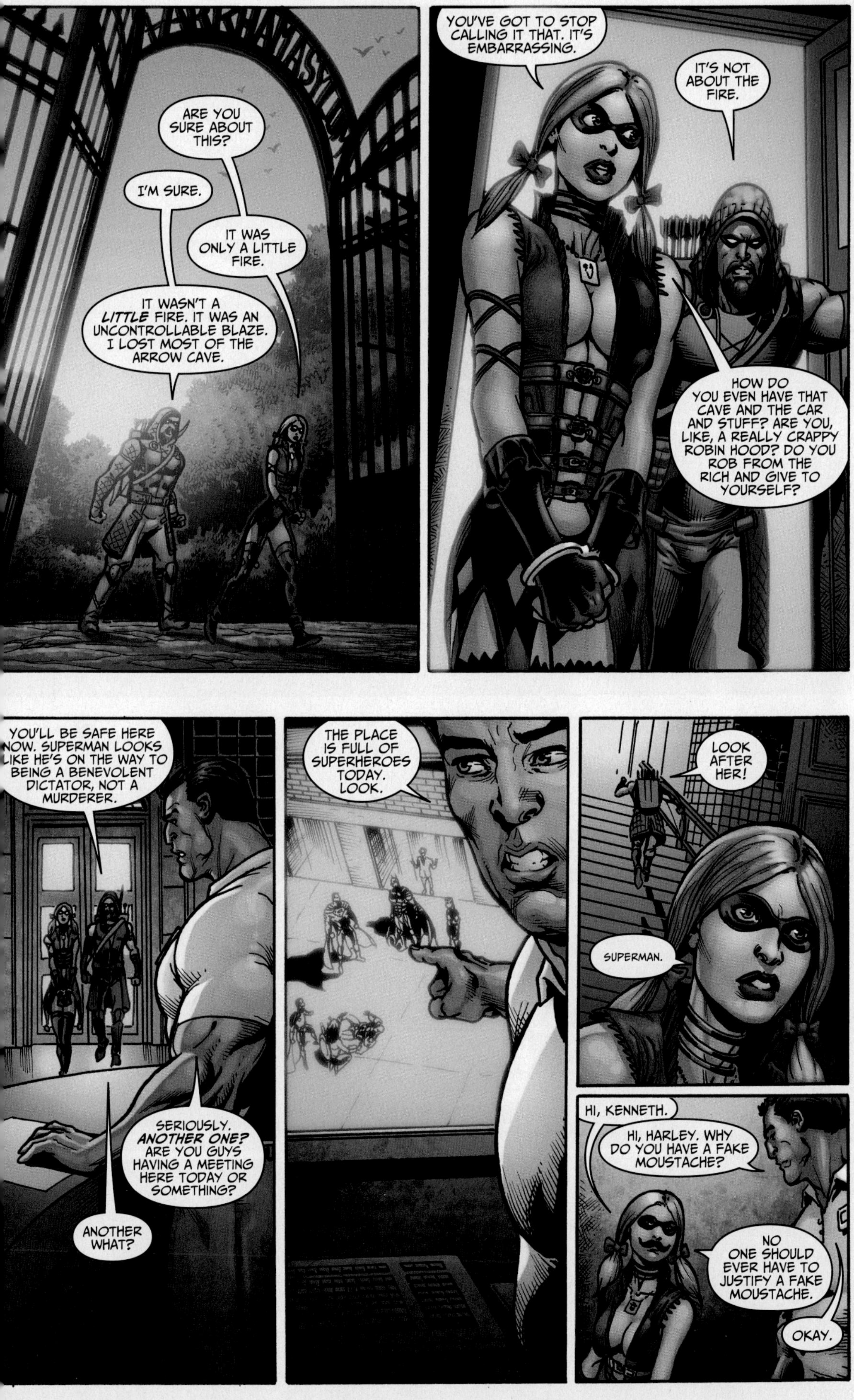
ARKHAM ASYLUM
ARE YOU SURE ABOUT THIS?
I'M SURE.
IT WAS ONLY A LITTLE FIRE.
IT WASN'T A *LITTLE* FIRE. IT WAS AN UNCONTROLLABLE BLAZE. I LOST MOST OF THE ARROW CAVE.
YOU'VE GOT TO STOP CALLING IT THAT. IT'S EMBARRASSING.
IT'S NOT ABOUT THE FIRE.
HOW DO YOU EVEN HAVE THAT CAVE AND THE CAR AND STUFF? ARE YOU, LIKE, A REALLY CRAPPY ROBIN HOOD? DO YOU ROB FROM THE RICH AND GIVE TO YOURSELF?
YOU'LL BE SAFE HERE NOW. SUPERMAN LOOKS LIKE HE'S ON THE WAY TO BEING A BENEVOLENT DICTATOR, NOT A MURDERER.
SERIOUSLY. ***ANOTHER ONE?*** ARE YOU GUYS HAVING A MEETING HERE TODAY OR SOMETHING?
ANOTHER WHAT?
THE PLACE IS FULL OF SUPERHEROES TODAY. LOOK.
LOOK AFTER HER!
SUPERMAN.
HI, KENNETH.
HI, HARLEY. WHY DO YOU HAVE A FAKE MOUSTACHE?
NO ONE SHOULD EVER HAVE TO JUSTIFY A FAKE MOUSTACHE.
OKAY.

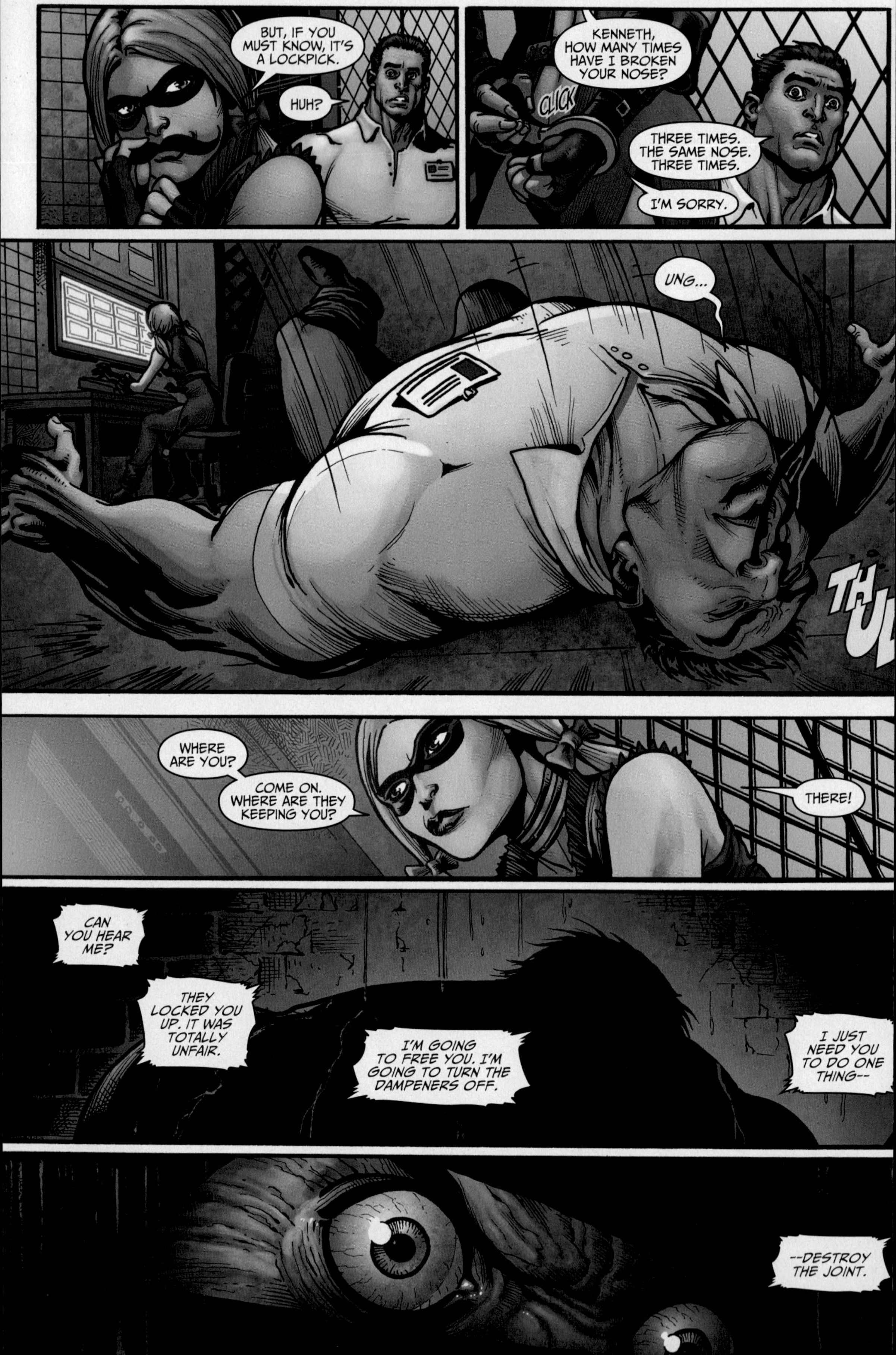
BUT, IF YOU MUST KNOW, IT'S A LOCKPICK.
HUH?
KENNETH, HOW MANY TIMES HAVE I BROKEN YOUR NOSE?
CLICK
THREE TIMES. THE SAME NOSE. THREE TIMES.
I'M SORRY.
UNG...
WHERE ARE YOU?
COME ON. WHERE ARE THEY KEEPING YOU?
THERE!
CAN YOU HEAR ME?
THEY LOCKED YOU UP. IT WAS TOTALLY UNFAIR.
I'M GOING TO FREE YOU. I'M GOING TO TURN THE DAMPENERS OFF.
I JUST NEED YOU TO DO ONE THING--
--DESTROY THE JOINT.

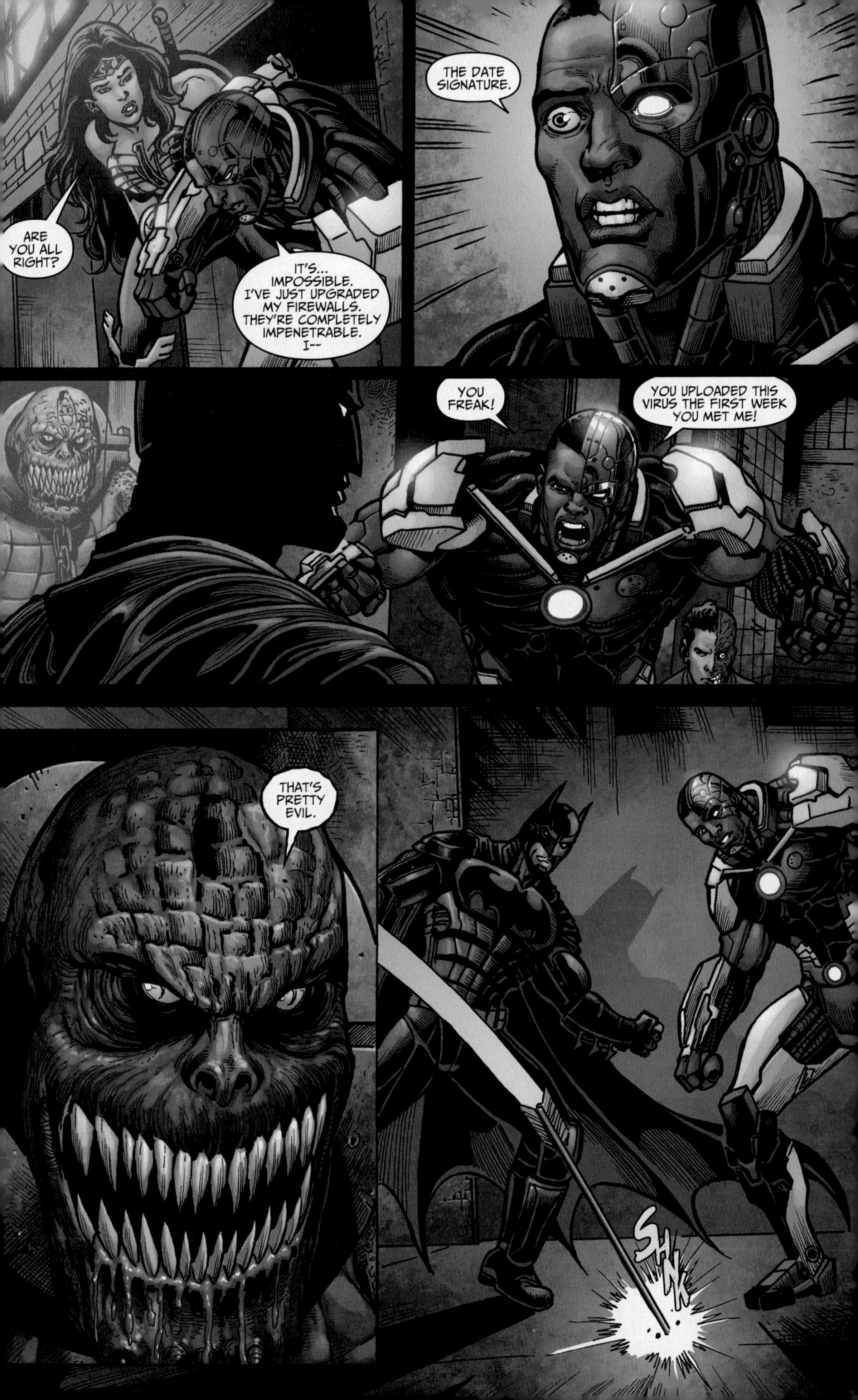
ARE YOU ALL RIGHT?
IT'S... IMPOSSIBLE. I'VE JUST UPGRADED MY FIREWALLS. THEY'RE COMPLETELY IMPENETRABLE. I--
THE DATE SIGNATURE.
YOU FREAK!
YOU UPLOADED THIS VIRUS THE FIRST WEEK YOU MET ME!
THAT'S PRETTY EVIL.
SHUNK

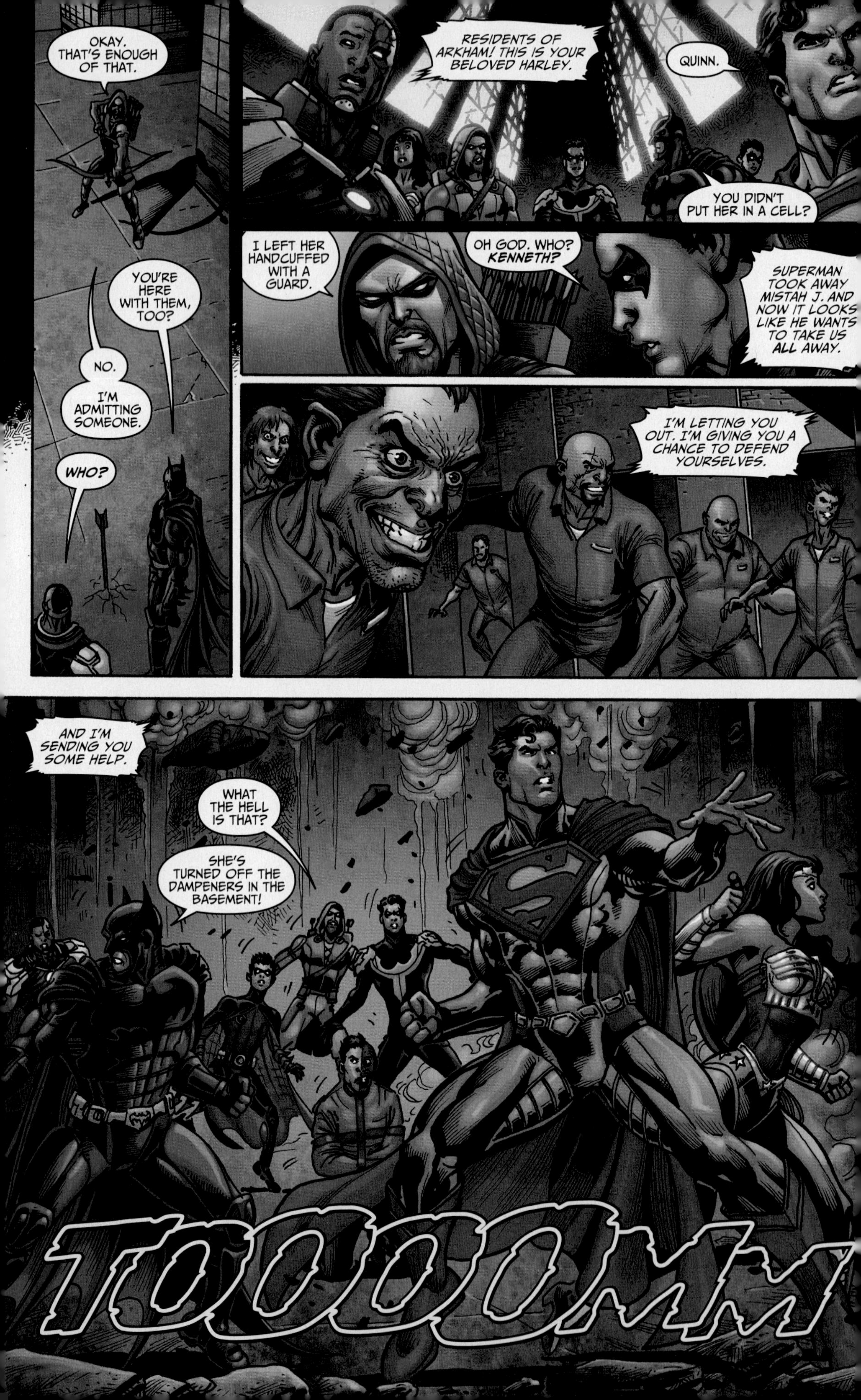
OKAY. THAT'S ENOUGH OF THAT.
YOU'RE HERE WITH THEM, TOO?
NO.
I'M ADMITTING SOMEONE.
WHO?
RESIDENTS OF ARKHAM! THIS IS YOUR BELOVED HARLEY.
QUINN.
YOU DIDN'T PUT HER IN A CELL?
I LEFT HER HANDCUFFED WITH A GUARD.
OH GOD. WHO? KENNETH?
SUPERMAN TOOK AWAY MISTAH J. AND NOW IT LOOKS LIKE HE WANTS TO TAKE US ALL AWAY.
I'M LETTING YOU OUT. I'M GIVING YOU A CHANCE TO DEFEND YOURSELVES.
AND I'M SENDING YOU SOME HELP.
WHAT THE HELL IS THAT?
SHE'S TURNED OFF THE DAMPENERS IN THE BASEMENT!
TOOOOMM

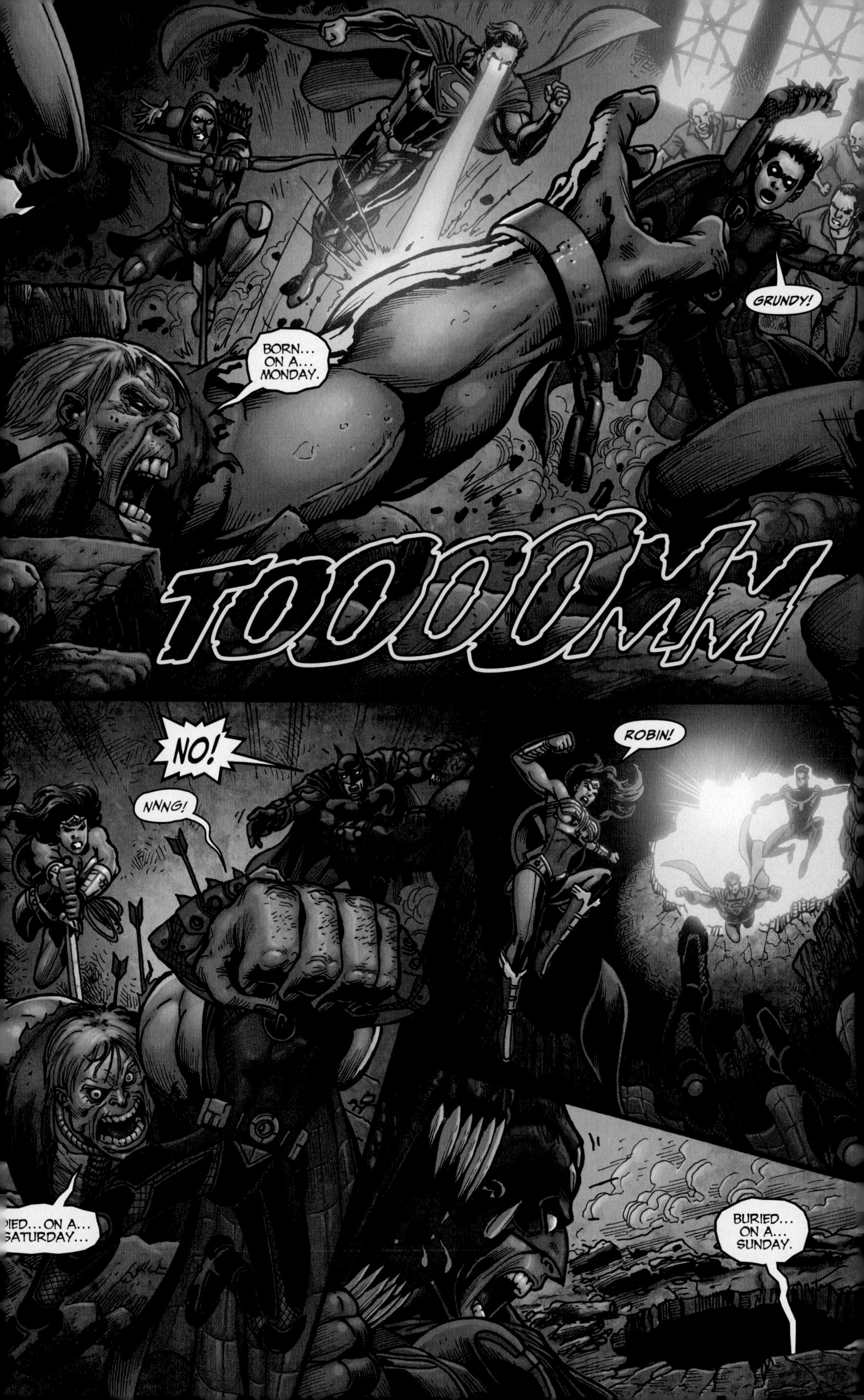
GRUNDY!
BORN... ON A... MONDAY.
TOOOOMM
NO!
ROBIN!
NNNG!
DIED...ON A... SATURDAY...
BURIED... ON A... SUNDAY.

PART SIX

Mike S. Miller David Yardin Jheremy Raapack Pencillers

Mike S. Miller Jheremy Raapack LeBeau Underwood Jonas Trindade David Yardin Inkers

Cover Art by Mico Suayan & David López and Santi Casas of Ikari Studio

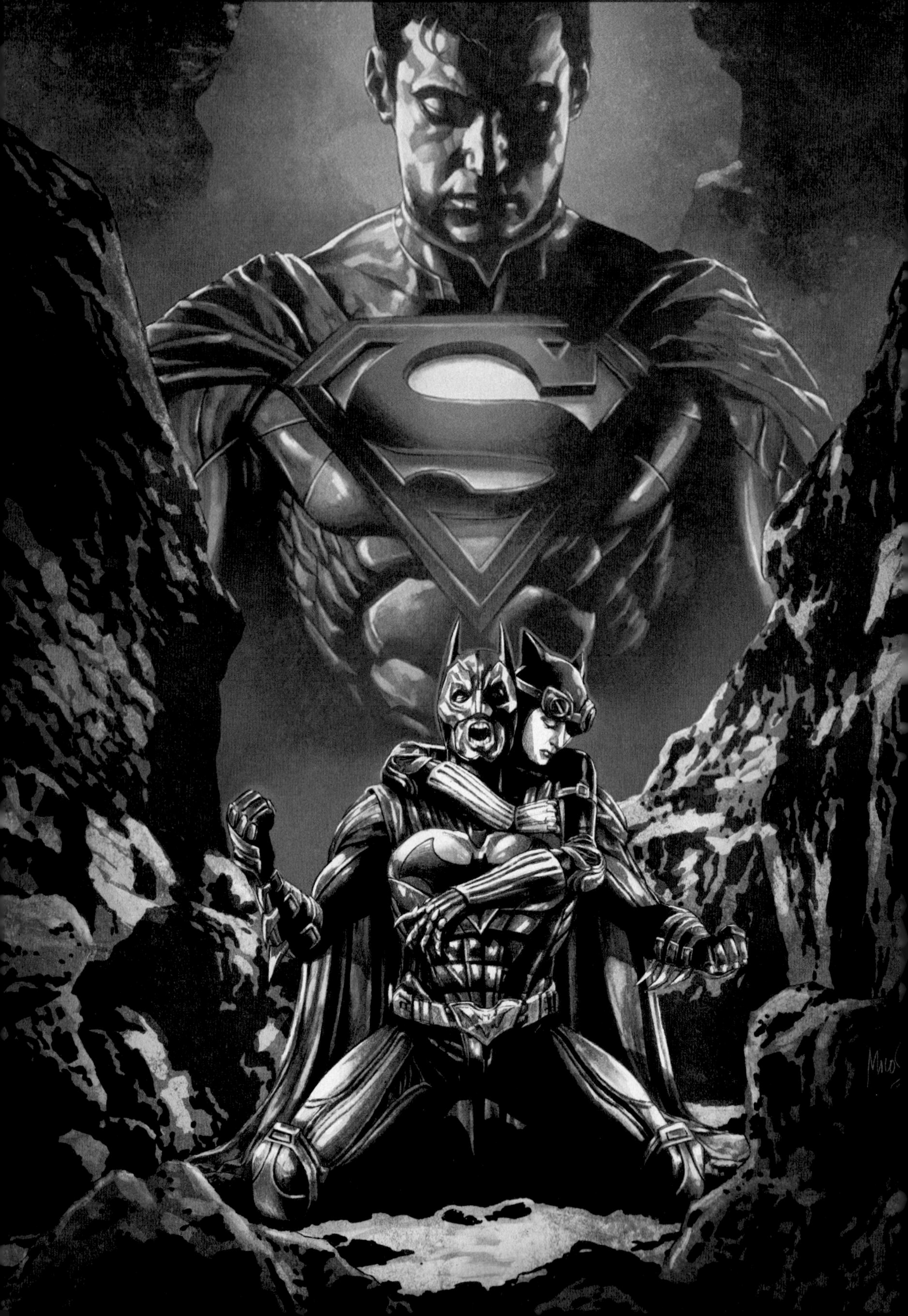

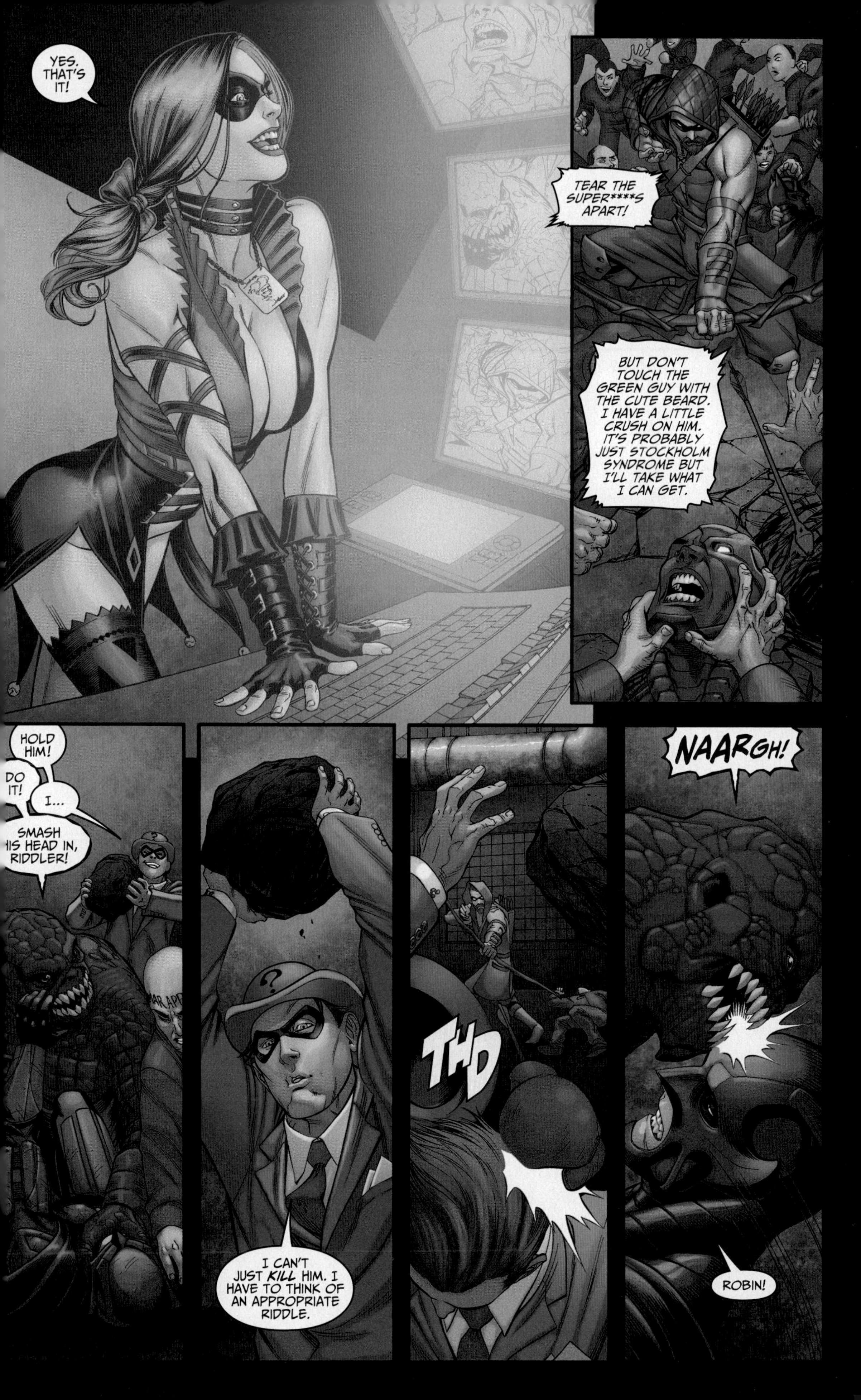
YES. THAT'S IT!
TEAR THE SUPER****S APART!
BUT DON'T TOUCH THE GREEN GUY WITH THE CUTE BEARD. I HAVE A LITTLE CRUSH ON HIM. IT'S PROBABLY JUST STOCKHOLM SYNDROME BUT I'LL TAKE WHAT I CAN GET.
HOLD HIM!
DO IT!
I...
SMASH HIS HEAD IN, RIDDLER!
I CAN'T JUST KILL HIM. I HAVE TO THINK OF AN APPROPRIATE RIDDLE.
THD
NAARGH!
ROBIN!

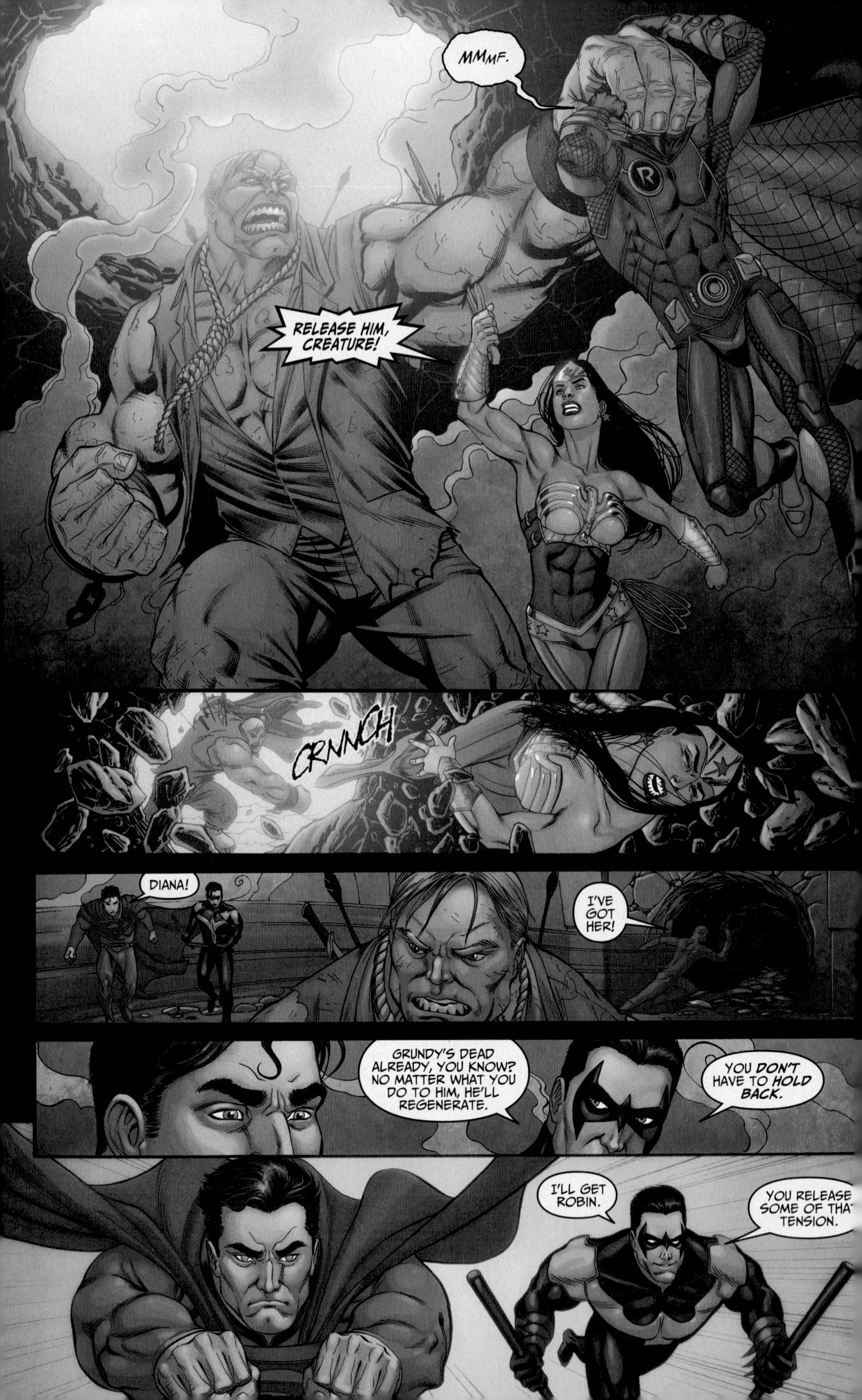
MMMF.
RELEASE HIM, CREATURE!
CRNNCH
DIANA!
I'VE GOT HER!
GRUNDY'S DEAD ALREADY, YOU KNOW? NO MATTER WHAT YOU DO TO HIM, HE'LL REGENERATE.
YOU DON'T HAVE TO HOLD BACK.
I'LL GET ROBIN.
YOU RELEASE SOME OF THAT TENSION.

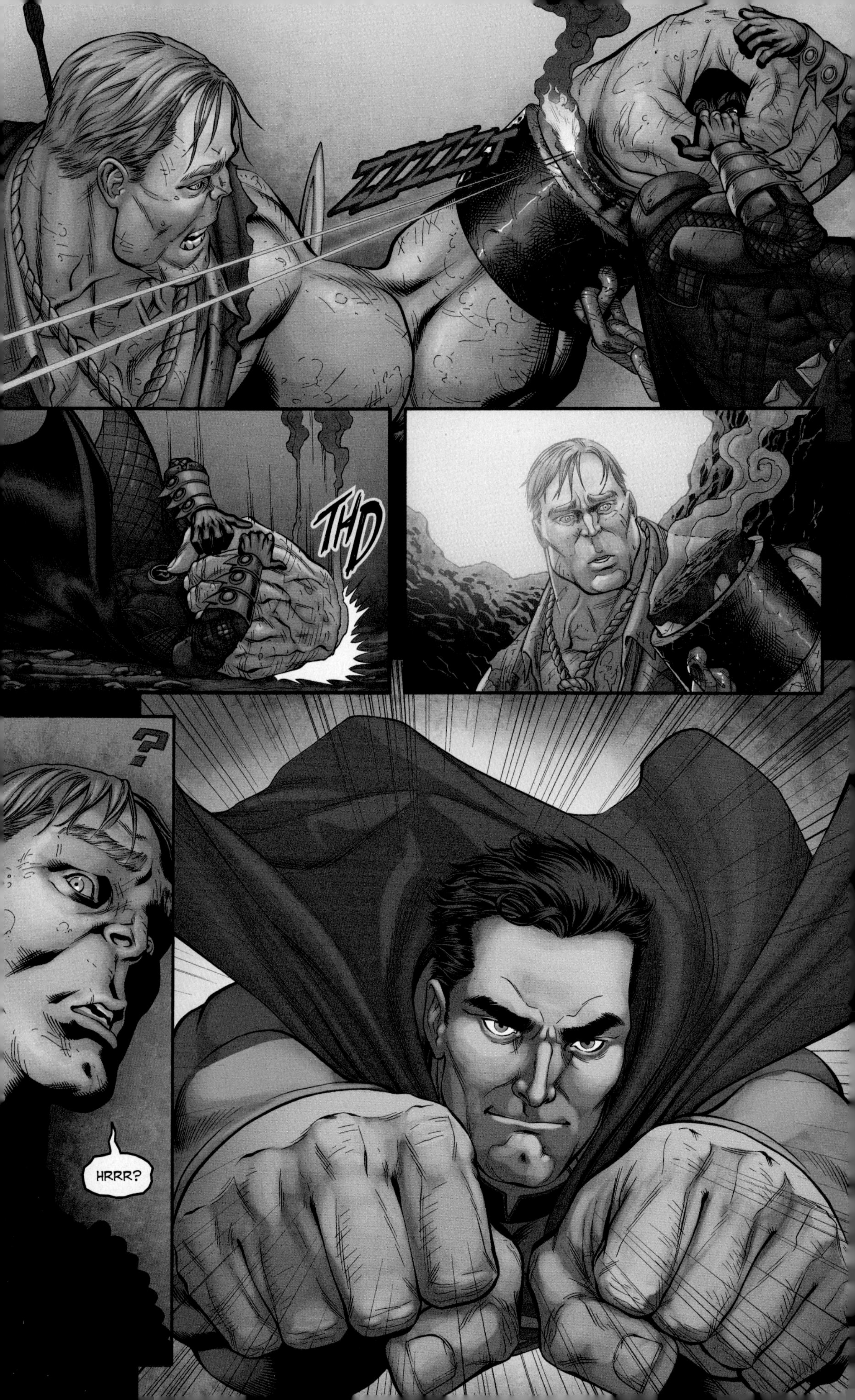

ZZZZT
THD
?
HRRR?

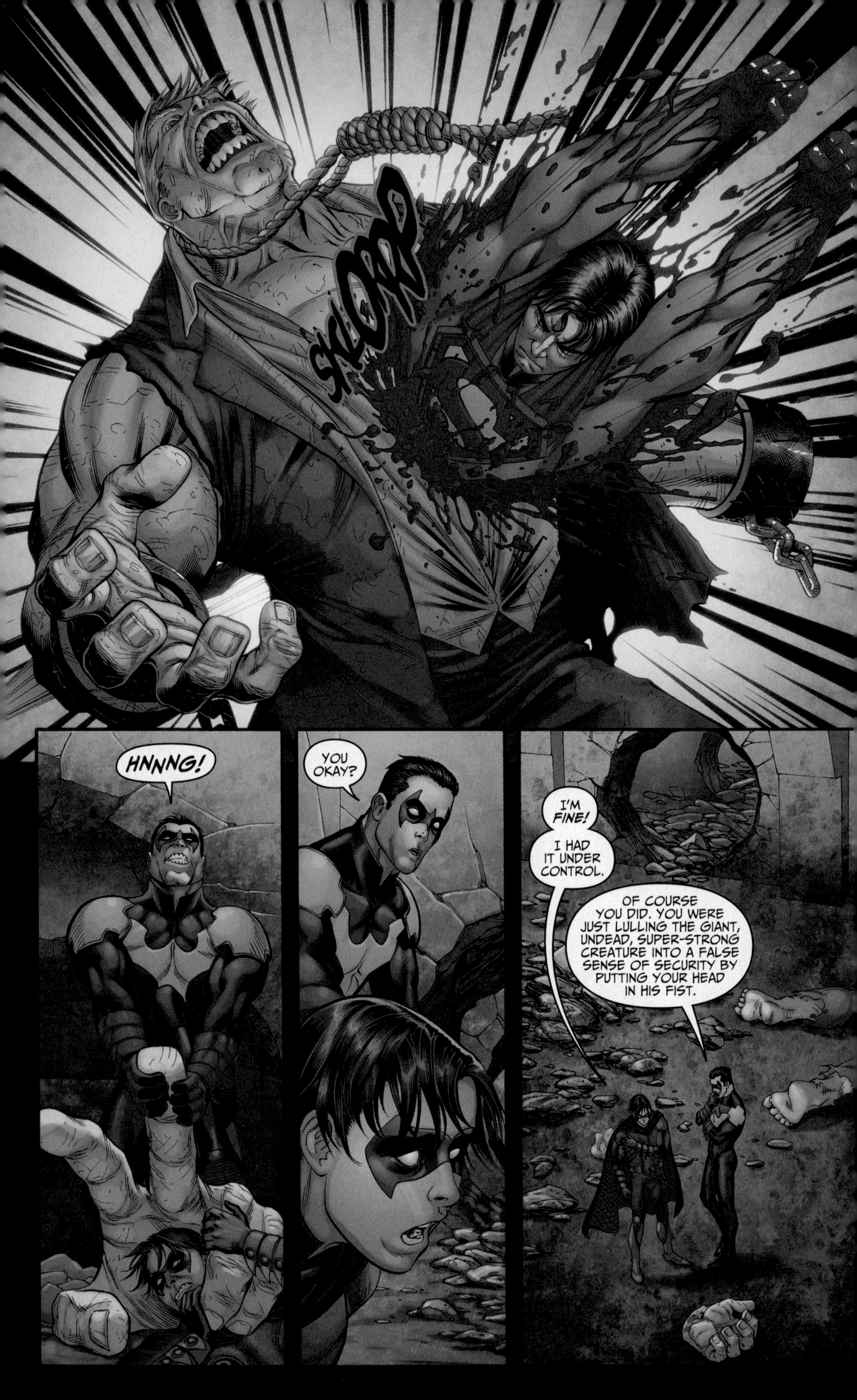
SKLOOP
HNNNG!
YOU OKAY?
I'M FINE!
I HAD IT UNDER CONTROL.
OF COURSE YOU DID. YOU WERE JUST LULLING THE GIANT, UNDEAD, SUPER-STRONG CREATURE INTO A FALSE SENSE OF SECURITY BY PUTTING YOUR HEAD IN HIS FIST.

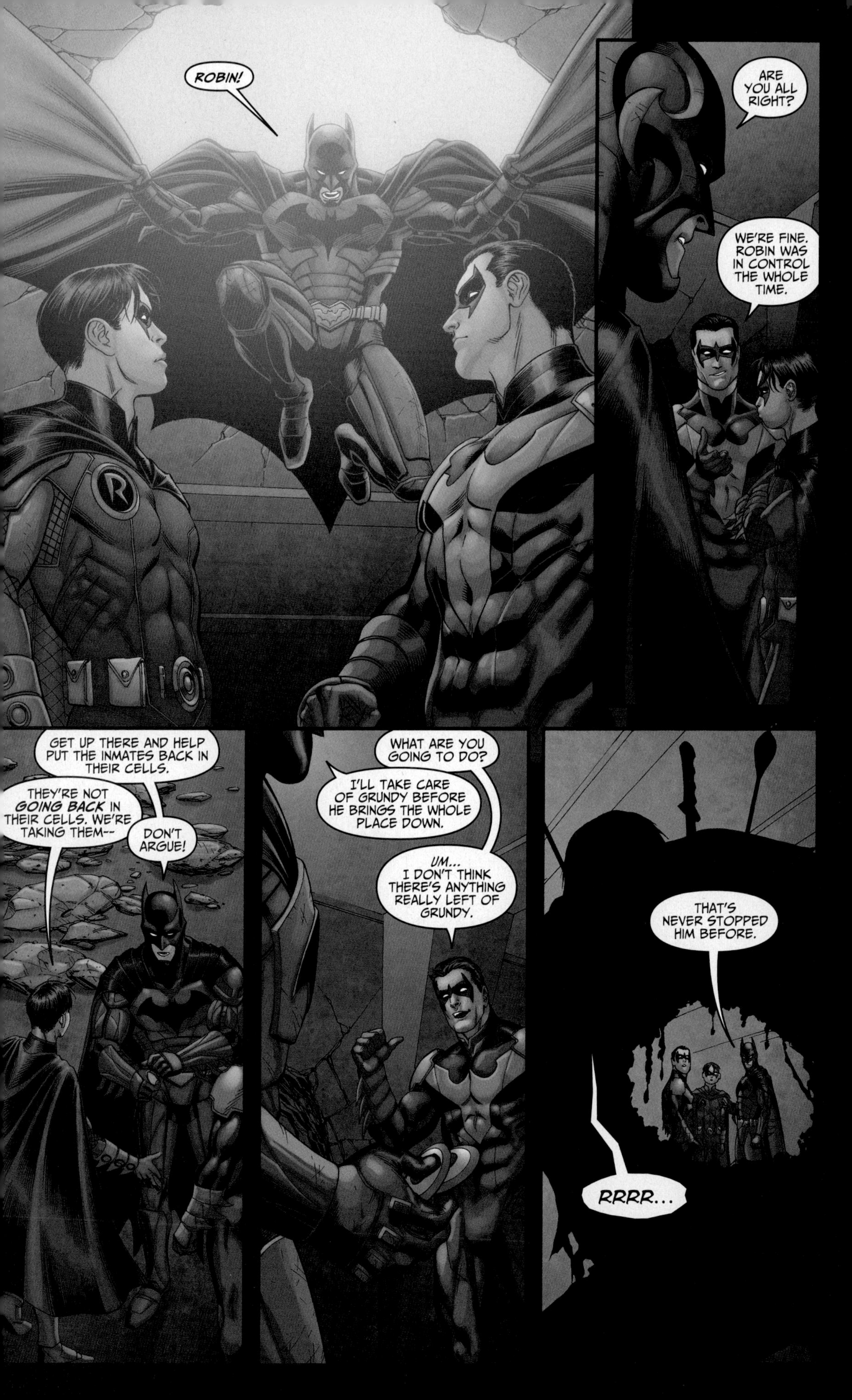
ROBIN!
ARE YOU ALL RIGHT?
WE'RE FINE. ROBIN WAS IN CONTROL THE WHOLE TIME.
GET UP THERE AND HELP PUT THE INMATES BACK IN THEIR CELLS.
THEY'RE NOT *GOING BACK* IN THEIR CELLS. WE'RE TAKING THEM--
DON'T ARGUE!
WHAT ARE YOU GOING TO DO?
I'LL TAKE CARE OF GRUNDY BEFORE HE BRINGS THE WHOLE PLACE DOWN.
UM... I DON'T THINK THERE'S ANYTHING REALLY LEFT OF GRUNDY.
THAT'S NEVER STOPPED HIM BEFORE.
RRRR...

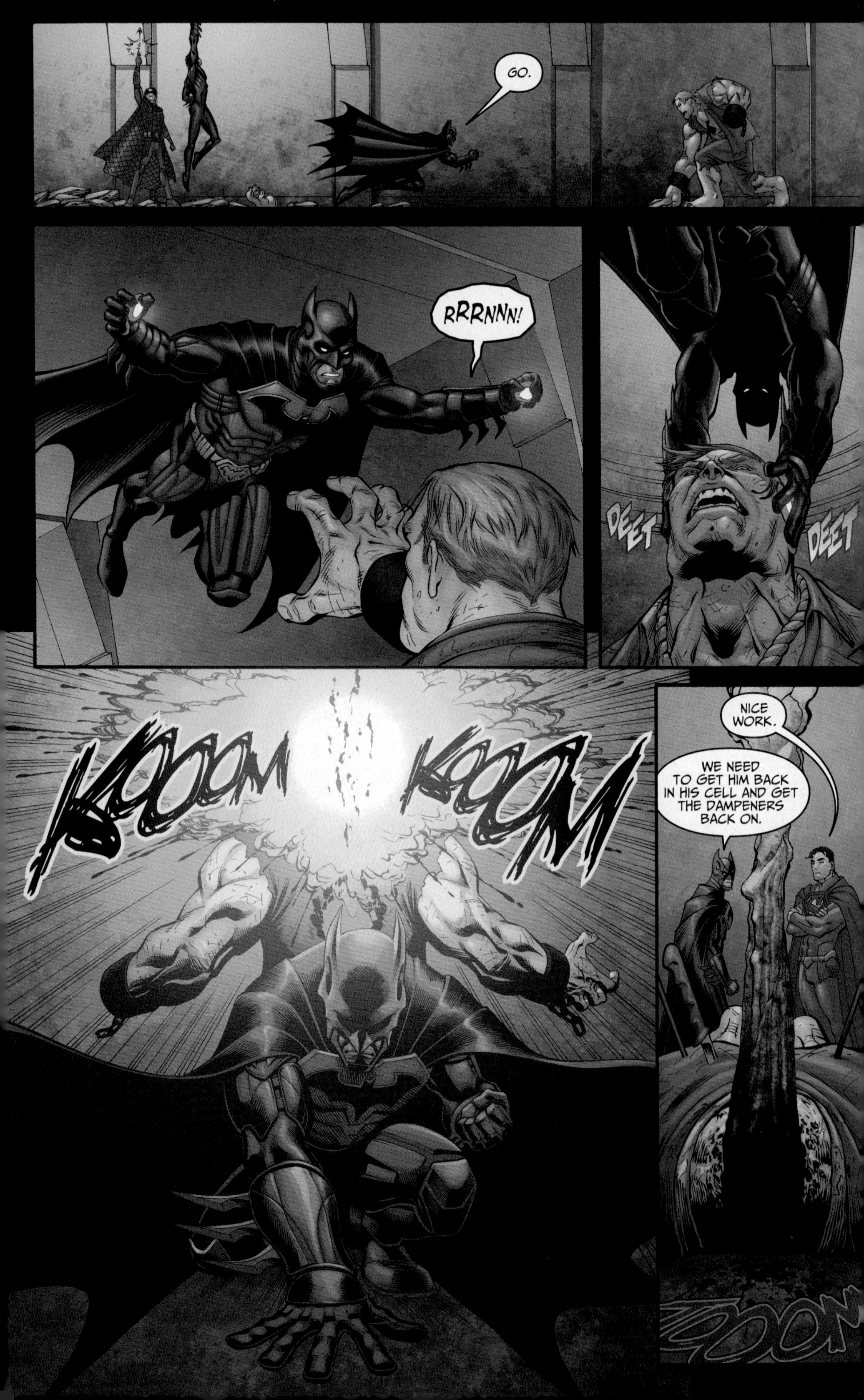
GO.
RRRNNN!
DEET
DEET
KOOOM
KOOOM
NICE WORK.
WE NEED TO GET HIM BACK IN HIS CELL AND GET THE DAMPENERS BACK ON.

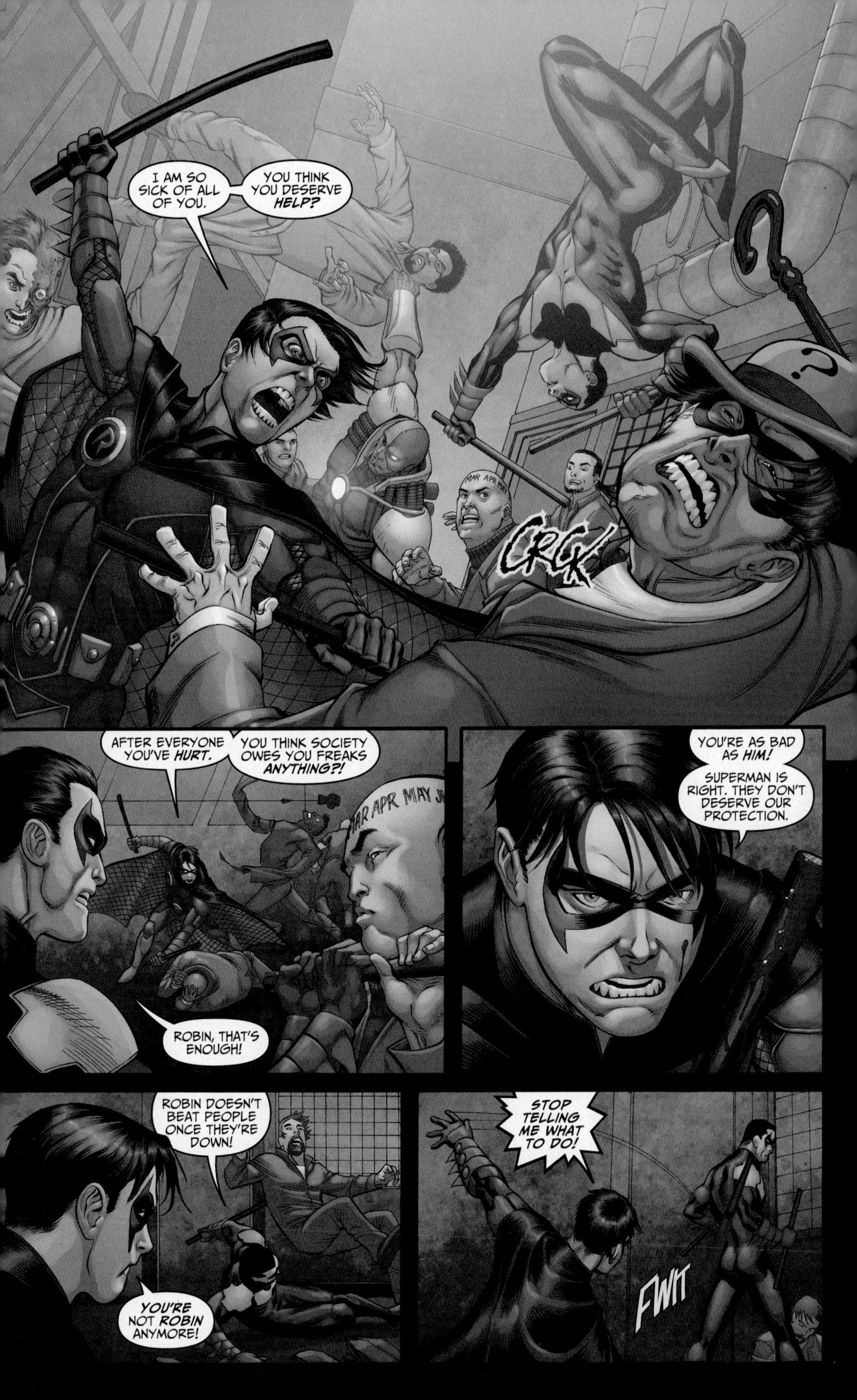
I AM SO SICK OF ALL OF YOU.
YOU THINK YOU DESERVE *HELP?*
MAR APR MAY
CRCK!
AFTER EVERYONE YOU'VE *HURT.*
YOU THINK SOCIETY OWES YOU FREAKS *ANYTHING?!*
MAR APR MAY JU
ROBIN, THAT'S ENOUGH!
YOU'RE AS BAD AS *HIM!*
SUPERMAN IS RIGHT. THEY DON'T DESERVE OUR PROTECTION.
ROBIN DOESN'T BEAT PEOPLE ONCE THEY'RE DOWN!
YOU'RE NOT *ROBIN* ANYMORE!
STOP TELLING ME WHAT TO DO!
FWIT

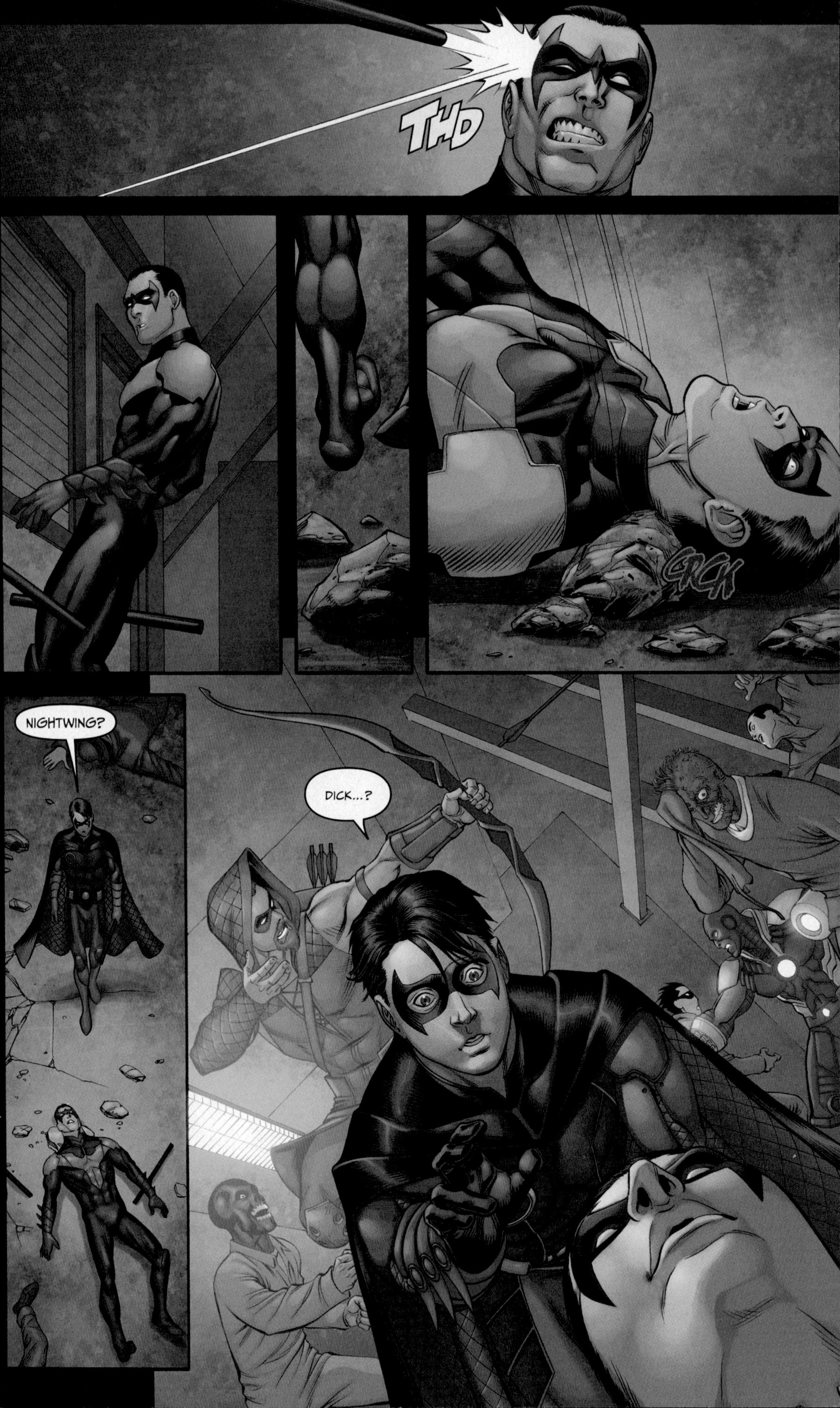
THD
CRCK
NIGHTWING?
DICK...?

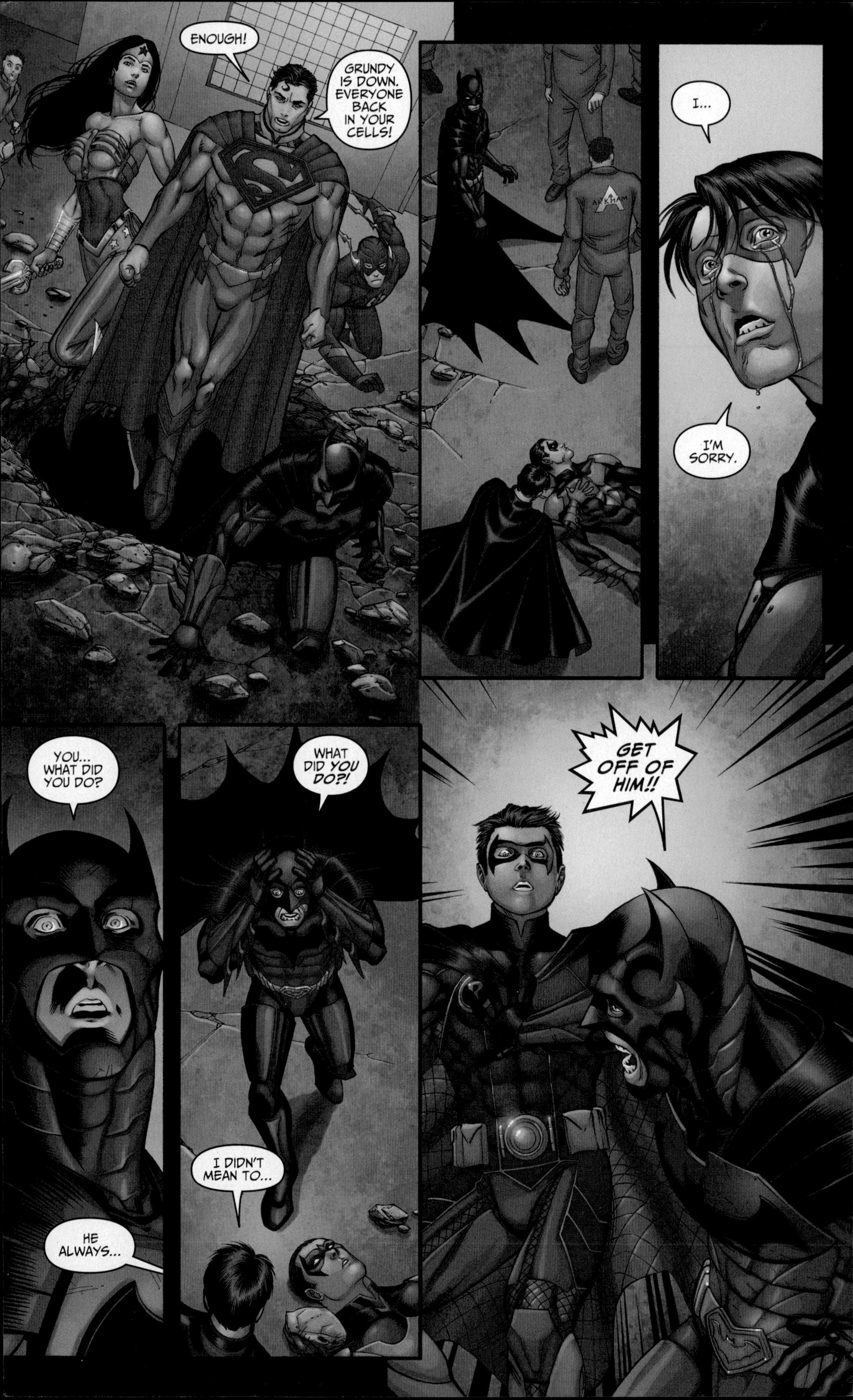
ENOUGH!
GRUNDY IS DOWN. EVERYONE BACK IN YOUR CELLS!
I...
I'M SORRY.
YOU... WHAT DID YOU DO?
HE ALWAYS...
WHAT DID YOU DO?!
I DIDN'T MEAN TO...
GET OFF OF HIM!!

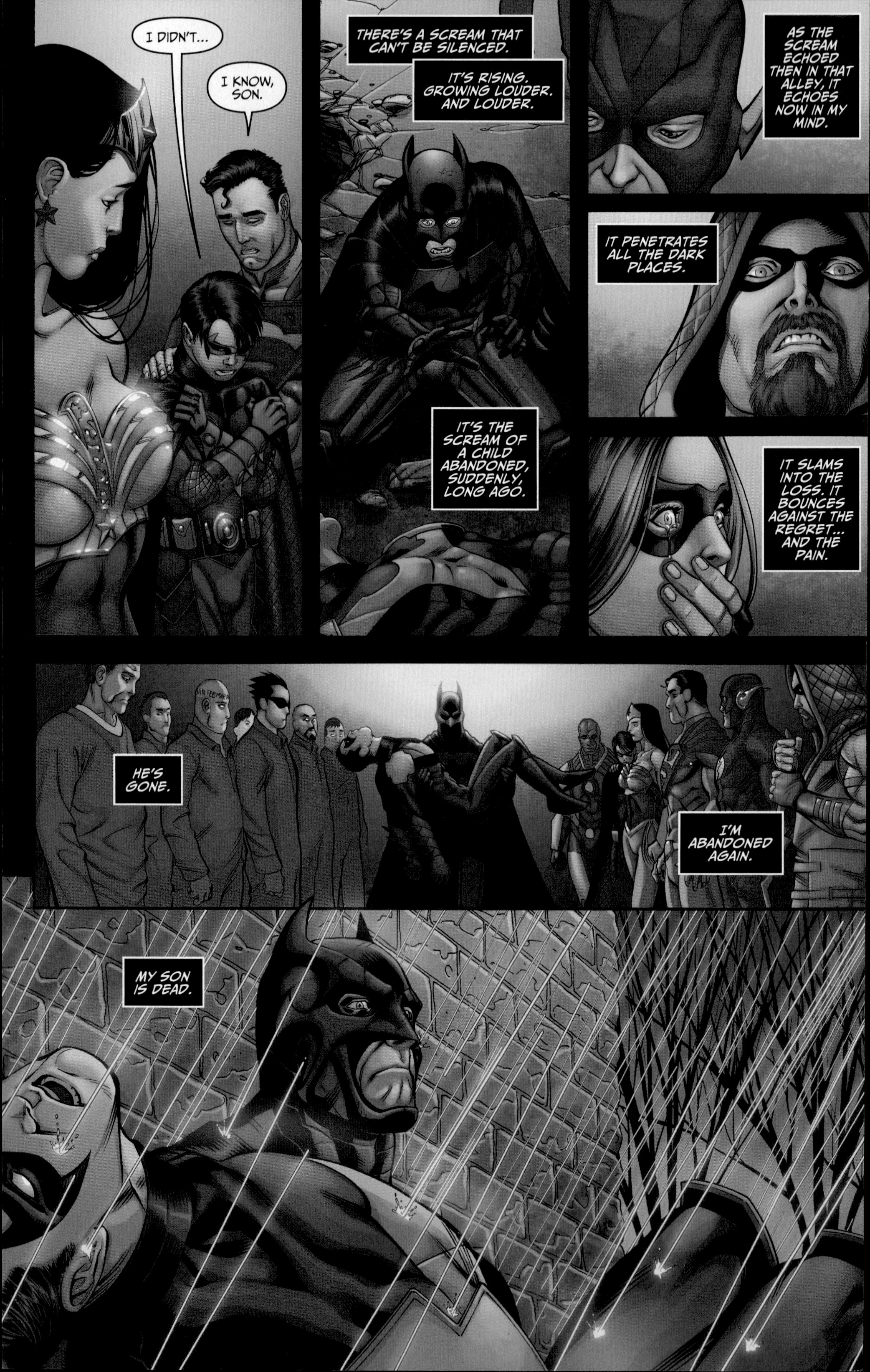
I DIDN'T...
I KNOW, SON.
THERE'S A SCREAM THAT CAN'T BE SILENCED.
IT'S RISING. GROWING LOUDER. AND LOUDER.
IT'S THE SCREAM OF A CHILD ABANDONED, SUDDENLY, LONG AGO.
AS THE SCREAM ECHOED THEN IN THAT ALLEY, IT ECHOES NOW IN MY MIND.
IT PENETRATES ALL THE DARK PLACES.
IT SLAMS INTO THE LOSS. IT BOUNCES AGAINST THE REGRET... AND THE PAIN.
HE'S GONE.
I'M ABANDONED AGAIN.
MY SON IS DEAD.

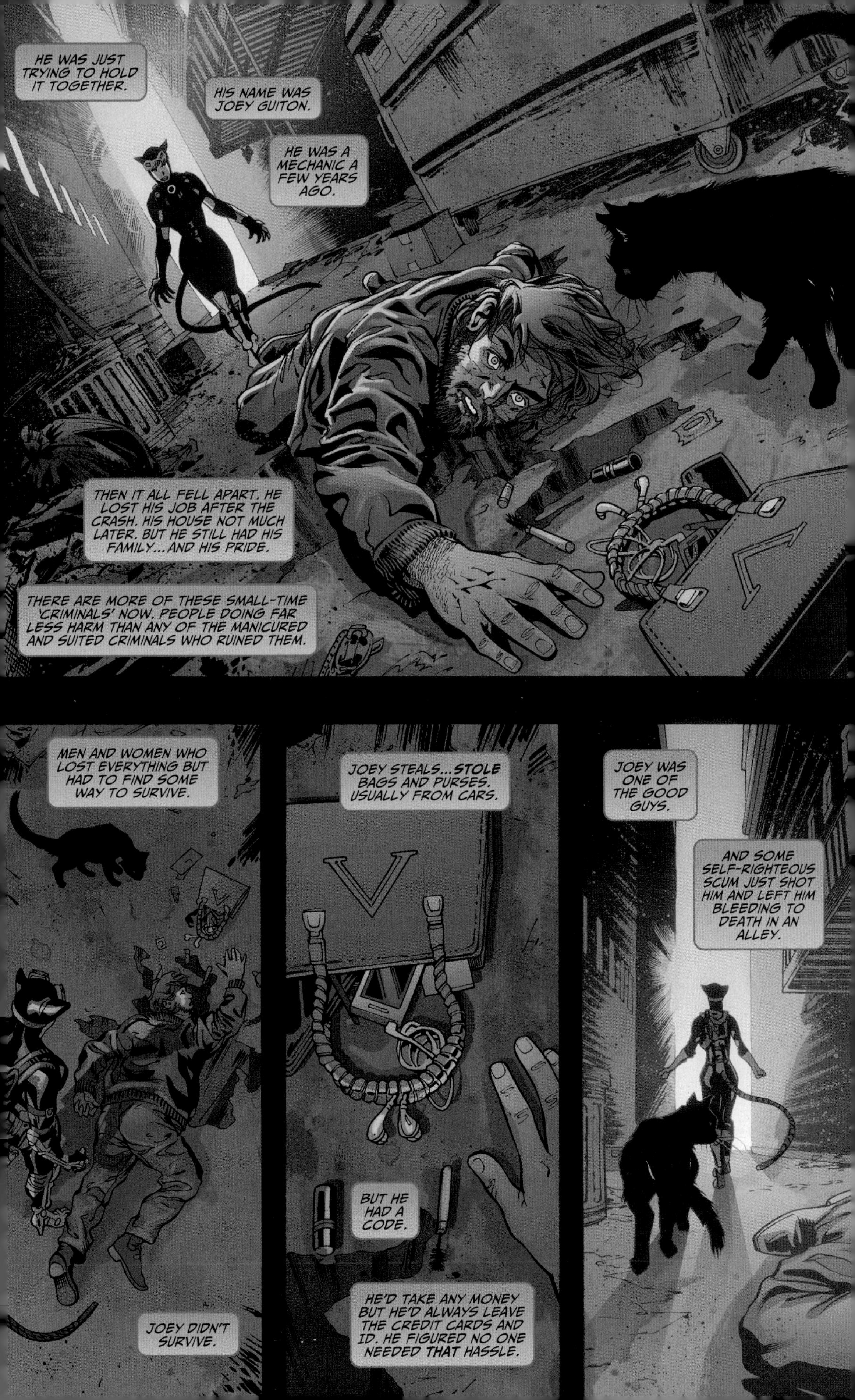
HE WAS JUST TRYING TO HOLD IT TOGETHER.
HIS NAME WAS JOEY GUITON.
HE WAS A MECHANIC A FEW YEARS AGO.
THEN IT ALL FELL APART. HE LOST HIS JOB AFTER THE CRASH. HIS HOUSE NOT MUCH LATER. BUT HE STILL HAD HIS FAMILY...AND HIS PRIDE.
THERE ARE MORE OF THESE SMALL-TIME 'CRIMINALS' NOW. PEOPLE DOING FAR LESS HARM THAN ANY OF THE MANICURED AND SUITED CRIMINALS WHO RUINED THEM.
MEN AND WOMEN WHO LOST EVERYTHING BUT HAD TO FIND SOME WAY TO SURVIVE.
JOEY DIDN'T SURVIVE.
JOEY STEALS...STOLE BAGS AND PURSES. USUALLY FROM CARS.
BUT HE HAD A CODE.
HE'D TAKE ANY MONEY BUT HE'D ALWAYS LEAVE THE CREDIT CARDS AND ID. HE FIGURED NO ONE NEEDED THAT HASSLE.
JOEY WAS ONE OF THE GOOD GUYS.
AND SOME SELF-RIGHTEOUS SCUM JUST SHOT HIM AND LEFT HIM BLEEDING TO DEATH IN AN ALLEY.

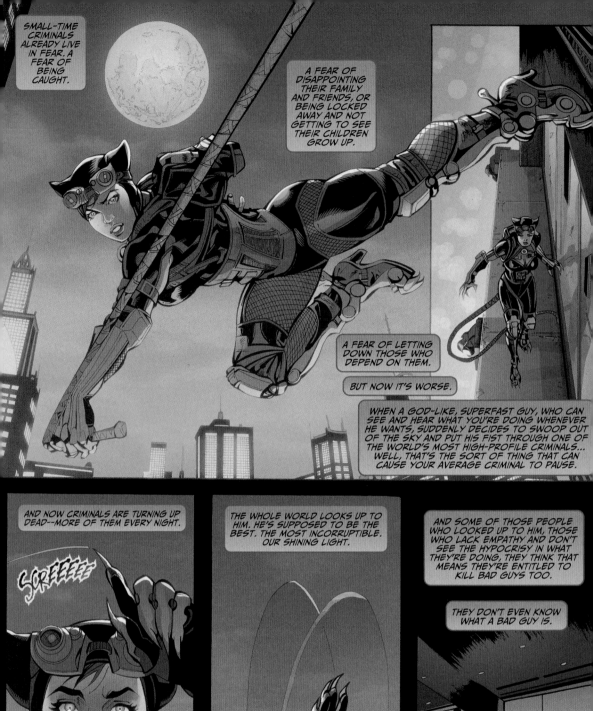

SMALL-TIME CRIMINALS ALREADY LIVE IN FEAR. A FEAR OF BEING CAUGHT.

A FEAR OF DISAPPOINTING THEIR FAMILY AND FRIENDS, OR BEING LOCKED AWAY AND NOT GETTING TO SEE THEIR CHILDREN GROW UP.

A FEAR OF LETTING DOWN THOSE WHO DEPEND ON THEM.

BUT NOW IT'S WORSE.

WHEN A GOD-LIKE, SUPERFAST GUY, WHO CAN SEE AND HEAR WHAT YOU'RE DOING WHENEVER HE WANTS, SUDDENLY DECIDES TO SWOOP OUT OF THE SKY AND PUT HIS FIST THROUGH ONE OF THE WORLD'S MOST HIGH-PROFILE CRIMINALS... WELL, THAT'S THE SORT OF THING THAT CAN CAUSE YOUR AVERAGE CRIMINAL TO PAUSE.

AND NOW CRIMINALS ARE TURNING UP DEAD--MORE OF THEM EVERY NIGHT.

SCREEEEE

AND IT'S ALL SUPERMAN'S FAULT.

THE WHOLE WORLD LOOKS UP TO HIM. HE'S SUPPOSED TO BE THE BEST. THE MOST INCORRUPTIBLE. OUR SHINING LIGHT.

AND HE JUST MURDERED A CRIMINAL AND DIDN'T ANSWER FOR IT.

AND SOME OF THOSE PEOPLE WHO LOOKED UP TO HIM, THOSE WHO LACK EMPATHY AND DON'T SEE THE HYPOCRISY IN WHAT THEY'RE DOING, THEY THINK THAT MEANS THEY'RE ENTITLED TO KILL BAD GUYS TOO.

THEY DON'T EVEN KNOW WHAT A BAD GUY IS.

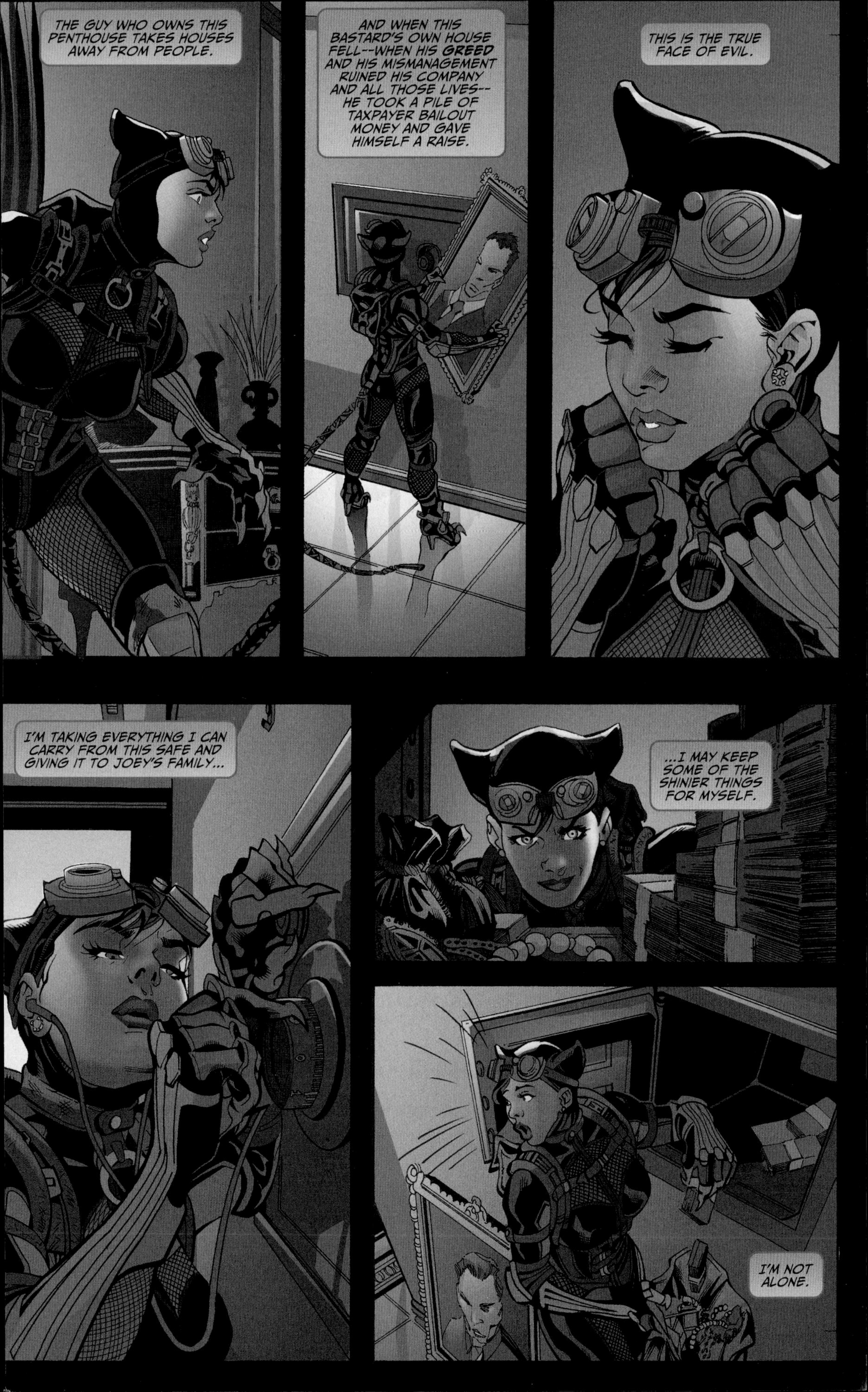
THE GUY WHO OWNS THIS PENTHOUSE TAKES HOUSES AWAY FROM PEOPLE.
AND WHEN THIS BASTARD'S OWN HOUSE FELL--WHEN HIS GREED AND HIS MISMANAGEMENT RUINED HIS COMPANY AND ALL THOSE LIVES--HE TOOK A PILE OF TAXPAYER BAILOUT MONEY AND GAVE HIMSELF A RAISE.
THIS IS THE TRUE FACE OF EVIL.
I'M TAKING EVERYTHING I CAN CARRY FROM THIS SAFE AND GIVING IT TO JOEY'S FAMILY...
...I MAY KEEP SOME OF THE SHINIER THINGS FOR MYSELF.
I'M NOT ALONE.

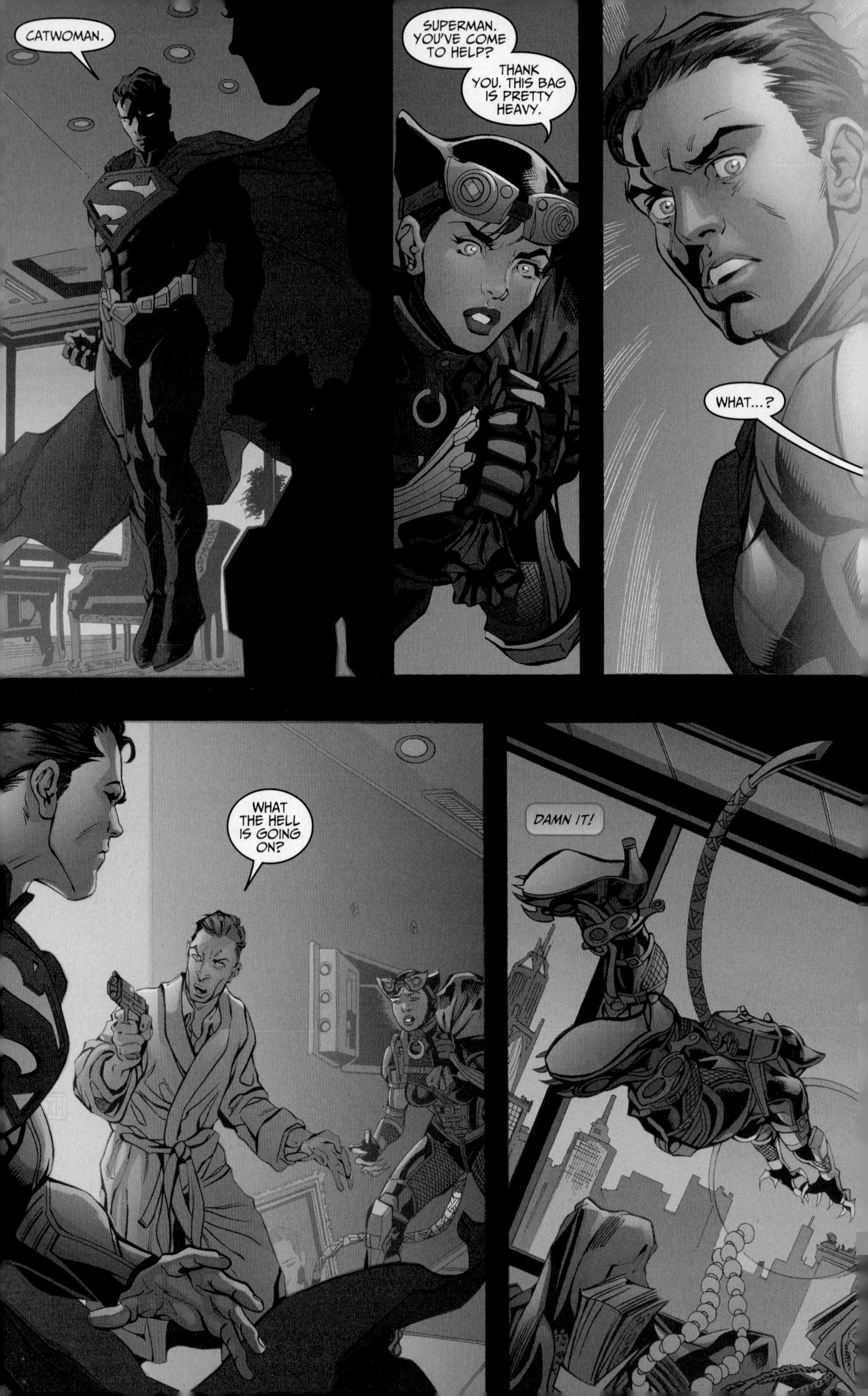
CATWOMAN.
SUPERMAN. YOU'VE COME TO HELP?
THANK YOU. THIS BAG IS PRETTY HEAVY.
WHAT...?
WHAT THE HELL IS GOING ON?
DAMN IT!

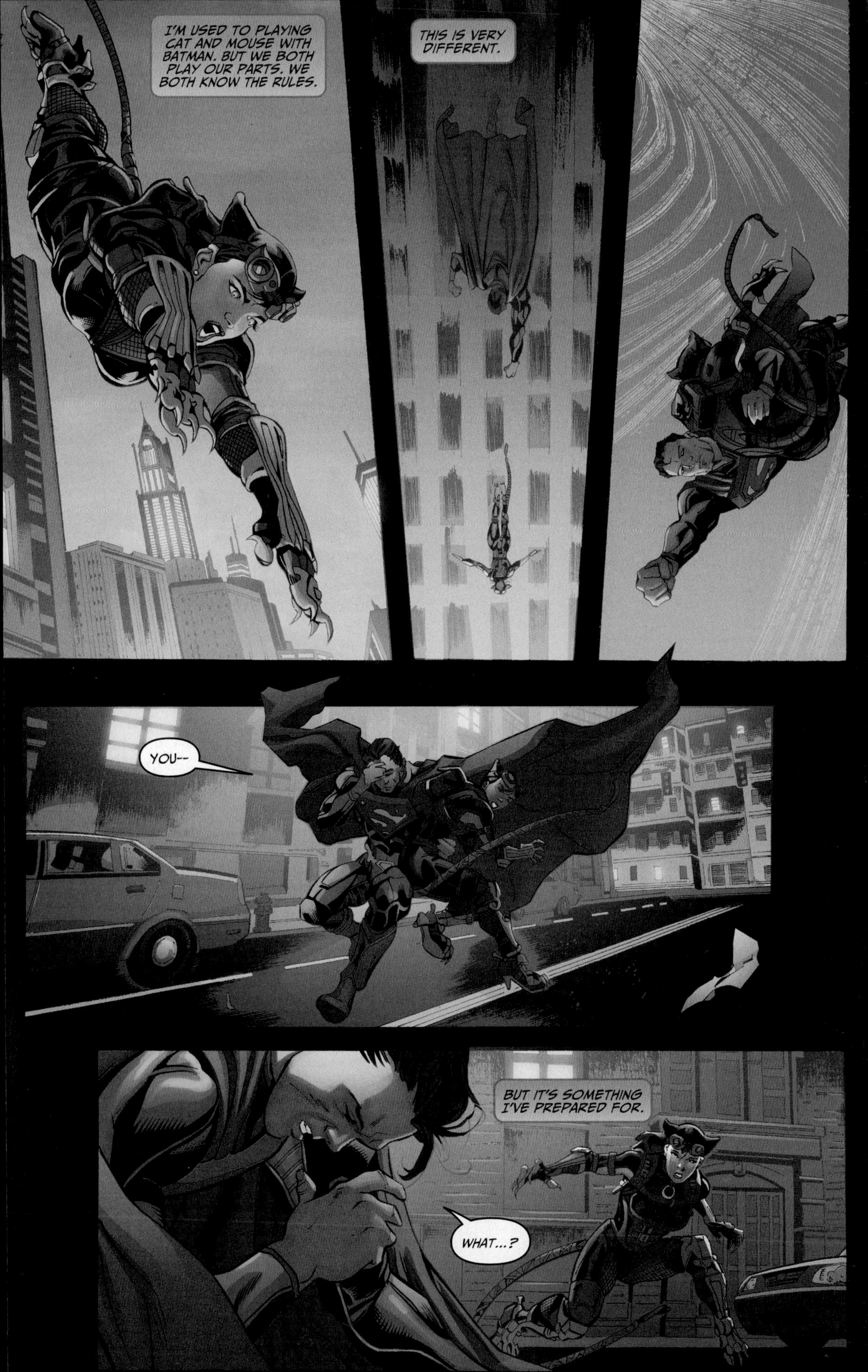
I'M USED TO PLAYING CAT AND MOUSE WITH BATMAN. BUT WE BOTH PLAY OUR PARTS. WE BOTH KNOW THE RULES.
THIS IS VERY DIFFERENT.
YOU--
BUT IT'S SOMETHING I'VE PREPARED FOR.
WHAT...?

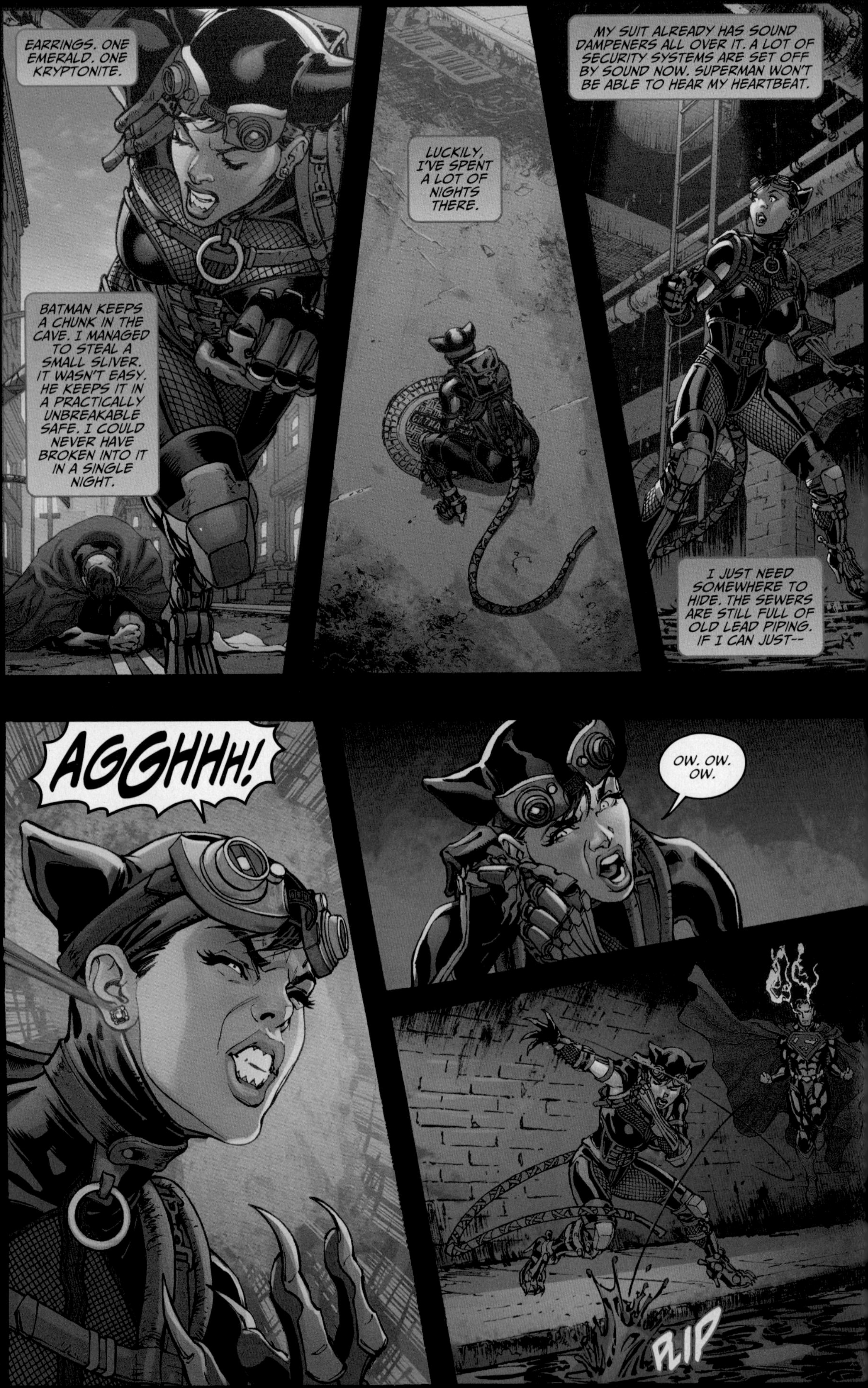
EARRINGS. ONE EMERALD. ONE KRYPTONITE.
BATMAN KEEPS A CHUNK IN THE CAVE. I MANAGED TO STEAL A SMALL SLIVER. IT WASN'T EASY. HE KEEPS IT IN A PRACTICALLY UNBREAKABLE SAFE. I COULD NEVER HAVE BROKEN INTO IT IN A SINGLE NIGHT.
LUCKILY, I'VE SPENT A LOT OF NIGHTS THERE.
MY SUIT ALREADY HAS SOUND DAMPENERS ALL OVER IT. A LOT OF SECURITY SYSTEMS ARE SET OFF BY SOUND NOW. SUPERMAN WON'T BE ABLE TO HEAR MY HEARTBEAT.
I JUST NEED SOMEWHERE TO HIDE. THE SEWERS ARE STILL FULL OF OLD LEAD PIPING. IF I CAN JUST--
AGGHHH!
OW. OW. OW.
PLIP

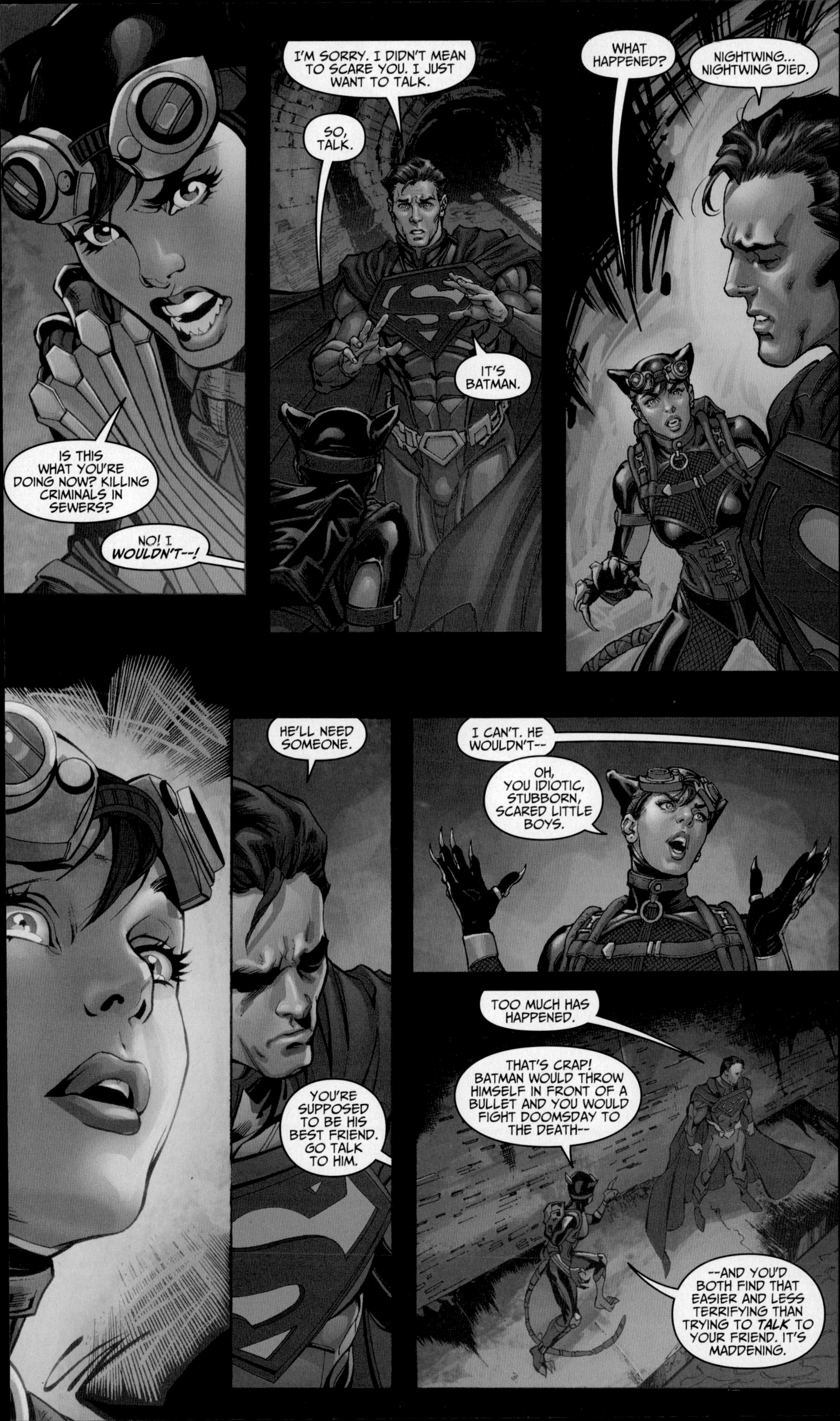
IS THIS WHAT YOU'RE DOING NOW? KILLING CRIMINALS IN SEWERS?
NO! I *WOULDN'T--!*
I'M SORRY. I DIDN'T MEAN TO SCARE YOU. I JUST WANT TO TALK.
SO, TALK.
IT'S BATMAN.
WHAT HAPPENED?
NIGHTWING... NIGHTWING DIED.
HE'LL NEED SOMEONE.
YOU'RE SUPPOSED TO BE HIS BEST FRIEND. GO TALK TO HIM.
I CAN'T. HE WOULDN'T--
OH, YOU IDIOTIC, STUBBORN, SCARED LITTLE BOYS.
TOO MUCH HAS HAPPENED.
THAT'S CRAP! BATMAN WOULD THROW HIMSELF IN FRONT OF A BULLET AND YOU WOULD FIGHT DOOMSDAY TO THE DEATH--
--AND YOU'D BOTH FIND THAT EASIER AND LESS TERRIFYING THAN TRYING TO *TALK* TO YOUR FRIEND. IT'S MADDENING.

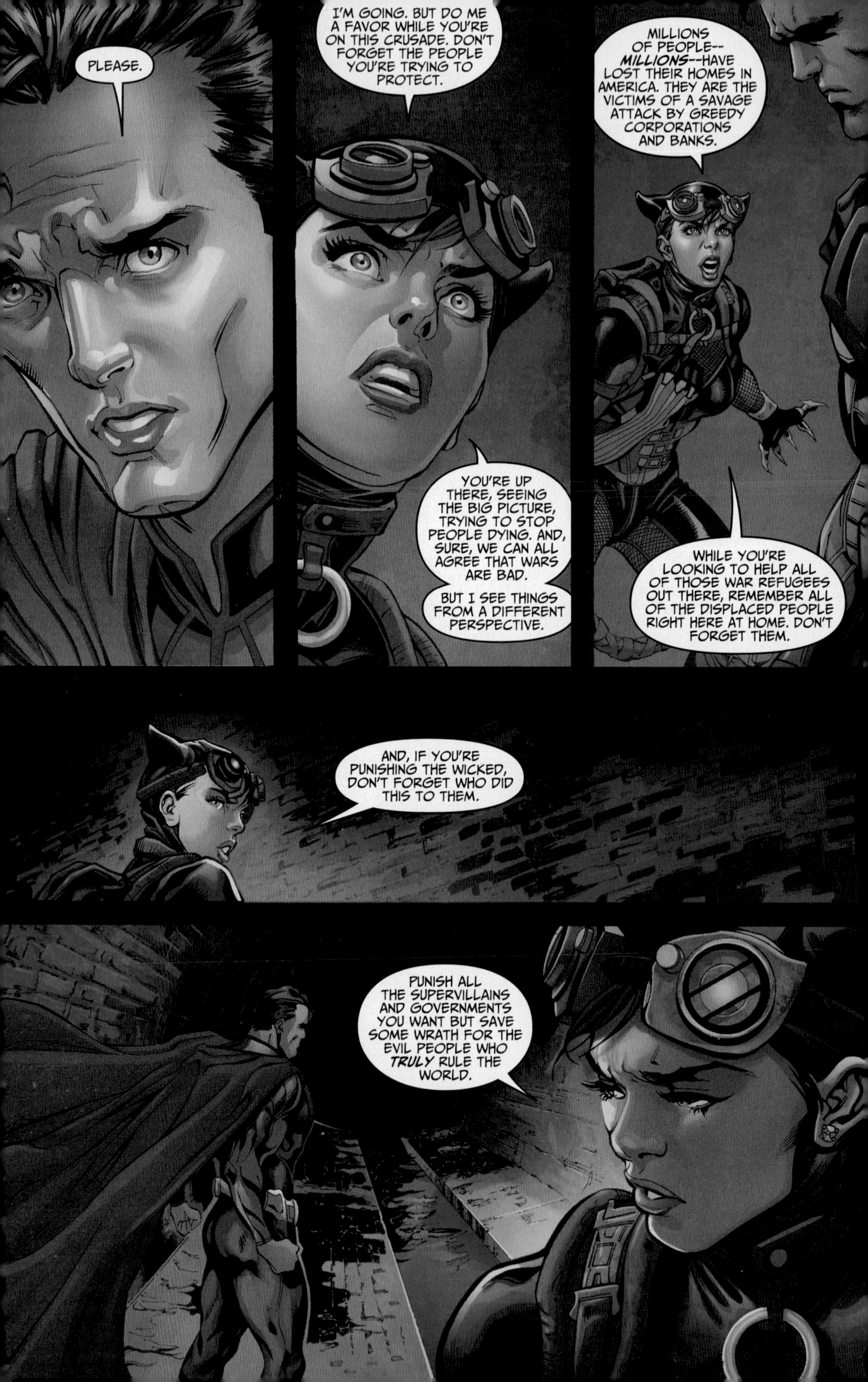
PLEASE.
I'M GOING. BUT DO ME A FAVOR WHILE YOU'RE ON THIS CRUSADE. DON'T FORGET THE PEOPLE YOU'RE TRYING TO PROTECT.
YOU'RE UP THERE, SEEING THE BIG PICTURE, TRYING TO STOP PEOPLE DYING. AND, SURE, WE CAN ALL AGREE THAT WARS ARE BAD.
BUT I SEE THINGS FROM A DIFFERENT PERSPECTIVE.
MILLIONS OF PEOPLE-- *MILLIONS*--HAVE LOST THEIR HOMES IN AMERICA. THEY ARE THE VICTIMS OF A SAVAGE ATTACK BY GREEDY CORPORATIONS AND BANKS.
WHILE YOU'RE LOOKING TO HELP ALL OF THOSE WAR REFUGEES OUT THERE, REMEMBER ALL OF THE DISPLACED PEOPLE RIGHT HERE AT HOME. DON'T FORGET THEM.
AND, IF YOU'RE PUNISHING THE WICKED, DON'T FORGET WHO DID THIS TO THEM.
PUNISH ALL THE SUPERVILLAINS AND GOVERNMENTS YOU WANT BUT SAVE SOME WRATH FOR THE EVIL PEOPLE WHO *TRULY* RULE THE WORLD.

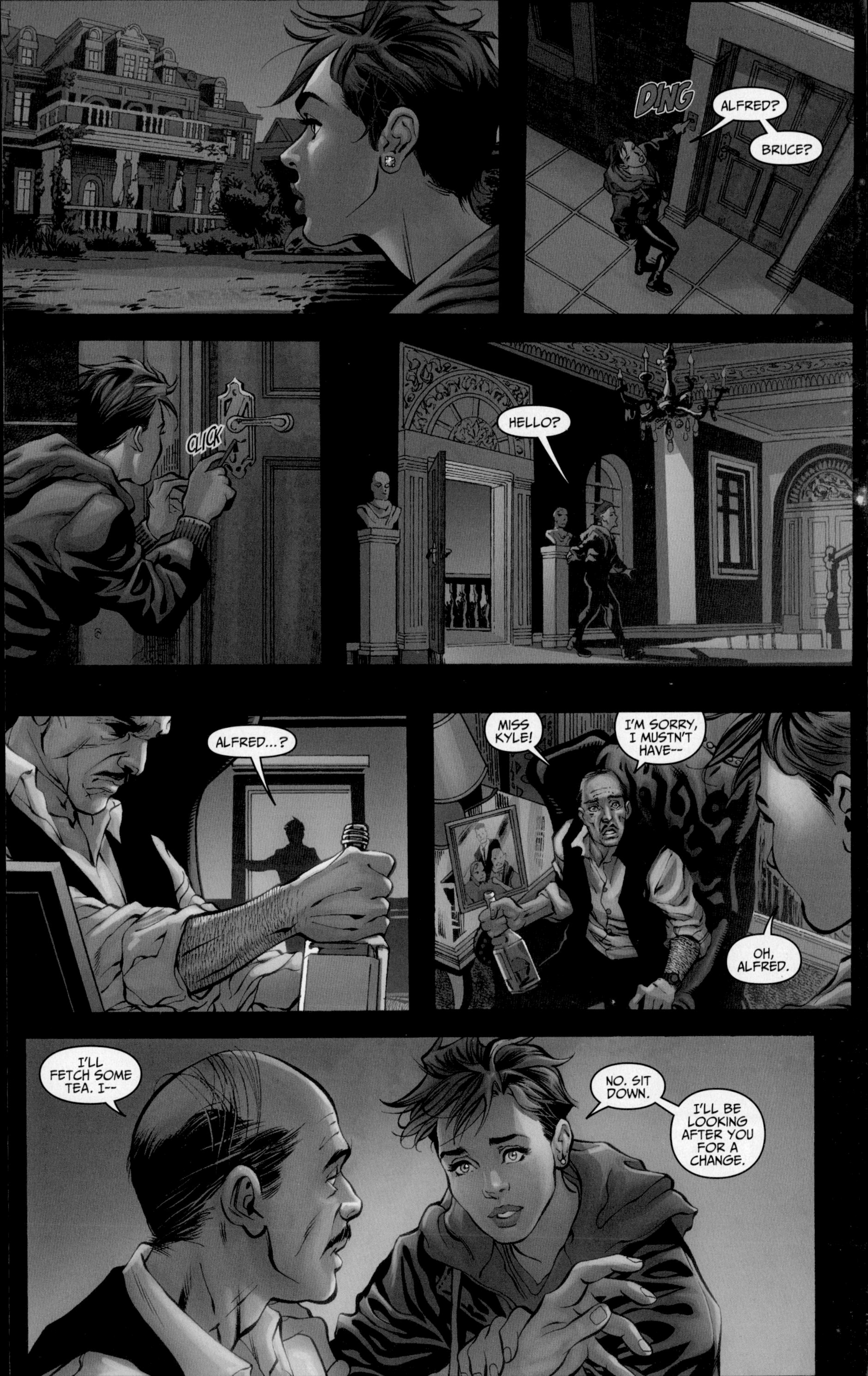
DING
ALFRED?
BRUCE?
CLICK
HELLO?
ALFRED...?
MISS KYLE!
I'M SORRY, I MUSTN'T HAVE--
OH, ALFRED.
I'LL FETCH SOME TEA. I--
NO. SIT DOWN.
I'LL BE LOOKING AFTER YOU FOR A CHANGE.

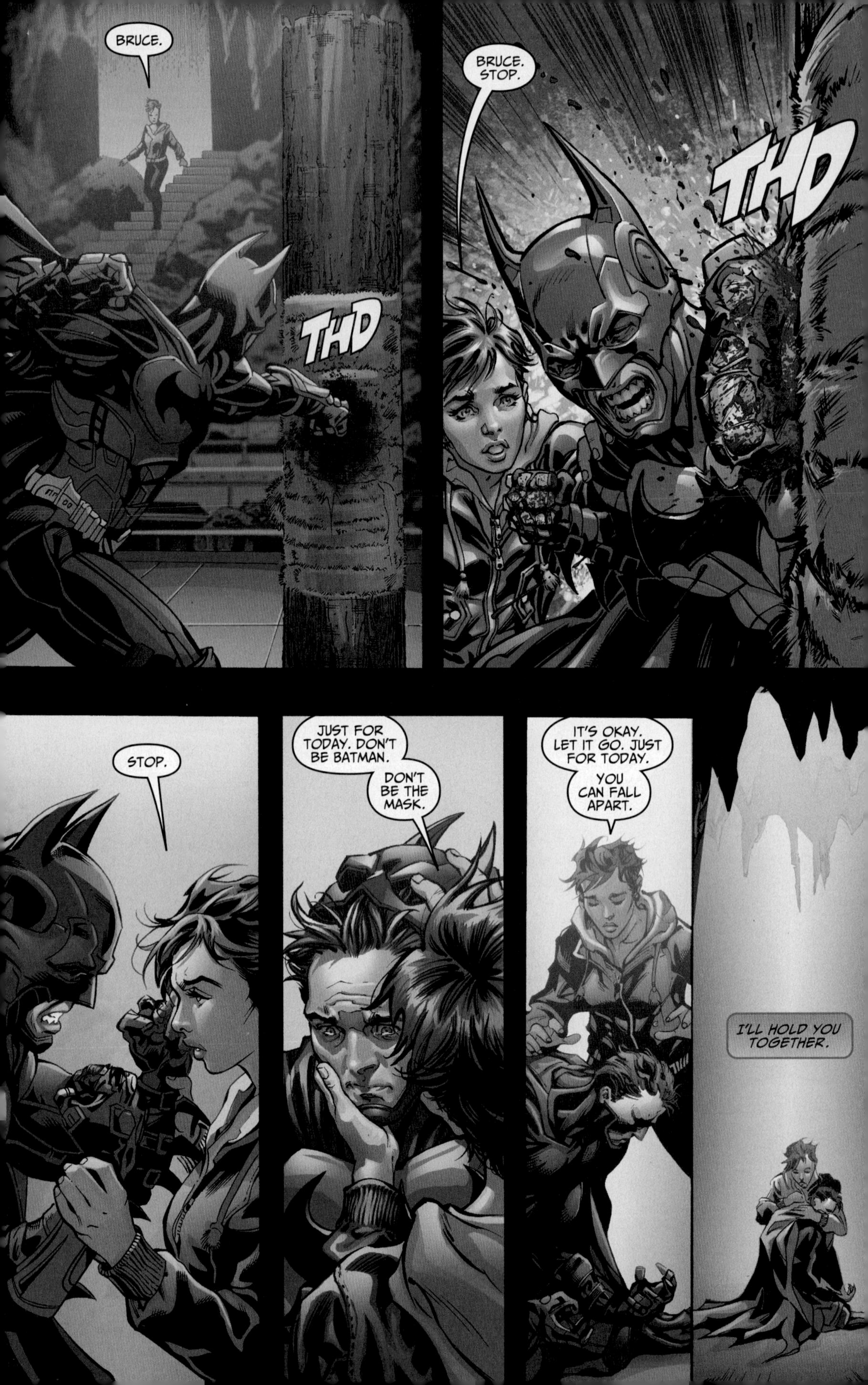
BRUCE.
THD
BRUCE. STOP.
THD
STOP.
JUST FOR TODAY. DON'T BE BATMAN.
DON'T BE THE MASK.
IT'S OKAY. LET IT GO. JUST FOR TODAY.
YOU CAN FALL APART.
I'LL HOLD YOU TOGETHER.

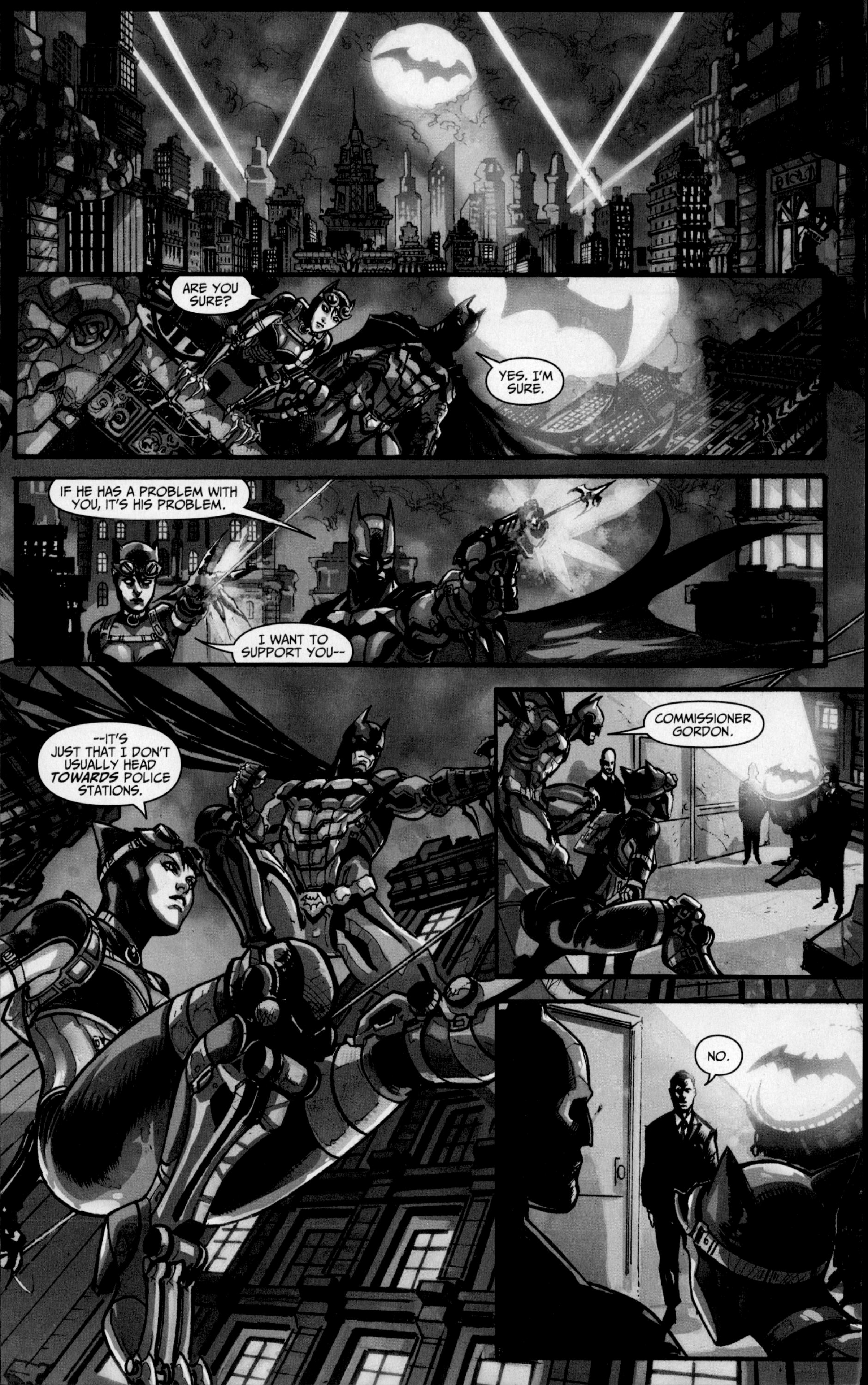
ARE YOU SURE?
YES. I'M SURE.
IF HE HAS A PROBLEM WITH YOU, IT'S HIS PROBLEM.
I WANT TO SUPPORT YOU--
--IT'S JUST THAT I DON'T USUALLY HEAD TOWARDS POLICE STATIONS.
COMMISSIONER GORDON.
NO.

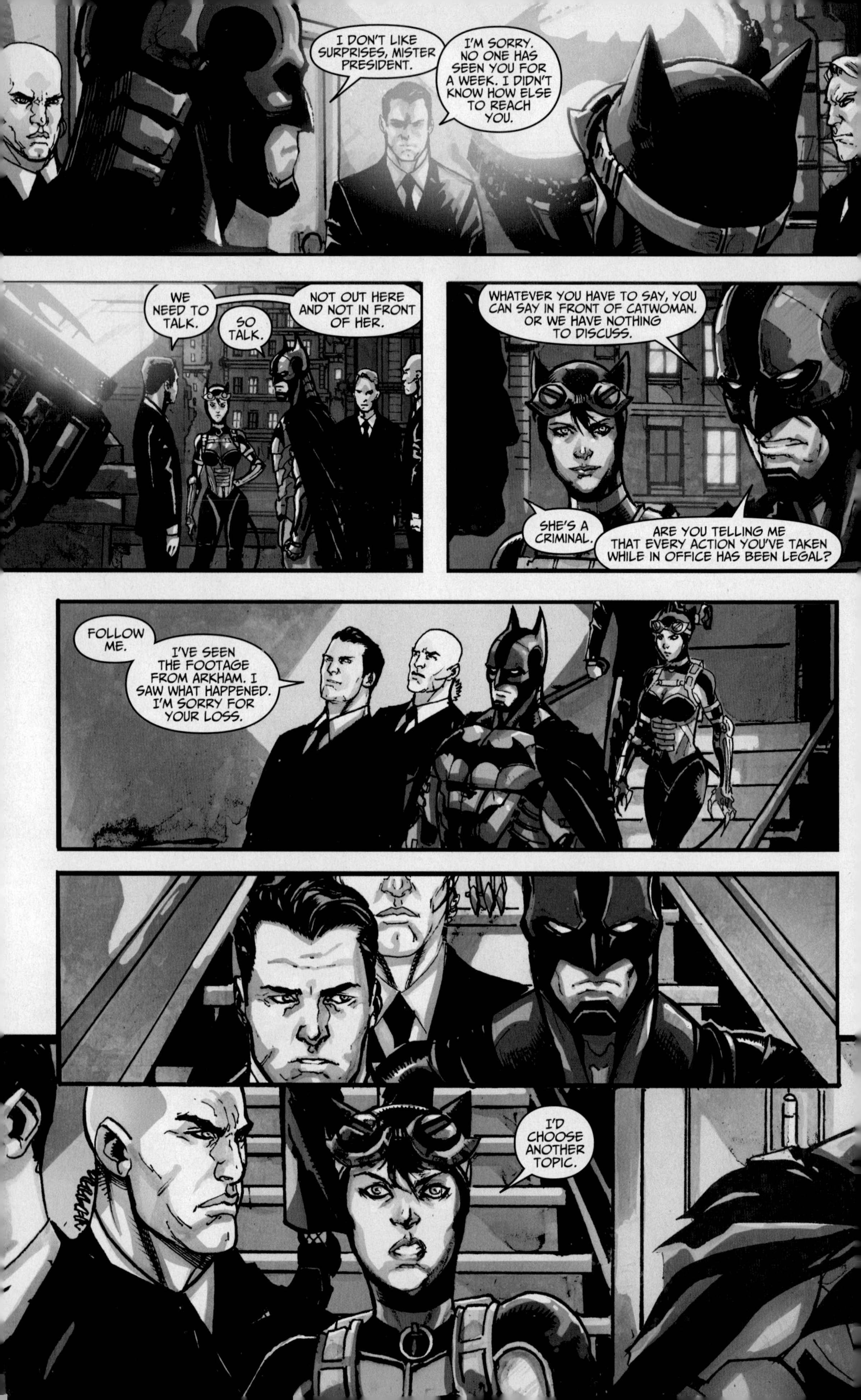
I DON'T LIKE SURPRISES, MISTER PRESIDENT.
I'M SORRY. NO ONE HAS SEEN YOU FOR A WEEK. I DIDN'T KNOW HOW ELSE TO REACH YOU.
WE NEED TO TALK.
SO TALK.
NOT OUT HERE AND NOT IN FRONT OF HER.
WHATEVER YOU HAVE TO SAY, YOU CAN SAY IN FRONT OF CATWOMAN. OR WE HAVE NOTHING TO DISCUSS.
SHE'S A CRIMINAL.
ARE YOU TELLING ME THAT EVERY ACTION YOU'VE TAKEN WHILE IN OFFICE HAS BEEN LEGAL?
FOLLOW ME.
I'VE SEEN THE FOOTAGE FROM ARKHAM. I SAW WHAT HAPPENED. I'M SORRY FOR YOUR LOSS.
I'D CHOOSE ANOTHER TOPIC.

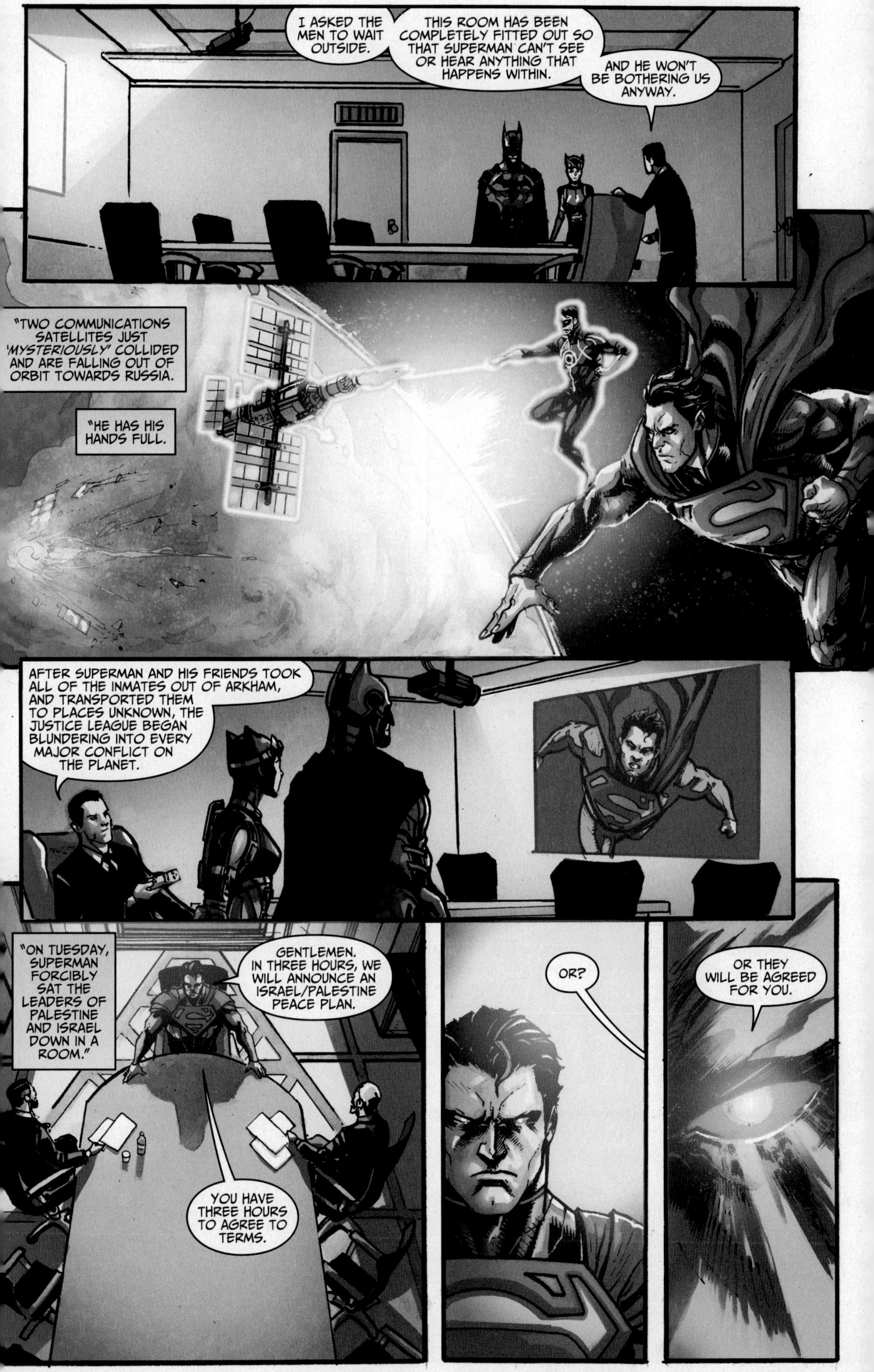
I ASKED THE MEN TO WAIT OUTSIDE.
THIS ROOM HAS BEEN COMPLETELY FITTED OUT SO THAT SUPERMAN CAN'T SEE OR HEAR ANYTHING THAT HAPPENS WITHIN.
AND HE WON'T BE BOTHERING US ANYWAY.
"TWO COMMUNICATIONS SATELLITES JUST 'MYSTERIOUSLY' COLLIDED AND ARE FALLING OUT OF ORBIT TOWARDS RUSSIA.
"HE HAS HIS HANDS FULL.
AFTER SUPERMAN AND HIS FRIENDS TOOK ALL OF THE INMATES OUT OF ARKHAM, AND TRANSPORTED THEM TO PLACES UNKNOWN, THE JUSTICE LEAGUE BEGAN BLUNDERING INTO EVERY MAJOR CONFLICT ON THE PLANET.
"ON TUESDAY, SUPERMAN FORCIBLY SAT THE LEADERS OF PALESTINE AND ISRAEL DOWN IN A ROOM."
GENTLEMEN. IN THREE HOURS, WE WILL ANNOUNCE AN ISRAEL/PALESTINE PEACE PLAN.
YOU HAVE THREE HOURS TO AGREE TO TERMS.
OR?
OR THEY WILL BE AGREED FOR YOU.

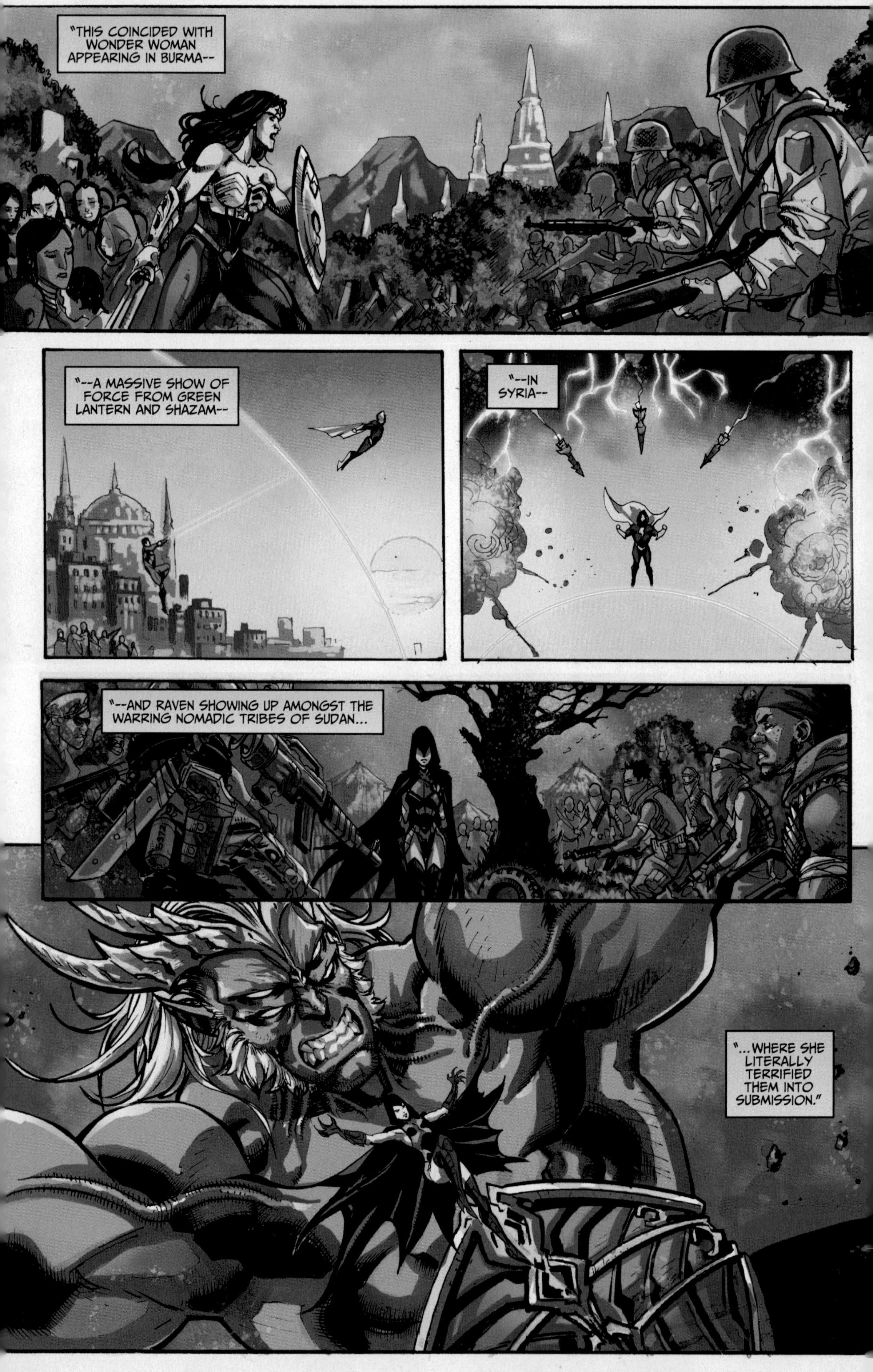
"THIS COINCIDED WITH WONDER WOMAN APPEARING IN BURMA--
"--A MASSIVE SHOW OF FORCE FROM GREEN LANTERN AND SHAZAM--
"--IN SYRIA--
"--AND RAVEN SHOWING UP AMONGST THE WARRING NOMADIC TRIBES OF SUDAN...
"...WHERE SHE LITERALLY TERRIFIED THEM INTO SUBMISSION."

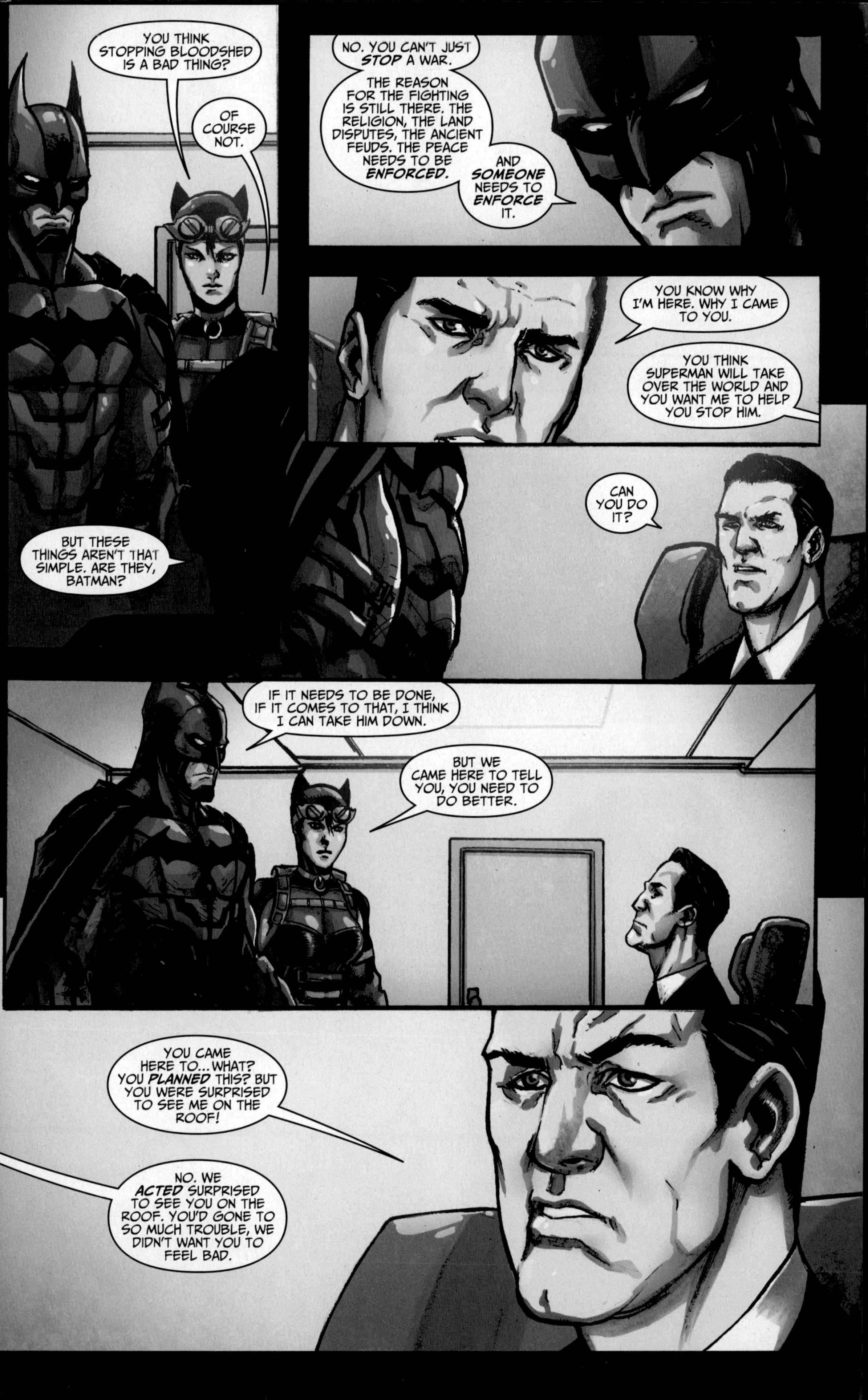
YOU THINK STOPPING BLOODSHED IS A BAD THING?
OF COURSE NOT.
NO. YOU CAN'T JUST *STOP* A WAR.
THE REASON FOR THE FIGHTING IS STILL THERE. THE RELIGION, THE LAND DISPUTES, THE ANCIENT FEUDS. THE PEACE NEEDS TO BE *ENFORCED*.
AND *SOMEONE* NEEDS TO *ENFORCE* IT.
YOU KNOW WHY I'M HERE. WHY I CAME TO YOU.
YOU THINK SUPERMAN WILL TAKE OVER THE WORLD AND YOU WANT ME TO HELP YOU STOP HIM.
BUT THESE THINGS AREN'T THAT SIMPLE. ARE THEY, BATMAN?
CAN YOU DO IT?
IF IT NEEDS TO BE DONE, IF IT COMES TO THAT, I THINK I CAN TAKE HIM DOWN.
BUT WE CAME HERE TO TELL YOU, YOU NEED TO DO BETTER.
YOU CAME HERE TO... WHAT? YOU *PLANNED* THIS? BUT YOU WERE SURPRISED TO SEE ME ON THE ROOF!
NO. WE *ACTED* SURPRISED TO SEE YOU ON THE ROOF. YOU'D GONE TO SO MUCH TROUBLE, WE DIDN'T WANT YOU TO FEEL BAD.

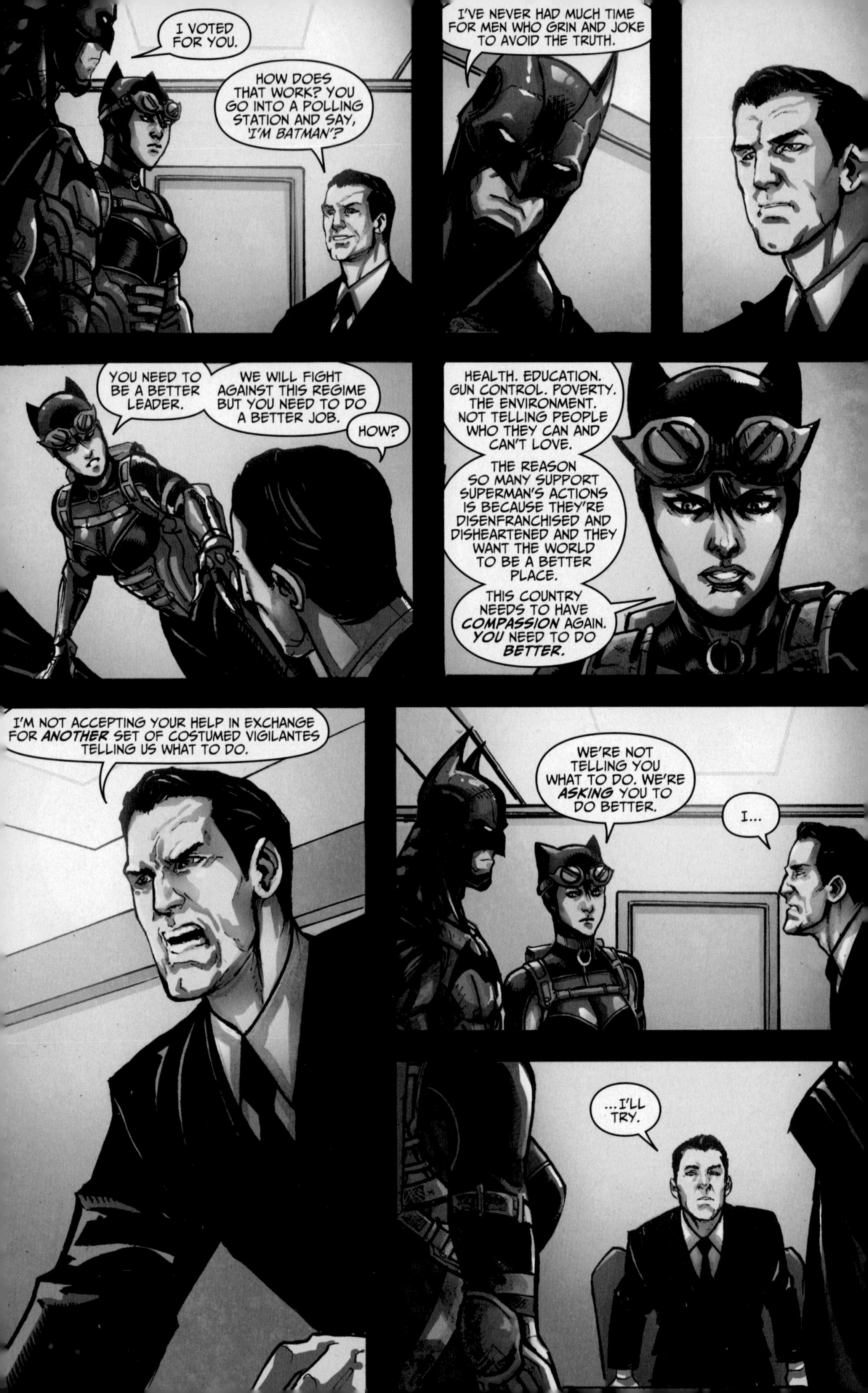
I VOTED FOR YOU.
HOW DOES THAT WORK? YOU GO INTO A POLLING STATION AND SAY, 'I'M BATMAN'?
I'VE NEVER HAD MUCH TIME FOR MEN WHO GRIN AND JOKE TO AVOID THE TRUTH.
YOU NEED TO BE A BETTER LEADER.
WE WILL FIGHT AGAINST THIS REGIME BUT YOU NEED TO DO A BETTER JOB.
HOW?
HEALTH. EDUCATION. GUN CONTROL. POVERTY. THE ENVIRONMENT. NOT TELLING PEOPLE WHO THEY CAN AND CAN'T LOVE.
THE REASON SO MANY SUPPORT SUPERMAN'S ACTIONS IS BECAUSE THEY'RE DISENFRANCHISED AND DISHEARTENED AND THEY WANT THE WORLD TO BE A BETTER PLACE.
THIS COUNTRY NEEDS TO HAVE COMPASSION AGAIN. YOU NEED TO DO BETTER.
I'M NOT ACCEPTING YOUR HELP IN EXCHANGE FOR ANOTHER SET OF COSTUMED VIGILANTES TELLING US WHAT TO DO.
WE'RE NOT TELLING YOU WHAT TO DO. WE'RE ASKING YOU TO DO BETTER.
I...
...I'LL TRY.

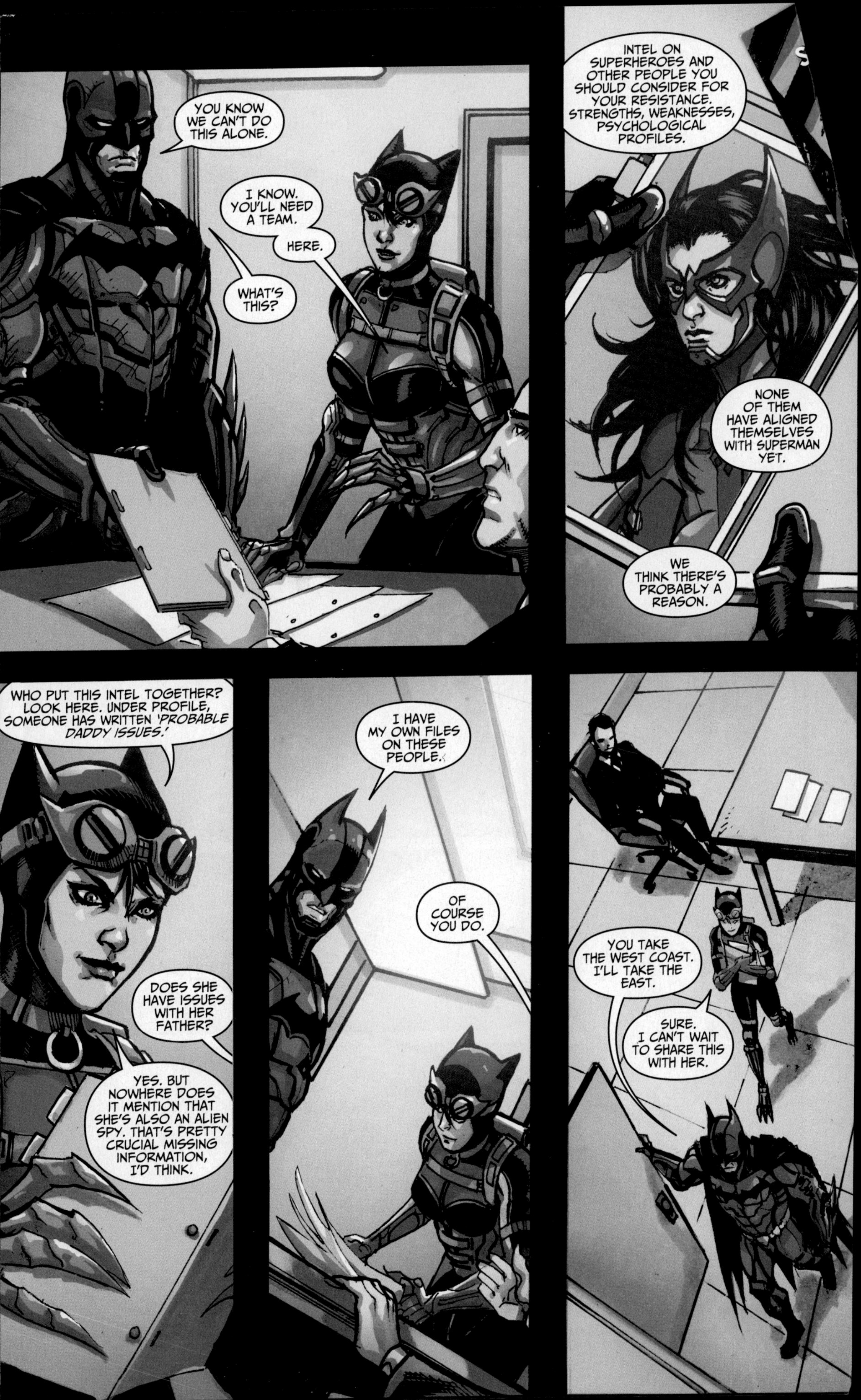
YOU KNOW WE CAN'T DO THIS ALONE.
I KNOW. YOU'LL NEED A TEAM.
HERE.
WHAT'S THIS?
INTEL ON SUPERHEROES AND OTHER PEOPLE YOU SHOULD CONSIDER FOR YOUR RESISTANCE. STRENGTHS, WEAKNESSES, PSYCHOLOGICAL PROFILES.
NONE OF THEM HAVE ALIGNED THEMSELVES WITH SUPERMAN YET.
WE THINK THERE'S PROBABLY A REASON.
WHO PUT THIS INTEL TOGETHER? LOOK HERE. UNDER PROFILE, SOMEONE HAS WRITTEN *'PROBABLE DADDY ISSUES.'*
DOES SHE HAVE ISSUES WITH HER FATHER?
YES. BUT NOWHERE DOES IT MENTION THAT SHE'S ALSO AN ALIEN SPY. THAT'S PRETTY CRUCIAL MISSING INFORMATION, I'D THINK.
I HAVE MY OWN FILES ON THESE PEOPLE.
OF COURSE YOU DO.
YOU TAKE THE WEST COAST. I'LL TAKE THE EAST.
SURE. I CAN'T WAIT TO SHARE THIS WITH HER.

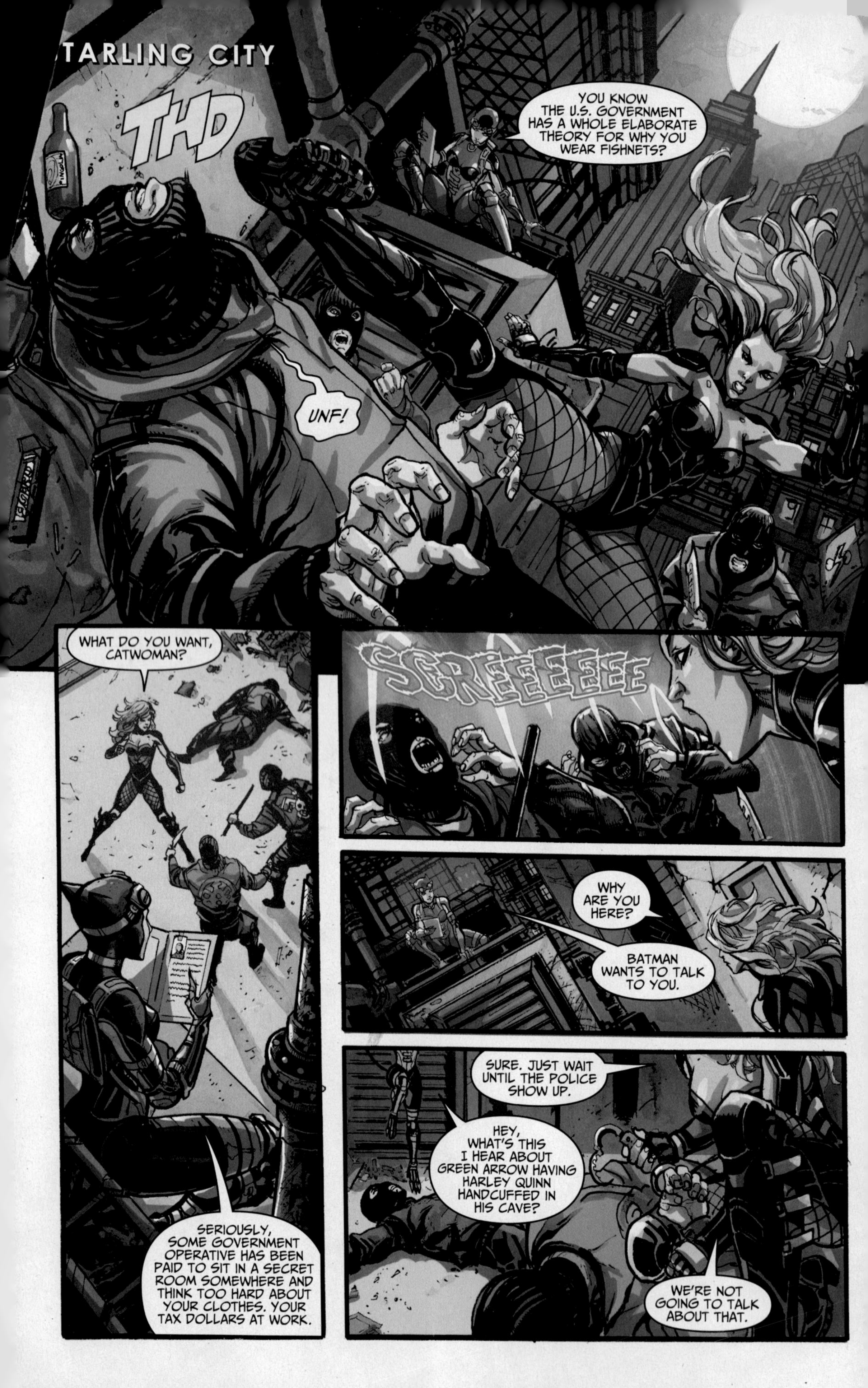

TARLING CITY
THD
YOU KNOW THE U.S. GOVERNMENT HAS A WHOLE ELABORATE THEORY FOR WHY YOU WEAR FISHNETS?
UNF!
WHAT DO YOU WANT, CATWOMAN?
SERIOUSLY, SOME GOVERNMENT OPERATIVE HAS BEEN PAID TO SIT IN A SECRET ROOM SOMEWHERE AND THINK TOO HARD ABOUT YOUR CLOTHES. YOUR TAX DOLLARS AT WORK.
SCREEEEEEE
WHY ARE YOU HERE?
BATMAN WANTS TO TALK TO YOU.
SURE. JUST WAIT UNTIL THE POLICE SHOW UP.
HEY, WHAT'S THIS I HEAR ABOUT GREEN ARROW HAVING HARLEY QUINN HANDCUFFED IN HIS CAVE?
WE'RE NOT GOING TO TALK ABOUT THAT.

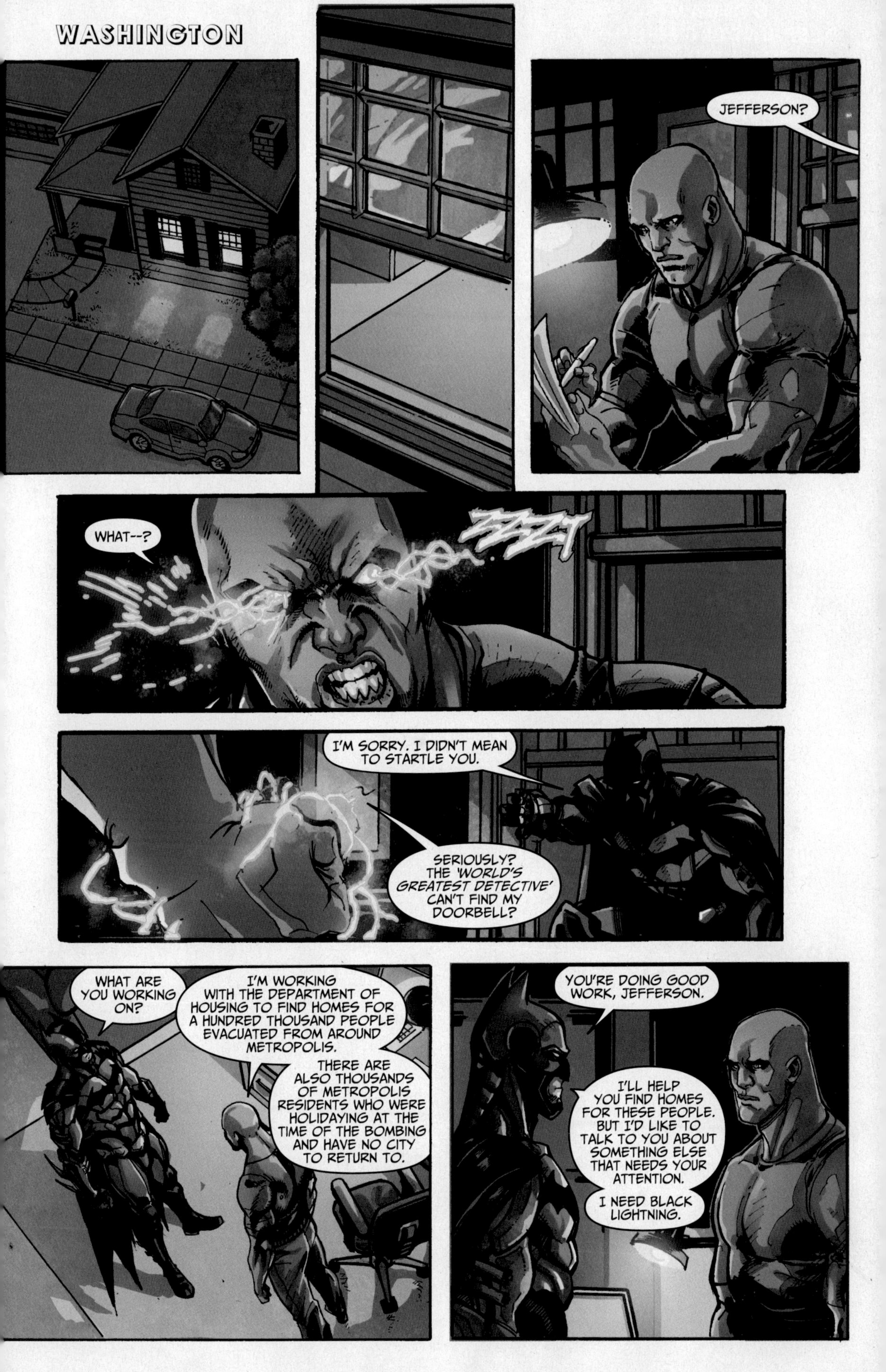
WASHINGTON
JEFFERSON?
WHAT--?
ZZZZT
I'M SORRY. I DIDN'T MEAN TO STARTLE YOU.
SERIOUSLY? THE 'WORLD'S GREATEST DETECTIVE' CAN'T FIND MY DOORBELL?
WHAT ARE YOU WORKING ON?
I'M WORKING WITH THE DEPARTMENT OF HOUSING TO FIND HOMES FOR A HUNDRED THOUSAND PEOPLE EVACUATED FROM AROUND METROPOLIS.
THERE ARE ALSO THOUSANDS OF METROPOLIS RESIDENTS WHO WERE HOLIDAYING AT THE TIME OF THE BOMBING AND HAVE NO CITY TO RETURN TO.
YOU'RE DOING GOOD WORK, JEFFERSON.
I'LL HELP YOU FIND HOMES FOR THESE PEOPLE. BUT I'D LIKE TO TALK TO YOU ABOUT SOMETHING ELSE THAT NEEDS YOUR ATTENTION.
I NEED BLACK LIGHTNING.

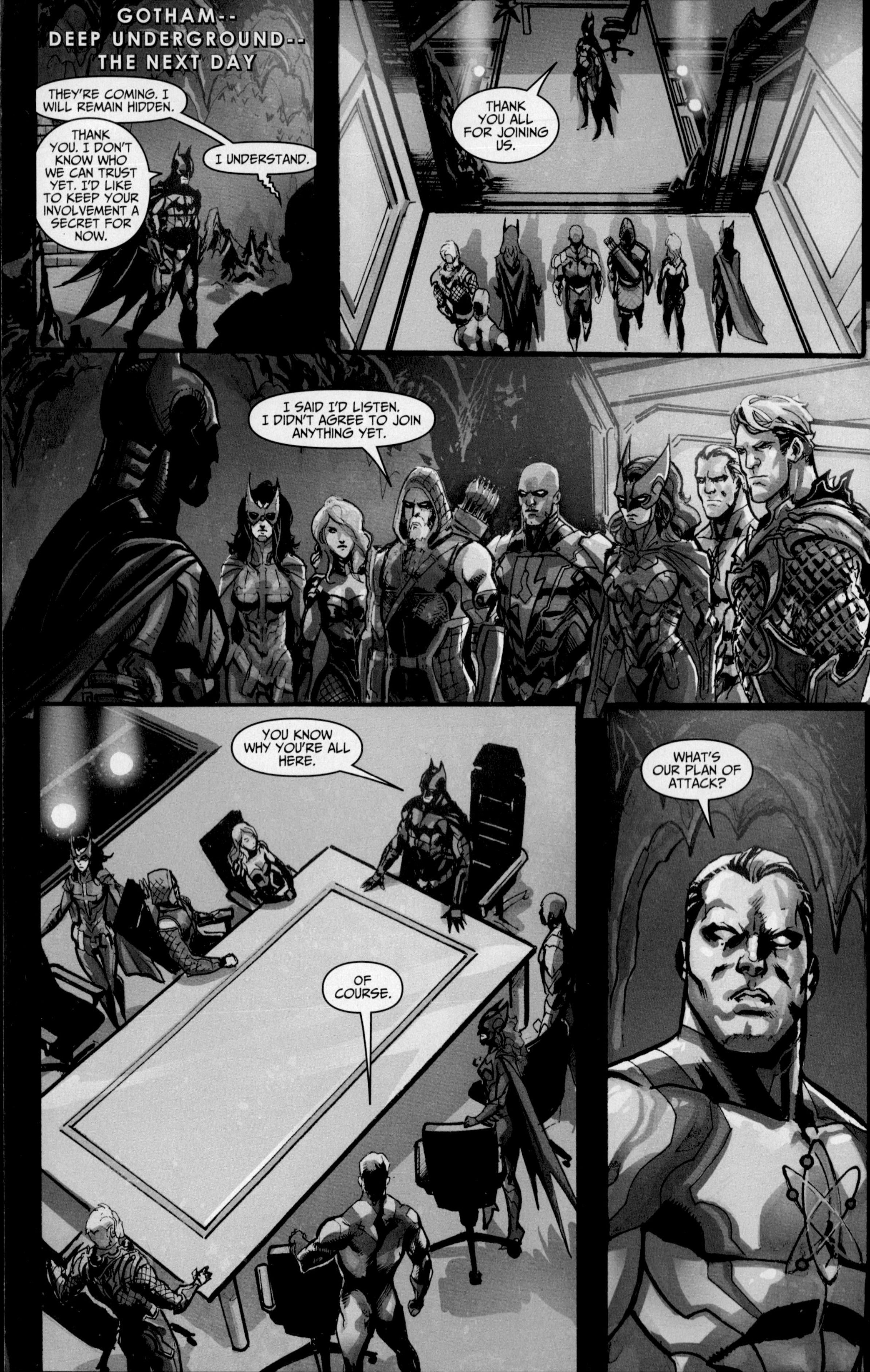
GOTHAM-- DEEP UNDERGROUND-- THE NEXT DAY
THEY'RE COMING. I WILL REMAIN HIDDEN.
THANK YOU. I DON'T KNOW WHO WE CAN TRUST YET. I'D LIKE TO KEEP YOUR INVOLVEMENT A SECRET FOR NOW.
I UNDERSTAND.
THANK YOU ALL FOR JOINING US.
I SAID I'D LISTEN. I DIDN'T AGREE TO JOIN ANYTHING YET.
YOU KNOW WHY YOU'RE ALL HERE.
OF COURSE.
WHAT'S OUR PLAN OF ATTACK?

Injustice #1 Game Varian

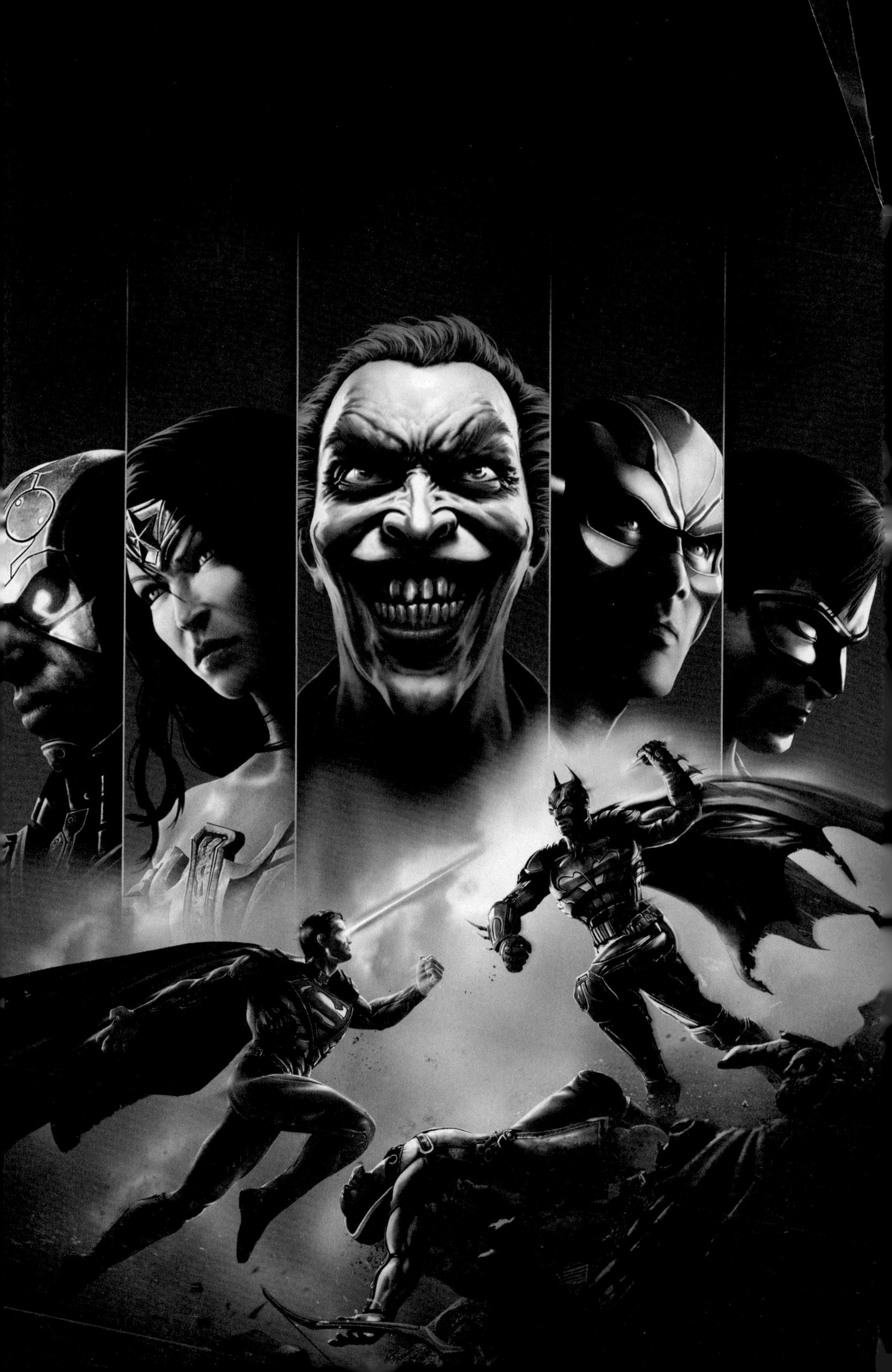

Injustice #1 3rd Printing Variant Cover

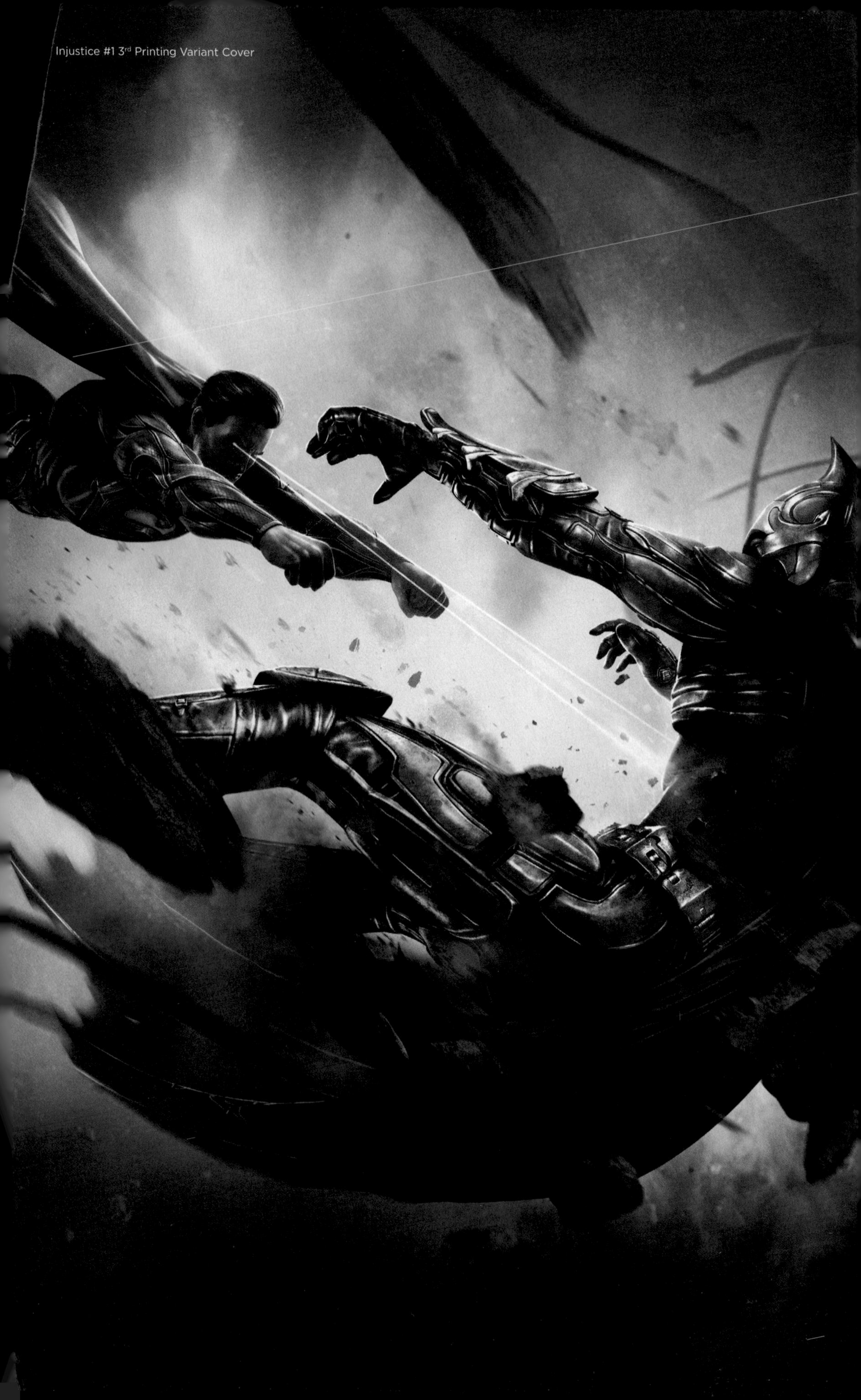

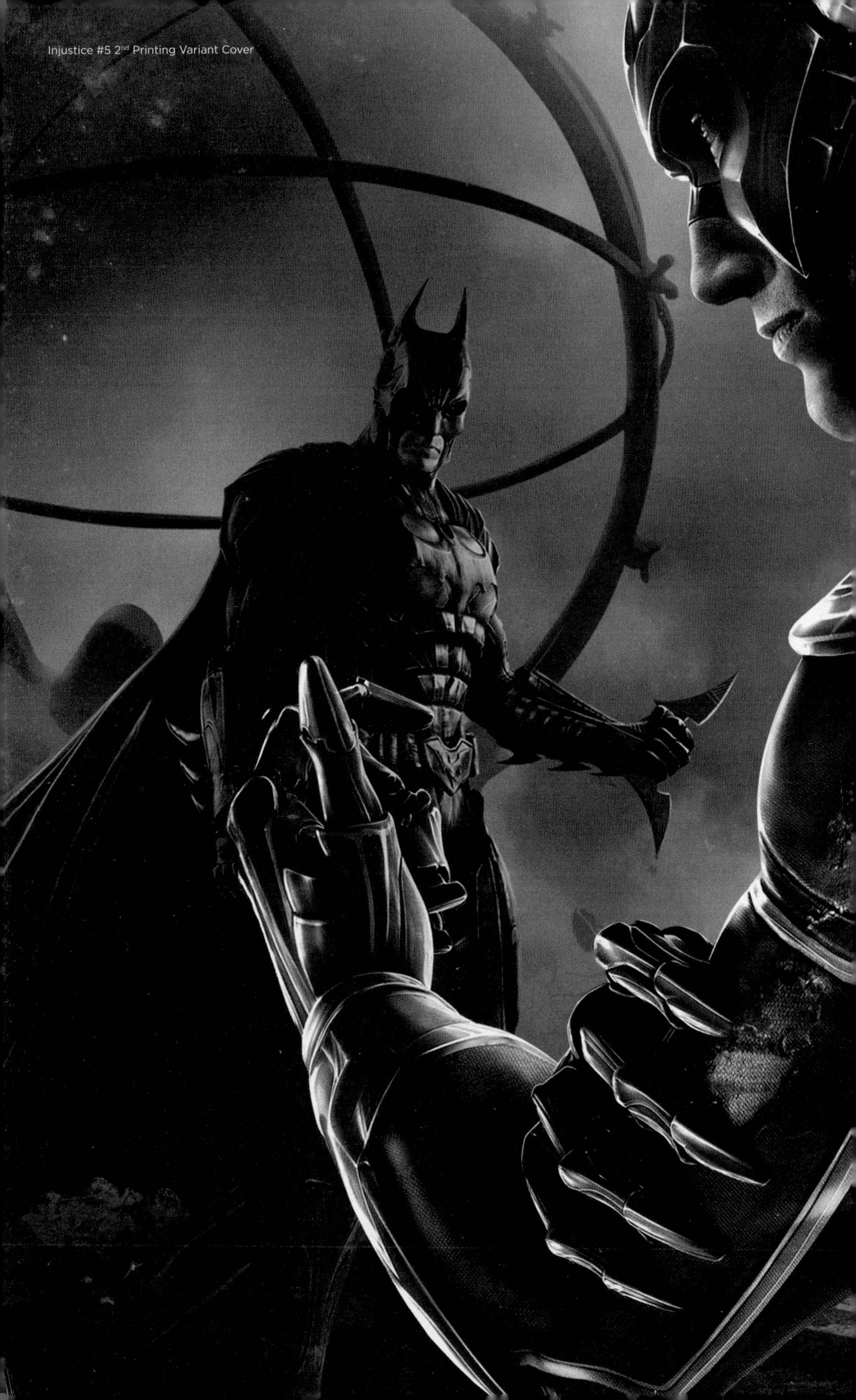

Injustice #5 2nd Printing Variant Cover

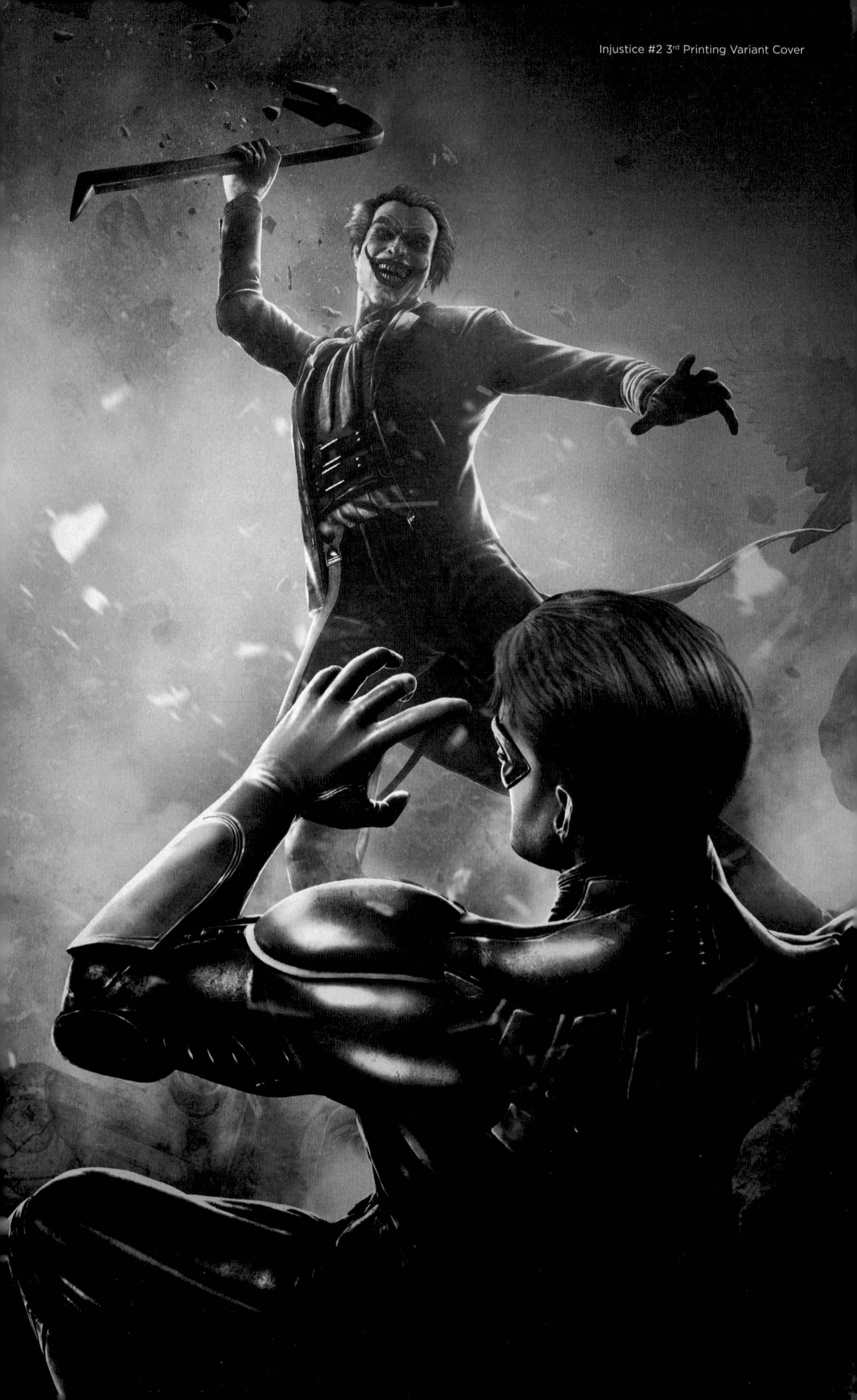

Injustice #2 3rd Printing Variant Cover